Language in South Africa

Impact: Studies in language and society

IMPACT publishes monographs, collective volumes, and text books on topics in sociolinguistics and language pedagogy. The scope of the series is broad, with special emphasis on areas such as language planning and language policies; language conflict and language death; language standards and language change; dialectology; diglossia; discourse studies; language and social identity (gender, ethnicity, class, ideology); and history and methods of sociolinguistics.

General editor

Annick De Houwer
University of Antwerp

Advisory board

Volume 14

Language in South Africa: The role of language in national transformation, reconstruction and development
by Vic Webb

Language in South Africa

The role of language in national transformation, reconstruction and development

Vic Webb

University of Pretoria

John Benjamins Publishing Company

Amsterdam / Philadelphia

Library of Congress Cataloging-in-Publication Data

Webb, Victor N.
   Language in South Africa : The role of language in national transformation, reconstruction and development / Vic Webb.
      p.   cm. (Impact: Studies in language and society, ISSN 1385–7908 ; v. 14)
   Includes bibliographical references and indexes.
      1. Language planning--South Africa. 2. Language Policy--South Africa. 3. Sociolinguistics--South Africa. 4. South Africa--Languages. I. Title. II. Impact, studies in language and society.
P40.5.L352 S619 2002
306.44′968--dc21   2002025420
ISBN 90 272 1849 8 (Eur.) / 1 58811 189 X (US) (Hb; alk. paper)

John Benjamins Publishing Co. · P.O. Box 36224 · 1020 ME Amsterdam · The Netherlands
John Benjamins North America · P.O. Box 27519 · Philadelphia PA 19118-0519 · USA

Vir Linette

Contents

List of figures, tables, abbreviations, notes on terms, examples of languages, acknowledgements and maps

Abbreviations

ALASA	African Languages Association of Southern Africa
ANC	African National Congress
CentRePoL	Centre for Research in the Politics of Language
DACST	Department of Arts, Culture, Science and Technology
DET	Department of Education and Training
ELSA	English Literacy Skills Assessment
EFL	English Foreign Language (teaching)
ESL	English Second Language (teaching)
GEAR	Growth, Employment and Redistribution (Programme)
L1, L2 and L3	First language, second language and third (or foreign) language
LANGTAG	Language Plan Task Group
LiCCA	Languages in Contact and Conflict in Africa (a research programme)
LiSA	*Language in South Africa*
LSSA	Linguistics Society of Southern Africa
LoL/T	Language of Learning and Teaching
LP(P)	Language policy (and plan)
NGOs	Non-governmental organisations
OBE	Outcomes-based Education
PANSALB	Pan-South African Language Board
RDP	Reconstruction and Development Programme
SA	South Africa
SAALA	Southern African Applied Linguistics Association
SAALT	Southern African Association for Language Teaching
SABC	South African Broadcasting Corporation
SAIRR	South African Institute for Race Relations
SMMEs	Small, micro and medium enterprises
SWOT analysis	An analysis of the Strengths, Weaknesses, Opportunities and Threats regarding the implementation of a specific proposals
TESOL	Teaching English to Speakers of Other Languages

A note about the author

Vic Webb teaches the politics of language and sociolinguistics at the University of Pretoria. A former president of the *Linguistic Society of Southern Africa*, he was the international chairperson of the *Languages in Contact and Conflict in Africa* programme (LiCCA) from 1993 to 1996, which is directed at descriptions of the language politics of African countries. He was also a member of the main committee of *LANGTAG*, a government appointed body instructed to describe the framework within which a comprehensive national language plan can be developed.

He is presently director of **CentRePoL** (*Centre for Research in the Politics of Language*) at the University of Pretoria, and is involved in a number of research projects, such as *The case for multilingualism as a developmental resource*; *Language, educational effectiveness and economic outcomes* (with François Grin of the University of Geneva); and *An audit of the language behaviour of Science and Mathematics pupils in ten Gauteng schools* (with Helma Pasch, University of Cologne).

Webb has worked at the University of Pennsylvania in the USA (1980/81), the Universität – Gesamthochschule – Duisburg, Germany (1992) and the Katholieke Universiteit van Leuven, Belgium (1995). He has edited a number of books (e.g. *Afrikaans ná Apartheid* in 1992 and *Language in South Africa. An input into language planning for a post-apartheid South Africa. The LiCCA(SA) Report* in 1995), written about 70 scientific articles and presented papers at linguistics conferences in the USA, Germany, Belgium, the Netherlands and, of course, in southern Africa. He has recently editing an undergraduate text-book in linguistics which has an explicitly African orientation, with Kembo-Sure of Kenya.

Contact details
  E-mail: vwebb@postino.up.ac.za
  CentRePoL, Human Sciences Building 15–18, University of Pretoria,
    0001 Pretoria, Republic of South Africa

Brief notes on the use of selected terms

African language: Language which originated in Africa, or is spoken only or mainly in Africa. In this sense, the Bantu languages, the Khoi-San languages and Afrikaans are *African languages*. In South Africa this is the term usually used to refer to the Bantu languages.

Bantu language: A language family within the group of African languages, with a distinctive linguistic structure (see p. 76). In South Africa, this term is stigmatised and thus not generally used to refer to these languages. Instead, the term *African language* is used to refer to these languages.

Bilingualism: A state of knowing two languages. In South Africa, this term generally refers to a knowledge of Afrikaans and English.

Centralized language: Language used with secondary (high) functions in formal, public life. (p. 89)

Dominant language: Language with high status, used in most of the high, public domains and functions, despite the fact that it may be the first language of a statistical minority or even almost no one's first language; usually used instead of citizens' first languages. The term thus does not refer to a statistical concept. In a situation of diglossia, this is the H language.

Ethnic language: Language which has the primary function of symbolising ethno-cultural identity; often a language which has not been standardised, or recognised as appropriate in high-function, public contexts.

Ex-colonial language: Language of the former colonial rulers. In Africa, English, French and Portuguese are the main ex-colonial languages. These languages are often still the dominant languages of official use.

First language: The primary language of a person, generally known very well. In South Africa, this term is commonly used in non-black communities, but does not seem to have much usefulness in black South African communities, and overlaps confusingly with concepts such as *primary language, home language, mother-tongue*, and, by analogy "*father-tongue*".

Foreign language/third language (opposed to *first language* and *second language*): Language seldom (if ever) heard in everyday life; language to which one is not exposed in every-day life. If studied, it would be used/heard only in the school classroom. In South Africa, French, Portuguese and German would be foreign or third languages.

Functional literacy: A person's ability to control his/her environment on the basis of his/her proficiency in the written form of a particular language. (p. 202)

Home language: Primary language of the home and its environment. Once again, possibly a rather inappropriate concept in black South African communities.

Indigenous language: Language which originated within a country, and used mainly within the country; endoglossic, not exoglossic, from the "outside", from "foreign soil". In South Africa, the Bantu languages have come to be known as "indigenous". English is certainly non-indigenous (though it does have indigenised varieties), with the position of Afrikaans ambiguous, since it is historically a "derivative" from Dutch and mutually comprehensible with it (in their standard varieties), yet is regarded as a distinct language. However, it is not used outside Africa in a significant degree.

Language of wider communication (LWC): A lingua franca, used in international communication and/or across community/language boundaries. Not community-bound. In South Africa, English is the main LWC in specific high-function domains. Zulu is also an LWC (in other domains), as is Afrikaans.

Language proficiency: Ability to communicate in a language, referring both to the productive aspect (the ability to construct meaningful written and/or oral "texts") and the receptive aspect (the ability to interpret written and/or oral "texts"); usually varies in extent, from a basic interpersonal communicative skill, to a cognitively higher-level communicative skill.

Major language: Used in this book to refer to a language with official status, and with significant numbers of first-language speakers. South Africa has 11 "major" languages.

Majority language: A statistical concept, referring to speaker numbers.

Marginalised language: Language seldom used in high-level, public functions, thus having little prestige and a low economic value (including low educational, political and social value). In South Africa the Bantu languages are marginalised languages, to varying degrees. Opposed to *centralised* language.

Minor language: Both a statistical concept ("low speaker numbers") and a functional concept ("none or only a few public functions").

Mother-tongue: Metaphorically, one's primary, best-known language. In South Africa, this concept is stigmatised because of its association with

Apartheid and the latter's doctrine of "mother-tongue education", which was perceived as part of the strategy of dividing communities (in order to obtain/retain control). The term has little meaning or relevance in black communities, since the "mother-tongue" of black South Africans is, culturally seen, the "father-tongue". (pp. 70, 196)

Multicultural: A situation characterised by multiple ethno-cultural identities (see "pluricultural").

Multlingualism: A knowledge of more than two languages in the case of individuals, and, societally, the presence of more than two languages; a particular attitude to public life, related to the political philosophy of pluralism. (p. 31)

National language: A language which functions as a symbol of a national socio-political identity (see page 153).

Official language: Language statutorily specified as the language of state administration, of official government business (see page 152).

Pluricultural: A situation characterised by multiple ethno-cultural identities. Preferred to the term "multicultural" because it does not suggest the recognition of communities which are culturally regarded to be internally homogeneous and having discrete boundaries in respect of other communities.

Primary language: First language of everyday usage, and thus need not be one's "mother-tongue, or first language of particular domains. In South Africa the primary language of academic activity is English.

Second language: A language which is acquired after learners' first languages, normally in a natural or spontaneous way, particularly since these learners are widely exposed to it in public places and in the media. Opposed to *third language/foreign language*. In South Africa English is a second language in most urban areas, but a third (or "foreign") language in most rural areas.

South African languages: Languages used as first languages by significant numbers of South African citizens. The concept stands in opposition to "languages found in South Africa".

Standard language: A variety which is codified, exists primarily in written form, legitimated by authorities, used in formal domains, used across community boundaries and accepted as a norm by members of the constituting language communities. Standard languages can exist at different levels of standardisation, particularly as regards the acceptance of the norms, their knowledge in the relevant community, and their use by community members.

Language standardisation: The process whereby a standard language is established. The process is usually deliberate, with prescribed norms for appropriate usage in formal contexts. Standardisation is usually associated with power, with the linguistic variety of the economically and politically most powerful community often forming the basis of an ensuing standard language.

Well-known language/language known well: A language of which people possess the basic grammatical, textual, functional and sociolinguistic competence.

Working language: The official language preferred by an institution for purposes of business. In South Africa, English is the working language of many state institutions and businesses. Akin to the notion "thread language" proposed by the South African National Defence Force (Chapter 4).

Examples from South Africa's languages

Tshivenda	Nyambo nnzhi	Tindzimi	Nyambo dza Afrika
Xitsonga	Maremu o kala	Maremu	Maremu ya Afrika
Sepedi	Dipolelo tše dintšhe	Dipolelo	Dipolelo tša Babaso
Setswana	Dipuo tse ngata	Dipuo	Dipuo tse Bantsho
Sesotho	Dipuo tse dintsi	Dipuo	Dipuo tsa Bantsho
isiNdebele	Amalimi amanengi	Amalimi	Amalimi we-Afrika
Siswati	Tilwimi etinengi	Tilwimi	Tilwimi te-Afrika
isiZulu	Izilimi eziningi	Izilimi	izilwimi zase-Afrika
isiXhosa	Iilwimi ezinenzi	Iilwimi	Iilwimi ze-Afrika
Afrikaans	Baie tale	Tale	Afrikatale
English	Many languages	Languages	African languages

Assistance with this list was obtained from: Lufuno Netshitomboni, Abbey Tshinki, Refilwe Malimabe and Buti Skosana from the University of Pretoria

Notable linguistic features
i.   The similarity in the Sotho/Tswana roots for "language" vs. the Nguni roots vs. the roots for Tsonga and Venda, as well as for "many" in the Nguni languages.
ii. The consistent word order difference between the Bantu languages vs. the two non-Bantu languages: noun + adjective vs. adjective + noun.
iii. The explicit presence of a (post-nominal) possessive marker in the Bantu languages (*ze* in Xhosa).
iv. The difference between the indefinite number adverb of Afrikaans and English. The Afrikaans word *baie* is a non-Germanic borrowing from Malayo-Portuguese, due to the importation of large numbers of slaves from east Asia in the 17th century.

Acknowledgements

I would like to express my appreciation to various people.

First of all, I would like to acknowledge my gratitude towards academic office bearers at the University of Pretoria, in particular successive chairs of the Department of Afrikaans (and linguistics) at the University, for their support, both for funding and the freedom to pursue my academic interests.

Secondly, I have to mention particular colleagues: William Labov, from the University of Pennsylvania, who drew me to sociolinguistics; René Dirven, formerly from the Gerhard Mercator University of Duisburg, Germany, who persuaded me to become involved in the politics of language; Ayo Bamgbose (Nigeria), Sammy Beban Chumbow (Cameroon), Herman Batibo (Tanzania and Botswana) and Kembo-Sure (Kenya), who generously accepted me as a friend and supported me professionally in many ways, particularly in the context of LiCCA; the late Kas Deprez, with whom I spent three months of stimulating challenge at the Catholic University of Leuven, Belgium; Ekkehard Wolff of the University of Leipzig, for warm support in many ways; and François Grin, formerly of the European Centre for Minority Issues and the University of Geneva, for the intellectual discipline he always insists upon.

Thirdly, there are the many friends and colleagues in South Africa, particularly within the context of the Linguistics Society of Southern Africa, as well as my masters students in Applied Linguistics and African Languages at the University of Pretoria.

I am also grateful to Kees Vaes from John Benjamins Publishing Company, his anonymous readers, and Annick De Houwer, for her valuably stern criticism through which *Language in South Africa*, I hope, acquired added value.

Finally, Linette, for the many hours of academic talk — about culture, and writing, and editing, and futurism, and so many more things.

Vic Webb
10 May 2001

Map 1. Political map of South Africa, with provinces.

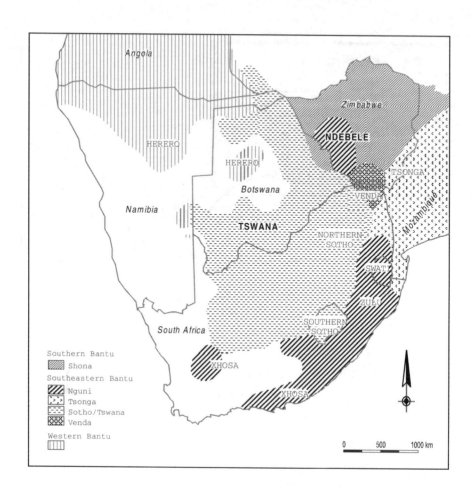

Map 2. Language map of the Bantu languages of Southern Africa.

Preface

The title of this book indicates quite accurately what it wants to do: it wants to discuss the role which language, or, more properly, languages, can perform in the reconstruction and deve lopment of South Africa.

The approach followed in *Language in South Africa* (*LiSA* for short) is characterised by a number of features:

a. it wants to be factually based and
b. theoretically informed, yet
c. acknowledges that an ideological point of departure is inevitable in the present South African context

In South Africa language is a common topic of debate, and many people have quite definite views on what the country needs, linguistically seen. Many of these views, however, are not sufficiently well-informed, and many are simply speculative and emotional. A specific example of such views is the generally negative attitude to the use of the Bantu languages as languages of learning and teaching. In a recent telephone discussion, for example, a senior employee of a non-governmental organisation directed at community colleges stated quite bluntly that any proposal to use these languages for training purposes was "nonsense". The language debate in South Africa also does not demonstrate the necessary insight into the nature of language political processes, such as language attrition, maintenance, spread and development, language policy construction and language policy implementation, and the nature of the inter-relationship between language and society at the macro-level. More serious is the insufficient appreciation for the fundamental role of language in public life. Decision-makers in the public and private sectors of society do not seem to take note of the basic role of language in educational development, and thus in economic performance and political growth, and, in fact, in national recon-struction and development.

Productive debate can obviously not be conducted in such a scenario, and *LiSA* hopes to provide information, bring home the need to base analyses, generalisations and "predictions" on validated findings, and to stress the need to conduct language planning within a justified framework. Additionally, it would like to demonstrate to the Government of South Africa the need for trained language planners.

Secondly, *LiSA* has a clear ideological point of departure. It was written with the assumption that language planning is basically a political act, and that the explicit acknowledgement and justification of such an ideological commitment can contribute positively to the debate on policy options. In this way the language planning process can become subject to more exact justification. The ideological framework within which *LiSA* was written is non-arbitrary, namely the Constitution of South Africa and its related documents, as is described in Chapter 2. The rest of the book follows logically from this basis, asking what must happen to the language situation in the various domains of public life, given the need to implement the political philosophy underlying the Constitution and the associated need for transformation and development.

LiSA also wants to contribute towards establishing the *politics of language* as a field of academic training and scholarly inquiry in South Africa. Internationally, language planning and the politics of language is a well-established field of study, covered in the work of Fishman (1970 and 1971), Ruben and Jernudd (ed., 1971), Fasold (1984), Cooper (1989) and Weinstein (ed., 1990), for example. In South Africa, too, the sociology of language has been the focus of research since the early seventies, with Prinsloo (1972, 1984, ed.), and Hauptfleisch (1974), Steyn (1980) and Alexander (1989) being important contributions. However, it has not yet become a field of undergraduate study. If the Government of South Africa accepts the importance of language planning for the country, a need for trained language planners will arise, which means that training programmes in language planning (and the politics of language generally) need to be available, particularly at the undergraduate level at South African universities. *LiSA* would like to contribute towards the development of this field of study in the country, in particular as regards information on the interrelationship between language and public life, the nature of strategic planning, language political processes, the analytical and descriptive instruments used in the field, and the sociolinguistic facts relevant to language planning in the country.

Post-democratic South Africa offers a unique opportunity for language planning scholars. The country has given statutory recognition to eleven languages as official languages at the national level, it has accepted a progressive Constitution and a Bill of Rights, and there is a strong commitment to transformation and reconstruction in all domains of public life. The problems which South Africa have to resolve are not unique. All African states face similar challenges, as do most so-called third-world countries and even many others, too. If South Africa manages to handle the language issue in an effective way, giving meaningful substance to linguistic pluralism in every-day life, it could make a useful contribution to the resolution of similar problems across the world.

The logic underlying the construction of this monograph can be described as follows: Chapter 1 argues that there are a number of serious educational, economic and political problems in the country; that language plays some role in these problems; and that the problems will not be resolved in a "natural" way, "sorting themselves out". State intervention is necessary, provided in the form of language policy development and language planning. Chapter 2 then describes the macro-contexts within which language planning in South Africa should be undertaken; Chapter 3 provides an overview of the available information relevant to the planning process. From Chapter 4 onwards, the language planning position in a number of public domains is discussed: Chapter 4 deals with the situation in state administration, Chapter 5 with national integration, Chapter 6 with education, Chapter 7 with economic activity, Chapter 8 with the promotion of the Bantu languages, and Chapter 9 with language management.

CHAPTER 1

Invisible voices

The problem of language in South Africa

Introduction

16 June is "Youth Day" in South Africa, a holiday celebrated for the first time in 1995.

"Youth Day" was established by South Africa's Government of National Unity, which came to power on April 27, 1994. The day recalls the events which took place on 16 June 1976, when Soweto schoolchildren erupted in protest against the apartheid policy of the government of the day. Although the main reasons for the protest were political, the direct trigger was a decision by the National Party Government that Afrikaans should be a compulsory medium of instruction in the secondary schools of the former Department of Bantu Education, along with English. Teachers and students rejected this decision, arguing that the teachers and pupils weren't proficient enough in Afrikaans, that text-books were not available in Afrikaans, and that the people directly affected by the policy decision had never been consulted. The Government, of course, rejected the objections of the teachers and pupils, and there was a direct confrontation between protesting pupils and police. In the country-wide protests which followed more than a hundred people died.

June 16 1976 is one of the most important dates in the sociolinguistic history of South Africa, and, also, as it turned out, in the political history of the country. It showed very dramatically how central language is in the national life of the country.

The language factor is equally central in the public life of all the other African states. Consider, for instance, the information contained in Table 1.1. The figures in Table 1.1 clearly show three things: firstly, that the indigenous languages of the people of Africa have no role (or almost no role) in the official domains in their countries; secondly, that the official language of public communication in all these countries is a language originating from the colonial period (usually English, French or Portuguese), and thirdly, that generally only

Table 1.1. Estimated knowledge of English, French and Portuguese in selected African states[1]

State	Population (in millions)	Number of languages	Official language(s)	Knowledge of the ex-colonial languages (%)
Ivory Coast	16	?[2]	French	35[3]
Kenya	29	42	English, Swahili	20[4]
Lesotho	2.3	4	English, Sesotho	Very low
Mozambique	18	24	Portuguese	24.4[5]
Namibia	1.8	About 14	English	Less than 10%
Nigeria	111	400	English[6]	About 30
Tanzania	29	135–150	English, Swahili	5
Uganda	19	30–41	English	40% "understand" English

about 30% of the citizens of these states "know" the official languages of their countries.

The impact of these three facts becomes clear if one takes into account that access to educational development and economic opportunities, participation in political life and social advancement is directly controlled by language: if one does not understand the language used for explaining concepts and ways of reasoning one cannot develop cognitively; if managers and workers do not share the language of the workplace, the occupational mobility of the latter will be adversely affected; if the language of tender applications for Government contracts is a language in which entrepreneurs have insufficient proficiency their chances of being awarded contracts are exceedingly slim (in all probability non-existent); if citizens do not have a proper knowledge of the language of political debate they cannot influence decisions which bear directly on their future in any meaningful way; and if one does not control the languages of social prestige and success fluently, one will remain a member of the underclass.

It is important to keep in mind that the type of language knowledge required for educational development, access to economic opportunities, and so on, is relatively "advanced". An ability to handle basic interpersonal communication (what the Canadian educational linguist, Cummins, called BICS: basic interpersonal communication skills, 1979) is not adequate in any way. What is required is a linguistic proficiency which will allow high-level cognitive performance (as in abstract, objective thought; processes of analysis, inferring, hypothesising and problem-solving; processes of control: planning, monitoring and evaluation);

the possession of developed affective skills (such as empathy for people who differ from you, respect for their right to be different, and the ability to act socially responsibly); and the ability to perform high-level social tasks (e.g. to obtain the meaningful co-operation of people in joint ventures of mutual benefit), and so forth. (In the domain of formal learning, Cummins called this level of language proficiency CALP: cognitive academic language proficiency.)

Given that this point has some validity, it seems clear that, since about 70% of the population of the African states does not know the language(s) of power in their countries, the majority of the citizens of these countries does not have access to their national rights and privileges. The language politics of African states therefore contributes to the disadvantaging of their own citizens, and is an obstacle to development. This is also the case in South Africa, and this book wants to deal with language and national development in South Africa. It argues that the present language situation is a barrier to meaningful social, political and economic transformation and reconstruction, that the country has to be transformed linguistically in a quite radical way, and that the Bantu languages[7] will have to play a far greater public role than before.

This first chapter provides a general overview of the problems in the language politics of South Africa. It discusses, first, problems in the educational, economic and political domains in which language plays some role (that is, what it calls language-related problems); after which it provides an overview of a number of language problems; and then closes by pointing out the need for language planning.

Language-related developmental problems in South Africa

Like many African countries, South Africa has several rather serious national problems, such as poverty, unemployment, inadequate housing, under-effective health services, violence and corruption. Another, equally typically African problem it has, is the inadequate development of its human resources. In all these problems, language plays an important role.

The role of language in under-development can be demonstrated in a number of crucial domains, as will be shown fully in later chapters. In this chapter the issue will be dealt with in a brief, introductory way, in order to indicate the nature and extent of the problem. The following domains will be covered:
– The non-democratisation of knowledge and skills

- Low productivity and non-effective performance in the workplace
- The inadequate development of democracy, the persistence of manipulation, discrimination and exploitation, the lack of national unity and the conflict potential of a divided society, and
- The possibility of linguistic and cultural alienation, contributing to the loss of the wealth contained in its diversity.

The non-democratisation of knowledge and skills

The notion "(under-)development" is rather controversial, since people either tend to evaluate development only in material terms (for example by per capita income or the gross domestic product), or from the perspective of their own beliefs, attitudes, norms and values, i.e. ethno-centrically. In this way an individual who is materially poor but wholly at peace with his environment may be viewed as un(der)developed, whilst a materially extremely wealthy individual who is stilted by stress and anxiety, is deemed highly developed. Clearly, a deeper, more flexible approach is needed, which makes provision for different kinds of development in different contexts, for instance: one measure for economic development, another for educational development, a third for political development, and so on. In the absence of an appropriate and generally accepted "measurement" of development, the more traditional approach will be followed in dealing with South Africa in this discussion, i.e. "development" will be measured from a "western perspective". Such an approach, though contestable, can be motivated on the grounds that the South African people seem to want to become industrialised, technologised and "modernised". It therefore seems reasonable to measure its degree of "development" with the measures of a modern, technologised society.

Looked at from this perspective, a large section of the people of South Africa are underdeveloped. South Africa is ranked 93rd in the *Global Human Development Ratings* by the United Nations Development Programme (Africa Institute, 1996: 24) with a Human Development Index (HDI)[8] of 0.65 (black South Africans: 0.462[9]) as compared with first-rated Canada's 0.932. This is no surprise, if one considers facts such as the following, collected from a variety of sources:

a. In 1992 the mean period of schooling for the population over 25 was 3.9 years, and in 1995 there were still 7 million black South Africans with 7 years or less of formal education — South African Institute of Race Relations, 1997.)

b. The drop-out rate for 1988 for the first school year in "black" schools was 16.2% (South African Institute of Race Relations, 1990: 828)
c. In 1993 the pass-rate for black pupils at the end of the final year in the formal school programme (grade 12) was 39%; in 1994 only 13% of the black pupils in their final school year passed well enough to be admitted to university study. (According to a report of the former Department of Education and Training — previously named the Department of Bantu Education, the department formerly responsible for the education of black pupils in the time of Apartheid, a large proportion of black pupils who had obtained their standard 10 (grade 12) certificates in 1993 was not fully literate, adequately prepared for the labour market, or able to be trained thoroughly.)
d. In 1992 14% of the teachers in the Department of Education and Training schools did not have a teaching diploma, and 57% were said to be under-qualified.
e. In 1994 only 1.7 million black South Africans had some form of post-matriculation training, and only 3000 had degrees.

Clearly, therefore, the educational development of the majority of black South African pupils was far below its potential in the time of Apartheid. (This is still the case, as will be shown in Chapter 6.)

There are a number of reasons for this distressing situation in the country's formal education, such as the enormous impact of colonialism and Apartheid on the belief of the black youth in their own abilities, the culture of violent protest against the authorities which was part of the struggle against apartheid (and the accompanying legitimisation of violence), the fact that many school children grew up in an illiterate or semi-literate environment with almost no exposure to the world of learning, that the daily chores of many learners (especially in rural areas) keep them from studying, that teachers were/are underqualified, that school classrooms were/are overcrowded, that the basic provision of educational facilities (such as training material, laboratory facilities and libraries) were (and are) wholly inadequate, and so on. In the context of all these factors, language seems rather secondary. However, I believe that it plays a vital role, and it can be helpful to focus on its role in educational development.

The major contribution of language to educational underdevelopment relates to the over-estimation of English in the black communities and the under-estimation of the Bantu languages as instruments of learning.

It is plain common-sense that cognitive development can only occur in and through a language the learner knows very well (see also Chapter 6). Cognitive skills, such as the ability to understand the central purpose of a text or to summarise its main line of argument, the ability to select information and to organise it into a new coherent whole, the ability to discover and formulate generalisations, the ability to understand abstract concepts and to manipulate them in arguments, the ability to recognise relations between events (e.g. cause and effect), and so on, can only develop in and through a language in which learners are highly proficient. Generally, such a language is the learner's first (or primary) language. (In South Africa this language was generally referred to as the child's "mother-tongue". However, this term has become stigmatised because it was commonly used by the former government in relation to the Apartheid education system.)

In spite of this generally accepted view black parents in South Africa overwhelmingly prefer English as the language of learning and teaching for their children, for the simple reason that English is equated with success and opportunity. Parents argue, quite rightly, that their children will only be successful in life in South Africa if they know English, since English is the dominant language of all public domains in the country. They then argue, wrongly, that the only way their children can acquire English effectively is if it is used as language of learning. This is a typical case of putting the cart before the horse: the development of cognitive skills does not take place because the language of development is not known well-enough, and English is not acquired effectively because learning skills have not been developed adequately. If the other route is followed: using a Bantu language for cognitive, affective and social skills development, both sets of negative consequences may be reversed: general learning skills may be better developed and, as a consequence, English may be acquired more effectively.[10]

The inadequacy of the English proficiency of school pupils can easily be demonstrated:

Firstly, there are the following findings of a 1986 research project in primary schools in Kwa Zulu/Natal (Odendaal 1986):

a. Fifth grade pupils could generally not understand questions such as: "Where is your home?" "Have you come far?" "What does your father do?" and "In what standard are you?"

b. 21.6% of the primary school teachers said their fifth grade children could not understand them when they used English as teaching medium.

c. 83.5% of these teachers said that the pupils could not understand their text-books.

A second example is the finding in a 1996 survey among teacher trainees in the four northern provinces of South Africa (newspaper report, without details about the source) that although English was to be their language of learning and teaching, only 5% of them were functionally literate in English, and could use English as an instrument of meaningful learning.

Thirdly, consider the following letter written by a Zulu-speaking pupil in her fifth school year, the year in which the switch is usually made to English as language of learning and teaching:

> *22 July 1988*
> Dear Teacher
> Man tomorrow I go to town gave me some bus fere I go to town to seven to by a shoes and sosks and trauers and kep to (ready?) a happy Satardy on Saturdy man com Saturdy to It a cake, and drink some coke and it Some food and orenge appel good by man I ??
> Yours sincerely.

It is not possible to decipher this letter completely, but the following is an approximate rewrite:

> Dear Teacher
> Tomorrow I go to town. (Someone) gave me some bus fare. I will go to town at seven to buy shoes, socks, trousers and a cap on Saturday. On Saturday (I will) eat a cake and drink some coke and eat some food and oranges and apples. Good-bye, man.
> Yours sincerely.

This child had been studying English for three or four years at school, and lived in Amanzimtoti in KwaZulu/Natal, which is largely an English environment, which means that the child had some exposure to English in her daily social interaction.

Finally, consider the following text, written by a fourth year university student in a TESOL course and who was an English teacher in rural South Africa, in an examination answer to a question about the role of memory in second language learning:

> Memory help us to recall about the previous events which are very importan in our lives. If was not of memory we could be able to have good people in subjects like Mathematics and Reporters, Journalists who passed History as a subject which need more of passed events even though some could be of current. Even Lawyers and Advocates they refere to the past events in judging people in courts.

Quite clearly, therefore, despite a history of 150 years of English teaching in South Africa (Hartshorne 1992) and vast expenditure on the English language business ($10 billion in 1989 internationally), on items such as the development of educational material for English teachers, curriculum development, teacher training, English language teaching methods, and research on the issue) black South Africans have not been able to acquire the necessary proficiency in English to use it effectively as an instrument of meaningful access to education. Knowledge, skills and opportunities could therefor not be meaningfully democratised in the country.

The reasons for the preference for English among black South Africans are reasonably self-evident: English is a world language, it provides access to almost all the sources of knowledge (school textbooks) and pleasure (literature, television, films), it is the most important language of work in the country, it allows one to communicate with billions of people all over the world, it is the language of the most successful people in the Western world, and it is the language of the struggle against apartheid. However, in South Africa the value of English has been completely over-estimated; in fact, a simple knowledge of English is often equated with "success" and "being civilised", as is apparent from the following quotes:

> (T)o be educated and trained means having acquired knowledge and expertise mainly through the medium of English. — Prof. Abram L. Mawasha, University of the North, 1988.
>
> Most (black people in South Africa) have come to hate their languages and consider them irrelevant to the education process. — Prof. C. T. Msimang, former Professor of Zulu, University of South Africa, 1991.

A knowledge of English is rated so highly in the black communities that parents believe that their children **need** to be taught through the medium of English, a view which is denied by experiences in most non-English-speaking countries outside the African continent, where English is learnt as a second or a foreign language, without these people being less successful or less civilized than any other people.

The other side of the coin (the "bad penny") is the total underestimation of the Bantu languages. Speakers of these languages argue that they are inappropriate for formal educational development, that no one can get a job with these languages (that is, that they have very little economic value), that they already "know" these languages, and so forth. What they don't take into consideration is that the issue is not language, but cognitive, affective and social development, and that the effective development of these skills will contribute to success across a wide spectrum. They also overlook the likelihood that the development of linguistic skills in the first language (generally a Bantu language) should lead to the more effective acquisition of English (since learning skills are more highly developed). At the same time, they should also take note of the link between the success rate for learning in a second language with "balanced bilingualism", which means, inter alia, that the first language should not be asymmetrically related to the second language (such as English).

It would make far better sense for personal and national development if the parents of black school children elected to use a Bantu language for educational development. This is also the view of a Ghanaian sociologist currently teaching at a South African university, Kwesi Prah, who states quite bluntly:

> One cannot underemphasize the fact that unless the generation of knowledge, discourse and knowledge transfer is effected in the language of the masses the conditions of the masses cannot be transformed (1995a: 86).

It is unlikely, however, that black parents will significantly change their views about the "best" language of learning for their children without Government intervention (for example in the form of comprehensive information campaigns to the parents of school-going children), because these languages have become highly stigmatised, and are perceived as worthless by most of their speakers.

Low productivity and ineffective performance in the workplace
South Africa's economic performance is characterised by a number of negative features, such as the poverty of a large proportion of the population, disparities in the distribution of wealth, and the marginalisation of 75% of its population, namely black South Africans. This is apparent from Table 1.2 below. There are, of course, a variety of reasons for this situation, with one certainly being the political situation of the past. In the context of this monograph, however, the question is whether language had or has any role in this situation in any way.

Not surprisingly, policy-developers and decision-makers in the public and the private sectors never consider language to be a factor of any significance in economic or political planning. For example, in the Government's macro-economic policies, neither the *Reconstruction and Development Programme* (the RDP) or the *Growth, Employment and Redistribution* policy (GEAR) makes any reference to language. Insofar as the political and business leadership in this country (and in Africa as a whole) is concerned, language is not considered to be important in the areas of formal, public life.

This is a rather serious mistake, as can easily be made apparent:

– As an instrument in the management of information (for example its transfer, distribution and access), language is central to good management,

Table 1.2. The economic marginalisation of the black communities in South Africa

Poverty (1998)	61% black South Africans (23 million) is poor (earn less than R948.55 per month per household of 4); 1% white South Africans is poor.
Average annual per capita income (1991)	White South Africans: R21 218; Asian: R7 087; Coloured: R3 931; black: R2 369.
Disparities in the distribution of wealth	Top 5.8% account for 40% of total consumption; bottom 40% account for less than 10%.
Skills shortage	8% to 42% increase in proportion of organisations experiencing shortages of skilled staff: 1993 to 6/1997

SAIRR: *South Africa Survey 1997/1998*

whether in the public or the private sector, and is fundamental in the production of goods and services, and in their delivery (as in buying and selling), that is, as a consumption factor;

– As an instrument of education and training, language is vital to the development of vocational skills and thus to productivity and competitiveness; and

– As an instrument in the socialisation of people, language is important in establishing the norms and values required for the development of work commitment and effectiveness, instilling a sense of institutional loyalty (and ownership), and developing a sense of security, which are all essential ingredients of good governance and good business.

The importance of language becomes apparent if one considers the over-all prosperity of the citizens of the country, their quality of life, and their access to the economic opportunities available to them. Then it quickly becomes clear that language can be a gate-keeper, a discriminator, which facilitates participation and sharing *or* acts as a barrier to accessing opportunities. This is what has happened in South Africa: language has become **a barrier** between the majority of citizens in this country and economic prosperity, an instrument of discrimination (in providing selective access to economic participation and occupational mobility), and to education and the development of people's knowledge, skills, norms and values. This happens both through the dominance of English in the formal economy of the country, and through the non-use of the Bantu languages.

The likely negative effect of the language situation on productivity and effectiveness in the workplace is indicated by research findings on communication in the workplace in 1987 in the Port Elizabeth/Uitenhage area by Kruger

(1989). He found that:

a. 85% of the communication between employers and employees was white/
    black interaction, yet only 4% of the white workers (mainly managers)
    knew Xhosa.[11]
b. Nearly 50% of the training officers couldn't speak Xhosa, and 22% used
    only English for training purposes.
c. 60% of the organisations did absolutely nothing to encourage white em-
    ployees to learn Xhosa or to learn about the Xhosa.
d. 50% of the organisations did not make information on pension schemes,
    insurance and savings available in Xhosa. (Some of the reasons given were:
    that translation is time-consuming and costly; that black people were in
    any case illiterate, and that Xhosa was not a technical language.)
e. Of the 200 labourers interviewed about 50% preferred Xhosa as workplace
    language, 20% preferred English and 15% Afrikaans

Thus: Afrikaans and English were (and are) over-empowered whereas the
Bantu languages were (and are) still marginalised.[12]

In an article in *The RDP Quarterly Report* in June 1996 on the South African
Government's policy for economic growth, the **Growth and Development
Strategy**, it was stated that the Government aims to "eradicate poverty, remove
wealth disparities between people, de-emphasise racial ownership, foster rapid
economic expansion and, in the process, cement social and political peace."
This the government wants to achieve by a massive investment in education
and training, job creation, competitiveness in international markets, and the
development of a system designed to draw the "poorest members of society
into the economic mainstream" (page reference no longer available). It is quite
obvious however that this aim can in no way be achieved if English is to be the
only language of economic activity, and if the "languages of the majority" do
not play some part in public life. The country cannot do without a policy and a
practice of multilingualism. The (nine official) Bantu languages have to be
transformed into languages of learning, access, production, trade, decision-
making, etc. If this does not happen South Africa cannot become a meaningful
global competitor with a "competitive edge" nor will it succeed in its goal to
redistribute wealth and to raise the quality of life of all its people.

Slow political development
From the perspective of Western democracy, South Africa is politically still
underdeveloped.

It is true: Judged within the context of the last 350 years of political life in South Africa, enormous changes have taken place over the past 10 years. The country now has a democratically elected government and its second democratic elections took place peacefully and effectively in 1999; political parties who oppose the Government are allowed to function freely; the laws and structures of racial segregation have all been scrapped; and the rule of law is gradually being established. Yet, there is still very little evidence of *meaningful* citizen participation in political decision-making; there are very few signs that important values and beliefs of democracy, such as respect for fundamental human rights, respect for opposing points of view and the acceptance of decisions which may be contrary to sectional interests, exist to a meaningful extent. Furthermore, the national community is still deeply-divided, with a very strong potential for inter-group conflict and frequent signs of racial intolerance (particularly apparent in private conversations).

South Africa's political underdevelopment is understandable. No modern state can effect changes which European communities took hundreds of years to establish in four or five years. Belgium, for example, is still undergoing constitutional change, despite having existed as a state for 170 years. Political, social and economic transformation necessarily take a long time.

It is easy to show that language played an important role in South Africa's slow political development.

First of all, South Africa's recent past provides many examples of the role of language in manipulation, discrimination and exploitation. Besides the use of language to ensure party political support (the National Party and Afrikaans), the strongest demonstration of the use of language for *manipulative purposes* was, of course, the policy of apartheid: whilst pretending that the philosophy of separateness was culturally based, the National Party government divided the culturally similar black people on linguistic grounds, whereas the culturally dissimilar white people (and also the culturally disparate Indians) were each politically grouped together. Since the policy of apartheid was a clear case of dividing people in order to retain control over them, it is a good example of language-based political manipulation. *Discrimination* on linguistic grounds is also easy to illustrate: The fact that Afrikaans and English were so exceptionally dominant before 1994 led to their use for discriminatory purposes. This was especially so through the linguistic restrictions applied in particular occupations, like radio and television reporting, and through the appointment of people on the basis of their proficiency in the formal standard varieties of Afrikaans and English. Though these restrictions no longer apply since the recent onset of democratisation in South Africa and, particularly, the take-over of public media power by black South Africans (reporters on radio and television are no longer expected to follow the Standard South African English norms exclusively) there is still a very real chance that English, with its exceptionally high standing in both the leadership and the general community, may continue to be an instrument of discrimination. As regards *exploitation* on linguistic grounds, Brown (1995) discusses the practice on the South African gold mines of using Fanagalo, a pidgin which presumably arose on the Natal sugar farms and which is generally perceived by black people as symbolising subservience, "boss-labourer"/"superior-inferior" relations (Adendorff, 1995), as medium of worker communication. Mine-workers from outside the "Fanagalo area" were formally taught the pidgin with specially produced grammars and dictionaries. This language policy of the mining industry was obviously designed at increasing efficiency and production. It also meant, though, that since workers were not given the opportunity to acquire English (or Afrikaans) adequately, they were severely restricted with respect to job promotion. This can be interpreted as exploitation, as a practice of keeping the black labour force in subservient positions and of ensuring cheap labour. An alternative option could have been for the mine management to have taught all their workers English, which would, eventually, also have served the interests of productivity, whilst at the same time have increased their occupational (and social) opportunities. Today, another option is that the Bantu languages be used as the working languages of the mining industry, particularly at the lower and middle levels.

There are many more domains in which one will find unfairness in general, such as the court, where all the proceedings were (and are), in Afrikaans and/or English (despite the possibility of an interpreter for languages other than Afrikaans and English); in rural health services where medical doctors and psychologists are usually unable to examine patients in a language which the patient knows, and in farming, where farm labourers are expected to perform their tasks through the language of the farmer.

Language has also played a role in the lack of *national unity* and the presence of *conflict potential*. Despite the advent of political "democracy" in 1994, South Africa is still a deeply and complexly divided society, and there is still evidence of tension between the races and between ethnic communities (also, variously, between social groups such as gender groups, age groups, religious groups, and so on, as one finds universally). This is due to pre-colonial conflicts (between the Khoe, the San and the Bantu-speaking people), colonialisation and apartheid. In all these cases of conflict and division, language played some part. As mentioned earlier, language (along with race) was a basic divider of society in apartheid South Africa. This was even artificially controlled, with language boundaries erected in the interest of political goals. In this regard Herbert (1992) writes: "the 'North Sotho (sic)[13] language is a fiction' (quoting van Warmelo). Governmental creation of ethnic groups and standard languages has been used to justify apartheid policy; for example, Lebowa is designated as a 'homeland' for the Northern Sotho people who themselves came into existence only through the legislative action of apartheid policy. Linguistic autonomy here and elsewhere has more to do with socio-political criteria than linguistic ones." (p. 3.)

Today, there still seems to be a more or less clear correlation between language, race and class in the country, as expressed in Table 1.3 (oversimplified and slightly manipulated to emphasise some sort of implicational relationship).

The exact role of language as an element of socio-cultural identity (and thus a potential source of division and conflict) in South Africa has not yet been systematically investigated. However, a number of observations can be made about the social meaning of the South African languages.

The perception of language as an identity marker in South Africa differs between communities. In some Afrikaans-speaking communities, for instance, Afrikaans is regarded as an indispensable part of socio-cultural life (and is expressed through statements of extreme language loyalty and "language love"), whilst in others it is perceived as "merely a tool of interaction". In the mainly black communities it is regarded as a symbol of oppression, acting as a trigger for intolerance. These meanings can lead to conflict, as can be illustrated by recent conflict between the Government and educational and cultural leaders in the white Afrikaans community about the demand of the latter for single-medium schools (that is, Afrikaans-medium schools), and for control over aspects such as the determination of school curricula, prescribed texts and the appointment of teachers.

English, on the one hand, is a symbol of liberation for some, whilst it seems

Table 1.3. The relationship between race, class and language in present-day South Africa

	Indian people	White people	Coloured people	Black people
Higher class	English	English	English	English
Middle class	English	English, Afrikaans	Afrikaans, English	English
Working class	English	Afrikaans	Afrikaans	Bantu language

This chart demonstrates the asymmetric ethnolinguistic division of power in the country.

to be becoming, on the other hand, a site of contestation, particularly due to the insistence that a specific set of language norms (namely "British English") be applied.

In the Bantu language communities ethnic self-awareness and even linguistic nationalism also seem to be emerging, albeit in small degrees. An example is the recent formation of a committee for marginalised languages. Despite the recognition of Tsonga, Venda and Swazi as national official languages, these three language communities, along with the (Southern) Ndebele-speaking people, have formed a **Committee for Marginalised Languages**, mainly, I think, because of feeling threatened by the "five big" Bantu languages (Zulu, Xhosa, Pedi, Tswana and Sotho/Southern Sotho — see Chapter 3). The seriousness of their intentions becomes apparent from the following statement by Hlengani Mabasa, chairperson, in a written submission to the *Language Plan Task Group*, set up by the Government in 1995/6 to describe a framework for the development of a comprehensive national language policy. He says that the present debate on language policy and planning in South Africa

> implicitly tells the people who do not speak these languages (the marginalised languages — VW) that the languages are of very little, if any value at all. This could further stigmatise the people who speak the "minor" official languages, hence, perpetuating tribalism. To succeed in social and economic life, people who speak the "minor" official languages will be increasingly under pressure to run away from their languages and cultural practices to associate themselves with one or two of the "major" official languages. Alternatively, this may lead to a rise of **ethnic demagogues** (emphasis original) among the people who speak the marginalised languages, unleashing extreme forms of ethnic chauvinism which may result in unwanted ethnic clashes." (p. 6.)

Another interesting example comes from the descendants of the Khoe-San people.[14] In 1652, with the arrival of the Dutch in South Africa, the Khoe-San population numbered between 300,000 and 500,000, according to estimates. By 1955 there were about 55,000 according to the South African paleo-anthropologist, Philip Tobias (1996, unpublished conference paper). Today, less than 200 people speak a Khoe-San language in South Africa (excluding neighbouring Botswana and Namibia). (Personal communication by Khoe-San linguist, A. Traill.) Since 1994 these people (who were classified as "coloureds" in the time of Apartheid), seem to be developing a sense of distinct ethnic self-awareness. This is firstly evident from a 1996 conference organised by the South African Government to revitalise Khoe-San identity (26–27 September 1996). The express aim of the conference was to debate the pre-history of the Khoe-San, their present socio-cultural position and the future of Khoe-San culture. Papers were read by paleo-anthropologists, archaeologists, anthropologists, historians, a geneticist and a linguist. Topics covered included: *Khoisan identity and definition, Rock Art and the World of Ideas, Khoekhoe cultures and their impact, Current state of Khoisan Heritage Conservation* and *Cultural Rights, Human Rights, Land Rights: Present and Future.*

A second example of re-awakening Khoe-San self-awareness is the following statement to the United Nations Working Group of Indigenous Populations (July 1996) in support of the argument of the *Griqua National Conference of South Africa*[15] for self-determination. The basis for Griqua self-determination, it is stated, involves:

> "recognition of aboriginality; representation at all levels of government; traditional leadership-status; the restitution of flagrantly violated treaties; the return of all GRIQUA land usurped by colonial powers but now inherited illegally by the nation-state of South Africa and compensation for untold suffering, genocide and ethnocide inflicted on the GRIQUA and their KHOISAN ancestors as culturally, linguistically, socially, economically and politically deprived, disempowered and almost decimated aboriginal, autochthonous and indigenous people of southern Africa." (p. 1 of the statement)

Today, organisations such as the *South African San Institute* (established in 1996) and the *Working Group of Indigenous Minorities* (with its headquarters in Namibia) work towards the recognition and promotion of the Khoe-San people (see Crawhall, 1998).

Given these examples of ethnic consciousness it is clear that questions of identity are of particular importance in the country. Obviously, a future language policy/plan will have to pay proper attention to the conflict potential of language, and the Government needs to make clear decisions about the establishment of structures within which language and cultural rights can be meaningfully recognised and the ethnolinguistic conflict potential be managed (see also Chapter 2). Language tolerance and language nationalism is, after all, acquired knowledge, and not biologically determined or inherited behaviour patterns. Ethnic tolerance can therefore be cultivated.

In addition to the problem of slow political development, the political developments of the past ten years will almost certainly have sociolinguistic consequences, which will ultimately have to be addressed in a comprehensive language policy. Harald Haarman (1995) discusses the sociolinguistic consequences of the disintegration of the Soviet empire, the rise of new nation-states in eastern Europe, trans-national integration in the European Union, the movement of work-seekers across state borders and the migration of refugees. He focuses particularly on the impact these events had and are having on the construction of group membership and individual identity, as well as on the increase in ethnic friction and growing nationalism. He then discusses the role of language in these processes (specifically as a symbol of identity and as an instrument in the construction of identity). The same types of changes have occurred in South Africa. Here, also, a former political order has disintegrated (structurally and functionally, albeit not attitudinally), a new "trans-national" integration process has to be built up, there is a general movement of work-seekers across the country, and there is an increasing incidence of in-migrating refugees. Here too, new group membership and new individual identities have to be constructed, and national integration has to be developed. In these political processes language can be an important factor.

As an illustration of the sociolinguistic consequences of political developments in South Africa, one can consider two further cases. First, there is the question of Afrikaans. In 1994 the white Afrikaans-speaking group lost all political power (undoubtedly for ever), and they are at present involved in a serious reanalysis and redefinition of who they are and what their position is in a non-racist society in which black people have all the political power. It is possible that Afrikaans could become an important instrument in a process of political redefinition. Secondly, the relations between linguistic communities in the Northern Province are also interesting from a language political perspective. Before 1994, Venda, Tsonga and Pedi all had the status, rights and privileges of being official languages in their own, clearly defined political spaces (in the so-called national states and homelands — see Chapter 3). Each was, in some sense, a "majority" language. Now, with the "unification" of the Northern Province, they find themselves grouped together in a new political space, the Northern Province. Although they are all three official languages at the national level, they are not necessarily official languages at the *provincial* level (according to the 1996 constitution), and they will therefore have to compete for (meaningful) official recognition as well as for the rights and privileges they formerly enjoyed. This situation could conceivably lead to increased socio-political awareness, a redefinition of group membership and group relationships, and a new definition of political identity (even, possibly, as a *politically oppressed community*). (See also the discussion above of the *Committee for Marginalised Languages*, comprising Venda, Tsonga, Ndebele and Swazi.)

Finally, the role of language in establishing a particular political discourse needs to be considered. As is well-known, language is a carrier or conveyer of socio-cultural values and beliefs and a socialising instrument, and as such has a re-ifying power. In the time of Apartheid, the meanings of words like *ethnicity, culture* and *development* obtained specific content, co-determining people's perception of reality (see Esterhuyse, 1986). In 1989, Mkhatshwa (published in 2000) discussed the use of language as a control mechanism at a conference on language and struggle (du Plessis and van Gensen, 2000), writing (2000: 37): "Language is used to promote the interests of the dominant social classes. Thanks to their ownership of the means for socialisation and of the media of mass communication, the media has become a formidable tool for propaganda, disinformation and mental coercion. What is even more alarming, is the manner in which language is deliberately distorted either to deceive or mystify. We only need to select a few words at random: *reforms, tricameral system,* the *Great Indaba, citizenship, consultation, law and order, terrorist, own affairs, Third World, homelands, democracy, separate but equal.*" (See also Willemse *et al.,* similarly 1989/2000.) Today, of course, language is also used with a similar function, particularly evident in politically correct language usage, that is, the use of politically appropriate terms such as *transformation, equity, equality, affirmative action in the sense of correcting past imbalances, transparency,* and *sustainable development.* If one has developed the "skill" of using these words, you are listened to, otherwise you are ignored and marginalised.

The issue of language and politics is of central concern for all African states. This is particularly clear if one considers their extreme linguistic and ethnic diversity (as in Nigeria, Kenya, and most other states), their colonialized past, and the impact on them of globalization. These three realities combine to produce a series of very serious problems for African states, for example:

- The need for state-wide administrative control requires, logically, a single language of wider communication. The most suitable candidate for this function is generally considered to be the ex-colonial language. However, through such a choice African states are denying their intellectual and spiritual independence, proclaiming their dependence on their former rulers, and destroying their integrity, which is an ironic twist to the independence tail, to say the least.

- Political sovereignty requires national integration and national loyalty, however, this is made difficult by the ethnic tensions in African states, as demonstrated in Nigeria (the Biafran war), Ruanda, and the Democratic Republic of the Congo. How should the conflict potential of ethnic diversity, expressed, very often, through language, be managed? How can state-building and nation-building take place in such situations? Can language play a meaningful role in boundary maintenance, the creation of new identities and resocialization? In the European nation-states lexicographers played an important role in nurturing distinctive languages and in creating the myth of a linguistically homogeneous state and a single national language. Can this also happen in African states?

– Africa is experiencing a desperate struggle to decolonise itself, to rid itself of its utter economic dependency on the Western world, and to free itself from its cultural bondage. However, one of the most conspicuous and overt markers of its colonised mind and soul is the strong presence of English, French and Portuguese. Why does Africa have this apparent total commitment to the ex-colonial languages and an inability to develop its own languages as languages of higher functions? What are the likely consequences of such attitudes?

– Africa is, of course, also subject to globalization, and is therefore sure to react emotionally to this phenomenon, by, for example, a spirit of relocalization, a need for closure, and a need for personal involvement. This introduces the question of language and ethnicity into the equation, particularly, on the one hand, the fact that closure implies increased ethnic identification, and, on the other, the fact that involvement implies using a language which will facilitate involvement (which cannot be an ex-colonial language).

The possibility of linguistic and cultural alienation
The symbolic meaning of languages in South Africa also plays a role in linguistic and cultural alienation.

Sub-Saharan African communities are generally characterised by a low esteem of their own cultures, and this, plus the process of language contact, has the potential, also in South Africa, of leading to language and cultural shift and language death/the loss of cultural diversity.

There are several examples of language shift in the South African language situation. A first example is the almost total shift from the Khoi and the San languages (the first languages of this sub-continent) to Afrikaans (at the time more correctly called "Cape Dutch"), Xhosa and Southern Sotho, accompanied, to some degree, by the loss of their distinctive cultural identities. (An interesting question is what language they would use today, if any, to express their cultural identity, were they to succeed in "revitalising" themselves as a separate community, as discussed above.) A second example is the shift in the former Indian communities of Natal away from Hindi, Gujarati, Urdu, Tamil and Telegu to English (see Mesthrie 1992 and 1995). A third, rather ironic example of language shift, is provided by Davey and van Rensburg (1993). This concerns the elimination of Afrikaans from a Tswana community in Tlhabane, near Rustenburg in the North-West Province. Although native speakers of Afrikaans (and non-speakers of Tswana), these (black) people were forced to relocate themselves in a Tswana-speaking area by the Group Areas Act of the previous government on racial grounds. As a consequence their children lost their native language and gradually (and against their own wishes) became Tswana-speaking. Today, practically no one in the community speaks Afrikaans. Further examples are the shift away from Afrikaans (and towards English) in the so-called coloured community in the Western Cape (Scheffer 1983), and in the formerly Afrikaans-speaking Indian community in Pretoria (Noor Mahomed, 1998). There may also be some shift towards English in the black communities.

The present constitution guarantees the principle of multilingualism and the development of respect for different languages and cultures, but the practical implementation of this philosophy may prove very difficult, as will be discussed more fully in later chapters. At this point it is interesting to take note of the possibility that the smaller official languages may, in some ironic way, be more disadvantaged than they were in the time of apartheid. The pre-1994 government ensured (albeit for the wrong reasons) that learners who were, for example, speakers of Venda (which has about 700,000 speakers nation-wide), could study their first language during the time allotted to such subjects within the school programme. Even though there may only have been three Venda-speaking pupils in a particular grade, provision was still made for them. Today, the right to study Venda as a school subject is constitutionally enshrined. However, the Department of Education has a ruling which limits such a possibility to cases where there are a minimum of 35 pupils. In the urban areas of Gauteng this is often not the case, and such pupils are thus obliged to study one of the major Bantu languages. In the long run such children may lose their knowledge of their parents' language, with predictable long-term consequences.

The phenomenon of language shift, added to the *de facto* increase in monolingualism in official contexts (the use of English as the major medium of government and public communication), makes the occurrence of linguistic and cultural alienation possible, leading, possibly, to linguistic and cultural death. When this happens and communities lose their "roots", they could also lose their sense of identity and of belonging, and become settings for serious social and psychological disturbances, such as alcohol misuse, sexual abuse and violence.[16]

Language problems in South Africa

The basic proposition in the preceding section was that there are several serious problems in South Africa which are somehow language-related. In order to resolve these problems through, for instance, language planning, note has to be taken of the language problems in the country, since these may act as obstacles to problem-solving attempts. In this section, therefore, attention is given to language problems in the country.

Language problems which may act as obstacles in resolving language-related problems include the following:

a. *The dominance of English*
The effects of the dominance of English have already been discussed. These effects flow from the over-estimation of the language, which could contribute, as suggested above, to retarded or restricted educational development, blocked access to economic opportunity, lower productivity and efficiency in the workplace, blocked access to political participation, the possibility of discrimination and manipulation, and, finally, pose a threat to the country's linguistic diversity.

In my opinion, whilst not forgetting that English is an important asset to the people of South Africa, that most South Africans have a serious need to acquire it, and that English is supported by strong natural economic, political and social forces, it is necessary to restore the balance of power between English and the other South African languages, that is, English also needs to undergo affirmative action, a process of redressing (past) imbalances. This is especially important because educational development (and thus economic growth) is conditioned, at least partially, by balanced bilingualism (between the L1 and English), by skills development in the first language and by the social standing of the minority language[17] (i.e. languages other than English).

b. *Low proficiency in English*
Given that English has such a central role in public life in South Africa, it is of great public importance that people should be adequately proficient in it. As demonstrated above: though it could possibly be true that a sizeable percentage of South Africans have a basic communicative ability in English, the level of proficiency in it is largely inadequate for the functions it has to perform. It is essential that this problem be addressed, either by vastly improved English second language teaching, or (paradoxically) by a radical upgrading of the Bantu languages and their teaching (see Chapter 6 for further discussion).

c. *Insufficiently adapted Bantu languages*
In general the Bantu languages have an extremely low status, as indicated above. They have almost no economic value (in more than just a monetary sense) and their speakers do not believe that these languages can serve as useful instruments of learning, economic activity, social mobility, or any other serious public business. They argue, without any appropriate linguistic justification, that these languages do not have the necessary (lexical and registral) equipment or status for use in the secondary domains of life, and that it makes no sense to study them at school or to try to give them more significant instrumental value. Their only use, they suggest, is as instruments of personal social interaction, cultural activity and religious expression.

There are various possible reasons for this lack of belief in Africa in the value of their own possessions. Following Omotoso (1994: 15 and elsewhere), the reasons could include such long-term factors as slavery, the culturally destructive impact of the work of Christian missionaries, colonialism (and in South Africa: Apartheid), and the pan-Africanist movement. A major programme of language revalorisation is clearly necessary (see Chapter 8, and Webb 1994a and b).

It is essential that committed development programmes be instituted in at least two areas. First of all, the study of the Bantu languages as first languages needs to be radically revised. In the same way as learners find the study of English as a first language valuable, so learners should find the study of the Bantu languages valuable, challenging and stimulating. First language study provides a unique opportunity to develop learners' cognitive, affective and social skills, and this should also constitute one of the main objectives of L1 teaching in the Bantu languages. Their syllabuses, learning materials and the didactic practices in L1 teaching thus need serious attention. Secondly, the technicalisation of the Bantu languages equally needs immediate attention. It is necessary that the myths associated with these languages be dismantled, for instance that the current lack of technical terms in them is a serious obstacle to their high-level use.

d. *Difficulties with establishing multilingualism*
In spite of the central role given to multilingualism (and pluralism in general) in the current constitution the country is experiencing an increasing practice of monolingualism:

- Government decision-makers and senior state administrators seem to be in favour of using only English in public domains, as is apparent from proposals that English be the sole working language of parliament and the court (see Chapter 4)

- The Government is exceedingly hesitant to give practical effect to the recognition of cultural and linguistic rights (see Chapter 5)
- In the domain of education there is an overwhelming preference for English as language of learning and teaching as well as a subject of study (see Chapter 6)
- In the economic sector the use of English only is taken as self-evident, with the interrelationship between the use of one language (English) and productivity and competitiveness not even questioned (see Chapter 7)
- The public media is strongly English-oriented

The basic reason for the increasing monolingualism is the power of English. However, given the government commitment to multilingualism[18] one would have expected a stronger attempt to promote it. The fact that such a stronger attempt is absent may be due to other reasons, such as (a) ignorance of the fundamental role of language in public life[19]: that language can obstruct access, provide access selectively or facilitate access to basic rights and privileges; (b) insensitivity to the needs of people who are not fully proficient in the dominant language of public life (particularly true of people who grow up in a largely monolingual world[20]); and (c) the (subconscious) decision of people who know the language(s) of power, to retain privileges exclusively for themselves (see Chapter 4, as well as Webb 1999a).

If the government is serious about language equity and promoting multilingualism it has to address the problem of increasing monolingualism. This means, first of all, deciding what the concept means.

In African states a policy of multilingualism cannot refer to "creating a multilingual society", simply because this is the natural state of affairs in these societies anyway. "Multilingualism" must mean, first of all, promoting *individual multilingualism* (so that the members of the society can communicate with one another because they share competence in overlapping languages); secondly, establishing a *multilingual attitude and way of thought;* and, thirdly, creating a *multilingual official or public society* (where all the major languages of the country are used for the **high public functions**).

Given the tendency throughout Africa to describe African countries as "English-speaking", "French-speaking" or "Portuguese-speaking", in contrast with their real multilingual nature (**no** African country is any one of these three), it is necessary to change attitudes and ways of thinking about the multilingual reality of Africa, to be positive about the potential of multilingualism, to promote the principle of multilingualism as well as the languages involved, and to create knowledge of these languages and a respect for their existence.

It is also necessary to understand that there are different categories of multilingualism in different countries. Multilingual states are not multilingual in the same way. Many European states, for example, are very multilingual, particularly in the sense of housing many languages, but this type of multilingualism is very different from that of African states. Britain, France, Germany, the Netherlands, and so forth all have sizeable communities whose first language is foreign (Asian, Southern or Central European, African), and the presence of these communities do pose problems. However, in African states the "minority languages" are statistically by far in the majority, and their existence poses very different problems, which therefore need to be handled very differently.

A particular facet of the problem of multilingual communities is the restricted ability of citizens to communicate *cross-culturally* on a meaningful level. In South Africa, this inability is the result of at least the following:
–   the absence of a national lingua franca at the basic levels and in the basic domains of public life
–   underdeveloped multilingualism, with most non-black citizens having a knowledge only of Afrikaans and English and therefore incapable of communicating with members of the black communities in a Bantu language, and
–   the absence of training in cross-cultural communicative skills in school language learning programmes (for example, dealing with cultural differences in interpretative schemata, conflicting contextualisation clues, and conflicting discourse conventions — see Chapter 6)

A final problematical aspect of a policy of official/public multilingualism is the question of the costs involved. Clearly, it is economically impossible to adopt a policy which aims at full linguistic equality, with all government communication and services in all 11 languages. On the other hand the constitutional language stipulations require obedience to at least the spirit of multilingualism in all public domains. How this can be done, given the restricted material and human resources available, is a serious matter, which will require a very creative approach (see Chapter 7 for a further discussion of cost-estimation).

e. *The politicisation of the country's languages*
The problem of politicised languages (and asymmetric power relations, discussed above) manifests itself in many ways, for example in the unevenness in

the knowledge of the country's languages; in the strong ethnic nationalism associated with especially Afrikaans;[21] in the negative socio-political meaning of Afrikaans in many communities; in the generally exceptionally positive socio-political meaning of English; in the generally exceptionally negative socio-educational meaning of the Bantu languages, and in the strong drive towards linguistic "purism" (in Afrikaans, English, Zulu, as well as the other languages).

In general, there is a strong degree of linguistic/ethnic intolerance in the country, with extreme stigmatisation and stereotyping of the different language communities. This is particularly the case with the different racial groups, but is also found with regard to language communities. Many white Afrikaans-speaking South Africans are markedly antagonistic about their English-speaking cohorts, whereas white English-speaking people can be as viciously one-sided, with negative references to Afrikaans-speaking persons formulated in "linguistic" terms ("There's this Afrikaner cow …"). Ethnic intolerance is also mirrored in race-directed reference terms, which relate, of course, to South Africa's history of racial conflict. For instance: Afrikaans-speaking whites are called *rock-spiders, hairy-backs* or *Boers* (which has a pejorative meaning for some but evokes fierce pride in others[22]); English-speaking South Africans are negatively referred to as *rednecks, souties* (from the Afrikaans name for epsom salts) and *the English*; black South Africans as *kaffirs* (a name publicly banned by the former president of the country); Indians as *coolies*; and the coloured people as *boesmans* ("Bushmen") and *hotnots* (from "Hottentot", a name formerly used to describe the descendants of the Khoe). Even terms such as *Bantu, Khoi* and *San* have negative connotations, and it is pointed out, for example, that "san" is a Khoe word which formerly meant "tramp", "rascal", "vagabond" or "forager". Naming is an instrument in the exercise of power (or perhaps a way of handling perceived threat), and as such needs to be dealt with, for example in public education programmes.

As regards linguistic nationalism, Afrikaans provides a good example. (Webb and Kriel, 2000.) Although Afrikaans has strong historical roots in the country's coloured (formerly largely Khoe-San, slave and mixed) communities, it was appropriated by the white political intelligentsia of the past as an instrument of political mobilisation. In the process Afrikaans was ideologised and mythologised into a "White Man's language", its standardisation re-classified its non-white speakers as speakers of non-standard Afrikaans, the language was "purified" of foreign elements (especially English elements) and it became a symbol of a particular socio-cultural identity (the Afrikaner). This latter association has become so strong that Afrikaner leaders saw any "change" in

Afrikaans (for instance regarding its public functions or the acceptance of "non-standard" elements as standard) as a threat to the integrity of the Afrikaner's cultural identity. As one can expect, Afrikaans acquired a schizophrenic nature, with a clear alienation between "cultured", or better still: culturalised, formal standard Afrikaans and colloquial Afrikaans, as described by Ponelis (1992). This internal division led to language-internal conflict, which has had serious educational consequences for children who grew up in coloured working class families (see de Villiers 1992).[23]

Since 1994, significant changes have befallen Afrikaans. Part of its serious loss of public functions (its functional public demise) is that its use in public forums (at conferences and workshops) generally means that no one listens to the speaker, or takes him/her seriously. On the other hand, its intellectually developed young speakers (students, young academics) consciously make use of English words, using, thus, a strikingly code-mixed variety, for example:

> *Dis 'n absolutely stunning song, gesing met great gutso!*
> (It's an absolutely stunning song, sung with great gutso!)

It seems they feel a strong emotional need to signal their detachment from a past they are historically bound to.

The politicised nature of the South African languages is an important factor since it has several consequences. Firstly it means that these languages cannot perform their social functions fully (such as serving as instruments of national unification, or effective instruments of access in public domains). Secondly, it obstructs both horizontal and vertical lines of communication, and thirdly it means that languages may play a role in future conflict.

The politicisation of the country's languages has, of course, also led to the politicisation of other (language related) phenomena, such as the issue of language of learning and teaching (in particular the principle of mother-tongue instruction) and ethnicity, as already mentioned.[24] The degree of their politicisation is such that it is at present difficult to debate them publicly, since any support for the use of a first language as language of learning and teaching, or concern expressed about threats to the country's linguistic and cultural diversity is immediately interpreted as an attempt to reinstate apartheid, to divide people, keep the disadvantaged disadvantaged and to retain political control in "white hands".

f. *Language standardisation*
Language standardisation is basically also a political issue, and as such it warrants separate attention.

The question of standardisation is crucial for more reasons than just the fact that a standard language functions as a set of practical guidelines for appropriate linguistic behaviour in formal public contexts. Given the politicisation of the South African situation language norms determine the content of language teaching programmes, can determine career appointments, can act as basis for discrimination, and can affect the degree to which people are taken seriously in public debate. "Proper language", it seems, is quite commonly used as an indication of one's cognitive abilities and the degree to which one is "civilised": even slight "deviations" from "correct pronunciation" can brand you as a "lesser person". This is likely to be a common experience among black South Africans, especially with regard to their "inability" to conform to the norms of "British" English. This was particularly apparent during public reaction to the use of radio broadcasters whose English was not considered up to standard in 1994/5.

The issue of what should be accepted as appropriate English in formal public contexts in South Africa is still a big issue. Whilst English is generally accepted as the language of public preference, there are differences about "what English". At a 1995 conference a young black South African delivered a paper entitled: "English? Yes. But whose English? Your English? Or mine?", and he made it quite clear: "We" are governing this country now, and we will decide what English is acceptable. If "you" don't like our decisions you can leave the country quite easily. There are no lions at the Johannesburg International Airport, and an air ticket to London is relatively cheap. This attitude is, of course, extreme, but it does illustrate the intensity of the debate, which is understandable, given the colonial experience.

A second emotional issue is the debate about the harmonisation of the Nguni and Sotho languages. In the 1950s a proposal was made that the Nguni and Sotho languages be harmonised, that is, that two varieties common to the constituting languages in the two language families should be developed, as one way of facilitating closer unity between the different language communities in the black sectors of the population. This suggestion was revived by Alexander in 1989, and it has since been debated quite heatedly, but is often wrongly interpreted. The proposal envisages the creation of two common written varieties for the two language families in the country (the Nguni languages: Zulu, Xhosa, Swazi and Ndebele) and the Sotho languages: Pedi, Sesotho and Tswana) to be used in school text books and in formal documents. The proposal certainly has a political undertone ("black unity"), but also has clear economic advantages, particularly in the sense that school textbooks could then be produced in only two Bantu "languages" instead of seven (Venda and Tsonga being excluded as non-Sotho and non-Nguni). It has the support of some sociolinguists, but is rejected by many leading persons in the Bantu language communities, mainly, it seems, because harmonisation is perceived as a threat to their socio-cultural (and political?) identity. This perception is sociolinguistically unfounded, because the proposal is not intended to be subtractive, to "take anything away" from any community. Rather, it has an additive aim.

A third example of problems with standardisation concerns the selection of the basic variety for the standardisation of the Bantu languages. In most cases the "natural" standardisation route was chosen: the use of a dominant dialect as the basis for standardisation. This was the case with Pedi, which was based on the Pedi dialect, Venda, which was based on Tsiphani, and Zulu. However, a consequence of this approach is that language-internal tension is building up, with speakers of the non-standard dialect feeling marginalised, as is shown in the dissertation work of T. Z. Ramaliba at the University of Pretoria in respect of Venda.

g. *The scarcity of language practitioners*

The preceding discussion emphasised the need for the large-scale linguistic transformation of South Africa. For this to happen in any meaningful way will require, among a number of things, the availability of well-trained language practitioners. Language teachers, people who produce effective language-learning material, copy-writers, editors, proof-readers, specialists in document design, translators, interpreters, lexicographers, terminographers and language planners are needed.

At present there is a lack of training programmes to produce specialists and workers in these areas, with few training centres (such as universities and technikons) equipped to provide the necessary training. In fact, training in linguistics in the country is also relatively elitist and Euro-centred, in the sense that such programmes are directed by British and US definitions of what constitutes a linguistic problem and what knowledge and skills linguists can be expected to require. Webb and Kembo-Sure (2000) is an attempt to contribute towards changing this situation.

The need for language planning

In the South African language debate the view is often expressed that the language issue should be allowed to follow its "natural" course, and that "natural" social, economic and political forces will eventually resolve the problems discussed in this chapter. This is, of course, an uninformed position, since it does not take into consideration the interests which control the "natural" forces, nor does it consider the possible negative consequences (continued disparities in the distribution of wealth, the potential for ethnic conflict, and so on) necessarily attached to such a position. In fact, the realities of the "natural" social, economic and political forces in the country make it imperative that the government intervene, and develop policies and plans to handle the necessary linguistic transformation of the country.

State intervention in the linguistic transformation of the country in the form of language planning is a necessary (but not sufficient, see Chapter 2) condition for the effective governance of a multilingual state. If the problems discussed above are to be handled in a meaningful manner, South Africa (like every African state) needs a comprehensive national language policy, an associated language plan, and a set of specific strategies for the implementation of the plan and the evaluation of its implementation efforts.

Language planning in the South African context is discussed more fully in Chapter 2.

Notes

1. The sources for these figures come variably from: Sow and Abdulaziz (1993) and the Africa Institute (1996) in general; Fermino (1996) for Portuguese; Ndoleriire (pers. comm.) for Uganda; Batibo (1995: 68) for Tanzania; and Pütz (1995: 160–1) for Namibia.

2. Information not available.

3. Griefenow-Mewis (1992) reports that, although 35% of the Ivoreans over the age of 6 are said to "know" French, less than 6% spoke a variety of French which could be understood abroad.

4. Kembo-Sure (1991: 246) states that "not more than 5% (of Kenyans) can be said to have some competence in English".

5. Heine (1992) puts the fluent knowledge of Portuguese in the former Portuguese colonies at less than 5%.

6. Igbo, Hausa and Yoruba are recognised as *national* languages.

7. The term *Bantu language* is controversial in South Africa, with black people associating it directly with apartheid (cf. the concept *bantustans*, the name generally used to refer to the political entities within which black South Africans were expected to "govern themselves"). However, in the international linguistics literature *Bantu language* is the general technical term, and it will therefore be used in this text in preference to *African* (which is technically misleading, since many African languages are not also Bantu languages), and *Black*, which unnecessarily emphasises race.

8. The HDI is based on longevity, knowledge (adult literacy, mean years of schooling) and standard of living (purchasing power).

9. It is, of course, objectionable to distinguish between races. However, race is still very much a factor in South Africa.

10. It would therefore make sense if the British Council and the US Information Service were to support the development of a culture of mother-tongue instruction.

11. Xhosa is a Bantu language of the Nguni family, spoken in South Africa by 8 million people, mainly in the Eastern Cape. (The languages of the country will be discussed more fully in Chapter 3.)

12. This is, of course, a metaphor, since languages are not "powerful"; it is their speakers who are powerful or powerless.

13. More properly "Northern Sotho", today called Pedi (or Sepedi) — see Chapter 3.

14. No full consensus exists regarding the spelling of the term Khoe-San, and it is spelt as Khoe-San, Khoesan, Khoi-San, Khoisan.

15. The Griqua are descendants of the Khoe.

16. Since our understanding of the link between language, culture and society is limited, a statement such as this has no predictive power. It is nevertheless an issue worth serious consideration.

17. Concepts such as this one will be discussed in Chapter 3.

18. See the view of the former Minister of Arts, Culture, Science and Technology, Dr. Ben Ngubane: "I want to urge that we need to devise national strategies to find real ways in which our linguistic diversity can form part and parcel of South Africa's development programmes ... and examine how South Africa's multilingualism can prove to be a resource." (Department of Arts, Culture, Science and Technology, 1996: 2.)

19. As Sue Wright notes: "Language is built so into the economic and social structure that its fundamental importance seems only natural and the majority do not need to reflect how central language is to their lives. ...Were we (i.e. the British) to live in a state where the linguistic situation was more complex and a subject of greater public debate, we would have a better awareness of how language empowers or obstructs, we would appreciate how language can mould a world view, we would know the importance of planning for communication." (1994: 2)

20. This is particularly the case with Europeans who are speakers of English, French and German in Britain, France and Germany respectively, as became apparent to me when a director of a Goethe Institute branch stated at a conference in Brussels in 1995 that "multilingualism was bad".

21. Public figures have even expressed a willingness to fight physically for Afrikaans.

22. Afrikaans-speaking white people refer to themselves variably as *Afrikaners, Afrikaans-speaking people* or *"Afrikaanses"*, which reflects their uncertainty about who they are. (The latter term is a new coinage which means something like: "those who are Afrikaans", and arose because of the heated debate about whether Afrikaans-speaking coloured people qualify for the name *Afrikaner.*) Being *Afrikaans-speaking* is not considered a linguistic term, but a socio-political issue.

23. There may also be a north-south division (Western Cape vs. the northern provinces) within the Afrikaans-speaking community. In the south, Afrikaans-speaking people (who are considered to be more liberal and also constitute the majority of the local population) seem to feel less threatened and less concerned with language maintenance. The validity of this distinction, its substance and the possible reasons still have to be studied.

24. Both of these phenomena were central components in the apartheid system.

CHAPTER 2

Exploring the maze

Language policy and language planning for South Africa: the frameworks

Problem-solving, as we know, needs to be approached within a specific conceptual framework. In the case of the language-related problems mentioned in Chapter 1 two frameworks are necessary, namely the theory of language planning, and the political philosophy within which the country is governed. These frameworks constitute the "macro-contexts" within which the linguistic transformation and reconstruction of the country have to be approached. This chapter first discusses the theory of language planning, and then describes the relevant political macro-context, which is constituted by the country's national ideals, the reconstruction and development programme and the Constitution.

The theory of language planning

The description of the theory of language planning[1] provided in this chapter covers a definition of language planning and a brief discussion of the value of language planning for resolving language-related problems.

A definition of language planning

The concept of language planning which is used in this book is based on an exposition by the Swiss "language economist", François Grin. (Grin has done considerable work on the inter-action between language and economy.) Grin (1996: 31) describes language planning as follows:

> Language planning is a systematic, rational, theory-based effort at the societal level to solve language problems with a view to increasing welfare. It is typically conducted by official bodies or their surrogates and aimed at part or all of the population living under its jurisdiction.

Though this description of language planning needs refinement (see later), it does highlight some of the central features of the process, as illustrated below.

Language planning is directed at solving problems with a view to increasing welfare

The problems which need to be solved through language planning in South Africa (see Chapter 1) include: centralising communities who have been disadvantaged over a long period of time, facilitating the educational development of marginalised people, stimulating economic growth and redistributing national wealth, promoting reconciliation between groups who are deeply divided and between whom there is a measure of distrust and even antagonism, restructuring the organs of government, maintaining effective public administration and providing equitable state services.

The focus of language planning is the socio-economic, educational, political and cultural welfare of society. It is important to emphasise this point since language planning is often considered to be primarily concerned with language maintenance and/or promotion. Language planning, however, is (or should be) concerned with language mainly in its role as a barrier to community welfare. The reverse of this relationship is also applicable: language promotion cannot be accomplished in isolation — for example: the Bantu languages of South Africa cannot really be promoted (acquire parity of esteem or equitable treatment) independently of the communities in which they are used, for instance through devising literary competitions for these languages. Nor does it help much to simply decree that certain languages will henceforth have parity of esteem and equitable treatment. Language promotion will only occur meaningfully if the languages concerned acquire *value*, in particular *economic and educational value*, something which is dependent upon the economic and educational prosperity of the **communities** that use these languages.

Language planning is theory-based

Language planning is based on "theories" about two constituent factors, namely language, and planning, and the interrelationship between language and public life.

As regards language, the features which need to be considered are the nature of the linguistic system and the nature of language knowledge (grammatical, functional and sociolinguistic competence), the way in which language is used in the communication process, its role as an instrument for the transfer of information, its psychological functions (for instance as instrument in people's cognitive and affective development), its social functions — in particular in the socialisation process (acquiring values, attitudes, perceptions and norms) and in facilitating social participation and binding, and in its symbolic function (for instance in identity construction). In planning language behaviour for increased welfare, languages are resources.[2]

The second constituent factor for which a theory is needed is the planning activity. The framework within which language planning should be conducted is the strategic planning framework, which can be diagrammatically represented as in Figure 2.1.

The nature of this framework and the way in which it works will be illustrated from the South African situation. The discussion refers to national language policy development.

Language policy development firstly has to be linked directly with the *vision* a country has set for itself, that is, the national ideals which the country, through its government, wishes to achieve. For example, the South African Constitution expresses the desire that the country develops into a liberal democracy. Any language policy decision proposed as part of a future policy must necessarily be consonant with developing a democracy.

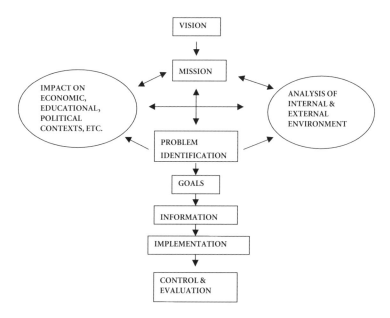

Figure 2.1. The strategic planning framework

The *mission* of a government has a similar role to play. A governments' mission, which can be said to be expressed in the country's constitutional stipulations, consists of the broad goals the government wishes to achieve in relation to its various areas of jurisdiction. In the South African case, the decision to promote eleven languages as official languages can be regarded as a mission statement.

The third factor in the planning framework is the set of *problems* which acts as obstacles to the realisation of the country's vision and its mission. These need to be identified, and information has to be collected about them and about the *internal* and *external* contexts in which these problems are situated. In the case of language policy development for South Africa, the internal environment, for instance, refers to the sociolinguistic realities of the country, and the external environment to issues outside the language issue which have a bearing on the language policies of the country.

Given the information referred to above, language planners are then in a position to formulate specific objectives, or *goals*, which need to meet the criterion of being a clear expression of the country's vision and mission and of contributing towards a resolution of the identified problems. The set of language policy goals constitute, in effect, the language policy of the government and should have the status of a legal document.

The next element in the framework is the plan of *implementation;* that is, the detailed plan according to which the specific goals of the policy are to be achieved. The language plan describes who does what, where, how and with what resources, and specifies the necessary management mechanisms and implementation strategies, the required resources (human, financial, technological and social), time schedules, support services, and how complaints should be mediated.[3]

The plan of implementation should obviously also contain performance indicators, which will enable supervisory agencies to determine the effectiveness of policy implementation. A language policy will thus include *control* and *evaluation* measures, directed in particular at determining the degree to which the country's vision and the governments' mission have been realised.

The final constituent factor in a theory of language planning is the interrelationship between language and language policies, and public life. This is the area of study called the "politics of language" in this book. At this stage insight into the relationship is tentative and inadequate, as is demonstrated by the inability of language professionals (such as the *sociologists of language*) to make significant predictions about the socio-political fate of languages, for example, under what conditions a particular language will atrophy and die. The problem is that there are too many variables which affect the public life of languages, and that effective instruments for the close study of language political processes have not been developed, so that scholars in the field of language politics have to rely mainly on case studies and the research findings of smaller and larger research projects.

Language planning is rational

Language debates are often rather emotional and ideological, and this makes it difficult to effect effective policy development. It is thus necessary to insist on language planning being a rational exercise, based on reasoning and factual material and subject to objective justification. Developing language policy requires deciding which languages must be used for which official functions, that is, one should first determine which official functions have to be performed, and then decide which languages would be most appropriate for those functions. Furthermore, planners must be fully informed about all the relevant facts, such as the precise sociolinguistic realities of the situation which needs to be transformed, the exact goals they are expected to achieve, and the resources available to them. Usually this requires that language audits be undertaken of the communities involved, as well as strategic analyses of the internal and the external environments of these communities.

Language planners obviously also have to be aware of available research findings, of the principles of the planning process, and of scholars' knowledge and understanding of the interrelationship between language and society at the macro-level, as argued above.

Language planning is authoritative

Language policy implementation is a difficult task, since it is difficult to change people's patterns of language use, language norms, language attitudes and beliefs about language. To succeed, language planning needs strong backing by political leaders, effective policies and strong government bodies. Policies need to be formalised in legislation (as acts, ordinances, and bylaws) or issued as regulations, instructions, proclamations, administrative rulings and decisions of law courts. In addition, specialised organisations and institutions are necessary if the state is to penetrate society in a significant way, as Human (1998: 36) points out. Traditionally, government bodies are quite static and re-active, and "designed" to resist change and to maintain the status quo (Human, 1998: 46). If the South African government is determined to implement the constitutional decisions (to be discussed further down) the machinery of government will have to adopt a radically pro-active approach and become, in itself, an agent of social change.

Language planning is systematic

Language planning is systematic, that is, it is undertaken in an organised, step-by-step way. The framework described in Figure 2.1 may be adapted into a process approach, represented in Figure 2.2:

Policy phase	Problem identifica-tion	Collection of relevant data	Correlate with vision & mission	Policy options & estimate of cost-effectiveness	Policy implementation & evaluation
Actors					
Actions					
Resources					
Time-table					

Figure 2.2. Phases in language policy development

Some criticism of Grin's "definition"

The exposition just given of language planning has two weaknesses, from the South African perspective: (a) the absence of any reference to the manipulative potential of language planning, and (b) the absence of any reference to the role of communities in the construction and implementation of language policy.

The first shortcoming does not need much comment, since the history of language planning in South Africa (as discussed in Chapter 1) provides sufficient comment. Language policy and planning should be a non-technicist activity, sensitive to the potential of language for hegemonic goals, to its use as an instrument of power, discrimination, manipulation and exploitation. As regards the second shortcoming, explicit mention should be made of the need for a bottom-up approach. Language planning is, essentially, a top/down activity — it needs to be authoritative, requires governmental resources and needs to be effectively managed. However, if language planning does not have the support of the communities it is intended for, it cannot succeed (without excessive force). To be effective, language planning needs to be complemented by a bottom/up approach. A bottom/up approach does not necessarily mean that people from grass-roots levels have to be actively involved in the process. It does mean though that the interests of the general public have to be served, and not just the interests of government. Language planning must take explicit note of the wants and needs, the views and attitudes, and the linguistic competencies of the general public. In addition, language policy development as well as implementation needs the direct involvement of citizens, through awareness and information campaigns, and with continual dialogue between government agencies, the private sector, labour organisations and the union movement, non-governmental organisations and any other bodies which are involved (see also Eastman, 1982, who discusses these two approaches extensively).

Can language planning make a difference?

An issue which also needs to be addressed is whether language policy and language planning has the potential to play a meaningful role in the transformation of South African life.

Grabe (1993/4: vii–ix) provides a useful overview of developments within language policy and planning. He points out (by implication) that during the eighties, one would probably have had to say that language policy and planning theory was not able to provide a framework within which constructive strategies for handling complex and deep-seated national problems could be devised. At that time language policy and planning theory was, in general terms:

a. practised in a monolithic way, with language policy and planning directed at single languages
b. seen as a wholly linguistic exercise, and
c. directed mainly at the national level and concerned mainly with the selection of a national official language.

However, certain international events have changed the theory and practice of language planning, such as the disintegration of the USSR, the economic and political integration of Western Europe, and migration patterns in Europe and the USA, with more foreigners effectively penetrating the economic worlds of the working classes. Thinking about language politics has been influenced by these developments, and there is a far wider acceptance of linguistic diversity, there is widespread support for the rights of minority languages, and the integrity and legitimacy of non-standard varieties (the "vernacular") is taken as given by language planning experts.

Language policy and planning theory reflects these developments in:

a. having become pluralistically oriented, that is, practised with explicit reference to all the variables in a given context (such as all the languages)

   b.   recognising the centrality of political considerations, looking at language in its broader socio-political context, accepting that language is more than just a reflection of society, but is also socially constitutive (and as such can contribute to correcting social injustice), and in

   c.   being directed at all levels of public administration, such as the regional and local levels, as well as large corporations (and institutions, such as universities and schools).

Given the acceptance of an extended role for language planning in public life, it is also important to realise that its power should not be over-estimated — language planning cannot, in and of itself, change anything (see Webb 1999c). It is a necessary but not a sufficient condition for social transformation. Firstly, referring to the process as *language* planning can be misleading, and may contribute to creating unfounded expectations. "Language planning" should rather be seen as *people* (or community) planning, with the emphasis on the educational, economic, political and social development of people. Secondly, if language planning is not congruent with the will of the leaders of a society and with the will of the society itself, nothing will change.[4] Language planning can, though, perform a facilitating role, creating a framework within which language can perform its fundamental developmental role. Given the changes in thinking about the process discussed above, and given congruence between the leadership and society, language planning can, potentially, contribute meaningfully to reconstruction in South Africa.

The macro-contexts of language planning

Earlier in this chapter the point was made that language policy development needs to be sensitive to higher-level issues (such as the vision and mission of the government). These issues will be discussed under the headings of the *national ideals* (the vision), the *reconstruction and development programme*, (vision as well as mission), and the *Constitution* (vision as well as mission). However, first the global context will be discussed — an important context not mentioned above, but equally significant for language policy development.

The global context
The "global context" refers to the political and economic forces which operate on a global level. These forces are contained in the "new economy" and the

information age. As the National Committee for Higher Education (NCHE) Report (1999: 61) points out, the work place is increasingly becoming knowledge-driven and knowledge-dependent. The formal education system must therefore produce "learning individuals", people equipped with knowledge and skills which will enable them to learn how to handle developments and problems which they have never encountered before. "(K)nowledge and the pursuit of knowledge have become key factors shaping the structures and dynamics of daily life." (p. 66).The modern world is also characterised by the extensive use of computer technology, participatory forms of work organisation (team work), and more educated labour (in particular multiskilling and the "continuous deployment of new knowledge"). This calls, states the Report, "for training in broad, generic and transferable skills enabling workers at all levels to deal flexibly with varied problems, tasks and new technologies" (p. 66).

It is clear that if South Africa (and Africa as a whole) wants to become part of the global economy and become competitive internationally, and wants to prevent itself from lagging further behind, educational institutions have to produce graduates who possess a wide array of knowledge, possess high levels of generic, transferable skills (are "multiskilled"), and are "learning individuals". Education has an enormous task, and language-in-education policies and practices may not be allowed to be obstacles in striving towards achieving these aims.

The national ideals

The vision of what South Africa wants to be, its "national ideals", were formulated by the political leaders who debated the democratisation of South African society in 1992 and 1993, and are described in various sections of the present Constitution (Act 108 of 1996), for example in the Preamble of the Constitution (see further down), the Founding Provisions and the Bill of Rights. These ideals include establishing a democracy, promoting equality and human rights, developing the people of the country, administering the country effectively, implementing affirmative action, developing national unity, and retaining the country's cultural diversity.

These national ideals imply the acceptance of a socio-political framework of pluralism. As is well-known, complexly multicultural national societies can opt for different models of government, such as *segregation:* the division of the country into ethno-political entities, as in the time of Apartheid; *integration:*

the creation of a new (single) cultural identity (a melting-pot option); and *assimilation:* the absorption of the different socio-cultural identities which constitute a country's cultural realities into an existing, dominant cultural identity. The South African political negotiators opted for *pluralism:* the recognition of cultural diversity as a formal constituent of political structure in a unitary state. The choice of a pluralist model of state must not be confused with the former policy of segregation. Whereas the policy of Apartheid was a negative response to demographic diversity, the present political leaders handle pluralism positively, implying (at least) the following: (a) the formal recognition of the country's cultural and linguistic diversity (without accepting the apartheid conception of this diversity as consisting of separable socio-political entities, with clear, distinctive boundaries); (b) the reflection of the country's diversity in government organisation, its structures, institutions and policies; (c) the active support for religious, linguistic and cultural equality; (d) the elimination of all statutory discrimination (based, for example, on language or cultural identity); and (e) the positive management of the conflict potential among socio-cultural communities.

The manner in which these ideals can be realised in regard to language will be discussed more fully in later chapters. A preliminary remark is necessary about the *style* which the Government wants to adopt for policy development and the construction of planning programmes. The Government has committed itself to a consultative, transparent and publicly responsible style of government. This approach has at least two implications for language policy construction and language planning. Firstly, it makes a multilingual approach self-evident, since *bilateral* communication between Government and the public is at the heart of this approach to public administration. (Communication with the public in one language only, for instance English, would spell the death of "open government".) Secondly, as also pointed out above, it commits the Government to adopting a "bottom-up" approach to planning, which means that all sectors which have a stake in language policy and planning have to be consulted.

The reconstruction and development programme

The next major context within which language policy formulation must occur is the South African Government's *reconstruction and development programme* (the RDP).

The RDP ties in directly with the national ideals, but has a distinct role in national life. It is based on six inter-linked principles, which together constitute the political and economic philosophy of the Government. The RDP is directed at nation-building and democratisation, it wants to be an integrated and sustainable programme, be people driven, be directed at general peace and security, and wants to link reconstruction and development (ANC, 1994: 4–7). The RDP is a strategy for the development of the country's human, natural and financial resources, and it is designed to play a concrete role in the lives of the citizens of the country, in the sense of creating employment opportunities, operationalising citizenship, breaking down social barriers and instilling tolerance and respect. Working within the RDP implies co-ordinating public programmes into a coherent and purposeful whole, meeting the aspirations of the citizens and involving their direct participation (in government institutions and programmes), and recognising that national development cannot occur in an unstable society.

The degree to which the RDP expects the citizens of the country to be involved in its projects appears from the following quote from a Government publication (*South Africa Yearbook* 1996: 58):

> "The RDP's vision is one of democratizing power, which means that all South Africans must have access to power and the right to exercise their power. .....
> (M)ass participation in its implementation is essential. Trade unions, sectoral social movements and community-based organisations, especially civic organisations, must be encouraged to develop RDP actions and campaigns within their own sectors and communities. Trade unions and other mass organisations must be actively involved in democratic public policy-making."

However, as Lo Bianco (1996: 43) points out, the role of language and language policy in the reconstruction and development of the country is not covered in the RDP document. He argues, naturally, that if the active participation of a multilingual civil society is to be obtained, the society "will have to be addressed in (all) its languages". The RDP, he notes, relates directly to "public participation, education, cultural diversity, knowledge, creativity and skill ... each (of which is) self-evidently mediated by communication effectiveness" and literacy (p. 44). Furthermore, he says, there are employment sections which "require specific language planning and language or literacy training, (such as) tourism, welfare (and) human resource development" (p. 44). In fact, all training programmes are directly dependent on linguistic skills.

As pointed out in Chapter 1, the government outlined a new strategy in February 1996, the *Growth and Development Strategy*. According to Ciaran

Ryan (*The RDP Quarterly Report,* June 1996, p. 3) this programme aims to "eradicate poverty, remove wealth disparities between people, de-emphasise racial ownership, foster rapid economic expansion and, in the process, cement social and political peace." This the Government wants to achieve by improved education and training, creating jobs, becoming internationally competitive and drawing in the poorest members of society into the economic mainstream. (The current macro-economic policy of the Government, which contains similar objectives, is called GEAR: "growth, employment and redistribution".)

Even a superficial consideration of the RDP and the Growth and Development Strategy will show that there is no way in which they can be implemented without the full consideration of the role of language. In both programmes *communication* (between varying institutions and sectors) is fundamental, and the basic instrument of communication is, of course, language.

One gets the impression from public documents (including the Constitution, which will be discussed below) as well as from the "behaviour" of public persons (including politicians), that language is not taken seriously enough, that language is seen as relevant mainly in people's private lives, in cultural life (as "part of people's identity") and in religious life, but that it does not have much to do with education, the economy, or politics. This view of the role of language is seriously flawed, and urgently needs to be unmasked. A comprehensive, national language policy *must* address the role of language in the social and political reconstruction of the country and in its economic development.

The Constitution

The last component of the framework within which national language planning must be conducted is the Constitution.[5]

Democratic South Africa began with an interim constitution, negotiated by the participants in the multiparty negotiating process leading up to 1994, and to be replaced by a final constitution, which was to be developed by the Constitutional Assembly (that is the National Assembly and the Senate: 490 elected members). Included in the interim constitution was a set of 34 Constitutional Principles, which had to be adhered to in the writing of the final constitution. The final constitution was adopted in 1996 as Act 108 (certified by the Constitutional Court in December 1996) and came into effect immediately. The rest of this paragraph will discuss the relevant Constitutional Principles, the language stipulations and the Bill of Rights, as applicable.

The Constitutional Principles

The 34 Constitutional Principles described in the Interim Constitution of 1994 are discussed since they provide a clear indication of the framework within which the Constitutional Assembly operated. Five of the 34 are of direct relevance to language policy:

> III. The Constitution shall prohibit racial, gender and all other forms of discrimination and shall promote racial and gender equality and national unity.
>
> IX. Provision shall be made for freedom of information so that there can be open and accountable administration at all levels of government.
>
> XI. The diversity of language and culture shall be acknowledged and protected, and conditions for their promotion shall be encouraged.
>
> XII. Collective rights of self-determination in forming, joining and maintaining organs of civil society, including linguistic, cultural and religious associations, shall, on the basis of non-discrimination and free association, be recognised and protected.
>
> XX. Each level of government shall have appropriate and adequate legislative and executive powers and functions that will enable each level to function effectively. The allocation of powers between different levels of government shall be made on a basis which is conducive to financial viability at each level of government and to effective public administration, and which recognises the need for and promotes national unity and legitimate provincial autonomy and acknowledges cultural diversity.

From a language policy perspective these principles ensure the absence of discrimination on the basis of language, free access to information (also regarding state administration), a commitment to multilingualism (and multiculturalism), a commitment to recognising and protecting linguistic associations, and the right of provinces to adopt language policies which may differ from the national policy.

The constitutional language stipulations

Act 108 of 1996 (the Constitution of the Republic of South Africa) starts with a preamble, which is provided here as it describes the spirit in which the constitution should be read:

> PREAMBLE
> We, the people of South Africa,
> Recognise the injustices of our past;
> Honour those who suffered for justice and freedom in our land;
> Respect those who have worked to build and develop our country; and
> Believe that South Africa belongs to all who live in it, united in our diversity.
> We therefore, through our freely elected representatives, adopt this Constitution

as the supreme law of the Republic so as to —
Heal the divisions of the past and establish a society based on democratic values,
social justice and fundamental human rights;
Lay the foundations for a democratic and open society in which government is
based on the will of the people and every citizen is equally protected by law;
Improve the quality of life of all citizens and free the potential of each person; and
Build a united and democratic South Africa able to take its rightful place as a
sovereign state in the family of nations.
May God protect our people.
Nkosi Sikelel' iAfrika. Morena boloka setjhaba sa hesp.
God seën Suid-Afrika. God bless South Africa.
Mudzimu fhatutshedza Afurika. Hosi katekisa Afrika.

The *language stipulations* are contained in Chapter 1, the "Founding Provisions", along with the specification of the basic values upon which the new
society is to be built, the commitment to the constitution as the supreme law of
the land, a stipulation about citizenship, the National anthem and the National
flag. The values upon which the state is founded are the following:

a. Human dignity, the achievement of equality and the advancement of
    human rights and freedoms
b. Non-racism and non-sexism
c. Supremacy of the constitution and the rule of law
d. Universal adult suffrage, a national common voter's roll, regular elections
    and a multi-party system of democratic government, to ensure account-
    ability, responsiveness and openness

The following are the language stipulations (p. 4):
Languages
6. (1) The official languages of the Republic are Sepedi, Sesotho, Setswana,
    siSwati, Tshivenda, Xitsonga, Afrikaans, English, isiNdebele, isiXhoza and
    isiZulu.[6]

    (2) Recognising the historically diminished use and status of the indig-
    enous languages of our people, the state must take practical and positive
    measures to elevate the status and advance the use of these languages.

    (3) a. The national government and provincial governments may use any
    particular official languages for the purposes of government, taking into
    account usage, practicality, expense, regional circumstances, and the bal-
    ance of the needs and preferences of the population as a whole or in the
    province concerned; but the national government and each provincial
    government must use at least two official languages.

b. Municipalities must take into account the language usage and preferences of their residents.

(4) The national government and provincial governments, by legislative and other measures, must regulate and monitor their use of official languages. Without detracting from the provisions of subsection (2), all official languages must enjoy parity of esteem and must be treated equitably.

(5) A Pan South African Language Board established by national legislation must —

a.   promote, and create conditions for, the development and use of -

(i)   all official languages;

(ii) the Khoi, Nama and San languages; and

(iii) sign language; and

b.   promote and ensure respect for —

(i)   all languages commonly used by communities in South Africa, including German, Greek, Gujarati, Hindi, Portuguese, Tamil, Telugu and Urdu; and

(ii) Arabic, Hebrew, Sanskrit and other languages used for religious purposes in South Africa.

A number of observations can be made about these stipulations (and the associated constitutional principles and the Preamble), namely:

a.   They commit the Government to a policy of multilingualism

b.   They commit the Government to the promotion of the Bantu languages

c.   The principle of "functional differentiation" in the implementation of language policy is accepted, which means that it is not the government's view that all eleven languages be used for all official functions in all domains of public life

d.   The implementation of the language stipulations must be controlled by legislation (or other statutory means)

e.   The implementation of the language stipulations is subject to a number of "escape clauses" (usage, practicality, expense, regional circumstances and the "balance of the needs and preferences of the population as a whole or in the province concerned"), which, in the absence of clearer definitions, could be used to undermine the language stipulations

f.   The language stipulations house a potentially contradictory situation, namely between the government's commitment to implementing a particular set of (policy) decisions and its commitment to obey the wishes of the people, which may surface in a multilingual policy being contradicted by the wish for the greater use of English.

The 1996 constitutional language stipulations differ from those of the interim constitution of 1994, and it may be useful to take note of some of these differences, since they give an indication of the thinking of the political leaders.

Besides being less specific (there is no reference to language use in parliament or to citizens' rights to use and be addressed in the official language of their choice in dealings with government institutions) and less repetitive, the two sets of stipulations differ as follows:

a. The 1996 stipulations do not contain the so-called non-diminution clause, which obligated the government to ensure that the rights and status of the former national official languages (Afrikaans and English) which existed at the beginning of 1994 would not be reduced. (This clause was seen by many as a way of ensuring that Afrikaans retained its privileges, which meant that an aspect of the legacy of apartheid was legally retained.[7]) This change opens the way for the non-recognition of Afrikaans as a provincial official language in, for instance: KwaZulu/Natal, the Northern Province, the North-West Province, and so on.

b. The 1996 stipulations operate with the notion of *equity*, rather than *equality* ("equal use and enjoyment"). This is an improvement, since the latter is impossible to implement if it is interpreted literally.

c. Whereas the interim constitution's language stipulations made frequent direct reference to *language rights* the 1996 version makes no explicit reference to them. The reason for this difference is probably that the issue of language rights is adequately covered in other sections of the constitution. In the same way, the 1996 stipulations do not prohibit the use of language "for the purposes of exploitation, domination and division" as was the case with the 1994 stipulations, since such linguicism is sufficiently covered by other clauses in the constitution (see Phillipson, 1992, on "linguistic imperialism").

d. The number of escape clauses increased in 1996. In addition to *usage, practicality* and *expense*, the 1996 Constitution also refers to *regional circumstances* and *the balance of the needs and preferences of the population as a whole or the province concerned* (p.4). Given the vagueness of these conditions (who determines the needs? how should the preferences be determined? what does a balance between these two matters look like?) they can easily be used to torpedo any language policy.

e. Whereas the 1994 constitution allowed the national government and the provinces to declare a single language as language of government, the present Constitution requires that at least two of the national official languages be recognised as languages of government in a province. This is a positive move towards more meaningful multilingualism.

The stipulation regarding the Pan South African Language Board also differs from the earlier version, particularly in being less specific. Once again, the reason is that the specifics are described in the parliamentary act which deals with the board. (The Pan South African Language Board is discussed in Chapter 9.)

The Bill of Rights
The Bill of Rights (Chapter 2 of the constitution) includes the following sections which are of direct relevance to language:

Equality (Section 9)
1. Everyone is equal before the law and has the right to equal protection and benefit of the law.
2. The state may not unfairly discriminate directly or indirectly against anyone on one or more grounds, including race, gender, sex, pregnancy, marital status, ethnic or social origin, colour, sexual orientation, age, disability, religion, conscience, belief, culture, language and birth.
3. No person may unfairly discriminate directly or indirectly against anyone on one or more grounds in terms of subsection (3). National legislation must be enacted to prevent or prohibit unfair discrimination (p. 7).

Education (Section 29)
1. Everyone has the right —
    (a)   to basic education …
2. Everyone has the right to receive education in the official language or languages of their choice in public educational institutions where that education is reasonably practicable. In order to ensure the effective access to, and implementation of, this right, the state must consider all reasonable educational alternatives, including single medium institutions, taking into account -
    (a)   equity;
    (b)   practicability
    (c)   the need to redress the results of past racially discriminatory laws and practices.

3. Everyone has the right to establish and maintain, at their own expense, independent educational institutions that —
  (a) do not discriminate on the basis of race;
  (b) are registered with the state;
  (c) maintain standards that are not inferior to standards at comparable public educational institutions (p. 14–15).

Language and culture (Section 30)
Everyone has the right to use the language and to participate in the cultural life of their choice, but no one exercising these rights may do so in a manner inconsistent with any provision of the Bill of Rights (p. 15).

Cultural, religious and linguistic communities (Section 31)
1. Persons belonging to a cultural, religious or linguistic community may not be denied the right, with members of that community —
  (a) to enjoy their culture, practice their religion and use their language; and
  (b) to form, join and maintain cultural, religious and linguistic associations and other organs of civil society.
2. The rights in subsection (1) may not be exercised in a manner inconsistent with any provision of the Bill of Rights (p. 15).

Access to information (Section 32)
1. Everyone has the right of access to —
  (a) any information held by the state ...
2. National legislation must be enacted to give effect to this right ...(p. 15).

Arrested, detained and accused persons (Section 35)
1. Everyone who is arrested ... has the right —
  (b) to be informed promptly ...
2. Everyone who is detained ... has the right —
  (a) to be informed promptly of the reason for being detained; ....
3. Every accused person has a right to a fair trial, which includes the right —
  (a) to be informed of the charge with sufficient detail to answer it ...
  (k) to be tried in a language that the accused person understands or, if that is not practicable, to have the proceedings interpreted in that language;
4. Whenever this section requires information to be given to a person, that information must be given in a language that the person understands (pp. 16–18).

Additional constitutional stipulations relating to language
In addition to the stipulations discussed thus far the constitution also makes provision for a *Commission for the Promotion and Protection of the Rights of Cultural, Religious and Linguistic Communities* (Section 185 of Chapter 9 of the constitution.) This commission is described as follows:

Functions of Commission
185 (1) The primary objects of the Commission for the Promotion and Protection of the Rights of Cultural, Religious and Linguistic Communities are —
(a) to promote respect for the rights of cultural, religious and linguistic communities;
(b) to promote and develop peace, friendship, humanity, tolerance and national unity among cultural, religious and linguistic communities, on the basis of equality, non-discrimination and free association; and
(c) to recommend the establishment or recognition, in accordance with national legislation, of a cultural or other council or councils for a community or communities in South Africa.
(2) The Commission has the power, as regulated by national legislation, necessary to achieve its primary objects, including the power to monitor, investigate, research, educate, lobby, advise and report on issues concerning the rights of cultural, religious and linguistic communities (pp. 101–102).

The Commission has not yet been established.

The constitution also provides for self-determination on cultural and linguistic grounds. It states (Section 235, Chapter 14):

> The right of the South African people as a whole to self-determination, as manifested in this Constitution, does not preclude, within the framework of this right, recognition of the notion of the right of self-determination of any community sharing a common cultural and language heritage, within a territorial entity in the Republic, or in any other way, determined by national legislation (p. 131)

Some evaluative comments

From the perspective of democratisation, the language stipulations of the new constitution are a significant improvement on the language policies of the preceding government: they recognise the need to centralise the major communities in the country through the recognition of all the languages of the country, and they establish principles which are basic to both the democratisation of the country and its social transformation. The question, however, is whether these stipulations are adequate and sufficient to effect the reconstruction and transformation of the national society. Evaluated from the perspective outlined in the first section of this chapter, it is clear that the set of stipulations cannot be regarded as a language policy; they are at most a description of the mission which the government is obliged to realise, the long-term (broad) goals. However, they do represent the first step in the process of developing a comprehensive national language policy. To advance beyond this step, a language policy proper needs to be constructed, that is a set of specific goals, based on information collected through analyses, and clearly linking the expected policy outcomes with the language-related problems which have to be resolved, the vision of the country and the mission the government wants to fulfil.

Almost seven years have passed since the acceptance of the constitutional language stipulations, which is too short a time to judge the government on its implementation of the stipulations. However, a number of remarks can be made.

First of all, the stipulations do not constitute a language policy, as pointed out above. They are at most a set of principles which must underpin any pursuant comprehensive national language policy.

Secondly, the exact justification for the decision to designate eleven languages as national official languages is unclear. It is clear that the decision was meant to give expression to the political philosophy of "unity within the diversity", that is, pluralism, which was accepted by all the participants to the constitutional negotiations. However, one needs to ask whether the same political goals could not have been achieved with alternative language stipulations. Would an explicit division between *official language* (or "working language in official contexts") and *national language* (see further in Chapter 5) not have achieved the same political aims?

The 1994 decision to recognise eleven languages as official languages at the national level came as a surprise to persons interested in the politics of language, since they generally expected English to be selected as the only official language (as the dominant political party, the African National Congress, the ANC, had proposed). The Afrikaans lobby had urged the retention of Afrikaans and English as national official languages, with the Bantu languages recognised at the regional level.

The selection of a national official language must technically be determined by the functions such a language has to perform, namely that it must enable the government of a country to maintain control over its citizens (in the sense of educating the youth, promoting national health, collecting taxes, preventing violence, mobilising civilians for purposes of national defence, and so forth), administer the country effectively, and dispense justice. An additional selectional criterion for the South African political leaders was that, given the serious national divisions, language should also serve as a means of promoting national unity and loyalty.

It is unlikely that the negotiation about South Africa's official languages was as "rational" as this. Given that the two sides were driven by opposing interests (the National Party government was concerned about its white Afrikaans support and the ANC by its opposition to Afrikaans as the symbol of apartheid), and that the two opposing language policy views were the National Party's preference for a continuation of the existing language policy (Afrikaans and English as co-official languages, with the Bantu languages as regional official languages) and the ANC's preference for the recognition of English as sole official language, the only way out of this impasse was, probably, the selection of Afrikaans and English along with all the indigenous languages of the country as official languages. If this is so, the choice of the eleven languages was not a "rational", sociolinguistic process, but political: the desire to come to a political settlement.

A third remark concerns the frequent criticism, generally from uninformed quarters, that an eleven language decision is impossible to implement, since all official functions cannot be performed in all eleven languages all the time, and since the necessary human and material resources are not available. However, if one reads the stipulations less superficially, it becomes clear that the writers of the constitution did not have such an interpretation in mind. Firstly, the constitution binds both the national and the provincial governments to two official languages,[8] and secondly, it replaces the notion of *equality*, which had been employed in the Interim Constitution, by the concepts *parity of esteem* and *equity*.

A fourth remark is more critical, and is based on Strydom & Pretorius (1999), and du Plessis (1999).

Strydom & Pretorius criticise the constitutional language directives for (i) lack of clear guidance on the language stipulations, (ii) confusion between the principles espoused (parity of esteem; equity; language promotion) and the practicality (or "qualifying") clauses (also called, albeit a bit harshly "escape clauses"), in particular as regards the hierarchical relationship between them, and (iii) the lack of follow-up measures (the enactment of laws), which should clearly explicate the purpose of the directives and provide a substantial basis for their implementation, thus giving credibility to the language stipulations. As examples of the lack of clarity they discuss the notion *official language*, pointing out that its non-definition (giving the term legal meaning) has allowed governmental institutions to reduce the official languages to "a mere non-binding status" (p. 9). As regards the potential conflict between the normative directives and the qualifying factors, they point out that the former obviously have precedence over the latter, meaning that "the purpose of the qualifying factors is not to release the state from the duty to fulfil this obligation" (Strydom & Pretorius 1999: 9). This means that these clauses may not be interpreted as "escape clauses"

Du Plessis (1999) takes a similar position, questioning the government's commitment to developing and implementing official multilingualism, suggesting that they have adopted "a laissez-faire approach regarding language matters" (p. 18), and adding that this stance was taken in order "not to enter into a debate on the unassailable position of English as the language of liberation" (p. 18).

A final remark relates to the language policy actions of the government pursuant to the adoption of the present constitution.

At the end of 1995, the government appointed an ad hoc committee to prepare a report on the framework within which a future comprehensive national language policy could be developed. This committee, generally called the LANGTAG committee (for: *Language Plan Task Group*), involved the direct participation through a network of sub-committees of about fifty language specialists (linguists, language planners, and language practitioners such as translators, interpreters, lexicographers and terminologists) and dealt with language equity, language development, language as an economic resource, language in education, literacy, language in the public service, heritage languages, sign languages and augmentative communication systems, and language services (in particular translation, interpreting and term-creation). In the course of its work, a number of workshops were held across the country, and the pre-final version of the report was debated at a national conference lasting two days. The final report was presented to the government in August 1996, and accepted by the cabinet soon afterwards.

Following the completion of the LANGTAG report, the task of language policy development was given to the Department of Arts, Culture, Science and Technology (DACST), the department which is formally responsible for language service provision and language planning. Over the past four years, this department has been drafting a language policy and plan, and has presented its proposals at a number of workshops.

At the end of March, 2000, DACST arranged a workshop during which a committee specially appointed to prepare a comprehensive national language policy for South Africa presented its proposal. Their proposal was accepted and subsequently formulated as the *South African Languages Bill*, which has since been presented to the cabinet for consideration. According to private sources, the cabinet has requested further refinement of the bill. The proposed bill has not been released for public comment, and so cannot be quoted in full. Its main proposals can be summarised as follows:

–   the national government must use not less than four languages for official work
–   these languages must be selected from each of four categories of official languages on a rotational basis
–   the categories of languages are: the Nguni languages (Ndebele, Swazi, Xhosa and Zulu); the Sotho languages (Pedi, Sotho and Tswana); Venda/Tsonga; and Afrikaans/English[9]
–   governments at provincial and local levels as well as institutions which perform public functions are subject to the policy provisions of the bill
–   the policy is applicable for legislative, executive and judicial functions
–   language units have to be established for each department of the national government and each province, which have to implement and monitor policy implementation, conduct language surveys and audits in order to assess existing language policies and practices and to inform the public about the policy, and
–   regulations concerning a language code of conduct for public officials have to be produced.

The bill also makes provision for intergovernmental co-ordination regarding language policies, legislation and actions relating to the promotion of multilingualism.

It is too early to comment on the bill, but the bill does seem to have initiated moves "in the right direction". Since 1994 official language practice has gradually become more and more monolingual, with English being used almost exclusively as official public language, and with little indication that state institutions are contemplating any meaningful implementation of the multilingualism prescribed by the constitution (see Chapter 4 for details). Since the acceptance of the proposal at DACST's March workshop and its reformulation as a bill, institutions at both local level and provincial levels as well as state departments have begun processes hopefully leading to language policy development. If these processes actually gain momentum, and if the requirements for effective policy development and the formulation of full-fledged policy implementation plans, which were described at the beginning of this chapter, are followed, it is likely that language planning in South Africa can become an interesting event.

Conclusion

The development of a really meaningful policy of multilingualism in South Africa could make a positive contribution to the African scene. Despite high level governmental support in public, language and culture have not been priorities in any African state, as is apparent from the fact that neither has figured in any five-year development plan of any government in Africa (see Webb 1994a). The support expressed for the development of indigenous languages and cultures in African states seems to have been lip-service. Practically all over Africa the ex-colonial languages still dominate government thinking. This is borne out by the following language policy situation:

Of the 48 sub-Saharan African states (thus excluding Algeria, Egypt, Libya, Morocco and Tunisia):

–   14 have an ex-colonial language as only official language
–   43 have an indigenous language as official language, but in addition to an ex-colonial language
–   Only 5 have no ex-colonial language as official language (Mauritania, Sudan, Eritrea, Ethiopia and Somalia), and
–   Only 1 African state has more than 2 official languages (South Africa) (Source: Africa Institute 1996: 8–9)

South Africa has statutorily accepted that the country is multilingual, has accepted that multilingualism can be seen as a positive resource, and has committed itself formally to a policy of multilingualism. To give concrete and meaningful content to these views will be difficult, but the country has no choice: making multilingualism work is non-negotiable. If democracy is ever to become meaningful in any degree in South Africa, knowledge and skills must be democratised, and citizens must have full access to all the rights and privileges of their country (which will be co-determined by the role of language as instrument of access). Multilingual language policy formulation and planning must simply succeed.

Notes

1. One should probably refrain from using the term "theory", especially since our understanding of the field and the conceptual apparatus developed for its study is rather restricted.

2. Languages are also resources in the sense of providing access to peoples' knowledge and insights. The Khoisan community provides a nice example: It is generally accepted that this community houses a vast knowledge of nature, for instance about the uses and dangers of roots and (desert) plants. If one wants to access this knowledge, proficiency in the languages of the community is essential (see also Heugh 1995, Lo Bianco 1996, Webb et al, 1996, and Crawhall 1998).

3. Human (1998: 154) illustrates this aspect of policy development with reference to raising the literacy level in a society. Such a policy decision, he says, needs to specify who the target community is, how many candidates will be accommodated, how many instructors will be involved, where and when the training will take place, for what language the training will provide, what training material needs to be available/developed, how long the literacy programmes are to last, how its success will be measured and what budget is required.

4. This view is neatly illustrated by the fact that Dutch was an official language in South Africa until 1983, along with Afrikaans and English. Yet no one even knew this, especially since Dutch had effectively "died out" in the country as a language of public use 70 or more years before. The existence of a particular language policy had no effect at all.

5. The Constitution was published in all eleven official languages. Quotations in this book are from the English version, unless explicitly stated otherwise.

6. These language names are in their Bantu forms. In this monograph the English forms will be used, thus: Pedi (also: Northern Sotho), Sotho (also Southern Sotho), Tswana, Swazi, Venda, Tsonga (also Shangaan), Afrikaans, English, Ndebele, Xhosa and Zulu (see also footnote 2, Chapter 3).

7. One must, however, acknowledge that the non-diminution clause also protected languages such as Venda and Tsonga, since it meant that they also had to retain their official status in their immediate regions. This fact is often over-looked in the language debate.

8. Note stipulation 6(3)(a): "the national government and each provincial government must use at least two official languages".

9. The logic in the categorisation is clear in the case of the first two (the languages being members of the same sub-families). Venda and Tsonga/Shangaan are grouped together because they do not belong to the two former sub-families, and Afrikaans and English are grouped together because most coloured, Indian and white South Africans know both (albeit to different degrees).

CHAPTER 3

The nature of things

A sociolinguistic profile of South Africa

Kembo-Sure, as first author of a chapter on "Languages in competition" in Webb and Kembo-Sure (2000), describes the complexities of Kenyan multilingualism by listing the linguistic demands his two sons have to face. Following his example, one could construct the following sociolinguistic situation in the South African context:

> Sipho Khumalo is the fourteen-year old son of a Zulu father and a Venda mother. His father teaches Public Administration at the Mamelodi campus of Vista University, and his mother looks after the family. They live in Mamelodi, a residential area on the outskirts of Pretoria, the administrative capital of South Africa, situated in the province of Gauteng. The community in Mamelodi in which they live is Pedi-speaking, so Sipho uses Pedi when he visits his closest friends. Sipho is in grade eight, the first year of the junior secondary school phase, and the language of the school is English. Since Pretoria has a large Afrikaans-speaking community, it means that he has a lot of exposure to Afrikaans outside his home environment, and will probably need it someday when he studies at the university or starts to work in a government office in the city. At home, Sipho is expected to speak English to his parents, since they want him to become fully proficient in this language. He accepts the need for this, but finds it a bit difficult because he is only exposed to English in the classroom. Travelling by taxi or going to the post office or a municipal office, he uses Pedi or Tswana. In the neighbourhood cafes and stores, which are owned by Indian traders, Fanagalo, a South African pidgin, is used. When he is alone with his mother, they often use Venda in talking to each other, because, she says, Venda is her language of comfort, security and relaxation. In church on Sunday, the sermon is in Pedi, although the preacher is actually an Ndebele. Sipho's grandparents on his father's side come from Mahlabatini in rural KwaZulu/Natal, close to Ulundi, the capital of that province, 500 kilometres away. His grandparents on his mother's side come from Thohoyandou, and speak Venda, a language not related to either Zulu or Pedi, and spoken four hundred kilometres away in the Northern Province. These grandparents know Pedi quite well, and they often laugh at the way Sipho and his friends speak the language, saying that Pretoria has really murdered the language of the Bapedi, which is a great pity, since they have such a rich tradition. What Sipho hasn't told them is

that some of the boys in his class are originally from Venda, but they have changed their names to sound more Pedi-like, since they're ashamed of their Venda connections.

On Friday nights, when he and his teenage friends walk around, looking for some fun, they usually guy around in Tsotsitaal, a variety which is an urban vernacular, typically used by street gangs, which sometimes has to be used, especially if you don't want people to suspect you think too much of yourself or you are a nerd. This is especially important when relatives from the Mahlabatini area visit Sipho and his family. The type of Zulu these people speak is so weird, it seems as if they have just emerged from Noah's ark. Unless you want to land in trouble with the gang, you really have to make sure that no one thinks you're from Inkatha country.

This imaginary (but not a-typical) language scene should give some impression of the wide array of languages black city-dwellers in South Africa are exposed to, and the linguistic demands made on them. In order to function effectively privately and publicly, among friends and in formal domains in society, a knowledge of a wide range of linguistic varieties is necessary, and one has to know which languages are appropriate in which situations and in which functions. In addition, it is necessary to keep in mind what the social (and also the political) meaning of each language is, since the languages are embedded in the politics of the country.

South Africa's languages are reflectors, conveyors and constituents of the complexly differentiated society. If its language politics is to be meaningfully transformed through language planning, note must obviously be taken of the country's sociolinguistic character. The purpose of this chapter is to provide such a sociolinguistic profile of South Africa.

The term *sociolinguistic profile* refers to a socio-political characterisation of the language situation in a state, region or community, or the language world of an individual. In this chapter it refers to the socio-political language situation in South Africa. Topics such as the following are covered in sociolinguistic profiling: the broad socio-political context, the languages of the country, language knowledge, the geographic, demographic and functional distribution of languages, national communication, corpus development, the public functions of languages, language planning institutions and completed language planning work.

A fully adequate sociolinguistic profile of South Africa cannot be provided, for a number of reasons: the precise boundaries between at least some of the country's languages are uncertain (making the enumeration of the languages problematical), there is a scarcity of systematically collected sociolinguistic facts, and obtaining reliable information about phenomena such as language attitudes (vs. opinions), language preferences, language knowledge, and people's perceptions of their sociolinguistic identity, is inherently difficult. A comment on the first reason only: besides the fact that there is often a mismatch between the official designation (naming, classification) of languages and the views of speakers "from below" about the identity (names, relationships) of the "languages" they use, there is also the fact that the naming and demarcation of South Africa's Bantu languages (as well as Afrikaans, and possibly even English) occurred artificially, on the basis of political considerations. In the 18th and early 19th century in northern modern-day South Africa, before white trekkers began moving into these areas, "Pedi", "Tswana", and so forth, did not exist. What was spoken, were the linguistic varieties of a wide range of "tribes", later linked with one another to form what was to be called "Pedi", "Tswana", and so on. Clearly, therefore, the sociolinguistic situation is more indeterminate than is conveyed by the statement that there are "nine official Bantu languages" in South Africa.

The socio-political context

South Africa is governed by a central government (of national unity), with limited powers awarded to the nine provinces of the country. It covers an area of 1 220 088 km². The official 1996 census placed the South African population at 40.5 million.

In the time of Apartheid the South African population was sub-divided along racial lines into "Asians", "Bantu", "Coloureds" and "Whites". The "Asian" group consisted mainly of people of Indian origin, but including some Chinese; the term "Bantu" referred to black persons (who today prefer to be called "Africans"); the classification "Coloured" was applied to people of "mixed" origin (through the mixing of indigenous Khoi, San, European settlers, and slaves from West and East Africa as well as the far East)[1]; and the "Whites", that is, descendants from Dutch, German, French, British and Portuguese immigrants from the seventeenth century onwards. The issue of race is a sensitive matter, and in (post-1994) democratic South Africa there is no longer any racial classification. Race continues to be a social and economic divider, however, and it is still necessary to take note of it in discussing issues of public nature, including language. The current racial distribution of the population is given in Table 3.1.

Table 3.1. Population distribution by race (1996 census)

Asian people	Black people	Coloured people	White people
1 045 596	31 127 631	3 600 446	4 434 697
2.6%	76.7%	8.9%	10.9%

Census in brief, 1998: 10

According to the 1996 census findings 53.7% of the South African population is urbanised. The racial distribution of the urbanised population is unknown, but is probably roughly as follows: 92% of the Asian population reside in urban areas, 75% of the black people, 86% of the coloured people, and 93% of the white people. The major metropolitan areas in the country are: Pretoria/Johannesburg/Vanderbijlpark; Cape Town; Port Elizabeth/ Uitenhage and the Durban/Pinetown/Pietermaritzburg area.

Colonial South Africa (before 1910) consisted of two British colonies (the Cape and Natal), and two Boer republics, the Orange Free State and the Zuid-Afrikaansche Republiek (the South African Republic, later the Transvaal). After the second Anglo-Boer war (1899–1902), the country was "united" to form the Union of South Africa (in 1910), consisting of four provinces: the Cape Province, Natal, the Orange Free State and Transvaal. From 1960 onwards the reigning government instituted homeland governments for the black people of the country, eventually establishing four so-called national states (the Transkei, the Ciskei, Bophuthatswana and Venda, each with its own "independent" parliament), and six so-called non-independent homelands (or "self-governing regions"), namely Gazankula (for Tsonga/Shangaan-speaking people), KaNgwane (Swazi-speaking), KwaNdebele (Ndebele-speaking), KwaZulu (Zulu-speaking), Lebowa (Pedi-speaking) and QwaQwa (Sotho-speaking). Since 1994 the homeland governments (both "independent" and "non-independent") have been disbanded, with South Africa re-constituted into nine provinces. The nine provinces of South Africa are indicated in Map 1 (p. xxvii).

The languages of the country

South Africa houses a large number of languages, of which eleven are considered to be official at the national level (see Chapter 1 for the socio-political description of the eleven languages). These eleven languages are Afrikaans, English, Ndebele, Pedi (Northern Sotho), Sotho (Sesotho or Southern Sotho), Swazi, Tsonga/Shangaan, Tswana, Venda, Xhosa and Zulu. In the constitution the names of the nine Bantu languages are written in their Bantu form, namely isiNdebele, Sepedi, Sesotho, siSwati, Xitsonga, Setswana, Tshivenda, isiXhosa and isiZulu.[2] These languages overlap demographically and geographically (though there are focal points); they are almost all also spoken in neighbouring states; and they are embedded in the politics of the country.

The LANGTAG Report (see Chapter 2) suggests that, in addition to the eleven official languages, about 70 more languages are used in the country. These include five Khoe and San languages, three Bantu languages (Northern Ndebele, which is not included under "Ndebele" in the constitution, Phuthi and Lobedu), 38 Bantu languages spoken by immigrants, migrant labourers and refugees from neighbouring countries, five Indian languages, four Chinese languages, two Eurasian languages, 14 European languages, five religious languages, Sign languages, and a variety of Augmentative and Alternative Communication Systems (AAC systems).

Counting languages is a difficult task, for many reasons: When is a variety a "dialect" and when a "language"? Are 50 speakers of a language (e.g. Japanese in the diplomatic community in South Africa) enough to qualify it as "a language of the country"? When does a "means of communication" such as a pidgin or an urban koiné (see Schuring, 1983 for Pretoria Sotho and Slabbert, 1994 for Tsotsitaal) qualify for counting? What about Fanagalo, which is widely used, especially in "master/mistress-servant" contexts, but which most black South Africans refuse to recognise as a "language"? And what do you do if the officially recognised ("canonised") languages of the country do not reflect the linguistic realities at grass-roots level? (Slabbert, 1994.) A further complicating factor is the ambiguity of certain terms commonly used in socio-linguistic profiling. The terms *mother-tongue/first language/home language* are problematical in the South African context. In Western communities these three terms are often synonymous, but this is not the case in the more traditional African societies. In the latter case *first language* is the language of the father and *mother-tongue* does not seem to be a significant concept. For example, if a Venda-speaking woman marries a Tsonga-speaking man and they live in Pretoria which is mainly a Pedi-speaking area, the children's *first language* will be Tsonga, their *home language* may be Venda (especially if the father is not home all the time) and the language used *most frequently* outside the home will be Pretoria-Sotho. It could be more appropriate to use the terms *primary* and *non-primary* language, but these could still provide an inaccurate profile. South African politics have also made the task of the language enumerator difficult. As mentioned in Chapter 1, Herbert (1992: 2–3) pointed out that some language boundaries seem to have been artificially introduced as part of missionary politics and the implementation of Apartheid. For example, Zulu and Xhosa are today considered distinct languages. However, "the development of a single standard for Xhosa and Zulu in the nineteenth century was prevented by competing interests and rivalry of different missionary groups and by political factors" (Herbert, p. 3). Another example concerns Swazi and Zulu, about which Herbert writes: "More recently, the differentiation between Swati and Zulu has been actively promoted as part of socio-political agendas whereas the actual structural differences between the two are no greater than the distance between two dialects of Zulu." (p. 3). A final example is the creation of Pedi, which is internally diverse enough to "raise some doubts about its essential unity", and which is so similar to Tswana that it is difficult to draw "any real boundary between Pedi and Tswana". Despite this, Pedi is claimed to reflect a distinct ethnic identity (p. 2).

It is therefore difficult to be precise about the number and identity of the languages of South Africa, and the version provided of the country's sociolinguistic profile in this chapter can therefore not be seen as definitive.

The sociolinguistic profile described in the rest of this chapter will also be biased in another way, namely in its almost exclusive focus on the official languages. The reasons for this decision are that the speakers of these languages number 99% of the country's total population and that the major concern of this monograph is with the use of these languages for development purposes.

Language families
The official languages of the country can be divided into two major language families. Firstly, there the *Bantu* languages, namely the Nguni languages (Xhosa, Zulu, Swazi and Ndebele), the Sotho languages (Pedi, Sotho and Tswana), and Tsonga/Shangaan and Venda, both of which are members of the south-eastern Bantu family, but are classified as neither Nguni nor Sotho, standing alone, as it were. The second major language family is the *Germanic* grouping — Afrikaans and English. As regards the non-official languages, there is the Khoi-San group, Indian languages, several European languages, several "mixed languages" and sign languages (see also Table 3.3).

Speaker numbers
Speaker statistics are generally dependent on official census surveys, undertaken by **Statistics South Africa**, the official government body for this purpose. Census surveys have been held regularly in South Africa (recently: 1970, 1980,

1985 and 1991), the latest being held in 1996. The following quotation from **Statistics South Africa**'s Report No. 03–01–11 provides information about the survey approach followed in 1996:

> INTRODUCTION
> In October 1996, South Africans were counted for the first time as citizens of a democracy. More than 100 000 people were employed to collect information on persons and households throughout the country using a uniform methodology. Census night, or the night of the count, was 9–10 October, 1996. In preparation, the country was divided into about 86 000 small pockets of land, called enumerator areas. An enumerator was assigned to each enumerator area to visit the structures within it.
> Questionnaires were made available in all 11 official languages. In addition, separate questionnaires were compiled for those living in hostels or in institutions, and for the homeless. The information collected was processed in nine provincial centres, employing about 5 000 people to work in shifts for nine months to code the questionnaires and capture the data on computer.
> ADJUSTING FOR UNDER-COUNT
> In every census, there are bound to be some people or households who are missed, or some people who are counted twice. During November 1996, a post-enumeration survey was undertaken to determine the degree of under- or over-count in Census '96. (Pages unnumbered.)

The 1996 census questions relating to language were:

> "6.1 Which language does (the person) speak MOST OFTEN AT HOME?
> 6.2 Does (the person) speak more than one language AT HOME?
> *(If "Yes") specify the language he/she speaks NEXT MOST OFTEN."*

Tables 3.2 to 3.5 provide the census statistics for the 11 official languages as home languages nationally, by province and population group as numbers and as percentages (excluding "other" and "unspecified", which means the percentages do not add up to 100).

In addition to the eleven official languages, Indian languages such as Hindi, Gujarati, Tamil, Urdu and Telegu, and European languages such as

Table 3.2. Speaker statistics by home language for the 11 official languages (1996 census)

1. Zulu	9 200 144 (22.9%)	7. Sotho	3 104 197 (7.7%)
2. Xhosa	7 196 118 (17.9%)	8. Tsonga	1 756 105 (4.4%)
3. Afrikaans	5 811 547 (14.4%)	9. Swazi	1 013 193 (2.5%)
4. Pedi	3 695 846 (9.2%)	10. Venda	876 409 (2.2%)
5. English	3 457 467 (8.6%)	11. Ndebele	586 961 (1.5%)
6. Tswana	3 301 774 (8.2%)		

Census in brief, 1998: 10

Table 3.3. The three statistically major home languages by province

Eastern Cape (6 302 525)	Xhosa 5 250 524 (83.8%)	Afrikaans 600 253 (9.6%)	English 233 376 (3.7%)
Free State (2 633 504)	Sotho 1 625 963 (62.1%)	Afrikaans 379 994 (14.5%)	Xhosa 245 101 (9.4%)
Gauteng (7 348 423)	Zulu 1 559 520 (21.5%)	Afrikaans 1 213 352 (16.7%)	Sotho 953 239 (13.1%) (English, 13.0%)
KwaZulu/Natal (8 417 021)	Zulu 6 658 442 (79.8%)	English 1 316 047 (15.8%)	Afrikaans 136 223 (1.6%) (Xhosa: 132 223)
Mpumalanga (2 800 711)	Swazi 834 133 (30.0%)	Zulu 706 816 (25.4%)	Ndebele 46 337 (12.5%)
Northern Cape (840 321)	Afrikaans 577 585 (69.3%)	Tswana 165 781 (19.9%)	Xhosa 52 689 (6.3%)
Northern Province (4 929 368)	Pedi 2 572 491 (52.7%)	Tsonga 1 102 472 (22.6%)	Venda 757 683 (15.5%)
North West (3 354 825)	Tswana 2 239 774 (67.2%)	Afrikaans 249 502 (7.5%)	Xhosa 178 931 (5.4%)
Western Cape (3 956 875)	Afrikaans 2 315 067 (59.2%)	English 795 211 (20.3%)	Xhosa 747 977 (19.1%)

Census in brief, 1998: 10–11

Table 3.4. Home language by population group

	Black	Coloured	Asian/Indian	White	Unspecified
Afrikaans	217 606	2 931 489	15 135	2 558 956	88 361
English	113 132	584 101	974 654	1 711 603	73 977
Ndebele	578 067	2 507	107	3 427	2 851
Pedi	3 674 320	2 173	319	1 316	17 718
Sotho	3 083 047	6 406	267	1 737	12 740
Swazi	1 006 804	1 553	201	316	4 320
Tsonga	1 745 216	883	306	736	8 965
Tswana	3 272 720	12 935	191	1 809	14 118
Venda	871 130	302	139	177	4 661
Xhosa	7 148 721	12 303	688	2 832	31 574
Zulu	9 132 569	8 502	1 787	3 448	53 838

Census in brief, 1998: 12–13

Portuguese, Greek, Italian, German, Dutch and French are also used by significant numbers of South Africans.

A brief sociolinguistic history of South Africa
The first inhabitants ("First People") of the southern African sub-continent
were the speakers of **Khoe** and **San** languages. Archaeological evidence indicates their presence along the southern coast of the country as early as 120 000
to 90 000 years ago. They were originally hunter-gatherers, with cattle being
introduced 2000 years ago presumably after contact had been made with Bantu
people in eastern Africa (present-day Tanzania), who were herders and subsis-
tence farmers. Thereafter the Khoe-San were divided into the San (also referred to as Bushmen), who remained hunter-gatherers, and the Khoe (also
referred to as Hottentots), who were herders.

The Khoe-San languages are unique in the sense that they are the only
languages in the world which had autochthonous clicks (later borrowed into
neighbouring south-eastern Bantu languages — Xhosa, Zulu and Sotho). It is
difficult to be definite about the number of Khoe-San languages spoken, and
about their interrelationships. Traill (1996) estimates that there were three
(unrelated) language groups, with four sub-groups, housing 16 separate languages. Crawhall 1998: 234–5 lists 6 "Khoe and San languages", three spoken in
communities on a daily basis, and three only by individual members of communities. Estimates of the former three quoted by Crawhall are that Nama is spoken
by about 6000 persons, !Xû by 3000 and Kxoedam by 1000.

Today the Khoe-San languages are spoken mainly in Namibia and
Botswana (but also in Zimbabwe and Tanzania). In South Africa they were
almost extinct by 1994, with no more than about 200 living speakers (Traill,
personal communication). After the Angolan war, in the mid-eighties, the San
who were recruited to fight on the South African side were resettled in South
Africa, thus increasing the presence of their languages in this country.

The demise of the Khoe-San people began soon after contact first with
Bantu immigrants after about 800 AD, and later with European settlers
(mainly Dutch), who "settled" in the southern tip of Africa from 1652. At that
time there were between 10 000 and 20 000 San living in South Africa, and
between 100 000 and 200 000 Khoe. Warfare (genocide), disease, poverty,
starvation, trade and intermarriage led to the total collapse of these people as
separate entities. Today they have become an underclass of labourers in rural
South African society. In the apartheid era they were classified as "coloured".
Recently, however, due to the freedom which democratisation brought to the

country, descendants of these people are increasingly objecting to being regarded as "coloured", saying that they have a distinct origin and history, and
should be recognised, once again, as Khoe-San (see the 1996 conference on the
Khoe-San peoples, referred to in Chapter 1).

The Khoe-San underwent almost total language shift, with their languages
being replaced by Xhosa, Sotho or Afrikaans. Today, only a handful of people
still speak a San language in the Kalahari Gemsbok Park, whilst Khoe-San
languages such as Nama, Kora and Gri are used by equally few people in the
Northern Cape (Richtersveld). In Namibia, however, there are more than 120
000 speakers of Nama, with Botswana also housing a considerable number of
San. One could argue that the Khoe-San languages today "live on", in a
manner of speaking, as borrowings in Afrikaans, Sotho and Xhosa, as well as in
place names.

The **Bantu-speaking people** arrived in southern Africa from around 800
AD, as part of their migration from Central Africa via the Great Lakes (Webb
and Kembo-Sure, 2000). The Bantu were herders and farmers (thus food
producers, not gatherers), and introduced an agricultural revolution which is
still being experienced on the continent (and currently moving through
Botswana) (Deacon, 1996).

The Bantu languages are a sub-group of the Niger-Congo language family,
and are therefore part of an estimated 400 separate languages. In southern
Africa there are about 35 Bantu languages, forming a south-western group,
and a south-eastern group. The Bantu languages of South Africa are part of the
latter (Van Wyk, 1966, Wilkes, 1978 and Bailey, 1995a), as indicated in Figure 3.1 (based on Bailey 1995a).

Next to Swahili (also a Bantu language which can be understood by 60
million people in 10 east African countries), the Nguni languages are the
widest known languages in the southern sub-continent, being intelligible to at
least 30 million people, with the Sotho languages intelligible to probably about
20 million.

Zulu, the best known Nguni language, was the language of a small tribe,
which became generalised through the military genius of one of the early kings
of the Zulus, Shaka (1790–1828), and his successor Dingane. Zulu today shows
relatively little diversity.

Xhosa houses a number of dialects, such as Ngqika, Gcaleka, Tembu,
Bomvana, Qwathi, Mpondomise, Hala, Zizi, Bhele, Gqunukwebe and
Ntlangwini. Written Xhosa is probably based on Ngqika and Gcaleka. The first
grammar of Xhosa was published in 1824 (Louw 1963: v).

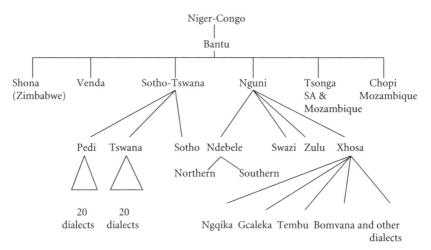

Figure 3.1. The Bantu languages of South Africa

The Ndebele of Zimbabwe and the speakers of Ngoni in Malawi and Tanzania are also Nguni. They are descendants of Mzilikazi, a military leader who fled from Zululand during the difeqane (or mfecane: wars by the Zulu's under the leadership of Shaka for political control during the 1820's), eventually moving to present-day Zimbabwe, Malawi and Tanzania.

The Sotho languages are also, of course, diverse. Sotho is relatively homogenous, but Pedi and Tswana each contain up to twenty dialects each.

Venda, which was standardised on one of its dialects, Tsiphani, is said to have six distinguishable varieties, whilst Tsonga has 5 dialects (Prof. C. Marivate, personal communication). Both these languages are related to languages in the neighbouring countries.

The present linguistic boundaries between the different Bantu languages were formerly of course not nearly as clear-cut as today, since the missionaries who produced orthographies for these languages, created boundaries between the languages of different communities, later reinforced by the South African governments (see the earlier quotations from Herbert). In modern-day urban South Africa new linguistic boundaries are being set up, and there seems to be growing conflict between urban and rural varieties of "the same language".

Geographically, the Bantu languages are relatively clearly defined, as shown in Map 2.

As can be seen on Map 2, a number of the South African Bantu languages are also major languages in neighbouring countries, for example Tsonga, also spoken in Mozambique, Venda, also spoken in Zimbabwe, Tswana (Botswana) and Sotho (Lesotho).

Before 1994, no Bantu languages had ever been official on a national level, though all nine current official languages were "official" in the homelands created under Apartheid rule, and were thus available for use in formal public contexts such as legislative institutions and courts of law.

Afrikaans goes back to the 17th century, when the Dutch established a community in the present Cape Town. The language spoken by the Dutch underwent considerable adaptation, particularly through use in the different local communities, notably those of the Khoe, the slaves from west Africa (Guinea and Angola), east Africa (Mozambique and Madagascar), and the far East (mainly India, and present-day Java, Bali, Timor and the Malayan Peninsula), and the French and German immigrants of the late 17th century (see den Besten 1989, Kotzé 1989, Webb 1993).[3] By the middle of the 19th century Afrikaans was the lingua franca in the Cape Colony (the present Western Cape, Eastern Cape and Northern Cape) in the lower classes of coloured and white people, alongside Dutch and English, which were the languages of the social elite and were used as high function languages. However, the political value of Afrikaans was discovered, and this lead to a movement from 1870 to promote its use in public domains (legislatures, state administration, courts of law, churches, schools). It became a national official language in 1925 along with Dutch (and English), and after 1948, when the white Afrikaans-speaking community gained political power in the Union of South Africa, Afrikaans was strongly promoted in public domains, eventually achieving functional equivalence with English. It is the first language of an equal number of coloured (that is, people of mixed origin, see Chapter 1) and white people, as well as some Asian and black people. Naturally, Afrikaans is not a homogeneous language, and several non-standard varieties exist, such as Cape Afrikaans, Orange River Afrikaans and the Afrikaans of millions of second-language speakers (Roberge, 1995, Van Rensburg, 1998). Since 1994, when the Afrikaans-dominated community lost political control, Afrikaans functionally became increasingly restricted, so that it is used seldomly in public forums today. A further striking feature of the language today is its strong stigmatisation in many black communities, which is due to its direct association with Apartheid.

Dutch continued to be an important language in the Cape Colony in education and, particularly, in religion. In the two Boer republics (the South African Republic and the Orange Free State) Dutch was also a language of government. In 1910, when the Union of South Africa was formed, Dutch and

English were designated official languages (with Afrikaans added to Dutch in 1925, as mentioned earlier). Dutch remained an "official language" in South Africa until 1983, when the ruling National Party introduced the so-called three-chamber parliament and had to change the constitution in the process. Today it is not used at all as a vernacular, except in the case of (recent) immigrants from the Netherlands.

The **"English presence"** in South Africa dates from the end of the 16th century when ships on their way to the far east stopped along the South African coast and traded with local people (mainly the Khoe). Later, in 1795, the British took control of the Cape by defeating its Dutch rulers, in order to protect their trading route to the east against threats from the French. They handed the Cape back to the Dutch in 1803 but then took control again in 1806, shortly after war with Napoleon's France started. In 1820 the British settled along the eastern borders of the Cape, near present-day Port Elizabeth, and in the 1840's and 1850's in today's KwaZulu/Natal. The British immediately dominated the public and economic domain, imposing their system of government (and taxation) and justice, their religion, and their public values and norms. Although the English ("British") government of the Cape Colony and Natal agreed to respect local language rights (including that of the Dutch) they also vigorously promoted the use of English in all public domains, and indirectly contributed in this way to the later movement promoting Afrikaans. English (in particular the standard variety) has maintained its linguistic links with British English quite remarkably. This does not mean, of course, that English has no diversity in South Africa, and there are varieties called Natal English, Eastern Cape English, as well as Afrikaans English, Indian English and now, more than before, "African English" (see Lanham 1978, Lanham and Macdonald 1979 and Lass 1995). In terms of its status English is by far the dominant language of the country, and is South Africa's most important non-primary language. It is the home language of 40% of the white people, a sixth of the coloured people, and practically all the Asian people.

The **Indian languages** arrived in South Africa from 1860 onwards, with indentured workers from India. In the course of just more than a century the Indian community underwent a massive language shift towards English, and today the descendants of these people use English as their first language, with the Indian languages serving mainly religious and cultural functions (Mesthrie 1992, 1995).

The history of intergroup relationships in South Africa has been largely a history of conflict — between the Khoe and the San, the Khoe and the Bantu, the Dutch (and their descendants, the Afrikaans-speaking whites), the English and the Bantu. These conflicts obviously had clear linguistic consequences. Some of the (linguistically) most important dates in the recent history of South Africa are the following:

Before 300	The Khoe and the San as original inhabitants, the "First People", spread across the entire country
From 300/800	Arrival of the Bantu in southern Africa, moving down along the eastern seaboard, and settling across the central and eastern parts of the country
1652	Establishment of a refreshment post by the Dutch government. Arrival of slaves from the west and east African coasts, and the far East
1659; 1673	First and second wars between the Dutch East India Company and the Khoe
1739	The Bushman War (between settlers and San communities)
1795, 1806	Arrival of the British with a formal take-over of control in the Cape
1811–1850	Border wars between white Afrikaans-speaking farmers, British settlers and the colonial (British) government on the one hand, and the Xhosa on the other in the eastern Cape/border area
1820	Arrival of British settlers in the eastern Cape
1820	Start of the Mfecane/Difaqane — migration of Bantu tribes southwards, westwards and northwards, fleeing from Shaka and his Zulu's, causing the displacement of numbers of tribes. Some of these tribes eventually settled in Zimbabwe, Malawi and Tanzania
1836	The Great Trek, which meant the movement of groups of Afrikaans-speaking farmers from the eastern Cape northwards, and leading to violent clashes with the Bantu, particularly the Zulu, the Ndebele and the Pedi
1867; 1870	Discovery of diamonds and gold in South Africa and the influx of foreigners mainly from British lower classes (for example Cornwall, Cumberland and Lancashire), but also from the USA
1880	First Anglo-Boer War; defeat of the British
1899–1902	Second Anglo-Boer War between Britain and the South Afri-

can Republic (1860–1902; the later Transvaal) and the Orange Free State (1854–1902); defeat of the Boer armies

1910	Establishment of the Union of South Africa following the defeat of the Boer republics in 1902, the granting of self-government to the Transvaal and the Orange River Colony by Britain in 1907, and extracted negotiations between the four colonies from 1908
1948–1994	Afrikaans-speaking white people control South Africa politically
1959	Act passed for the establishment of Bantu self-government (the homelands policy, "bantustans", later referred to as national states)
1961	Police opened fire on a crowd of black people who had gathered to protest against the compulsory carrying of identity documents ("pass books") at Sharpeville in present-day Gauteng, killing 69 people; the establishment of the Republic of South Africa outside the British Empire/Commonwealth
1976	Protests by school children in Soweto against the unilateral decision of the Government that Afrikaans be used as medium of instruction for three of the six subjects in "black" secondary schools (see Chapter 1)
1994	End of white rule in South Africa and the establishment of democratic government, under the control of black people; acceptance of 11 official languages at the national level

Language knowledge

This section aims to provide information on the knowledge of South Africans
of the eleven official languages of the country. It is difficult to provide accurate
information on the number of people who can be said to "know a language"
(or who claim to know it), since "knowing a language" can cover such a wide
span, for example from being able to interact with someone at a very elementary level, to being able to read or write a language, to being able to follow
national news broadcasts, to knowing what is appropriate speech behaviour in
particular contexts. The information provided in this section therefore cannot
be regarded as definitive in any way. Nevertheless, it has some usefulness.

As regards knowledge of Afrikaans and English, Schuring (1995: 86, Table 11) and Kotzé (1995) both quote information based on the 1980 census, which found that 44% of the population at that time knew Afrikaans, and 40% English. (Schuring, 1993: 15–16, using information from the 1991 census statistics adjusts his figures to 42.31% speaking competence in Afrikaans, and 42.35% speaking competence in English.) By 1991 this situation had changed, as shown in a media release (SSD 5/112e) of the Central Statistical Service, p. 5, which states that approximately 49.1% of all persons of seven years or older speak, read and write English, and 43.8% Afrikaans.

Available information on knowledge of the Bantu languages is more dated. The statistics provided in Table 3.5 for these languages were calculated by using the *percentages* provided in a survey by researchers at the South African Human Sciences Research Council in 1975 regarding the ability of respondents to speak them (well or poorly). (The investigation involved 3653 respondents nation-wide from the so-called black communities between the ages of 15 and 54; see Schuring and Yzel 1983). The *actual numbers* provided in the table are based on the statistics of the 1991 census. The table includes the figures given above for Afrikaans and English.

The information supplied in Table 3.5 does not differentiate between different levels of proficiency in the different languages. The degree of linguistic proficiency in a particular language has to be determined by using validated tests, but this has not been done adequately.

Table 3.5. Estimated knowledge of the 11 official languages (source described above)

Language (see Table 3.2 for home language speaker numbers)	Estimated number of persons who know the languages as non-home languages in millions	TOTALS: (Home language speakers, Table 3.2, plus estimates of previous column; in millions)
Zulu	15.7	25.0
Xhosa	11.0	18.0
English	14.1	17.6
Afrikaans	10.3	16.00
Pedi	9.1	12.8
Sotho	7.9	11.0
Tswana	7.7	11.0
Tsonga	3.4	5.1
Swazi	2.4	3.4
Venda	1.7	2.6
Ndebele	1.4	1.8

An attempt to determine proficiency was made by the research section of the South African Broadcasting Corporation in the early 1990's, and was reported on in van Vuuren and Maree 1994. In this test respondents were asked the following three questions: *Which day of the week is it?* (basic level); *How many years have you been living in this house?* (intermediate competency), and *When you are listening to a piece of music being played on the radio or at a party, which instrument do you most like to hear?* (complex competency). The test, of course, does not lie in the "correctness" of the answers to these questions, but in the ability to "decode" the questions, to understand the syntactic relations in each and to answer them appropriately.

Some of their findings, which incorporate Pedi and Zulu, are provided in Table 3.6.

Table 3.6. Differentiated language proficiency (Adapted from van Vuuren and Maree 1994)

	Afrikaans	English	Pedi	Zulu
No understanding	41%	31%	52%	35%
Up to basic level	25%	2%	1%	2%
Up to intermediate level	12%	21%	2%	13%
Up to complex level	21%	47%	44%	49%

The information presented in Table 3.6 means, for example, that 35% of the population (of respondents) cannot understand any Zulu, and that 65% do have some "knowledge" of Zulu, distributed as tabled, with 49% being able to understand complex sentences in Zulu.

Though clearly more informative than the census data, the value of this information is still very restricted, for at least four reasons: (a) the testing procedure is doubtful, (b) the investigation did not involve rural communities, (c) it did not distinguish between advantaged and disadvantaged people, and (d) the test is linguistically seen extremely superficial: language knowledge involves far more than the "test" assumes. It is for example highly unlikely that 47% of the total population of South Africa can use their English skills for any meaningful task beyond basic interactional skills, such as higher educational development and for access to the major higher domains of life. (In fact, it is probable that English is a meaningful instrument to only about 25% of the black people of this country, as argued in Webb 1995, and as is discussed in Chapter 1 and again in Chapter 6.)

Incidence of multilingualism

Up till 1990, when the present democratisation process started, the term *multilingualism* was seldom used. The general concept was *bilingualism*, which was used to refer specifically to "a knowledge of Afrikaans and English", and not to "knowledge of (any) two languages".

The incidence of bilingualism (in the above sense) in South Africa in 1980 according to Schuring (1995) is given in Table 3.7.

Table 3.7. Knowledge of both Afrikaans and English ("bilingualism") as a % of the total South African population by race

Asian people	Black people	Coloured people	White people	Average
29	21	51	74	31

Today Asian, coloured and white South Africans are still only "bilingual" in this sense: they know only Afrikaans and English. Black people however, are multilingual, with 69% of the urban population who know 3 or more languages (24% up to 5 languages), generally including Afrikaans and English (van Vuuren and Maree, 1994). Here one also has to ask, however, what it means to say that someone "knows five to six languages". What communicative functions can such a person perform with his/her knowledge of these languages?

Though it may be true that the multilingual skills of South Africans are of a restricted nature, multilingualism remains a valuable asset for a number of reasons: a knowledge of more than two languages gives access to the considerable knowledge and skills (of diverse nature) available among the millions of speakers of these languages, multilingual people possess a more developed facility for handling cross-cultural contact, and they have an empathetic attitude towards speakers of languages other than their own, which is a skill often lacking in the make-up of people who grow up in largely monolingual environments, or environments which are dominated by a single language.

Geographic distribution of the South African languages

Afrikaans is nationally distributed, with concentrations in the Western Cape and the Free State (see Map 1, South Africa showing the nine provinces of the country). English is in the main an urban language, being numerically dominant in Cape Town, Durban, Pinetown, Pietermaritzburg and Johannesburg. The Bantu languages are strongly represented in both rural and urban areas, but with reasonably strong concentrations in specific geographic regions. The geographical distribution of the Bantu languages was given in Map 2.

As regards the distribution of the official languages across the nine provinces, the 1996 census gives the information contained in Table 3.8.

Table 3.8. Distribution of the official languages as home language across provinces in percentages (rows total 100%)

	Eastern Cape	Free State	Gauteng	KwaZulu/ Natal	Mpuma- langa	Northern Cape	Northern Province	North West	Western Cape
Afrikaans	10.3	6.5	20.9	2.3	4.0	9.9	1.9	4.3	39.8
English	6.7	1.0	27.4	38.1	1.6	0.6	0.6	1.0	23.0
Ndebele	0.2	0.8	19.6	0.2	59.0	0.0	12.4	7.3	0.5
Xhosa	7.3	3.4	7.6	1.8	0.5	0.7	0.1	2.5	10.4
Zulu	0.3	1.4	17.0	72.4	7.7	0.0	0.4	0.9	0.0
Pedi	0.1	0.1	18.6	0.0	7.9	0.0	69.6	3.6	0.0
Sotho	4.5	52.4	30.7	1.5	2.9	0.2	1.8	5.5	0.5
Swazi	0.1	0.4	9.1	0.7	82.3	0.0	5.6	1.7	0.1
Tswana	0.0	5.2	17.4	0.1	2.3	5.0	2.1	67.8	0.1
Venda	0.1	0.2	11.4	0.1	0.4	0.0	86.5	1.4	0.0
Tsonga	0.0	0.8	21.8	0.1	5.6	0.0	62.8	8.9	0.0

Source: Statistics SA: *Census in brief*, 1998, Table 2.11

The Language Atlas of South Africa (Grobler, Prinsloo and van der Merwe, 1990) describes the geographical distribution of the languages of the country based on home languages. Though useful, it has restricted value, for several reasons: It is based on the 1980 census information and thus represents the situation within the state structures of Apartheid (thus ignoring, for example, the presence in "South Africa"[4] of millions of Xhosa-speakers, Venda-speakers and speakers of Tswana, who were statutorily citizens of "foreign countries"), it uses only information on first language speakers, and it represents only the statistical situation, thus without reference to the functions of languages or their status.

A similar, but more valuable, instrument of sociolinguistic importance is computerised data-bases. An example of such a system is the data-base of GISLAB (the Geographical Information System laboratory) of the University of Pretoria. It contains all the information gathered in the 1991 census, and it is therefore possible to construct spatial representations of, for instance, dominant and secondary languages per district (or province or nationally), percentages of speakers of a language per district/province/country, and patterns of geographic language distribution. It is also possible to relate language knowledge to other demographic dimensions, such as income patterns or levels of education. The usefulness of this information for planning purposes is clear.

A last source of information, which appeared in 1996, is the *Socio-economic Atlas for South Africa. A demographic, Socio-economic and Cultural Profile of South Africa*, compiled by specialists at the Human Sciences Research Council, the Education Foundation and the University of South Africa. As a computerised data-base it has all the advantages of the GISLAB data-base of the University of Pretoria mentioned above.

Demographic distribution

For the purposes of this monograph *demographic distribution* refers to sociolinguistic information pertaining to different groups in the national community, specifically racial groups, ethnic groups, socio-economic classes, age-groups, urban vs. rural people and any other social group which may relate significantly to the politics of language.

The differences between racial groups regarding both knowledge of languages (particularly English) and multilingualism has already been mentioned. There are also differences regarding language attitudes between the races, but these have not been studied systematically (except in relation to Afrikaans and English, see Khalawan 2000). It is reasonably certain, however, that the language of the intellectual, political and economic leadership among black people is English.

As indicated in Chapter 1 (in the discussion of the correlation between language, race and class), the linguistic world of the higher classes is mainly English, with the Bantu languages being mainly the languages of the working class. Afrikaans is used throughout the socio-economic spectrum.

Regarding the urban/rural dimension, the available information is given in Table 3.9 (based on the 1991 census data; home language speakers, in millions).

Table 3.9. Urban/rural distribution of four South African languages in millions

	urban	rural
Afrikaans	4.90	0.90
English	3.30	0.14
Pedi	0.83	2.90
Zulu	3.06	5.30

Age is certainly also a significant variable regarding language knowledge, but has not been researched yet. Very little of value is thus known about the demographic distribution of the country's languages, and extensive further research is required.

Language functions

The functional distribution of the South African languages is discussed in slightly more detail later on, and here only a general remark will be made: until 1994 Afrikaans and English were both used in all public domains, but with Afrikaans the preferred language in official contexts. The Bantu languages were *statutorily* recognised as official languages in the so-called national states and self-governing regions, but this fact had very little real meaning. Since political democratization (in 1994) Afrikaans is being used less and less in official contexts (as one can understand) and is thus undergoing gradual functional decline. English, on the other hand, is rapidly becoming the only language of official use at all levels of Government and in all state and semi-state departments.

If the present South African government is at all serious about democratization it will have to pay special attention to the extended use of the Bantu languages in public life.

Language status

The South African linguistic scene, as in any other multilingual country, is characterised by a-symmetric power relations. For example: English is a powerful language — it has enormous prestige and status and has a central place in public life. The Bantu languages, on the other hand, have very little prestige in the public arena and can be described as marginalised. It is difficult to find appropriate terms to describe the language political character of the country, since the usual terms can be ambiguous in the African context: the terms *major language* and *minor language*, for example, could be interpreted statistically, geographically *or* socio-politically. English, for instance, is not a major language of South Africa in statistical or geographical terms, and the Bantu languages are, generally speaking. However, socio-politically, the situation is reversed. Because of this ambiguity the terms *centralised* and *marginalised* languages will be used in this monograph.

In general terms the status and social meanings of the languages are as follows:

English is valued for its usefulness as an instrument for international contact and communication, as a means of access to all domains of human achievement, as a symbol of prestige and civilisation, and as a language of wider communication in formal public domains within the country and within large parts of Africa. Since English-speaking South Africans were largely opposed to Apartheid, it is regarded as a politically "neutral" language.

The equation: *a (mere) knowledge of English = "success, being civilised"* is strongly operative in large sections of South African society. It is a demonstrably destructive equation, and it is essential that attempts be made to normalise the expectations of English. This idea does not mean in any way that the role of English in national life or the personal lives of individual South Africans should be diminished. It does mean, however, that there should not be such an exclusive focus on English as a language of education, and that the Bantu languages should play a more constructive role.

Afrikaans has an ambivalent status. Many of its white speakers see it as the embodiment of their socio-cultural identity, and argue that it has the same instrumental value as English, even internationally, since Afrikaans can be understood in the Netherlands and parts of Belgium (as well as former Dutch colonies). For many non-Afrikaans-speaking South Africans, on the other hand, Afrikaans is stigmatised as the "language of the oppressor", and since 1994, when white (Afrikaans-speaking) political control came to an end, a process of demise set in, and Afrikaans has increasingly become functionally restricted regarding high-level public domains. An interesting indication of the attitudinal ambivalence in the case of Afrikaans is provided in a quotation from a work by the celebrated Afrikaans poet and painter, Breyten Breytenbach. He describes the mammoth monument erected in celebration of Afrikaans in Paarl, a Western Cape town (regarded as the "birthplace" of Afrikaans), as

> "a granite penis erected against the flank of the mountain above Paarl, that finger in the eye, ...an abomination and ... an insult to anybody's aesthetic feelings ... an incredibly obtuse and insensitive and arrogant insult to the non-Afrikaner people of South Africa" (1984: 219).

It is also true, though, that Afrikaans is still accepted by all communities (at least until relatively recently) as a useful instrument of the workplace (see Khalawan, 2000, on the attitudes of black learners in their final school year towards Afrikaans as a school subject).

The *Bantu languages* are widely used for private communication but have a very low public status in general. This is apparent from remarks such as the following:

> In South Africa, people who come from the Northern Transvaal, the Vendas, when they come into Johannesburg they hide the fact that they are Vendas, they don't speak in Venda. People who come from the same area, the Tsonga, when they come into areas like Johannesburg, hide this fact (Wally Serote, a poet and a leading figure in the ANC, 1989, quoted by Woods, 1995), and

> The pathetic consequence (of the policy of mother-tongue instruction in black schools in South Africa) is that most of them (i.e. the black people) have come to hate their languages and consider them irrelevant to the education process (C. T. Msimang, 1991).

Ironically, the "recognition" of the Bantu languages as official languages in the former self-governing regions and the "national states" probably led to some elevation in their status within their own communities, though this has not yet been investigated. Equally ironically, the strengthening of the position of the Nguni and Sotho languages, combined with the on-going debate about the harmonisation (unification) of these two sets of "languages" (see Chapter 8), seem to be stimulating linguistic consciousness in the Venda, Tsonga, Southern Ndebele and Swazi communities, as evidenced by the creation of the *Committee for Marginalized Languages*, which was discussed in Chapter 1.

Language attitudes

Language attitude studies have tended to concentrate on Afrikaans and English. Proctor and Vorster (1974) reported on "black attitudes" to Afrikaans and English, using the matched guise technique, and Hauptfleisch (1974) and Scheffer (1979) described attitudes to them in white and coloured communities respectively, using the survey questionnaire method. Webb (1993) provides a survey of language attitude studies in South Africa up till 1991.

A door-to-door survey undertaken nationally by the Human Sciences Research Council in 1992 among 2000 South Africans older than 18 about the importance of languages (precise reference unavailable) produced the information provided in Table 3.10.

Table 3.10 confirms the observations made in the previous section on the status and social meaning of the South African languages. If one considers the fact that English is the home language of only 8.5% of the national population, it is clearly a very prestigious language in the country. Afrikaans (home language of 14.3% of the national population) is relatively far behind in second

Table 3.10. Three most important and second-most important languages at national and local levels in %[5]

Most important at **national** level		English:	64.7	Afrikaans:	14.6	Zulu:	5.8
Second most important at **national** level		Afrikaans:	27.0	English:	23.4	Zulu:	19.2
Most important at **local** level	Black respondents	English:	45.7	Zulu:	16.1	Pedi:	8.7
	White respondents	English:	51.1	Afrikaans:	48.6	–	
2nd most important at **local** level	Black respondents	English:	25.4	Zulu:	20.5	Afrikaans:	19.9
	White respondents	English	46.0	Afrikaans:	41.9	Zulu:	4.6

Source: *Human Sciences Research Council* 1992 (full reference not available)

place. Given that Zulu is the home language of 22.7%, it is understandable that it is quite strongly placed among the Bantu languages. A surprising aspect, however, is the relatively poor position of Xhosa, which has a large user population (17.7%) and is strongly represented in the ruling political party, the African National Congress (ANC).

A similar array of attitudes appears from sociolinguistic fieldwork in 2000 in two residential areas in the Pretoria region, Atteridgeville and Mamelodi, which were formerly both "black" townships. 300 respondents were involved in a research project being undertaken by Strydom, a doctoral student in Linguistics at the University of Pretoria, and their responses are provided in Tables 3.11 to 3.15. In all four tables the same language evaluations are expressed: perceptions of the value of English are overwhelmingly positive, no Bantu language is viewed as having much value, and the position of Afrikaans has deteriorated to a level on a par with the Bantu languages, except as a language of the workplace. The differences between the Bantu languages can be ascribed to their presence in the townships as home languages: the statistically strongest Bantu language in Pretoria is Pedi, followed by Zulu and Tswana, but with Zulu stronger in Mamelodi and Tswana in Atteridgeville. The relatively poor status of Xhosa is at least partly due to its "absence" as a language of the Pretoria area. These relationships are demonstrated generally in Tables 3.11 to 3.15.

A Friedman test of the significance of differences in multiple comparisons of the languages involved in **Tables 3.12, 3.14** and **3.15** shows that English is deemed significantly more important as a subject of study than any of the other languages (except Pedi and Tswana in Atteridgeville), that it is significantly more valuable than any other language for getting a job and is even deemed significantly valuable in both residential areas (which are non-English-speaking) for getting respect.

Table 3.11. Language the President should use in addressing the nation as %, in A(tteridgeville) and M(amelodi)[6]

	Eng	Pedi	Tsw	Sot	Zulu	Xho	Nde	Afr.	Swa	Tso	Ven	All
A	86.7	3.3	0.7	0.7	1.3	1.3	1.3	0.0	0.0	0.0	0.0	0.6
M	66.7	4.7	2.0	0.0	4.7	0.7	0.0	0.7	0.0	0.0	0.0	4.7

Preliminary computer data, Strydom 1999

Abbreviations: Tsw = Tswana; Sot = Sotho; Xho = Xhosa; Nde = Ndebele; Afr = Afrikaans; Swa = Swazi; Tso = Tsonga; Ven = Venda; All = the use of all the languages, i.e. the percentage of people who would prefer the President to use all eleven languages.

Table 3.12. Mean scores awarded to the importance of studying particular languages at school (1 = Important, 2 = Unsure; 3 = Unimportant)

	English	Pedi	Tswana	Afrikaans	Zulu	Xhosa
Atteridgeville	1.00	1.14	1.28	1.60	1.46	1.84
Mamelodi	1.00	1.50	1.92	1.64	1.82	2.35

Preliminary computer data, Strydom 1999

Table 3.13. Preferred language if all magazines, books and newspapers could be printed in ONE language as %[7]

	Eng	Pedi	Zulu	Tsw	Afr	Nde	Swa	Tso	All
Atteridgeville	79.7	5.4	1.4	1.4	1.4	1.4	0.7	1.0	5.7
Mamelodi	67.3	4.7	8.0	2.7	0.7	1.3	0.0	0.0	14.6

Preliminary computer data, Strydom 1999

Table 3.14. Mean scores for value of languages for getting a job (1 = valuable, 3 = not valuable)

	English	Afrikaans	Pedi	Tswana	Zulu
Atteridgeville	1.02	1.29	1.65	1.76	1.76
Mamelodi	1.15	1.60	1.85	2.13	2.02

Preliminary computer data, Strydom 1999

Table 3.15. Mean scores for value of languages for obtaining respect (1 = valuable, 3 = not valuable)

	English	Pedi	Tswana	Zulu	Afrikaans
Atteridgeville	1.07	1.17	1.22	1.42	1.58
Mamelodi	1.34	1.57	1.90	1.85	2.00

The language attitudes obviously reflect the power relations between the country's main languages. This situation constitutes a rather serious problem, since it makes the linguistic transformation of the country very difficult, and represents a major challenge to attempts to promote the use of the Bantu languages as, for instance, languages of learning and teaching in formal education.

Language growth and language shift

A reasonably reliable indicator of sociolinguistic status is provided by language growth (or decline) and language shift. Schuring (1993: 11–12), using data from the 1991 census, provides the following information on the "growth" of the South African languages over the period 1946 to 1991:

Three of the major languages **decreased** in relative speaker numbers:

- *Afrikaans* shows a *decrease* in home language speaker numbers from 19.4% of the total population to 15.03% (As Table 3.2 above shows, the percentage for 1996 was 14.4.)[8]
- *Sotho* shows a *decrease* from 7.7% to 6.7% (but up in 1996: 7.7%, Table 3.2), and
- *Xhosa* shows a *decrease* from 20.95% to 17.03% (but up in 1996: 17.9%, Table 3.2).

Four of the major languages increased in relative speaker numbers:

- *English* shows an *increase* in primary speaker numbers from 8.58% of the total population to 9.01% (but down to 8.6% in 1996, Table 3.2),
- *Pedi* shows an *increase* from 6.86% to 9.64% (1996: 9.2%),
- *Tswana* shows an *increase* from 5.15% to 8.59% (1996: down to 8.2), and
- *Zulu* shows an *increase* from 18.11% to 21.96% (1996: 22.9%).

A number of factors should be kept in mind in interpreting these data. Firstly, there is reason to question the validity of the 1991 census survey since inadequate efforts may have been made to enumerate communities in informal settlements and rural areas. Secondly, the data date from before 1994, a date which represents a serious change of direction in South Africa.

Language shift has occurred to some extent from Afrikaans to English (Hauptfleisch 1977; Scheffer 1979), and to an almost total extent from the Indian languages in Natal to English (Mesthrie, 1995). (See also Chapter 1.)

The social hierarchy of a country's languages is also apparent from patterns of diglossia, code-switching, linguistic mixing, borrowing and language accommodation. These phenomena have not been studied systematically in the South African context, but it is likely that it will be found that English is generally the donor rather than the receiver. For example, in a diglossic situation English will be used for the high functions; code-switching and code-mixing will involve switches and mixing with English; borrowing will be from English, and linguistic accommodation will be towards English.

Language preference patterns
As indicated in Chapter 2, the South African Constitution compels language policy developers at all three levels of Government to "take into account usage, …regional circumstances and the balance of the needs and preferences of the population as a whole or in the province concerned…: Municipalities must take into account the language usage and preferences of residents." (Constitution, p. 4). This stipulation will obviously lead to language audits being undertaken at all levels of government, which will mean that far more information is likely to be available at some future date than at present. Very little information is available at present, with much of it not being very useful. An example of the type of data currently available, is presented in Table 13.16.

Table 3.16. Language use in Soweto (in the 80s)

	Home language (%)	Ability to read and understand (%)
English	0.4	78.6
Zulu	36.9	56.0
Afrikaans	0.0	51.6
Sotho	19.0	44.1
Tswana	19.5	35.6
Xhosa	8.9	31.0
Pedi	6.8	24.6
Tsonga	3.6	6.7
Venda	3.0	5.6

Source: Schuring 1993: 14

Once again, the dominance of English is demonstrated. However, the position of Afrikaans (with no home-language speakers in Soweto) was also quite strong at the time, despite the Soweto protests against it in 1976 (with posters such as "Kill Afrikaans!"). The status of the Bantu languages is as expected. An interesting aspect is their mutual relationships, especially compared to Pretoria, where a different distribution of these languages as home languages prevails (see Table 4.8).

Literacy

The degree of illiteracy in South Africa is difficult to specify, because of a lack of exact information, and because its calculation is dependent upon the definition of literacy used. The LANGTAG report on literacy (1996: Chapter 5, authored by a team led by Prof. A. C. Nkabinda) puts the adult illiteracy rate at 29% (literacy being defined as a grade 7/standard 5 level of school education — i.e. seven years of schooling, at about age 13). If grade 9 is taken as the defining point the rate will obviously be lower. The report also estimates that a total of nearly 10 million people are presently in need of adult literacy training and basic education (pp. 138–9; see also Chapter 1).

An insight into the seriousness of the problem is provided by the following findings in tests of the literacy skills of teacher trainees in rural and urban South Africa, carried out by Hough & Horne, a private firm of literacy assessment consultants. They found that only 5% of the rural students, who would have to use English, a second or third language for them, as medium of instruction, had the required English literacy skills. In the case of the urban students (total assessed: 5924), who had all completed their secondary school training, they found the following decrease in English literacy skills from 1990 to 1997, by year of final school year:

Table 3.17. % students who possessed the expected English literacy skills by final school year

1990	1991	1992	1993	1994	1995	1996	1997
51	35	33	31	28	25	24	22

It is difficult to explain the decrease, and one can only assume that the struggle against Apartheid and the accompanying disruption of formal education (expressed in slogans such as "No education before liberation!"), especially after 1976, was an important contributing factor.

National communication

In countries dominated by a single language, such as Britain and Germany, private and public communication between social categories is usually in the general lingua franca. In a multilingual country such as South Africa this can only be the case if the majority of the people know one particular language.

This is not the case, as was indicated above. In South Africa national communication must therefore occur multilingually.

Of course, a situation may develop in which a general lingua franca gradually develops. This may be happening with English, which is already the medium of communication in particular domains, such as the national political debate, tertiary (and increasingly, secondary) education, and the public media. (Recently, the Government announced that it is considering declaring English as the main language of the court and of parliamentary debate; whilst the national broadcaster has decided to broadcast cricket, a national sport in the country, only in English. However, Tables 4.12, 4.13, and 6.10 to 6.13 suggest that this may not be a wise decision.)

Corpus development

Afrikaans and English are highly standardised, codified and technicalised, with the other official languages standardised and codified to a lesser degree, and also less technologised. The standardisation of Ndebele and Swazi has only recently begun. Another feature of the standardisation of the Bantu languages, is that there seems to be a degree of language-internal conflict, particularly in the sense that their standard varieties do not yet seem to be generally accepted and used in formal contexts (see also Chapters One and Eight.)

Grammars have been written for most of the Bantu languages, and there are a number of dictionaries available in each. (See Poulos 1990, and Poulos and Lourens 1994, for grammars of Venda and Pedi respectively, and see the LANGTAG report on the development of the (South) African languages (Chapter 2), especially pages 82–85).

An interesting aspect of the standardisation of the Bantu languages is that they were initially standardised by missionaries, which had a variety of consequences. Later on, the South African government created language committees (called "Language Boards" from the late 1950's) to handle the development of their orthography and to create new technical terms. An overview of this work is provided in the LANGTAG report, pp. 67 to 75 (see Chapter 9).

The Khoe-San languages have also been documented, with grammars (or grammatical notes), dictionaries/word lists, and teaching material (Traill, 1996).

Mention must also be made of *Fanagalo*, a pidgin which arose in Natal (presumably mainly on the sugar cane farms) due to the necessity of communication between English sugar farmers, indentured Indian labourers and the

Zulu-speaking local population, and was later imported by the mining industry as a means of communication between mine workers of divergent linguistic
origin. The mines consequently codified Fanagalo, producing grammar books
and dictionaries in it. Fanagalo remains, however, a highly stigmatised means
of communication. (Adendorff 1995.)

The democratisation process in South Africa has presented language planners with a considerable challenge, namely the fact that many speakers of the
major languages are alienated in varying degrees from the standard varieties, so
that the latter are (or can become) instruments of elitism and discrimination.
Various proposals have been made to handle this problem, such as the
harmonisation of Nguni and Sotho (Alexander 1989), the replacement of one
set of norms (such as standard British English) with another (such as "Black
South African English") — see Webb 1997; and the adaptation of non-standard forms in the standard (e.g. Cape Afrikaans forms in standard Afrikaans —
van Rensburg 1992) (see also Chapter 1). There are clear arguments for and
against each of these positions at various levels of the debate (linguistic, sociolinguistic, linguistic politics), which will be dealt with in Chapter 8.

Public functions and domains

National languages

The South African constitution designates no languages as "national languages". It is also unlikely that any single language will develop into a *de facto*
"national language", particularly in the sense of Fasold (1984: 74), i.e. as a
symbol of national identity, as a link with a glorious national past, and so on.
This issue is discussed more fully in Chapter 5.

Official languages

South Africa has eleven official languages at the national level. At the provincial
(regional) level legislatures have the right to select their province's official
languages from the list of national official languages. A number of them have
done so: Gauteng selected Afrikaans, English, Zulu and Pedi; the Western Cape
Afrikaans, English and Xhosa, and the Free State Afrikaans, English, Sotho and
Xhosa. This issue will be dealt with more fully in Chapter 4.

At the level of local government very little has happened as yet, as is
reported in Chapter 4. The following quotation from a newsletter of the
Northern Pretoria Metropolitan Sub-Structure , the "NPMSS", (vol 2/2, April

1996, p. 4), however, illustrates an aspect of the language policy problem. The editor writes (translated from Afrikaans): "The estimated number of residents of the NPMSS is currently between 400 000 and 500 000. The preferred language of communication of 90% of the residents of the NPMSS is English. As regards official publications or activities of the Council of the NPMSS, it is self-evident that they cannot occur in Afrikaans AND English, or even in all 11 official languages. That will simply be too expensive for the rate-payer." The implication of this point of view is clear: the newsletter will in future have to be in English only, despite the fact that such an approach is in essence in conflict with the spirit of a multilingual approach, and the statistics available, see Table 4.8, especially for Soshanguve, which is situated in the NPMSS.

This view is illustrative of the more general problem in South Africa with a multilingual approach: Policy decision-makers operate in isolation of each other and without full consideration of the macro-context or the micro-context.

As indicated in Chapter 1, South Africa does not yet have a comprehensive language policy. It is therefore not yet clear what the government has in mind in connection with the 11 national official languages. It is, of course, unrealistic to think in terms of all eleven languages being used equally at national level for all official functions. At the same time it would be unconstitutional to allow one language (which would be English, of course) to develop into the only official language at national level. This issue is discussed more fully in Chapter 4.

As pointed out in Chapter 1, the democratisation of the country implies the transformation of the state administration into an institution in which the Bantu languages will have a dominant role. Formerly, Afrikaans and English were the main languages of government, the state administration, the security services, postal and telegraphic services, transport and the electronic media (Prinsloo, 1995 and Smit, 1995). It will be interesting to observe the nature of the change-over as well as the possible obstacles (such as the use, in practice, of English as main language of internal state administration, which would be unconstitutional).

Education

All 11 major languages are sufficiently developed, and have the necessary status to be used as media of instruction at the junior primary school level. In practice, only Afrikaans and English are used in the senior primary phase, secondary school, and throughout the tertiary level. (Two universities are apparently "experimenting" with the use of selected Bantu languages -Xhosa and Tswana — at university level.)

The choice of medium of school instruction was a serious problem in South Africa in the former political dispensation, causing widespread controversy, especially in the so-called black schools (schools controlled by the former Department of Education and Training, generally referred to as "DET schools"). As indicated in Chapter 1, the political unrest which started in Soweto in 1976 was at least partly caused by the unilateral decision of the then Minister of Bantu Education to enforce the use of Afrikaans as a medium of instruction in half of the high school subjects in the DET schools. Today, the policy on medium of instruction in all these schools has changed, allowing a free choice from day 1 of the school programme. The medium of instruction, however, is still an issue today, with many former white Afrikaans schools claiming that it is their constitutionally enshrined right to have single-medium Afrikaans schools, whereas the government rejects this interpretation of the constitution. This issue is debated more fully in Chapter 6.

The question of medium of instruction has also become a serious issue at the tertiary level. The government's view is that tertiary institutions (teacher training colleges, technikons — "technical universities", and universities — totalling 37, with about 600 000 students) are national assets and therefore have to admit all qualifying students. Given the right of students to demand that training programmes be available in their languages of preference, and given the language politics of the country this has meant that, since 1994, all tertiary institutions which formerly used Afrikaans as the major medium of instruction (i.e. five of the 21 universities) have gradually been switching to using English in addition to Afrikaans.

The issue of language of teaching at tertiary level has been quite an emotional matter, especially in the Afrikaans community. Some of the institutions concerned rejected the demand to teach also in English, pointing out that the use of Afrikaans can be constitutionally, sociolinguistically and historically justified, and cannot be seen as a denial of anyone's fundamental rights, since intending students are generally in a position to choose an alternative training institution. In any case, they argue, why is there no pressure on the (16) historically English universities to provide tuition in any other language besides English?

The five (historically Afrikaans) universities have, in the main, all made changes to their language policies, with most of them opting for at least an equal use of English. Only Stellenbosch University in the Western Cape is insisting on the right to use Afrikaans as its main language of teaching at the undergraduate level.

The judiciary
Despite the drastic changes in the constitutional language stipulations the major languages of law are still Afrikaans and English, both as regards the formulation of laws and in the courts of law. A system of interpreters is available for interpreting from Afrikaans and English into the Bantu languages, and vice versa. This system is, however, not satisfactory. As mentioned earlier, the Government seems to be considering making English the main (or only) language of the court.

Other domains
English, and decreasingly, Afrikaans, are the major (and generally the only) languages of middle to higher level trade, industry, finance, science and technology. The autochthonous languages are used only in some sports, in one or two local newspapers, regional radio programmes and, to some degree, on national television.

Language planning institutions

A number of language planning agencies look after the interests of the major languages. Two of these are the *Suid-Afrikaanse Akademie vir Wetenskap en Kuns* (the South African Academy for Science and Arts) for Afrikaans and the *English Academy* for English. Formerly, ten *language boards* were responsible for the nine Bantu languages (Xhosa having one in the former Transkei as well as one in the former Ciskei). These agencies deal with the standardisation of the languages, their codification, their technicalisation, the promotion of their literature and their study. The 10 language boards (for the Bantu languages) previously operated under the control of the Ministries of Education of the so-called national states and the self-governing regions and were therefore seen in some quarters as part of the apartheid system. This has led to their being perceived to be instruments of apartheid, and they have all been scrapped. At present a new language management system is being constructed, with the Pan South African Language Board (an independent national body) heading a reasonably elaborate system of provincial language committees and a set of national language bodies. This organisation is discussed more fully in Chapter 9.

Besides these agencies there are also state institutions such as the *National Terminology Service* and the *National Language Service*, as well as cultural bodies and private and semi-private language bureaux (in private concerns and municipalities). Non-governmental organisations (such as the *National Language Project*) and university programmes (such as the *Language Facilitation Programme* at the University of the Free State, and **CentRePoL** at the University of Pretoria) also deal with language planning issues.

Finally, language planning issues have received extensive attention from sociolinguists in South Africa. The systematic study of the politics of language goes back to at least 1972, with the doctoral work of Prinsloo in 1972. Since then, numerous publications have appeared, as is reflected in the bibliography of this book. Some of the noteworthy contributions have been Prinsloo 1972, Steyn 1980, Prinsloo and van Rensburg 1984 and du Plessis 1992. Early work dealt mainly with Afrikaans, but more recent work also deals with the Bantu languages, for example, Mmusi 1987, Masinge 1997 and Masunga 2000 (see Webb 1996 for an overview).

In conclusion, a diagrammatic representation of the 11 official languages of South Africa in terms of their power relations at different stages in their recent history is interesting. The first diagram below (Figure 3.2) represents, subjectively determined, the pre-1994 situation, Figure 3.3 the post-1994 situation, and Figure 3.4 the "ideal" situation (which never occurs of course, but could be something towards which governments could strive). Each language is presented as a circle, with the size of the circles roughly representing the power of the language, with regard to its political, bureaucratic and economic power.

Figure 3.2. Linguistic power-relations before 1994

In Figure 3.2 Afrikaans is on the bureaucratic centre-stage, with English of basic importance, especially in economic contexts, but with the Bantu languages all neatly controlled, in the service of Apartheid.

Figure 3.3 shows that English is all-powerful, with the nine Bantu languages officially recognised and thus in an improved position (no longer boxed-in, but more central and selectively larger in size), yet still with little significant public roles, being effectively nameless. Afrikaans, equally nameless and marginalised, is represented by a bigger circle because of its economic value.

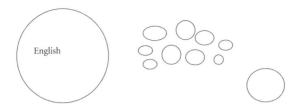

Figure 3.3. Linguistic power-relations after 1994

The "ideal" sociolinguistic situation

In an "ideal world", where the spirit of linguistic pluralism prevails and the principle of linguistic equity is implemented, all eleven languages should be in perfect harmony, equally valued, with no linguistic domination or subordination, with the speakers of each language not feeling any compulsion to switch language in the presence of speakers of any other language, and with social, economic and political power not being a determinant of language choice. Such a world could then be represented as in Figure 3.4.

The question to be debated is what the South African government should do to move in the direction of Figure 3.4.

Figure 3.4. The "ideal" linguistic power-relations

Notes

1. The Apartheid Government was unable to find a "definition" of the so-called coloured population group, and coloured people were generally classified negatively as being "non-black" and/or "non-Asian/Indian" and/or "non-European".

2. Following the tradition of referring to a language with the name customised in the language of use (thus "French", not "Français", and "German", not "Deutsch" in English) the anglicised forms of the Bantu languages are used in this monograph.

3. Their own languages were lost in the shift to "Afrikaans"/Cape Dutch.

4. Quotation marks are used to signify the exclusion of the so-called national states from South Africa.

5. Since only the first three choices are indicated in Table 3:10 the percentages do not add up to 100.

6. Percentages in Tables 3.11 to 3.15 do not total 100 because choices for combinations of languages were not included.

7. Data on the preferred language for listening to the radio and TV viewing also shows a strong preference for English (with 59% in Atteridgeville, for instance, in favour of its use as the only language, as opposed to 9%, for example, in favour of Pedi).

8. The census survey results are probably not wholly comparable, as explained later in the text.

CHAPTER 4

For the people, by the people

Language and state administration

The central role of language in governance need not be argued; it is self-evident. Effective communication between the political leadership (the cabinet) and the state administration, between individual government bodies and institutions, within these bodies and institutions, and between the government and its citizens, which are prerequisites for good government, occurs mainly through language.

In many of the leading countries of the world, such as the United Kingdom, France, Germany and Japan, language is not really a matter of special concern in state administration. These countries are dominated by one language and the choice of language for purposes of government is, in principle, not a problem. However, in countries which are complexly multilingual, and where language knowledge and proficiency are unequally distributed, the matter of language for purposes of government is not so simple, and the role of language in governance needs to be discussed.

A discussion of language and governance must cover at least two main issues, namely language in state administration, and language in national integration. These two aspects clearly overlap, and any distinction between them is bound to be arbitrary. However, the distinction will be maintained in this book, with the first being discussed in this chapter, and the second in Chapter 5.

In this chapter the following topics will be covered:
- The general tasks which have to be performed by a government and their implications for a language policy and language plan for state administration in South Africa
- Features of a multilingual policy and plan
- The process of language policy development for the Department of Labour
- The present state of language practice in South African public life
- Language policy proposals for specific state departments, in particular the defence force and the police services in South Africa

- Cost-estimation for language policy
- The need for a pro-active approach

The general tasks of government

Generally speaking, the basic task of a government is to ensure order, stability, peace and prosperity for all the citizens of the territory for which the government is responsible. In more specific terms a government must maintain the social order, manage the country politically, control public resources and facilitate the economic, educational, social and cultural life (and development) of its citizens.

The *maintenance of the social order* implies the protection of citizens against external threats, social protection (against poverty, ill health, violence and criminality), the management of internal conflict, and the regulation of social behaviour (controlling corruption, theft and fraud). In South Africa, with the establishment of a democratic government, "maintaining the social order" requires going much further. In fact, it means *reconstructing the social order*, breaking down racial barriers and inter-group suspicion, working towards some sort of national integration, and establishing new values, new attitudes, new beliefs, new perceptions, new norms, and so forth.

The *political management of a country* requires a measure of control over all sectors of civil society if the laws and policies of the government are to implemented effectively. In this regard communication is obviously fundamental. For example, if the present South African government is to succeed in its fight against HIV/AIDS or in the implementation of legislation and policies (e.g. on labour relations, skills development, employment equity, employment conditions, and the promotion of worker health and safety) languages and the modes and styles of communication will have a central role to play (see again further down).

The *management of public resources* implies the provision and maintenance of services (education, employment opportunities, housing, welfare, health care, water, electricity, transport, communication facilities, professional guidance for farmers, recreation, and so on), the collection of taxes, the management of state finances, the collection and distribution of information and the protection of the environment.

Allied to the management of public resources is the *facilitation of the economic, educational, social and cultural development* of the country's citizens.

This task, which is of especial importance in an emergent, third-world country such as South Africa, refers to the provision of effective educational programmes, the promotion of economic growth (the creation of wealth and its (re)distribution, job creation and capacity building), the promotion of the norms and values pertinent to an emergent economy and a modern democracy with a political philosophy of pluralism (work ethic, competitiveness and a striving towards occupational efficiency, productivity and professional loyalty, equity, acceptance of the rule of law, tolerance for ethnic, racial, linguistic and religious differences and respect for the environment), and the protection of the country's cultural wealth.

These responsibilities and obligations are performed within the context of a particular set of norms for political management. In the case of the South African government these (publicly espoused) norms are democracy, equity, the absence of all discrimination, affirmative action and tolerance for diversity along all demographic dimensions (such as gender, language, culture and religion). These values provide the basis for its authority, its right to make laws and to develop policy for the country, and its right to expect the citizens of the country to accept these laws and policies. Directly flowing from this is the need for a particular *style of government*. A democratic government, such as the South African government wants to be, is characterised by accountability, legitimacy and transparency. Robinson (1996) defines these styles as follows:

> Accountability denotes the effectiveness with which the governed can exercise influence over their governors
> Legitimacy is concerned with the right of the state to exercise power over its citizens, and the extent to which these powers are perceived to be rightly exercised, and
> Transparency is founded on the existence of mechanisms for ensuring public access to decision making. (p. 347)

Two particular aspects of this style of government are the commitment to consultation with the polity, and to demographic representativeness.

These tasks and "styles of governance" collectively imply one basic requirement of good government: the necessity for effective communication — communication by the government with all the people in the country so that citizens are informed about the policies of the government, and communication by the people with the government so that the government knows what the needs and views of the citizens are. A government needs to be aware of these needs and views. As Ranney (1987: 39) points out:

> If a nation's government simply does not know what demands its people are making, it can hardly deal with them satisfactorily. If it is dimly aware of the demands but unaware of their variety or intensity, it is not likely to deal with them very well. And if it does not cope effectively with the most urgent and widely supported demands, it risks anger, alienation, and perhaps rebellion from the groups it ignores. Consequently, governments need effective methods of articulation of interests. *Interest articulation* means the process of forming and expressing demands by political groups and transmitting them to government authorities. (Emphasis original.)

Good government presupposes the free and full exchange of information, and the full employment of negotiation, consultation and persuasion. Given this requirement, and given also the vital role of language as an instrument of access and equity, it is clear that extensively and complexly multilingual countries like South Africa, where the majority of the population do not have an adequate proficiency in the dominant language of public life (see Chapters One and Three), will have to employ all the major languages of the country for purposes of effective government. A government has to establish mechanisms and styles for government-citizen communication and has to develop citizens' knowledge of the procedures required for this type of communication as well as the skills to handle the relevant communication processes.

HIV/AIDS provides a dramatic example of the need for effective communication. According to a report of the South African Department of Health, released on 17 February 1999, 22.8% of the national population had contracted HIV in 1998, having risen from 0.73% in 1990. (The figure for KwaZulu/Natal was 32.5% for 1998.) In the same year it was estimated that between 23 and 33 per cent of all pregnant women in the country were HIV-positive, with 70 000 babies estimated to be infected every year, and (according to research done by the AIDS Training and Information Centre) 50% of the country's tertiary students are HIV-positive. Furthermore, although 71% of the pupils in the Eastern Cape believed HIV to be a threat in 2000, only 25% believed they could get infected, whilst 30% of the people researched who had only primary school education did not know how the disease was transmitted. (Reported in a national newspaper, *The Sowetan*, 14/08/2000.) Clearly, communication on AIDS has not been meaningfully effective. It is therefore essential that the Department of Health pay serious and immediate attention to their language policy (which does not yet exist) to ensure that information on HIV/AIDS is effectively distributed. In such a policy, the Department of Health must make sure that all factors relevant to effective public communication are taken into account, such as the languages/dialects used, the community's language attitudes, its levels of knowledge and understanding, cultural and social factors, local realities, styles and forms of interaction, accessibility of the information, feedback, participation by communities in the dialogue, and so forth.

The example of the HIV/AIDS issue illustrates a central question in this book: to debate what a multilingual policy for state administration involves. Questions that need to be discussed include:
– which policy options should be considered?
– what are the likely costs and benefits of each of the options?
– which languages should be used for which particular functions at which levels of official life and for which purposes?
– which resources are required for the implementation of the different policy options?
– which language development and language management measures are needed?
– do government employees/state officials have the necessary knowledge, skills and attitudes to implement such a policy?

Some features of a multilingual language policy and plan for state administration

In Chapter 2 the macro-contexts of language planning for South Africa were discussed, and the ideological vision and political mission which should guide such planning were described. This chapter will discuss the language planning tasks a government has to perform within the socio-political realities of the country, if the government is to be maximally efficient and effective.

Three features of a policy of multilingualism

To begin with, three features of a multilingual language policy for state administration need to be kept in mind.

Firstly, it must reflect the spirit of multilingualism, and English may not be the only language of official use. Governments and legislatures at all levels, all state bodies (also at provincial and local levels of government) and all parastatal boards, commissions, etc. must employ languages other than English in official functions, and state employees will have to know these languages, be skilled in using them in official communication, and be positive about multilingualism. In practice this largely means that the Bantu languages need to be centralised in state administration. In this connection, the observation made by Strydom and Pretorius (1999, see previous chapter) is pertinent, namely that the qualifying clauses in the constitution (the so-called escape clauses) must not be allowed to overrule the hierarchically superior stipulation of multilingualism.

Secondly, the principle of functional differentiation must be followed, which means that all 11 languages need not be used for all official functions in all contexts in all places at all times, but that language policies must differentiate on the basis of region and functional domain, provided they are multilingual in spirit.

Thirdly, policy decision-making may not be arbitrary, emotional or ideologically determined (in a negative way). It must be rational, systematic and formulated within a theoretical frame, with clear sets of assumptions, principles and aims, and based on sociolinguistic realities. A specific instance of non-arbitrariness is that the functional allocation of languages should allow for all three the functional dimensions or relationships relating to language use in public administration, that is, the domain of direct contact between state and citizens; inter- and intra-departmental official communication; and departmental record-keeping (for instance: archival records, the agendas and minutes of meetings, and so on). These three dimensions of communication make different demands with regard to language use, and language policy and language planning must therefore be differentiated according to these lines.[1] The paragraphs below describe a possible differentiation.

Communication with the public
One of the language stipulations of the interim constitution stated that "Wherever practicable, a person shall have the right to use and to be addressed in his or her dealings with any public administration at the national level of government in any official South African language of his or her choice." Although this clause is not explicitly included in the final constitution, the central idea it expresses can be used as a basis for (national) language policy, particularly since effective communication with the polity is a central part of good governance. Thus, all official interaction between the state and the civil community should in principle occur in any of the eleven official languages.

This policy decision should apply, for instance, to the annual reports of state departments, their mission statements and policy documents, government publications (*Government Gazette*, the *Provincial Gazettes*), official forms such as census forms and income tax forms, official documents (such as identity documents and passports), legislation, decrees and ordinances, press releases and public advertisements, pamphlets for national distribution (on elections, health care, educational decisions), and the letterheads on state stationary.

The same should apply to other instances of communication with the public (where the public are expected to respond), such as green papers and white papers (both draft legislation and policy). In the case of comprehensive publications such as the recent report of the *National Commission on Higher Education*, (which comprises 413 pages) executive summaries should be provided in all eleven languages. (The executive summary of the 1996 LANGTAG report,[2] which deals with language policy, was, ironically, translated into only *six* official languages, which is a poor reflection on the commitment of the department officially responsible for language policy, to multilingualism. It is unclear what the reasons for the decisions against the remaining five languages could have been.) Furthermore, advertisements of staff vacancies, interviews with applicants, negotiations with trade unions, worker organisations, professional associations, and professional advice (for example to farmers, small business entrepreneurs, medically and psychically ill people[3]) should all be handled in any of the eleven official languages.

Personal correspondence with civilians must, obviously, be in the official language selected by the civilian. In the case of a citizen who does not know one of these languages (which would be highly exceptional), the citizen will need to obtain assistance from someone who possesses the required competence.

The question of the language of legislation requires a comment. According to one view it is practical to select one language, for instance English in South Africa, as the first language of legislation, decrees and ordinances, with translations available in each of the other official languages. In the case of a legal dispute only the formulation in that one language need then be dealt with. Such a view can obviously not be accepted in a meaningfully democratic country, since it implies the subordination of the speakers of the other languages. It is therefore necessary that translations be done precisely, and that the formulation in every language then be given legal standing.

Internal communication
In the case of official tasks which are not directed at the general public, such as departmental training programmes, appointing, promoting, motivating and evaluating staff, internal newsletters, inter- and intra-departmental oral and

written communication,[4] the communication of internal regulations, instructions and directives, and job descriptions with their key performance indicators, the use of all eleven languages is possibly not required. The language policy in such contexts need only obey local constraints, such as the language knowledge of the government employees involved or the languages dominant in a particular region. (In KwaZulu/Natal, for example, state administration can be conducted almost wholly in Zulu and English.)

Internal record-keeping
Policy on internal record-keeping must also prescribe, in the spirit of multilingualism, the use of more than one language, even if a specific administrative task involves persons or institutions who share the same language(s). Examples of such tasks include compiling memoranda for ministers and the cabinet on public needs; requesting clarification on policies, missions and aims for senior administrators; evaluating policy implementation; devising control systems and directives, departmental budgets and departmental book-keeping and stock-keeping records; and the agendas and minutes of meetings. Language policy decisions in such cases may be differentiated by level, meaning that the languages prescribed for ministerial business could be different from that at the level of district offices.

The languages of internal record-keeping may, of course, be any of the eleven official languages, depending on the local or particular context. For instance, in the administrative capital of KwaZulu/Natal the language of record-keeping could be Zulu and English. (The tendency to opt for English for this function locally and/or nationally must be checked vigorously, since there can be no justification for such a decision.)

The proposed South African Languages Bill

As mentioned at the end of Chapter 2, the proposed South African Languages Bill has not yet been approved, and most state departments have not engaged in developing language policies. It is therefore not possible to provide an evaluation of any implementation.[5]

The proposed bill requires all state departments to develop language policies, stipulating that not less than four languages be used for all official business at the national level (selected on a rotational basis from each of four categories of the official languages). If accepted, the bill will compel bodies of state to "recognise the principle of multilingualism", to ensure that all the official languages "enjoy parity of esteem and be treated equitably", to "elevate the status and advance the use of the historically marginalised languages of South Africa" (p. 1 of the unnumbered proposed bill), to ensure "intergovernmental co-ordination and harmonisation of policies, legislation and actions relating to the entrenchment and promotion of multilingualism" (p. 4 of the proposed bill) and to establish language units which must, inter alia, "conduct language surveys and audits relevant to its sphere of activity with a view to assessing the appropriateness of an existing language policy and practice" (p. 8).

The bill seems to have been developed on the assumption that policy documents need not be very specific (and presumably, that decisions on specific issues and on specific measures should more appropriately be part of a plan of implementation). This is in my opinion a pity, since the language political situation in South Africa is serious enough to warrant a far more pro-active approach (as argued at the end of this chapter). It is important to keep in mind that the two most important language political challenges in South Africa (as elsewhere in Africa) are the negative status of the Bantu (or African) languages and the lack of understanding of the fundamental role of language in personal and public life. Any language policy proposal should address these two issues very vigorously. The policy should demonstrate to citizens that the Bantu languages are wholly suitable for use in any high-function public context, and that their use will most certainly lead to more effectiveness and efficiency and higher productivity in the state administration. In my opinion the following measures should form part of any language policy proposal:

- An "imperfect knowledge" of Afrikaans and English should not be used as a barrier to the occupational progress of civil servants
- A knowledge of at least one Bantu language must be required for appointments and promotion in the civil service
- The Bantu languages must be developed as instruments of technology and used in information pamphlets for the state's extension services with farmers, the provision of medical and psychological information to the public, legal advice, etc.
- The Bantu languages must be used as languages of staff training
- Bantu languages must immediately be introduced to perform prominent functions, initially at least in official letterheads, the names of buildings and public signs, such as road signs
- Programmes must be developed for training civil servants in handling the multilingual (and multicultural) reality of South Africa, and in handling ethnic nationalism and related phenomena

- The current language-skills needs in the civil service, and the staff-development programmes available to meet these needs, must be determined
- Positions must be created in every government body for language planners, editors, translators, interpreters and terminologists, and in-service language training programmes for such persons should be provided

The need for research and development

Besides the work of Cloete, 1965, Prinsloo, 1995 and Smit, 1995, very little is known about the sociolinguistic realities of the state administration. Research is necessary on:

- Patterns of language use in government departments. (Which languages are used for which functions?)
- The present state of language knowledge and expertise in government departments
- The language attitudes, expectations, views and beliefs of people in the public service
- The available human and physical resources (infrastructure) for language policy implementation

Without answers to these questions a sociolinguistically accountable plan of implementation is difficult to draw up.

The process of language policy development for the Department of Labour

Working within a specific theoretical and analytical framework (as described, for example, in Chapter 2, Webb et al. 1996; Webb 2001 and Webb & Grin 2000) and within the relevant language policy contexts to which all departmental language policy has to respond (the constitution and the South African Languages Bill), note should first be taken of the vision and the mission of the Department, so that the eventual language policy and plan act as facilitators, not as obstacles to the Department of Labour in performing its main task, that is to transform the labour market, improve vocational skills development, contribute towards better labour relations, facilitate employment equity, and facilitate social transformation.

A second preparatory task is to analyse the external and the internal environments of the Department as they relate to language policy development. A framework such as set out in Table 4.1 can be used:

Table 4.1. Environmental factors affecting decisions about language planning goals

External environment (beyond departmental control)[6]	Internal environment (within departmental control)

– International forces:
  – The information era
  – Global competitiveness
  – Increasing technologisation
– Constitutional language stipulations
– The SA Languages Bill
– Provincial language policies
– The sociolinguistic realities of the Department's clients (other Government institutions, communities and the labour market)
	– Departmental structures
	– The organisational culture of the Department
	– Inter- and intra-departmental relations
	– Departmental tasks, functions and policies
	– Financial resources
	– Human resources
	– The sociolinguistic realities of the Department (e.g. the language knowledge and linguistic skills of officials)

Analyzing the *external environment* of the Department includes the governmental language policy context, identifying the relevant global forces, defining the political, economic, social and technological contexts applicable to language policy development in the Department, and determining the sociolinguistic realities (linguistic character, usage, preferences, needs) of the **clients** of the Department (statutory bodies; private sector institutions; labour organisations; other government departments; the general public, and so forth). This process will obviously include consulting with other departments and institutions with which the Department co-operates, as well as consulting leaders of industry, labour organisations and community-based organisations.

Analyzing the *internal environment* of the Department includes determining its organisational culture (values, attitudes and perceptions); its structure, policies, functions, tasks and systems; its core objectives, needs and wants; the strategic issues relevant to it; its practices; the relevant industrial relations policies and processes; staff recruitment and selection policies and practices; staff development programmes; and its sociolinguistic realities (the linguistic knowledge and skills levels of departmental officials).

Following on the strategic analysis of the environmental factors which impinge on language policy development for the Department, it will be necessary to collect the sociolinguistic information and analyse it, using appropriate analytic tools. The collection of information about the sociolinguistic character of the internal and external environment can be handled within the frameworks described in Table 4.2 and Table 4.3 as an illustration. These tasks need to be supplemented with interviews with key role-players in the Department, a

Table 4.2. The sociolinguistic character of the Department's clients

Feature	Afrikaans	English	Zulu	Xhosa	Pedi	Tswana
Proficiency levels/Language knowledge *As L1 and L2 (all 4 modi)*						
Literacy levels						
Acquisition opportunities *As L1, L2, L3*						
Geographic distribution						
Demographic distribution *Rural/urban*						
Functions to be performed						
Languages required to perform the tasks and functions regarding the different categories of clients						
Language attitudes						
Language preferences, needs & wants						

Table 4.3. The sociolinguistic character of the departmental administrative staff

	Afrikaans	English	Pedi	Tswana	Zulu	Xhosa
Language distribution						
Language proficiency/knowledge, skills						
Top management						
Middle management						
Lower management						
Working language						
Meetings						
Agendas						
Minutes						
Memoranda						
Inter-institutional communication						
Intradept communication						
Lang. related functions to be performed						
Patterns of language behaviour in Dept.						
Language preferences						
Lang. acquisition programmes available						
Languages of laws, regulations and proceedings						
Reports						
Information brochures						
Newsletters, media releases						
Public notices						
Community services						
Availability of translation services						
Availability of interpretation services						
Editorial work						
Language management expertise						

nation-wide questionnaire survey, workshops on the issue, and consultation with representative officials of the Department.

The next step is to describe the *general and the specific goals/set the targets* which the departmental language policy should achieve in order to give effect to its vision, mission, functions, tasks and policies, describe the expected outputs and outcomes of the language policy, and specify measurable indicators of effective policy implementation. Besides specifying which languages should be used for which tasks and functions, the goals should also describe the linguistic knowledge and skills required to perform particular functions and tasks (for example, being able to write reports, lead workshops and seminars, conduct meetings, summarise reports, manage the work of commissions, and so forth), and list the types of linguistic knowledge and skills it seeks to develop in the labour market (such as worker organisations being able to draft statutes and handle bargaining).

The next step is to draw up a *business plan/plan of implementation* for the proposed language policy, indicating *what* needs to be done in order to realise the language policy goals, *how* these tasks will be performed, by *whom*, with *what resources*, *when* and *how*, and *how* policy implementation should be monitored.

A sub-section of the task of language policy development is to specify possible language policy options, with a list of the pro's and cons of each and an estimate of the likely costs of each option. The purpose of such a document is to enable the policy decision-makers of the Department to select the language policy best suited to their views on departmental policy.

The language-related tasks and functions of the Department of Labour for which language policy development has to provide.
The South African Department of Labour has to ensure:
a.   Communication between the national Department, the 10 provincial departments and the 221 labour centres, and with its more or less 6000 employees, facilitating co-operative, effective departmental administration through the participation of particularly black workers. These functions require effective communication between the Minister of Labour, the Director-General, Deputy Director-General, the Chief Directors, the Directors, the administrative officers, clerks, typists, security personnel and messenger staff. Given the probability that there is a wide disparity in the language knowledge and linguistic skills (in both the first and the second language,) of these employees, a language policy must be a facilitating instrument for obtaining staff co-

operation and involvement in training, policy implementation, the management of staff performance, conducting meetings, seminars, workshops, and improving staff's ability to respond effectively to clients — leading to the Department of Labour's improved performance in service delivery.

b.   Transformation of the departmental culture, especially in the sense of establishing particular values (e.g. work commitment), developing professional knowledge and skills, promoting institutional loyalty, and establishing a corporate culture.

c.   Distribution of information internally, e.g. about the goals and objectives of the Department, policies, plans, obligations, organisational structure, management techniques, performance evaluation, appointments and promotions, and handling grievances.

d.   Communication and co-ordination with
   – people outside the Department, e.g. about labour laws and policies
   – institutions regarding employee interests and with labour organisations (such as bargaining councils, trade unions, employer organisations)
   – co-operating institutions (Nedlac, the Employment Conditions Commission, the Commission for Employment Equity, the National Skills Authority, the Commission for Conciliation, Mediation and Arbitration, the Occupational Health and Safety Advisory Council, Unemployment Insurance Fund, Sectoral Education and Training Authorities (SETAs), Compensation Commission, etc.), and
   – the Human Rights Commission, the Commission for Gender Equality.

e.   Providing an integrated service delivery to the public and its institutional clients, leading to client satisfaction.

f.   The transformation of the labour market through the creation of a market environment which will support social development and economic growth, attract investment, enhance productivity, support small and medium enterprises (SMEs), and so forth. This task will also require the promotion and development of workers' vocational knowledge and skills, thus allowing them to respond to market demands. It is clear that the language issue is of central concern for policies on, and arrangements for training, through the National Training Strategy, the Industry Training Boards, and in consultation with the National Qualifications Framework and the South African Qualifications Authority. Transforming the South African labour market includes the capacity-building of workers, promoting bargaining skills, promoting the effective management of worker organisations; improving/promoting acquaintance with, and skills in, information technology. Transforming the labour market also includes eliminating discrimination, inequality and exploitation, which relates to language, e.g. the discriminative and exploitative role of Fanakalo in the mining industry and English in occupational mobility. Resolving potential labour disputes and conflict, for example the protests of the (white, Afrikaans) Mine Workers Union regarding the use of Afrikaans is also necessary.

g. Communication with international bodies (the International Labour Organisation, USAID and foreign governments).

h. The distribution of information to the general public and the labour market to raise the level of knowledge and awareness of the Department, e.g. its policies, its services, its publications (reports, brochures, booklets, videos, labour journals, briefings, newspaper articles, media releases (electronic and written media), publicity campaigns, and so forth).

Finally, a SWOT analysis[7] needs to be made of the language policy proposal. Table 4.4 provides an illustration of a hypothetical proposal:

Table 4.4. A generalised SWOT analysis of a language policy proposal for the Department of Labour directed at the use of Bantu languages for official purposes

Strengths	Weaknesses
Multilingual skills of the majority of employees Strong government, with legitimacy and 67% voter support Established administrative structures Effective communication system Established education system Technological facilities Research expertise available	Uncertain political & bureaucratic will Fear of possible high costs of language planning Inadequate supply of trained language workers Insufficient appropriate information Under-adapted Bantu languages
Opportunities	Threats
Climate of transformation/reconstruction & development Favourable demographic set-up	Globalisation Dominance of English Low self-esteem/negative language attitudes Escape clauses in the constitutional language stipulations Lack of appreciation for the role of language in public life

The present state of language policy development in the state administration

Notwithstanding some impressive achievements, which include their courageous decision to recognise eleven languages as official (reaffirmed in the final constitution of 1996; see Chapter 2); the LANGTAG process (see Chapter 2 and footnote 2), and the establishment of the Pan South African Language Board (see Chapter 9), the Government's record in language policy formulation and planning is not very encouraging.[8]

There are a number of general signs that official public life is gradually becoming more unilingual/English. Consider, first, the following proposals put forward by parliamentarians:

a. The proposal in 1998 (since abandoned) by the Speaker of Parliament and the Leader of the Council of Provinces that English be the main language of parliamentary reporting (and therefore that the agendas of meetings, all resolutions adopted at meetings, and all parliamentary speeches be recorded in English in Hansard, the official report of parliamentary proceedings)

b. The proposal by the Portfolio Committee for Defence that English be the only language of the South African National Defence Force, and that English be the only language of orders, training, general communication, control and co-ordination (February, 1998)

c. The serious discussion of using only English as the language of record in the court (February, 1998)

Consider further the following decisions by parastatal bodies:

d. The decision by the Post Office to use only English for internal business, with English as the language of meetings, the minutes of meetings, memoranda, notices, letters, and even of advertisements of employment opportunities (April 1998)

e. The telecommunication firm Telkom's similar decision in May 1998

f. The strong bias towards English in the programmes of the South African Broadcasting Corporation's television section, and

g. The decision in 2000 by South African Airways to use only English on its internal flights

Similar decisions were made in the private sector:

h. The Landbank (now called the Land and Agricultural Bank of South Africa) decided in 1997 that English would be its official language, despite the fact that the majority of its staff members were Afrikaans-speaking, and that 80% of its clients were also Afrikaans-speaking

i.   The Council of Real Estate Agents made a similar decision in 1997
j.   The ABSA banking group (which was and still is primarily Afrikaans) decided in 1997 to use English as language of internal business
k.   The editorial board of *De Rebus*, the official journal of the Society of Lawyers decided in 1997 to switch to English
l.   The official journal of nurses, *Nursing World*, decided to use only English as official language in 1997.

A significant mismatch between the constitutional language stipulations and actual language practice seems to be emerging in South Africa.

The government has, of course, been made aware of this mismatch, and has expressed concern. But its concern is not very convincing, as is apparent from the statement by the minister responsible for language policy in April 1998, i.e. the (former) Minister of Arts, Culture, Science and Technology, namely that the official status of languages should not be confused with the use of these languages, and that although 11 languages "must enjoy parity of esteem and must be treated equitably" this does not mean they must all be used (*The Citizen*, 14 April 1998, p. 6).

The extent of the increasing monolingualism is also described in the *South Africa Yearbook 1996* (3rd edition), which was compiled and published by the South African Communication Service (a government department):

> (T)here is a marked move towards unilingualism in the public sector..... In most government departments the medium of communication is English, and most meetings are conducted in English. This trend is also visible in official publications. Nationally important documents are increasingly being published in English only. These documents include white papers, proclamations by the President, notices by Cabinet Ministers and reports by commissions of enquiry. Acts of Parliament are being amended by Presidential proclamation in English only, with resultant differences between the English and Afrikaans texts of a particular Act.
> Documents published with a view to eliciting comments from the public also tend to appear in English only, for example draft bills and green papers. (p. 381)

The LANGTAG report (preliminary Final Report, 1996: 154–157) also discusses the "invisibility of the marginalised languages" (the Bantu languages) and thus the denial of access and equity to the speakers of these languages. It points out that in 1995 eleven of the 21 annual reports of government departments were published in English only, with seven published only in Afrikaans and English, and only two published in four or more languages. (The only government department which published its annual report in all eleven languages was the South African Communication Service. Even the department responsible for language policy, the Department of Arts, Culture, Science and Technology published its annual report in English only.)

There are, of course, a number of reasons for South Africa's (increasing) monolingualism. These include: a global tendency towards assimilation and homogenisation; the view that a policy of multilingualism will lead to unnecessary translation and interpreting costs; the belief that multilingualism will result in ineffective administration; the likelihood that most politicians and public administrators are not politically committed to a policy of pluralism, and the (unacknowledged) desire to retain the privileges which a knowledge of English guarantees for the benefit of the already privileged.

Some research findings
Research findings about government language policy development and implementation have also provided some negative indicators.

At the end of 1997, **CentRePoL**, a research centre in the politics of language at the University of Pretoria, approached the 27 state departments and the Public Service Commission with a written request (in English, of course) for information about their language policies. Thirteen replied, generally in very brief terms. Their responses (November 1997 to February 1998) can be summarised as follows:

– Six replied that they had no official language policy, but that their "working language" (for internal oral and written communication) was English. The six were the departments of Arts, Culture, Science and Technology; Constitutional Development; Finance; Land Affairs; the Office of the Deputy President; and Sport and Recreation. The first two of these departments reported that their annual reports were also published in some of the other official languages.

– Seven replied that they had adopted a language policy and that their official language (of formal documentation, meetings, internal communication, press releases, interviews with the media and annual reporting) was English: Agriculture; Education; Home Affairs; Public Service and Administration; the Public Service Commission, Public Works; and Welfare. In some of these departments provision was made for the use of other official languages in external communication and in the case of merit assessments and disciplinary hearings, but in most cases it was clear that English was to be the "anchor language". Where documents needed to be translated, the translations had to be from English.

– The following fifteen departments did not reply: the Office of the President, the departments of Labour, Housing, Correctional Services, Trade and Industry, Provincial and Local Government, Foreign Affairs, Safety and Security, Justice, Communication, Mineral and Energy Affairs, Intelligence, Water Affairs and Forestry, Environment and Tourism, Transport and Public Enterprises. (The labels and grouping of state departments have changed since the survey.)

The *Unit for Language Facilitation and Development* and the *Department of Constitutional Law and Philosophy of Law* at the University of the Free State conducted a more comprehensive survey in May and June of 1999. Their survey (questionnaire and telephone interviews) was conducted among 43 state departments and state institutions[9], and among 79 local government bodies in the Free State. Table 4.5 contains the findings for the state departments and institutions (du Plessis, 1999).

Table 4.5. Language policy in 27 state departments and 16 state/semi-state institutions in 1999, du Plessis (1999)

	27 state departments	16 institutions
Have developed and implemented a language policy	15	4
Have decided to use "mostly English"	15	10
Use English for all written communication	19	13
Also use Afrikaans	8	4
Also use a Bantu language	4	2
Use English for records	22	–

The language used for laws, regulations, notices and public forms was found to be English in more than half of the cases. In some cases (record-keeping and written communication by the state institutions) the Bantu languages were not used at all. The significance of this wholly skewed situation becomes apparent if one views it in the context of the linguistic distribution of first languages in the province: Sotho is the first language of 62.1% of the population, Afrikaans: 14.5% and English: 1.3%.

In addition to these findings, du Plessis (1999) also reports a dearth of language legislation over the past five years, with only 11 acts or decrees being passed, that dealt with the establishment of language management structures, the place names committee and public broadcasting.

Du Plessis' conclusion is, inevitably, that the government has adopted "a laissez-faire approach regarding language matters" (1999: 18).

Since the research work reported on in this paragraph, an advisory panel appointed by the Minister of Arts, Culture, Science and Technology, drafted the language policy proposal discussed earlier. The proposal was subsequently submitted for comment to all government departments in a revised form, further revised and then (as stated above) presented to Cabinet as the *South African Languages Bill*. The bill was discussed by Cabinet on 13 September 2000, who decided that further work on the bill needs to be done, "taking into account priorities and financial implications". This information (including the preceding quotation) was obtained from a document provided by the ombudsman on language affairs in the official opposition, the Democratic Alliance, who directed a series of questions to ministers in parliament in August 2000 on their departments' inputs to discussions of the proposed bill. 16 of the 27 ministries replied to the questions, four withdrew their answers and seven did not reply. The departments who did not reply were Communications, Correctional Services, Defence, Environmental Affairs and Tourism, Housing, Minerals and Energy Affairs, Public Enterprises, Public Service and Administration, Trade and Industry, Water Affairs and Forestry and Welfare and Population Development. The departments of Justice and Constitutional Development, the Ministry of the Presidency, Agriculture and Land Affairs, Public Works, Transport, Provincial and Local Government and Home Affairs stated that they had not been requested to submit inputs on the proposed bill (by the Department of Arts, Culture, Science and Technology). The remaining departments all responded positively, listing specific concerns (for example the cost and budgetary implications of the proposed legislation).

The language policy proposals of two state departments

As an example of departmental language policy development, the draft policies of the South African Police Service (SAPS) and the South African National Defence Force (SANDF), drafted in 1998, will be discussed.[10] Both were quite clearly intent on formalising multilingualism.

The SAPS draft policy contains clauses stipulating that the language to be used at official meetings should be the (official) language best understood by the members of the meeting, that such members should not be hampered in their participation by the language used, that members of the SAPS should be enabled to become proficient in the dominant languages of the region where they are stationed, that communication with the public should take place in the language of preference of the public, that training should occur in the language the trainees prefer, and that provision should be made for foreign languages and for sign language. The draft policy exhibits a striking sensitivity to the principle of multilingualism as well as the constraints on policy development.

However, in light of the constitutional philosophy and the needs of a multilingual society, the draft policy is not progressive enough, and, in fact, differs very little from the former bilingual set-up. The proposed policy requires that internal written communication be mainly in Afrikaans and English; notes and memoranda to the minister must be in English; legislation, government notices, green and white papers, annual reports, reports of Commissions of Inquiry, research reports, speeches by the National Commissioner, press releases, commemorative publications and brochures and pamphlets, must all be in Afrikaans and English (though translations can be made); radio communication and court proceedings must be in Afrikaans and English; and examinations must be taken in Afrikaans or English.

The draft policy of the SANDF (discussion document titled "Language policy for the Department of Defence", *Policy proposals, Draft 6*, 1998) is more comprehensive than that of the SAPS.

Before giving an overview of their policy it may be useful to consider the ethnolinguistic diversity of the members of the SANDF. Heinecken (1998b: 2) provides the following information (exact year unspecified, but presumably valid for 1997/8), which shows the distribution of members by language as a percentage of the total employees: Afrikaans 34.7, English 27.2, Ndebele 0.1, Swazi 0.72, Zulu 4.4, Xhosa 5, Sepedi 5.45, Southern Sotho 3.5, Tswana 6.35, Tsonga 0.96 and Venda 1.6. This ethnolinguistic distribution is not representative of the South African population and will certainly change within the next few years.

The development of a multilingual language policy for the SANDF is an extremely difficult task. Besides the fact that its members are ethnolinguistically very diverse, that it is separated into distinct service divisions (army, airforce, navy and medical corps), that it is a highly decentralised institution, and that its members are hierarchically strictly organised, communication along all dimensions often needs to be vitally clear, since command and control are central functions in the SANDF.

The language policy proposal of the SANDF displays a strong commitment to the principle of multilingualism (as well as the principles of human rights, non-discrimination and tolerance) and to the institutional needs of the SANDF, namely, command, control, management and training. It formally (and rather creatively) introduces a number of concepts and measures designed to meet these requirements, including: *link language*, a language which can be used at the local levels to ensure optimal communication; *language facilitator*, a member identified as a language resource person who can assist in on-the-spot interpretation and translation; and *thread language*, the "language used throughout the Department of Defence in order to facilitate general communication, command, control and co-ordination", the language which "will be used for formulating orders and instructions on behalf of the Minister of Defence. The thread language shall serve as a communication medium across decentralized Department of Defence elements".

The prime objective of the Department of Defence regarding language policy development is to "devise a common communication system by the use of a designated, single, thread language. This thread language ... will be supported by the use of appropriate link languages".

The proposed SANDF language policy contains a number of proposals which are explicitly directed at multilingualism: it states that the language of origin of a member may not be a barrier to appointment or to career progression, that documentation can be compiled in any official language, that any of these languages can be used for training purposes, that ceremonial documents will be in the recipient's language of choice, that members must be proficient in two languages and will be encouraged to acquire a third language, that corporate communication (articles, press releases, information boards and warnings) can be in any language, and that a Language Policy Monitoring Advisory Body must be set up.

If one reads the policy proposal a little more thoroughly, however, one discovers a proposal which has the potential to undermine the pluralistic future which the policy wants to create. The thread language, which is to be the central language of the SANDF, is to be English. As such, English will be the language:

– in which proficiency will be required for (senior) promotion
– in which all trainers and instructors must be proficient
– upon which the language used in basic training will be "based"
– of intermediate training and senior staff training
– of manuals, guides and aids
– in which language courses are provided
– in which all defence force documents must be summarised/translated

- in which all orders and instructions must be formulated (with translations or explanations in the link languages)
- which must be used as basis for all military terms
- which is preferred for communication between individuals as well as for "multi-addressee correspondence", and
- of all contractual documents (letters of appointment and training contracts)

It seems, then, that the concept *thread language* is in fact simply a disguise for English, and the impression the policy proposals make of being genuinely pluralist, is an illusion. This impression is strengthened by the fact that no other language (neither Afrikaans nor the Bantu languages) is mentioned in the policy document by name (they are referred to as "link languages", and once as "indigenous languages").

The language policy proposal of the SANDF undoubtedly goes much further than any other government department regarding the issue of multilingualism. However, given the dominant role awarded to English,[11] it is unlikely that the SANDF will really be able to establish any kind of meaningful "multilingual practice".[12]

Besides the noted shortcomings, both policy proposals also lack another essential element, a plan of implementation. Listing a series of decisions about language is not enough. Such decisions have to be translated into a plan which specifies precisely what actions have to occur, by whom they have to be handled, what resources will be made available to implement the decisions, when the actions must occur and how their implementation is to be evaluated.

At the end of this chapter the need for a pro-active approach to governmental language planning is discussed. It may, however, be appropriate to mention the gist of that issue in the context of this discussion of departmental language policy development. Given the philosophy of pluralism entrenched in the constitution and given the legacy of the colonial and apartheid governments of South Africa, a much stronger policy stance is necessary: transformation will not take place in any domain of public life if policies and their accompanying plans of implementation are not used vigorously as instruments of change. If policies are developed in a re-active way, that is as "reactions" to present conditions, and not pro-actively, as instruments of future change, transformation will not take place. The success with which governments, and in particular state departments, can be used to generate transformation has been demonstrated by every colonial government in Africa, as well as the

National Party government in the period 1948 to 1994. These governments were completely successful in establishing the supremacy of their beliefs, values, norms and visions, as well as their languages. The argument that the "public service" is not a "normative" institution, and that public administrators are there merely to "implement" government policy, is demonstrably not valid, nor wise.

Language policy at the provincial and local government level

Language policy at provincial level
As mentioned in Chapter 2, the constitution stipulates (Section 6 (3) and (4), 1996: 4) that provincial legislatures must decide on their own language policies, but that they may not use less than two languages for official purposes. In addition, provincial governments have to "regulate and monitor their use of official languages", making sure that "all official languages … enjoy parity of esteem and (are) treated equitably". Civilians may use any official languages in their dealings with these governments. The selection of languages "for the purposes of government" must take account of "*usage, practicality, expense, regional circumstances, and the balance of the needs and preferences of the population in the province concerned*".

These constitutional considerations are so vague that it would be possible to formulate a wide variety of policies, each of which would "reflect" these considerations. One could, for instance, ask: What usage? As first languages? Second languages? In what functions? In what domains? What "circumstances"? The status of the languages? Their functional value? The knowledge people have of these languages? What needs and preferences? And, who determines these needs and preferences? Very little sociolinguistic information is available on any of the features upon which the selection of provincial official languages has to be based, which means that officials are free to develop whatever "working language" situation they please. In addition, the "practicality clause" referred to in Chapter 2 equally provides state officials with considerable freedom of movement (and decision-making).

The South African Languages Bill is not much clearer in this regard, listing "interests, needs and aspirations of all affected parties" (Section 3(1)(e), 2000: 4) as guiding principle for provincial language policy development. The bill contains four proposals, though, that are more specific, namely by (a) demanding "intergovernmental co-ordination and harmonisation of policies, legislation and actions" (p. 4), (b) requiring in an explicit way that provincial and local government bodies implement the policy, (c) requiring that a language unit be established in every province, which is meant to manage the implementation of the provincial policies, and (d) prescribing that language surveys and audits be conducted "with a view to assessing the appropriateness of an existing language policy and practice" (Section 7(1)(c), 2000: 8). The effect of the proposed bill seems to have led to a degree of urgency at provincial (and local, — see below) level to begin with the process of language policy development. The obvious reason for this new purposefulness is that the language clauses of the constitution will become binding on all government bodies once it becomes an act of law.

Information on the status of language policy development in all nine provinces is not available. In the case of the Free State, Gauteng and the Western Cape the position is as follows:

The Free State Legislature (the provincial government of the Free State) accepted a three language policy for the functioning of the legislature (Afrikaans, English and seSotho — sic), with simultaneous interpretation facilities available from and into these languages as well as from and into Xhosa and Zulu.

On 9 December 1997, the Gauteng Legislature accepted all 11 official languages as official languages of the province, but decided that laws and official notices would be published only in four languages — Afrikaans, English, Pedi and Zulu. Their decision has not yet been enacted.

The Western Cape published a very impressive and comprehensive draft language policy in August 2000, in which it is proposed that Afrikaans, English and Xhosa be the official languages of that province and used for debates in the legislature, official records of debates (with translations where contributions were made in only one language), all legislation, official reports and resolutions, and all notices of motions in the Provincial Parliament. Provision is also to be made for the use of these three languages in the case of official advertisements, communication with and services to the public, internal communication and identification signs. Furthermore, language audits are to be undertaken of the sociolinguistic character of the province, provincial citizens' language identities, the needs and expectations of the province's language users, and the language proficiency in each provincial department as well as in local governments; a code of conduct is proposed, language acquisition opportunities for provincial employees are to be provided as well as translation and interpreting services, the implementation of the province's language-in-education policy is ensured and a commitment is made to the development of the three official languages.

For reference purposes, the first-language distribution in the nine provinces is provided in Table 4.6.

Table 4.6. Three principal languages as % of total population per province for 1996

PROVINCE	Population	First language	Second language	Third language
Western Cape	3,956,875	Afrikaans 59.2	English 20.3	Xhosa 19.1
Eastern Cape	6,302,525	Xhosa 83.8	Afrikaans 9.6	English 3.7
KwaZulu/Natal	8,417,021	Zulu 79.8	English 15.8	Afrikaans 1.6
Northern Cape	840,321	Afrikaans 69.3	Tswana 19.9	Xhosa 6.3
Free State	2,633,504	Sotho 62.1	Afrikaans 14.5	Xhosa 9.4
North West	3,354,825	Tswana 67.2	Afrikaans 7.5	Xhosa 5.4
Gauteng	7,348,423	Zulu 21.5	Afrikaans 16.7	Sotho 13.1
Mpumalanga	2,800,711	Swazi 30.0	Zulu 25.4	Ndebele 12.5
Northern Prov.	4,929,368	Pedi 52.7	Tsonga 22.6	Venda 15.5

(*Census in brief*, 1997; 10–11)

Information such as is contained in Table 4.6 is restricted in value, since it refers only to first-language speakers. Language knowledge among second-language speakers, the social meanings of languages and language attitudes, citizens' preferences and needs, and the demographic distribution of all the information also need to be considered. (The point about the demographic distribution is that younger generations or urban dwellers may differ markedly from their aged and rural cohorts. The plans of language policy implementation may have to relate to these variables.)

Language policy at the local government level
The proposed South African Languages Bill is also more specific than the South African constitution concerning municipal language policy development. The constitution only stipulates that municipalities must take into consideration "the language usage and preferences of their residents" (Section 6(3)(b), 1996: 4). This stipulation provides very little guidance, since information on the "language usage and preferences of their residents" is not generally available, and the question then is, who will decide what the language usage or the language preferences of residents are? Political leaders? Senior officials? Will they be guided by information on first-language speakers? If this were so, the main official language of Tshwane (the new name for what was called the "Greater Pretoria Metropolitan region" until 2000) must be Afrikaans (with 41% speakers), then Pedi (19.2% of the speakers), and thirdly, English (with 10.5%). Besides offering very little guidance, the consti-

tutional requirement places no obligation on local governments to support the linguistic transformation of (local) South African communities. In fact, it legalises the retention of the status quo, or, worse, the reduction of the country to increasing monolingualism, as can be demonstrated with reference to a court-supported decision by a large municipal government in a strongly Afrikaans-speaking community in Gauteng to use English for all internal as well as external communication (even in advertisements of job vacancies).

There was also very little concern among municipalities across the country to develop language policies. This is shown up in the research work reported on by Strydom and Pretorius (1999) (see also Chapter 2). They surveyed 79 local governments and report that 48 of them had no language policy (of which 46 did not plan to take rectifying steps). Those who reported having decided on a language policy indicated that they would use Afrikaans and English, as in the past. 32 municipalities stated that they use predominantly English. 74 of the local government councils reported having no policy on the promotion of the Bantu languages. The conclusions reached by Strydom and Pretorius (1999) include that:

- "There does not seem to be any unequivocal awareness of and commitment to the intent of the official clause as a binding directive for the promotion of multilingualism" (1999: 21)
- The *de facto* situation regarding "official language use" is dictated by the earlier sociolinguistic situation, with no indication that municipalities intend promoting the usage of the Bantu languages
- The development of clear, unequivocal language policy directives for local government is essential

The development of the South African Languages Bill has led to a rather dramatic change; in fact: (a) a bill is being debated, making language policy development at the local government level compulsory (Section 4(1) (a), 2000: 5, and Section 5(4)(b), 2000: 6), (b) provincial governments are instructed to support local governments regarding the development of language policies, and (c) municipalities are obliged to undertake language surveys and audits.

The City Council of Pretoria (who has since been incorporated into Tshwane, along with 15 other neighbouring municipalities) immediately responded to the bill, and organised a language summit in September 2000, directed at the mayors, politicians and top management from the 16 constitutive local councils as well as language practitioners from the Gauteng Province.

Four issues were discussed at the conference, namely the nature of municipal language audits, the South African Languages Bill, the views of the Pan South African Language Board, the role of the provincial legislature in supporting municipal language policy development, and the role of municipal community interpreters. The Tshwane Metro Council is currently considering the language policy development issue and deciding how it wants to handle it.

As an indication of the information local level governments will have to consider, Tables 4.7 to 4.17 are provided for the larger municipalities currently constituting the Tshwane Metro, based on information obtained in 1999 on request in electronic format from **Statistics South Africa**, the national body responsible for national statistics.

Table 4.7. Estimated distribution of population by race in selected former major municipalities incorporated into Tshwane in 1996

Former municipalities	Asians	Black	Coloured	White	TOTALS
Atteridgeville	0	92,000	0	0	92,000
Centurion	0	12,000	0	68,000	80,000
Mamelodi	0	155,000	0	0	155,000
Pretoria	20,000	65,000	24,000	417,000	526,000
Soshanguve	0	146,000	0	0	146,000
Elsewhere	516	34,214	1,728	44,732	81,190
Total: Tshwane Metro	20,516	504,214	25,728	529,732	1,080,190

Source: Statistics South Africa (SSA), 1999

Table 4.8. Speaker distribution by first language and residential area in major municipalities in 1996

	Afrikaans	English	Pedi	Tswana	Zulu	Tsonga	Sotho	Ndebele
Pretoria	343,000	110,000	82,000	33,000	25,000	21,000	18,700	11,000
Soshanguve	47	4	5,412	5,233	1,916	2,650		
Atteridgeville	178	172	41,459	10,320	7,363	1,870		
Mamelodi	9	0	83,931	?	24,108	?		
	343,234	110,176	212,802	48,553	58,387	25,520		
	41.4%	13.3%	26.7%	5.8%	7%	2.5%	2.2%	1.1%

Source: Statistics South Africa (SSA), 1999

As an indication of the uncertainty about language distribution Table 4.9 displays statistics supplied by the Pretoria City Council in the invitation sent out to participants in the language summit mentioned earlier. Their source is not indicated.

Table 4.9. Speaker distribution by first language as a % of the total population considered (*Information supplied by the Pretoria City Council*)

Afrikaans	English	Pedi	Tsonga	Tswana	Zulu
16.0%	9.9%	22.1%	–	20.4%	14.2%

Information dealing with the social meaning of the local languages is almost wholly unavailable. However, the data contained in Tables 4.10 to 4.17 (also provided in Chapter 3) provide some insight into the social dynamics of the local region. The information comes from the fieldwork of the doctoral student in the politics of language at the University of Pretoria mentioned above, and covered 300 respondents in two residential areas (usually called "townships") in Pretoria, namely Atteridgeville and Mamelodi.

Table 4.10. How well respondents in Atteridgeville and Mamelodi understand the following languages as a % of the respondents, by self-evaluation in 1999. (The % for the intervening levels of competency has been deleted.)

	Afrikaans	English	Pedi	Tswana	Zulu	Tsonga
WELL	15.0	54.7	51.7	41.0	39.0	13.0
NOT AT ALL	4.6	1.6	1.0	0.0	4.6	6.0

(Source: Preliminary computer data, Strydom, 1999)

Table 4.11. How well the above respondents speak the different languages

	Afrikaans	English	Pedi	Tswana	Zulu	Tsonga
WELL	13.6	53.0	51.0	42.3	45.7	11.3
NOT AT ALL	6.7	2.3	1.0	1.0	5.7	6.3

(Source: Preliminary computer data, Strydom, 1999)

Table 4.12. How well respondents read the different languages

	Afrikaans	English	Pedi	Tswana	Zulu	Tsonga
WELL	41.0	55.4	44.0	16.7	29.3	8.0
NOT AT ALL	8.3	4.3	11.0	1.0	5.3	46.3

(Source: Preliminary computer data, Strydom, 1999)

Table 4.13. How well respondents write the different languages

	Afrikaans	English	Pedi	Tswana	Zulu	Tsonga
WELL	14.6	55.0	21.0	15.3	26.0	6.3
NOT AT ALL	5.7	4.3	6.7	12.0	12.3	25.0

(Source: Preliminary computer data, Strydom, 1999)

Table 4.14. Mean scores awarded to the importance of studying particular languages at school (1 = Important; 2 = Unsure; 3 = Unimportant)[13]

	English	Pedi	Tswana	Afrikaans	Zulu	Xhosa
Atteridgeville	1.00	1.14	1.28	1.60	1.46	1.84
Mamelodi	1.00	1.50	1.92	1.64	1.82	2.35

(Source: Preliminary computer data, Strydom, 1999)

Table 4.15. Preferred language if all magazines, books and newspapers could be printed in ONE language, as a percentage of respondents interviewed[14]

	Eng	Pedi	Zulu	Tsw	Afr	Ndeb	Swaz	Tson	ML
Atteridgeville	79.7	5.4	1.4	1.4	1.4	1.4	0.7	1.0	5.1
Mamelodi	67.3	4.7	8.0	2.7	0.7	1.3	0.0	0.0	14.6

The abbreviated language names are: Tsw(ana), Afr(ikaans), Nde(bele), Swaz(i) and Tson(ga). The ML (multilingual) option refers to publications in several languages.

(Source: Preliminary computer data, Strydom, 1999)

Table 4.16. Mean scores for the value of languages for getting a job (1 = valuable; 3 = not valuable)

	English	Afrikaans	Pedi	Tswana	Zulu
Atteridgeville	1.02	1.29	1.65	1.76	1.76
Mamelodi	1.15	1.6	1.85	2.13	2.02

(Source: Preliminary computer data, Strydom, 1999)

Table 4.17. Mean scores for value of languages for obtaining respect (1 = valuable; 3 = not valuable)

	English	Pedi	Tswana	Zulu	Afrikaans
Atteridgeville	1.07	1.17	1.22	1.42	1.58
Mamelodi	1.34	1.57	1.90	1.85	2.00

(Source: Preliminary computer data, Strydom, 1999)

Properly controlled surveys and audits of local government regions, using instruments such as the frameworks displayed in Figures 4.1 and 4.2 could provide the relevant authorities with the information they need for the construction of socially meaningful language policies which will at the same time be expressions of the constitutional language stipulations. The co-operation of specialists in language planning would obviously also be a requirement.

The costs of pluralism in the state administration

A final issue to consider in dealing with language policy development for the state administration is the issue of cost-estimation. The general objection to official multilingualism is that it will cost too much, and the question thus needs particular attention.

The presumed cost of multilingualism has been calculated, and the following scenarios have been constructed for interpretation and translation services.

Interpreting
Wise and Hahndiek (1995) calculated the possible cost of interpretation services in parliament as follows:

Ideally, that is if a continuous service is to be rendered in all eleven languages in the General Assembly, the Senate (since supplanted by the National Council of Provinces) and one committee meeting room (thus in three localities) a total of at least 660 interpreters will be needed. This figure is arrived at as follows: To interpret from one language into each of ten other languages 110 interpreters are needed. This figure must be doubled to provide for relief (interpret for one hour, rest for an hour), giving 220 interpreters. In three localities 660 full-time interpreters are then needed. This figure is extremely large, given that the European Union employs 428 full-time interpreters and the United Nations in New York 114, according to Wise and Hahndiek (1995).

In practice, however, the situation need not be so dramatic. The fact is that members of the South African Parliament often choose to speak only English. For instance, from 25 to 27 May 1995 106 speeches were delivered in the National Assembly. The languages used were as follows: 13 in Afrikaans, 91 in English, 2 in Zulu and none in any of the other languages. In the (former) Senate 78 speeches were made on the same days: 10 in Afrikaans, 67 in English, and 1 in Xhosa. Thus the need for interpreters would be less than is "ideally" needed.[15] Furthermore, as Wise and Hahndiek (1995) point out, it is possible that a (short-term) policy could be agreed upon that would stipulate interpretation only into English (thus allowing all members to use any one of the official languages). This would require 30 full-time interpreters (three localities, interpreting every second hour). (If the mutual comprehensibility of the Nguni languages and the Sotho languages are taken into account, so that only two interpreters are needed for each of these language families, the total number of interpreters would be lower, of course.)

It must be accepted that interpreting will be a very costly matter. If the need for interpretation services in the provincial legislatures, the local government level and the country's courts is taken into account, the demand will indeed be big: Nine provincial legislatures need interpreters in each of their constituent forums, as well as the 698 non-racial local authorities, and the 431 magistrate's courts and 160 small claims courts (excluding therefore the Constitutional Court, the Appellate Division, the provincial divisions, and so forth).

Translation

A report commissioned by the Dept of Arts, Culture, Science and Technology in 1995 on the likely costs of the translation of government publications emphasised that the state is responsible for a large number of publications. Examples of these (and their frequencies, where available) are: Government Gazettes (774), departmental annual reports (22), state tender bulletins (600), statistical reports (30), commission reports (30), bills (774), green papers (18), white papers (16), patent journals (50), auditor-general reports (21) and acts of parliament (155). Furthermore, there are also the Hansard Report (of parliamentary debates), publications of the state archives, publications of the Master of the Supreme Court, Provincial Gazettes, notices, ad hoc publications (e.g. information pamphlets on housing and health), municipality reports (newsletters), municipal by-laws, agendas, tabellings, minutes, standing committee reports and select committee reports.

The commissioned report mentioned above calculated that the major publications would amount to 131,821,000 pages, which, if translated into only one language, would cost R43 million (including the costs of proof-reading, editing, duplicating, binding, storing and distributing).

If all publications were produced in all 11 languages the costs could amount to R340 million per annum; if only the 5 major publications were produced in all 11 languages at least R270 million; if only the 5 major publications were produced in four languages (Afrikaans, English, an Nguni language, and a Sotho language, i.e. translation into only 3 languages), the costs would be about R96 million. (Such a decision would, of course, lead to protests by the speakers of Venda and Tsonga, who already feel marginalised.)

Thus, according to these calculations, it is going to be very expensive to implement a policy of multilingualism meaningfully.

However, there is another side to the picture. The calculation of costs (particularly translation costs) is often "determined" in a very one-sided way, namely as "costs per translated word". The cost of Gauteng's four-language policy, for example, was determined at R0.80 per word. Approaching the matter in this way is tantamount to trivialising the issue. The fact is that the question of cost calculation is an intricate matter (see also Chapter 7). Firstly, the costs of all the factors which play a role in the production of goods cannot be calculated. For example, "the state of technology, consumers' preferences and tastes, and most of what can be described as cultural factors (including language) (are) recognised as influencing typical economic decisions but is itself not explicable by economic analysis. …" (Beukes, 1995: 2). Secondly, cost analysis often does not take non-material costs and benefits into consideration. Strauss (1995) points out: The (indiscriminate) application of cost-benefit analyses is problematic in at least three ways: cost estimation does not necessarily reflect "the value of related benefits"; their calculation is necessarily short-term (therefore does not reflect possible long-term losses); and the role of non-calculable benefits (e.g. the role of multilingualism in nation-building and the promotion of peace and stability) is not adequately considered. As an example, Strauss adds the following observation in relation to the costs of language learning: "In a more general economic theory the utilitarian approach (emphasising decisions where costs can be clearly identified and quantified) must be complemented with cultural considerations having to do with identity and solidarity." There must therefore be an "understanding of investment processes on which the returns are largely non-material." Thirdly, the cost of multilingualism needs to be balanced by the cost of monolingualism, which is, naturally, impossible to calculate in material terms. As Strauss (1995: 12, once again), points out: "Cost-benefit analysis is also not designed to take social inequalities into account". For example: Francophone African countries, who generally follow a language policy directed at the dominant use of French in their schools, "necessarily privilege an indigenous elite, since (their policies) spend 25% of the education budget on 12% of the pupils", and: "Multilingualism coincides with poverty especially when only a thin elite share a common or link language, while this language does not serve as a vehicle for economic and political relations among the people at large" (p. 7). Added to these costs are the consequences of ethnic conflict and social unrest due to linguicism (such as discrimination and exploitation, as was argued in Chapter 1).

The relationship between costs and (non-calculable) benefits is rather neatly illustrated by du Plessis (1994). Du Plessis discusses the decision of a state body responsible for local services, the Thukela Joint Service Council in Ladysmith, KwaZulu/Natal, to establish simultaneous interpretation facilities. The 70 members of this council speak Afrikaans, English and Zulu, and for interpretation services there is a need for 70 headsets, 70 microphones and a number of interpreting cabins for the interpreters. He calculates the costs of the service at R100,000–00 for the basic facilities, plus R8,000–00 per session for the interpretation service per meeting. Evaluating these considerable costs (particularly for a local government body) du Plessis reports that the establishment of the service has increased active participation in meetings since members feel better able to express themselves. In terms of costs du Plessis concludes (translated): "Calculate, first of all, what the costs of using English only will be in the long run in terms of the necessity for continual explanations, negative publicity, boycott actions, wilful go-slow actions, the resolution of misunderstanding, the loss of effectivity, the rebuttal of language conflict, the possibility of legitimacy crises, and so forth. If one were to translate these consequences of a monolingual policy into money terms, the initial financial investment in the democratic (and constitutional) facilitation of multilingualism is really quite minimal." (Page-reference not known.)

Conclusion: the need for a pro-active approach

In light of the considerations mentioned in this chapter, particularly the immensity of the task, it is clear that the linguistic transformation of state administration cannot be expected to succeed if it is simply left to occur "spontaneously". It has to be government driven.

Along with the formal education system, the state administration is the government's most valuable and most important agency in the reconstruction of South African society. The government has full jurisdiction over the Public Service and all its activities, and if it makes use of state departments as language policy and planning agents it can effectively give meaning to its ideals of democratisation, pluralism, development, equity and affirmative action, demonstrate that multilingualism and effective administration are not conflictual, and that multilingualism can, in fact, given a new-order conception of management (participant involvement and shared responsibility), facilitate effective administration.

In order to do this, however, the active involvement of the entire public sector will be needed. In fact, it will require state institutions to be *pro-active agents of reconstruction.*

State institutions are often thought about as "mere neutral instruments" of state policy implementation, which are subject only to practical considerations such as the availability of human and infrastructural resources and funding. This seems to be the view, for instance, of the Board of the South African Broadcasting Corporation. Their present language policy is too strongly pro-English, with only the nominal recognition of the other ten official languages. In terms of the spirit of the constitutional language stipulations their policy is clearly skewed. They explain this skewed policy in terms of mainly practical and financial considerations, and they justify their policy by pointing out that it is in accordance with the constitutional stipulations.

In a technical sense, their attitude is correct, one supposes. Their policy does indeed "obey" the constitutional stipulations, as well as the availability of human and material resources. However, given the commitment to large-scale reconstruction, government policies, I think, cannot be controlled by these considerations in a simplified way, to the extent, for instance, that the nation comes to accept that it needs to be a "victim" of existing conditions. *State policy formulation must be guided by the spirit of the over-all ideology, and must become a pro-active agent of reconstruction* (instead of being merely re-active). Given South Africa's past, and its present national ideals, the public service cannot simply be a (neutral) instrument for the implementation of government policy. It has a social responsibility, and must precipitate social transformation. Civil servants must act in terms of higher level moral codes, for example the norms and values expressed in the constitution (democracy, human rights, equality, non-discrimination and affirmative action), they are obliged to act in the *spirit* of the constitution and the government's Reconstruction and Development Programme and they must be actively guided by the principles of accountability, transparency and consultation.

Applied to language policies, this means that state language policies must not merely *reflect* the language stipulations of the constitution in a technical way, but must actively contribute to establishing the major decisions about the management of language in South Africa as a multilingual community. Government institutions must continually monitor the degree to which they have contributed to the promotion of multilingualism, the Bantu languages and a programme of linguistic affirmative action.

This approach to public management has clear consequences for a national language policy for state administration. It means that state institutions cannot decide to opt for only one (or two) language(s) of government on the grounds that it is demanded by effective administration, considerations of "practicability" or the availability of funding. It also means that the state administration must itself be a multilingual and pluricultural institution, which reflects the multilingual nature of South African society, and, indeed, acts as an agent of social reconstruction.

Notes

1. This chapter excludes language policy development in departments in which language plays a separately definable role in their domain of responsibility. The Ministry of Education, for example, needs clear language policies on the languages of learning and teaching in primary and secondary schools, language study, and the language requirements for students' performance certification.

2. The report submitted to the Cabinet in August 1996 in which a framework for the development of a comprehensive national language plan was described (see Chapter 2).

3. An interesting initiative of the Department of Arts, Culture, Science and Technology, is the development (following an Australian example) of a telephone interpreting system for the country (called TISSA). The purpose of the system is to facilitate communication between people who urgently need medical assistance, and doctors, but who can't understand one another's languages. By making telephonic contact with an interpreter the doctor can then provide assistance. The system is unfortunately not yet operational.

4. The Department of Labour can serve as an example, since it is involved in extensive formal contact and negotiation with a variety of statutory bodies (see further down).

5. At the end of April 2001, DACST and the Treasury called for applications to undertake a pilot costing study for the implementation of the proposed bill in three (unspecified) government departments. The report of the study was to have been completed by mid-July 2001.

6. These factors were mentioned in Chapter 2 and are also referred to in Chapter 8. A more complete list of external factors is provided in Taljaard and Venter (1998: 142): political, social, cultural, technological, legal, environmental and ideological factors, power, nationalism, religion, media, trade, international finance (the IMF; the World Bank), multinational and transnational corporations, globalisation, NGOs, resources, values, norms, ethics, crime and poverty. They could have added: "polluted" minds and spirits, population movement (urbanisation), and the rapid expansion of the Information Age and its transition to the Knowledge Era. All these factors have a demonstrable affect on language management.

7. A SWOT analysis lists the *strengths, weaknesses, opportunities* and *threats* which are likely to affect the successful implementation of a particular proposal. A SWOT analysis is a common analytical instrument in strategic planning.

8. There are unconfirmed suggestions that the political leadership of the country may have decided to follow a language policy *practice* of using only English for official business, and have no real intention of promoting the Bantu languages beyond their present role as languages of social interaction, cultural practice and religion.

9. Such as the Judicial Service Committee, the Public Service Committee, the Human Rights Commission, the Electoral Commission and the Public Broadcaster.

10. Given the South African Languages Bill discussed earlier both drafts will probably be adapted.

11. Before 1994 the central role of Afrikaans in the SA Defence Force was strongly counter-balanced by English. This (necessary) counter-balancing measure has now been considerably scaled down.

12. This possibility is supported by Heinecken 1998a: 16, who found that the following percentages of members of the different sectors in the SANDF were not frustrated by the lack of respect for their home languages: Army: 27; Airforce: 36; Navy: 49; Medical: 31; and that only 24% of the speakers of Afrikaans and 40% of the speakers of a Bantu language were not frustrated. (63% of the English-speaking members were not frustrated.) (The Airforce and Navy have both been predominantly English in South Africa.) These findings suggest two things: that English has already become the dominant language of the SANDF, and that the language issue can quite easily become a divisive factor.

13. Friedman tests of the significance of differences in multiple comparisons of the languages involved and applied to the information contained in Tables 11 to 13, indicate that English is generally regarded as significantly more important in the dimensions covered in the tables, than the other languages (Webb, 1999c).

14. Data on the preferred language for *listening to the radio and TV viewing* also shows a strong preference for English (with 59% in Atteridgeville, for instance, in favour of its use as the *only* language, as opposed to 9%, for example, in favour of Pedi).

15. In a discussion of interpreting costs in parliamentary debate the negative implications of the various options need to be seriously considered, for example the fact that the practice of speaking only English has a serious inhibiting impact on non-speakers of English, resulting in their non-participation in the decision-making process.

CHAPTER 5

The power of one

Language and nation

The power of language in interpersonal interaction is commonly experienced. Returning home to Pretoria one Sunday afternoon in July 1999 after a weekend visit to KwaZulu/Natal, I was stopped by traffic police for driving 100 kilometers per hour instead of the required 60 just outside the small village of Nqutu. In addition, I did not have my driver's licence with me. Two rather serious offences. I got out, and accompanied the Zulu-speaking traffic officer to his car, where he had recorded my speed. On the way I explained to him that we had travelled to KwaZulu to enable some German friends to experience the real Zulu's and to make them aware of the great Zulu history. I mentioned the palaces of King Zweletini Zulu, Ulundi, the provincial capital, the royal kraal of King Cetswayo, whose Zulu army defeated the British in 1789, and King Dingane, who had murdered the great Shaka and Piet Retief, the Boer leader, and 79 of his men in December 1838. My friends, I said, were really awed. I spoke Zulu to the traffic officer, which I had acquired as a child. My fine was going to be heavy, so I asked him whether we couldn't make some sort of plan. He said: What sort of plan? I said, well, anything — like ignoring one of my offences? He thought for a moment and then said "you can go", with no further prosecution. Talking about this experience later on, I realised more and more that it must have been my use of Zulu which had swayed the traffic officer.

Language has often been a factor in traffic transgressions. In the 1950's, a prominent Afrikaans-speaking cultural leader in English-dominant Natal steadfastly refused to heed traffic summons' if they were not issued in Afrikaans. Similarly, non-white offenders always knew exactly how to "soften-up" burly, Afrikaans-speaking traffic cops, addressing them throughout their interactions in Afrikaans as "my crown, my boss".

The problem of language and nation

In Chapter 4 it was pointed out that a discussion of language and state needs to deal with two main issues: state administration and nation-building. The latter issue is the subject of this chapter.

As discussed in Chapter 2, the political philosophy which underlies the South African constitution, and upon which the public life of this country is to be built, is pluralism. The government is therefore directed at establishing "unity within diversity", at developing national integration, at nation-build-ing. Furthermore, as has also been shown, the constitution is aimed at the recognition of human rights, the equality of all South African citizens, the promotion of respect and tolerance for all citizens and the furtherance of democracy and national unity. Similarly, the current government, and in particular the country's former president, has made serious attempts at creat-ing national pride and cohesion.

One of South Africa's many current problems, however, is the legacy of socio-political divisions within the country, the lack of national unity and the country's large conflict potential. Besides the extreme examples of the former (armed) struggle against Apartheid and the violence between supporters of the Zulu-based Inkatha Freedom Party and the African National Congress, there is also the general distrust between the races and a lack of meaningful co-operation between groups in the country. Despite the rhetoric of some leaders, there is very little justification for talking about "*a* or *the* South African na-tion". The South African people have never been united, do not share a glorious past, and do not have common norms, values or ideals in any signifi-cant degree. On the contrary, they have a history of military and political conflict and discrimination, they have a society which is deeply divided, is radicalised, and is characterised by inequality. And language, in various ways, reflects, conveys and strengthens these attitudes and tensions, continuing to be a constitutive factor in this regard.

The question language planning has to debate is how a national language plan (given the ability to implement such plans effectively) can contribute to bridging the gaps between racial and political groupings in the country, and to contribute to nation-building. How can language (or languages) contribute to national integration, to the construction of a new national identity, to estab-lishing national loyalty? Can they become symbols of national identity and national unity, and trigger emotional experiences of national attachment, much as is the case with the national flag and the national anthem? Can the

South African languages bind the people of the country together in any way? Or is multilingualism a barrier to national integration? More generally, is it at all possible to construct national unity in the context of complexly multilingual (and divided) societies?[1] This chapter aims to discuss these issues, in particular how language and language policy can contribute to nation-building in South Africa.

Before beginning, a brief historical note. Historically, the chances of language contributing positively towards nation-building in South Africa seem rather slim, for two reasons:

Firstly, the South African state, like most African states, does not have ethno-linguistically appropriate borders. The partitioning of Africa at the Berlin conference in 1884–5 (by non-Africans) occurred without serious consideration for the interests of the "tribes" of Africa, and boundaries were artificially and arbitrarily drawn around and through cultural and linguistic groupings who had no wish to be "joined together", or who would rather have remained apart.[2] South Africa was not part of that partitioning, but is nevertheless a product of the same type of process — "negotiations" between militarily and economically powerful European leaders and threatened or subjected indigenous leaders, and is thus an illustration of the same phenomenon: the Tswana live in South Africa as well as in Botswana, the (Southern) Sotho in South Africa and Lesotho, the Swazi in South Africa and in Swaziland, the Venda in South Africa and in Zimbabwe, and the Tsonga in South Africa and Mozambique. Although there were adjustments to the borders in the ensuing decades the problem of cultural diversity and divisions was not addressed. The South African state as such also has a history of "inappropriate" political borders. In 1910, with the creation of the Union of South Africa, four provinces were created (the Cape Province, Natal, the Orange Free State and Transvaal), based on the political history of the white citizens of the country. After the Afrikaans-supported National Party gained political control in the country in 1948, the provincial borders were maintained, but in the Fifties, with the formalisation of the homelands policy (of "grand" Apartheid), new political entities were introduced, based, supposedly, on cultural identities, but in reality reflecting the boundaries of the Bantu languages: Transkei, Ciskei, Venda and Boputhatswana. Now in post-1994 democratic South Africa new political borders have once again been created, with nine new provinces. Although the bases for the new division are not known, they may eventually prove to be more appropriate. Until 1994, however, South Africa can be said to have had an ethno-linguistically insensitive political division.

The ethno-linguistically insensitive grouping had at least two consequences for state-formation in Africa. One was that the newly independent African countries (including South Africa, which was later to become "democratised"), had to develop national integration and loyalty and to construct new identities across the realities of ethno-linguistic diversity. This was formerly never an issue. Now, in the modern European paradigm for state construction, which operated with the notion of the "nation-state", the development of "being Nigerian" had to be undertaken; being Yoruba, or Igbo, or Hausa, was not enough. Another consequence was that a national means of communicating with subjects had to be developed in the interest of "good governance", and the argument was that, in order to collect taxes, manage conflict, provide education, develop the economy, and so on, a single language had to be used, a lingua franca had to be established, to inform subjects about government decisions and to exert control over them. Since inter-ethnic relations are often tense in Africa, this "lingua franca" is usually the ex-colonial language, which is English in South Africa. However, as discussed in Chapter 1, 75% of the black South Africans have not had the opportunity to acquire English well enough to be functionally literate in it, that is, to be in control of their own destinies in and through the language.

The second reason for the slim chances that the language factor will contribute towards nation-building in South Africa, is that language has played a significant role in political control in South Africa, for manipulation, discrimination and division (note, for instance the remarks quoted in Chapter 1, Herbert 1992: 2), with languages (and their speakers) being selectively marginalised or centralised. Language was a strong instrument in the divisions in South African society, as also elsewhere in Africa (see Sure, 1997).

It is therefore possible that, politically, the language issue will rather be a barrier to nation-building in South Africa. If language policy (and planning) is therefore to contribute towards national integration, it will require a considerable degree of creativity and will-power from the Government, the nation-builders.

Factors in the equation

Given the facts and views described in the previous section it is not surprising that the role of language in nation-building in Africa is a contested matter, and that there are differences about all sorts of issues in the process. In order to contribute towards the debate it is necessary to start off with clear indications of what is meant by the basic terms which are pertinent to the discussion. In this section a description will therefore be given of what is understood by the terms *nation, nation-state, nation-building* and *national language.*

Nation

The term *nation* is ambiguous, and used with at least two meanings. The first meaning can be described in the words of Elaigwu and Mazrui (1992): (a nation is a) "stable, historically developed community of people with a territory, economic life, distinctive culture, and language in common" (p. 237), or, as Janson and Tsonope (1991: 9–11) formulate it: a nation is a group of people with a common origin, tradition and language. In this sense of the word, the Yoruba of Nigeria, the Gikuyu of Kenia and the Zulu's of South Africa are nations. The second meaning is: "the people of a territory united under a single government, country, state" (Elaigwu and Mazrui 1992: 237).

The distinction between the two meanings is quite common. Degenaar (1994: 328–9), for example, distinguishes between *nation one* and *nation two. Nation one,* he says, refers to a nation-state constructed on the basis of ethnic nationalism, and *nation two* to a state constructed on the basis of state nationalism or "citizen nationalism". This is related to Fishman's distinction between *nationalism* and *nationism* (1968), with the former referring to "the organisationally heightened and elaborated beliefs, attitudes, and behaviors of societies acting on behalf of their avowed *ethnocultural* self-interest" (Fishman 1989: 109), and the latter referring to "the aspiration for an independent state apparatus", and a "*politically* independent territoriality" (Fishman 1989: 39, 108, emphasis added).

It requires no argument to realise that no African state (with the possible exception of states like Botswana, Swaziland and Lesotho, which are in some degree monolingual) can be a "nation" in the first sense of the word. Inhabitants of African states are people of diverse origins, diverse political economies, diverse cultures and diverse languages, living in a single political space and governed by a single government, sharing, also, cultural characteristics with groups in neighbouring countries.

With reference to Africa it thus makes no sense to think of nation-building in terms of definition one, and the term *nation* will therefore be used only in the second meaning.

Nation-state

The term *nation-state* is generally used with the meaning of "a state consist(ing) of one nation speaking one language" (Janson and Tsonope 1991: 9–11), or a culturally (more or less) homogeneous state with a single socio-cultural identity and nationalism. This meaning may be more or less applicable to countries such as England, France and Italy (though their "unification" was hardly "planned", being partially the result of military conflict), but it is certainly inappropriate in African contexts, as mentioned above. Janson and Tsonope point out: "The European idea of a nation-state was completely absent in (southern Africa before the Europeans arrived)" (p. 9). The same applies to South Africa, whose cultural and linguistic diversity make it inappropriate to think in terms of a South African "nation-state". Instead, one should think in terms of a "political" unity, a national community of "South African citizens". The term nation-state will therefore not be used any further.

Nation-building

Once again, there is a conflict between the "European"[3] meaning of the term *nation-building* and its meaning in the African context, as Elaigwu and Mazrui (1992) demonstrate. They reject the view of nation-building as "the cultivation by a people over time of (common) political 'attitudes, beliefs and values', (with the) emphasis ... on the *'congruity of cultural and political identities'*", which they see as "a 'trend toward cultural homogeneity'" (emphasis added, p. 439). In many ex-colonial African states, where "groups of people were arbitrarily sandwiched into a territorial unit, which then formed a geopolitical entity called the state, there was no sharing of common 'values, beliefs, and attitudes'" (Elaigwu and Mazrui 1992: 439). The notion *nation-building* can therefore not be used with the meaning of the "homogenization of cultural and political identities" in the African context.

In this monograph the term *nation-building* will be used in the sense of Elaigwu and Mazrui (1992), to refer to

> two dimensions of identity. One is closely linked to state-building. We refer to the progressive acceptance by members of the polity of the legitimacy of the central government, and identification with the central government as symbol of the nation. This is the vertical dimension of nation-building ... On the horizontal dimension, nation-building involves the acceptance of other members of the civic body as equal fellow-members of a 'corporate' nation — a recognition of the

rights of other members to a share of common history, resources, values and other aspects of the state — buttressed by a sense of belonging to one political community. … Nation-building … is the widespread acceptance of the process of state-building; it is the creation of a political community that gives fuller meaning to the life of the state. (p. 429)

Implicit in this view of nation-building is the idea of *multiple identities*. In the modern state, whether in Europe or Africa, citizens have more than one identity, some of these identities being cultural and others political. In the same way as a citizen of Belgium can have a Flemish identity, be a Belgian and also a European, so citizens of African states can be Buthelezi's, Zulu's as well as South Africans.

Nation-building should not therefore be seen as involving the replacement of one identity with another, but as the *addition* of one identity to another. This point is also made by Elaigwu and Mazrui 1992, who point out that nation-building is not a process of *transferring* commitment and loyalty from smaller socio-political units (like "tribes") to larger political systems (like the state). It is, rather, "the *widening* … of horizons of identity of parochial units to include larger units such as the state" (1992: 438, emphasis added). Nation-building is an additive process, not a subtractive or replacive one.

National language

The concept *national language*[4] is also used quite ambiguously in the literature, and it is therefore necessary to be clear on how the term is to be used in this chapter.

The term *national language* must not be confused with the term *official language*.

In South Africa it is common to talk of "national official languages", and this is often taken to imply that these languages are "national languages" in one of the senses of this term (see for instance Cluver, 1992, and Janson and Tsonope, 1991: 11, who see a national language *inter alia* as the language in which the laws and administrative documents of the nation-state are written). In this book the term *official language* will be used to refer exclusively to the language of state administration (at national, provincial and local levels), official communication with the public, and legislation, and the term *national language* will be used in the nation-building context.

Secondly, it is necessary to clarify the content of the term *national language*. In the literature (e.g. Fasold 1984, Janson and Tsonope 1991: 11, Mvula

Webb 1992: 22 and Heine 1992: 25), the term *national language* is
at least four meanings:
ional language is a language which acts as a *symbol* of national identity
(such as English in England)

– A national language is a language of *national communication* (such as
Dutch in the Netherlands, or Sotho in Lesotho)
– A national language is an *indigenous language* of a country (such as Yoruba
in Nigeria), and
– A national language is a language officially (constitutionally) *designated as
such* (such as Swahili in Kenya).

Of these four meanings the first is the most problematical from the perspective
of this book, in particular as regards the identity the national language is
supposed to symbolise. There can be at least two symbolic values (as discussed
above): (a) that a national language is a symbol of a national cultural identity
(including what Fasold, 1984: 77 calls "authenticity" and "a glorious past"), or
(b) that it is a symbol of a national sociopolitical identity.

As already indicated the term cannot be used in the first sense in the case of
a pluricultural and multi-ethnic country like South Africa, especially given the
fact (as it was formulated at the beginning of this chapter) that the "South
African people have never been united, do not share a glorious past, and do not
have common norms, values or ideals in any significant degree" but, on the
contrary "have a history of military and political conflict and discrimination,
…is a society which is deeply divided, is radicalized, and is characterized by
inequality". If the term is to be used at all in the South African context it will
have to be in the Fishman (1968) sense of "nationism", that is, used as a symbol
of national political identity, as an entity which plays a role in the construction
of socio-political unity and loyalty.

The objection against the notion of a national language as a symbol
of cultural identity in African states also applies to Bamgbose's definition
(1991: 34) of a national language as "any language native to a country, … given
some measure of recognition by the government and … recognized by the
government as an instrument for achieving *sociocultural integration*, particularly at the national level" (italics added). Had Bamgbose excluded the notion
of "cultural" integration, and used the notion "sociopolitical" integration, his
definition would have been useful.

The other three meanings given above are also problematical: the second
in the sense that, if it were true, very few African states would be able to

recognize national languages (with Swahili in Tanzania being an exception); the third in the sense that indigenous languages may actually be divisive factors (see later on), and the fourth in the sense that statutory designations may be meaningless (next paragraph).

A third necessary remark is that the concept cannot, obviously, be an empty entity. Designating national languages in a constitution (the fourth meaning above), is obviously not enough. A national language must play a meaningful role in the socio-political life of a national community. It must not only be a *de jure* national language, but also a *de facto* entity, that is, not only the result of having been designated as such yet remaining "hardly more than a label which has no legal implications" (Heine 1992: 25). To be a meaningful entity a national language should have everyday significance, and be used, for example, in primary education or local government. As examples, Heine quotes Kenya (with Swahili), Senegal (with Wolof) and the Central African Republic (with Sango) — 1992: 25–7.

Discussing the meaningfulness of the national languages in Guinea, Heine (1992: 32) points out that "the national languages of Guinea are not second-class languages. They do play an important role in national life, as he explains with the following observations:

1. In communication between the government or the administration on the one hand, and the public on the other, the national languages are more important and more frequently used than French
2. Competence in one of the eight national languages is a sine qua non for employment in the civil service or for advancement in socio-economic status
3. Public sign-boards, certificates and other documents are issued both in French and …. in any of the eight national languages
4. Ninety-five per cent of the national radio broadcasts are in the national languages

A central component of the meaningfulness of a national language lies in its role in preventing a cleavage between horizontal and vertical communication, thus allowing upward mobility and genuine access to national rights and privileges, status and power. If "national languages" do not allow this, they can hardly be regarded as national languages.

Since many of the problems which South Africa experiences, such as colonialisation, ethnic rivalry and the exceptionally low esteem of the indigenous languages, are common to most African states, it may be useful to take critical note of how these states handle the question of national language. Did the concept *language language* play any significant role in state- or nation-building in these countries?

National languages and nation-building in African states

Thirteen African states have not officially designated any language as national, including Cameroon, Ivory Coast, Lesotho, Mozambique and South Africa, three have designated an ex-colonial language as national language (including Botswana), and 28 have chosen indigenous languages as national languages, including Angola (with 6), Burkina Faso (10), Ghana (9), Kenya (1), Nigeria (12, of which three, Hausa, Igbo and Yoruba, are also official), Zaire (10) and Zambia (7) (Abdulaziz and Sow, 1992).[5]

Despite the large number of African states who have opted for indigenous languages as national languages, language and culture is in reality not regarded as a serious issue in Africa. For instance, no African state has included either as a priority in any five-year development plan.[6] And Sow and Abdulaziz (1992: 530) write that:

> Even political leaders as clear-sighted as President Kwame Nkrumah of Ghana were reluctant to promote what they felt to be (the) vast number of 'backward' languages ... Those political leaders could not yet visualize Africans speaking and making themselves understood in languages other than English, French or Arabic!

One of the reasons for this situation is undoubtedly the vast degree of colonialisation in Africa. As Sow and Abdulaziz (1992: 523) point out:

> the authentic values of the past ... were being decried, ridiculed and debased in the face of new values imported by the European civilisations. ... The new ambitions of the colonized subjects took the form of wanting to live like the colonialists, dress like them, eat and drink like them, speak and be housed like them, and laugh and get angry like them, in short to have the same religious, moral and cultural yardsticks.

The official stipulation in African states of *national languages* thus seems to have had very little impact. In fact, it is not clear whether the choice of national languages in African states was ever seriously intended to contribute to nation-building. It is possible that it was rather their choice of *official language* that was motivated in nation-building terms, on the basis that a so-called "neutral" language (which is then usually the ex-colonial language) should be chosen for this function since, not being anyone's first language (e.g. English in Nigeria), it is expected to decrease the possibility of ethnic conflict.

Summary

To summarise the preceding discussion from the perspective of South Africa one could say that the country can only think of becoming a *nation* in the political sense, and *nation-building* can only be directed at constructing a state to which South African citizens can develop loyalty. The notion *nation-state*, in its traditional meaning, is inapplicable in the South African context. The relevance of the concept *national language* in South Africa will be discussed in the next paragraph.

The role of a national language in nation-building in South Africa

Given the discussion of the concept *national language* above the first questions to ask are what the function(s) would be of such a language in nation-building, and whether any South African languages qualify to be designated as such.

As regards the first question: (a) national language(s) may contribute in at least two possible ways to nation-building in South Africa. Firstly, it can serve as a symbol of a particular national political identity, in this case: "being South African", and helping to establish and promote a "national consciousness". In this regard a national language is like a national flag, anthem or dress. It is a symbol of the political nation. Secondly, a national language can contribute to nation-building by supporting political integration, in particular both horizontal and vertical integration, through facilitating communication between groups of people and between the élites and the non-élites (the masses), thereby breaking down the barriers which keep these entities apart.

The second question, whether any language in South Africa can perform these nation-building functions, can be discussed with reference to Bamgbose's six criteria for selecting a national language (1991: 19–29), applying the criteria to the 11 official languages of the country.

Bamgbose proposes the following six features as criteria for the selection of a national language, namely *nationalism, nationism, vertical integration, acceptability, population* and *language development status*. Briefly, he uses these features as follows:

Nationalism (N, p. 20):	authenticity and socio-cultural integration
Nationism (n, p. 20):	political integration and efficiency
Vertical integration (v.i., p. 22):	bridging the gulf between the élites and the masses

Acceptability (a, p. 22):   being acceptable to the different communi-
                                        ties in the state
Population (p, p. 24):   known (or used) by 40 to 50% of the
                                        population
Language development status (lds, p. 26):   used in publications, research, scientific
                                        translations, standardised, studied as
                                        school subjects, and used as languages of
                                        learning and teaching, etc.

Applied to South Africa (in a somewhat over-simplified way), these criteria predict that no South African language can individually perform the required functions at present (but can, of course, develop the means to do so):

Table 5.1. Evaluation of South Africa's major languages in terms of Bamgbose's six criteria

	N	n	v.i	a	p	lds
Afrikaans	n	n(y)	y/n[7]	n	y/n	y
English	n	y(n)	n	y(n)	y/n	y
Zulu	n	n	n	n	y	n/y
Xhosa	n	n	n	n	y	n/y
Ndebele	n	n	n	n	n	n
Swazi	n	n	n	n	n	n
Pedi	n	n	n	n	n	n
Sotho	n	n	n	n	n	n
Tswana	n	n	n	n	n	n
Venda	n	n	n	n	n	n
Tsonga	n	n	n	n	n	n

(Abbreviations listed above.)

No South African language (or languages) can be selected as national languages on the basis of Bamgbose's criteria. The question is thus: can language then play no nation-building role at all? Would it make no sense for the South African government to develop a language policy directed at utilising the languages of the country for nation-building purposes? I would argue that language can play a role, and will discuss my views shortly. First, however, the different possible policy options in this regard need to be considered.

South Africa can select between a number of policy options regarding the choice of national language. It can select an ex-colonial language, one of the indigenous languages, all or some of the Bantu languages, and no national language.

An ex-colonial language

If an ex-colonial language were to be selected as national language, the choice would have to be English.[8]

The arguments generally produced by African governments who support this option are that, at the time of independence, the state administration (and education) were already operating in the ex-colonial languages, that the indigenous languages are not yet adequately adapted for use in governmental functions, that "tribal" tension is a real possibility, particularly in the context of political instability, and that the ex-colonial languages are neutral languages (by which they mean no-one's first language).

Many counter-arguments have been raised against this line of thought. Bamgbose (1991: 23) points out, for example that this option

– equates national integration with a monolingual policy (one nation, one language)
– ignores the fact that the ex-colonial languages are politically non-neutral, having been used in the subjugation of the African people and now continue to be used for political advantage in that they divide the ruling élite from the masses, and could thus develop into instruments of ethnic domination, and similarly
– ignores the fact that the ex-colonial languages are culturally also not neutral, but function as conveyers of non-African values.

In regard to the first objection Bamgbose (1992: 18) mentions that the use of an ex-colonial language equates integration with *horizontal integration among the top 10–15% of the population*, which means that "the interest of the educated élites who form a minority in each country is equated with the interest of the nation" (p. 19). He could have added that such a choice can increase the blocking of access to rights and privileges, thus supporting élite closure, continuing inequity, thwarting democracy, and preventing full development and effective transformation. The simple fact is that less than 25%, on average, of the people in any African country have an adequate knowledge of any ex-colonial languages,[9] and these have therefore become instruments of discrimination and exclusion (see also Monsour 1993: 124–125, who lists the negative consequences for the people of Africa who have to conduct their public lives, e.g. communicating with political leaders, the state administration and in education, in ex-colonial languages).

These arguments also apply to English (and Afrikaans) as a possible national language in South Africa: English is not ethnically neutral (being the first language of a numerically and socio-economically significant portion of the population), nor is it politically or culturally neutral. It cannot thus promote vertical integration, and cannot develop into a symbol of political unity. Furthermore, it will probably also contribute strongly to the continued marginalisation of the majority of the African people in the country, and restrict their languages to inappropriateness for higher state functions, thus remaining relegated[10] to performing cultural, religious and personal functions. The choice of English as sole national language would undoubtedly ultimately cause tension and possibly even conflict, and have the opposite effect than national languages are meant to have.

One of the Bantu languages

It seems self-evident that the choice of national languages should become part of the process of decolonisation, of re-establishing the self, and of developing self-esteem and confirming cultural integrity. From this angle, it seems wisest to opt for a Bantu language as a national language.

The question is, of course, which Bantu language? The example of Tanzania cannot be followed, since there is no single language in South Africa which is known as widely as Swahili (95% of the population), and which is politically and culturally as "neutral" (being the first language of only 5% of the Tanzanian population). The information regarding language knowledge as first and "non-first" languages in South Africa was provided in Chapter 3. From that information, Zulu is the language of widest communication, being known by more than 50% of the South African population. However, Zulu, like all the other official languages, is socio-politically all but "neutral". The option of choosing a single Bantu language as national language is not viable.

All or some of the Bantu languages

The above option can be extended to all or a sub-set of the Bantu languages, but there are clear problems with such an option. The choice of all the Bantu languages (including the non-official Bantu languages) as national languages would reduce the question of national language to relative meaninglessness, whilst the selection of a sub-part of them, say those with official status, would lead to protests from the speakers of the non-official Bantu languages, such as Northern Ndebele and Shona. Were the "major" Bantu languages (with the largest speaker numbers, say, Zulu, Xhosa, Pedi, Sotho and Tswana) selected, there would be protests from the smaller official languages (Tsonga, Venda, Ndebele and Swazi). There would probably also be protests from the speakers of Afrikaans, who could argue that they are also speakers of "an African language" (on the basis of its origin, its speaker base and the lexical and metaphorical meanings it conveys in everyday discourse). This option may, in fact, lead to the non-integration into the mainstream community of the speakers of smaller languages, and even to conflict.

In summary: it is unlikely that the selection of any one South African language or any set of its languages can meaningfully perform the tasks required of a national language in South Africa. It seems that languages as such cannot perform the same functions as a national flag, an anthem, a national flower, and so on, being symbolic of national identity in any sense, whether cultural or political. It is therefore wise not to follow the example of many of the African states. The last option mentioned above, that *no national language* be designated, is probably the most appropriate decision.

If no language is officially designated as "national language", how can language perform a role in national integration and nation-building in South Africa?

Language and nation-building in South Africa

Language can play a sigificant role in nation-building within the context of a national language policy and plan directed at six basic issues. These issues are:
– The enhancement of ethno-linguistic self-esteem and equity
– National communication
– A culture of democracy
– The meaningful recognition of language rights
– The management of the country's conflict potential, and
– The protection of linguistic diversity

Before discussing each of these issues, it is perhaps useful to stress two other matters:

First, it is necessary to remember that the development of a language plan directed at nation-building must be based on the philosophy of pluralism. Given the South African constitution (see Chapter 2), with its explicit focus on "unity within the diversity", equity (of the 11 official languages) and the protection of cultural and linguistic rights, South Africa cannot adopt a policy of assimilation (to the dominant language and cultural community) as in the

South American countries, or a policy of national cultural integration as in the United States of America, with its so-called "melting-pot" approach, nor can post-1994 South Africa follow the example of Apartheid South Africa, with its policy of "ethno-linguistic" (read "racial") segregation, thus moving in the opposite direction of the proposal of this chapter.

Secondly, it is necessary to keep in mind that language planning (see Chapter 2), in and of itself, is not enough to achieve any nation-building aims, that the role of language planning must not be over-estimated and that it can at most be a facilitator, a framework, within which national objectives may be realised. As indicated at the end of this chapter, the attitudes of the political leadership and the commitment of the people of the country are crucial.

The enhancement of ethno-linguistic self-esteem and equity

The struggle in Africa against colonialism and, in South Africa, against Apartheid, is usually formulated as a struggle against political oppression and discrimination, and as the denial of basic human rights, such as access to proper education and occupational opportunities. However, language is also a site of struggle, and liberation can only be said to have been achieved if the languages of Africa are also "free". In Chapter 3, the low social value and stigmatisation of the Bantu languages in their first-language communities was discussed, and slavery, colonialisation and missionary work were mentioned as causal factors. If the South African community is to have any hope of becoming a nationally integrated entity, this situation has to change, and all the languages of South Africa, in particular the Bantu languages (including, of course, the Khoi and San languages) and their speakers, must free themselves of the (psychic) domination of English, must regain their self-esteem and re-establish themselves and their cultural integrity. An essential part of the struggle for freedom in South Africa (and, of course, elsewhere in Africa too), is the liberation of the languages of the country and the restoration of the human dignity of the people of Africa. Language planning should be part of this process of decolonisation.

Language equity (parity of esteem and equitable treatment) will be very difficult to realise in South Africa. Given the inequality between the present official languages with regard to status, functional value, resource value and speaker numbers (see Chapter 3) in real terms, and given the fact that language equity cannot be handled externally but that languages undergo expansion through the volition and vitality of their own speakers, achieving language equity will be a difficult challenge in the short-term. It is clear, however, that the government can make a substantial contribution to the linguistic transformation of South Africa, by policy development and implementation, by funding and supporting the promotion of the Bantu languages, by allowing extensive research work on the politics of language, by development projects, by upgrading their teaching and by the comprehensive expansion of their resources. The matter will be discussed in more detail in Chapter 8.

Promoting national communication

At present, cross linguistic communication is not effective in the case of speakers of the Bantu languages interacting with other South Africans. Cross-cultural communication generally occurs in English, often to the detriment of the Bantu-speaking persons, who have not been able to develop their English language proficiency well enough. Very few non-Bantu-speaking South Africans know the Bantu languages. In fact, most of them are not even able to pronounce the names of these compatriots of theirs, which is a reflection of the racist realities of the situation, a denial of human dignity and the right to recognition and respect, of these people.

Vertical and horizontal communication are a non-negotiable criterion for developing a common loyalty in a country. This is probably more so in South Africa than elsewhere in Africa, since the stark divisions and tensions of the past, and particularly the social hierarchicalization of South African society with its a-symmetric power relations, can only be addressed in a meaningful way if its citizens can communicate effectively with one another. This is the only way in which social transformation can really occur: through communication, and the consequent establishment of a commonality of values and norms, points of view, attitudes, loyalties and social practices. This is also the only way in which stereotypes, prejudices and misrepresentations can be broken down, and respect can be engendered for one another.

Given the sociolinguistic realities of the country, national communication can only become a reality if the citizens of the country know each other's languages. Since black South Africans already each know about five languages, individual multilingualism in South Africa effectively means that the white, coloured and Asian citizens need to attain effective competence in the Bantu languages. This can be achieved by requiring a credit in such languages for secondary school certification, and by requiring competence in the Bantu languages for appointment and promotion in the work place.

Equally important is the development of the cross-cultural communicative skills of all South Africans during their school careers. Since verbal communication is basically a process of negotiating meaning, participants in especially cross-cultural communication situations should have well-developed skills in particularly two areas: knowledge of culturally sensitive discourse rules and the ability to handle communicative derailment. These skills refer to discourse participants' ability to infer one another's communicative intent, and presupposes a knowledge of contextualization cues and interpretative schemata, as well as a knowledge of more superficial matters such as culturally different ways of greeting, giving and receiving compliments and apologies, initiating or closing conversations, changing discourse topics, talking loudly or whispering in public, and so on (see Chick, 1985 and Ndoleriire, 2000). Equally, a knowledge of each other' values, views, beliefs, struggles, needs and anxieties is necessary for effective communication.

As a final comment, the following quotation from Kashoki (quoted by Monsour 1993: 127) is applicable in a discussion of communicative skills in a nation-building context: That in multilingual Africa integration into the national system cannot be measured by the ability to speak the official language of the state, but rather by the ability to communicate in several of its local languages, and more specifically by the range of communicative functions the languages at a person's disposal can perform.

Promoting a culture of democracy

Language (planning) can also play a role in the country's democratization process. This issue must be approached from the perspective of what is meant by the term *democracy*.

For the purpose of this chapter, the term democracy[11] is used to refer to two issues, viz. the degree to which the citizens of the state are able to *participate* in the political life of the state, and whether the state has *legitimacy* for its citizens.

Participation in the political life of the state implies that citizens are involved in one of four ways, namely in (i) decision-making, in (ii) being consulted about issues that concern them, in (iii) being kept informed by politicians, and in (iv) being able to communicate their views to political leaders.

The present *de facto* language set-up does not allow for satisfactory citizen participation in the political life of the country in any of these ways. First of all, the language of political debate in the country is mainly English, which means that 75% or more of the black South African population cannot follow the arguments of politicians, evaluate their views or hope to influence political decisions in any way. Secondly, effective communication between the citizens and the state administration (especially in the case of written communication, for example in government forms and notifications) is not possible, since the major language of state administration is also English, which once again heightens the marginalization of the majority of the country's citizens (see also Chapter 4).

Clearly, a language policy will have to be evolved and implemented meaningfully which will give a far bigger role to the Bantu languages in all public domains, such as the political debate, state administration, the security services, health services, the legal system, the media, and the communication industry.

An especially vital field in establishing democracy is that of (primary) education. The democratization of knowledge and skills is essential for meaningful democracy. However, in African conditions, also in South Africa, the ex-colonial languages are generally preferred as language of learning and teaching (see Chapter 6). Empowerment through effective knowledge and skills development, as will be pointed out in the next chapter, can only really occur if the language of learning and teaching is a language which is well-known. Eyamba Bokamba, Ayo Bamgbose, Mubanga Kashoki, and many other African sociolinguists have stressed this view over and over again throughout Africa. Bokamba (1993), for example, emphasized this view with data from francophone African states, showing empirically that the drop-out figure in primary schools negatively correlates with the amount of expenditure in education, and pointing out that the situation is so bad that had the relevant ministries of education been business enterprises they would surely have been declared bankrupt for delivering such a low return on investment.

The principle of participatory democracy naturally also has a flip-side, viz. the responsibility of citizens to deal with their own problems. In the field of language planning this means that the speakers of the South African languages have to define their own language problems, make their own decisions on language maintenance, determine their own priorities, and seek their own funding from government sources and elsewhere (see also Chapter 8).

Legitimacy implies that the state (is seen to) serve(s) the interests of its citizens.

If the government wants to demonstrate its legitimacy through language planning it must develop a language policy which will facilitate the development of social and political unity, fulfil the needs of the citizens of the country for work, educational and economic development and cultural security, and develop among them a sense of ownership of the country.

As far as language planning is concerned, serving the interests of the citizens ought to mean:

a. That the state is prepared to deal with the real language and language-related problems of society, such as illiteracy, the high drop-out figure in schools, the low pass-rate, the inaccessibility of educational and economic opportunities because of language barriers, non-supportive language policies for rural development projects, and so on (Chapter 1)
b. That the state recognizes the language rights of all the citizens of the country and is prepared to fund the promotion of their languages
c. That the state promotes mutual respect and tolerance, and
d. That the state effectively prohibits the use of language for purposes of domination, manipulation or discrimination

Language and language planning can clearly play an important role in establishing meaningful democracy in both the participatory and the legitimacy dimension. However, whether this will become reality can only be determined once the government has developed and implemented comprehensive language policies.

Language rights

The meaningful recognition of language rights

In light of the statutory discrimination of the Apartheid era and its accompanying selective advantaging of one sector of the community, it is essential that a compulsory programme of equity be established, aimed at providing each member of the civic society with a feeling of value, of being a potentially meaningful member of that society. This means, *inter alia*, recognizing language rights.

Language rights is an issue of fundamental importance. In this regard it is necessary to recall the remark by Monsour (to be referred to again further down), namely that group rights are "profoundly symbolic and emotional" and that if a "government is corrupt and unjust and an individual is excluded from rewards, they will fall back on group loyalty and migrate or rebel" (1993: 132). Human rights are by definition adversarial, and need to be handled very circumspectly.

A simple acceptance of the principle of language rights is in itself relatively meaningless. It is necessary to indicate as precisely as possible what language rights entail in concrete terms, and to provide practical instruments to enable citizens to make these rights meaningful realities in their lives. It is therefore important that legal provisions specify exactly who the holders of the rights are and what legal sanctions can be imposed for their denial, and that funds be provided for acceptable court cases.

According to the constitution the citizens of South Africa have the following *language rights* in the case of the official languages:

- to have their languages promoted
- to use any official language in dealings with the national and the provincial governments
- to be protected by the state against exploitation, domination and division on linguistic grounds
- to select their own language of educational instruction
- to establish educational institutions based on a particular language (if such an action does not imply racial discrimination)
- to be informed of police action in the language of one's choice, in the case of a detained or arrested person,
- to be able to follow court proceedings in a language s/he understands (and to have court records kept in such a language), in the case of a person involved in court action
- to have access to state information, and
- to self-determination through organs of civil society on the basis of language.

The constitution therefore recognises citizen's rights to linguistic security, to obtain access to the rights, privileges, status and power of the common society, to receive respect for their linguistic identity, to perform their cultural practices in the language of their choice, and to study their languages and have them researched.

Listing language rights is a relatively easy task. Making them everyday realities is much more difficult. To achieve this, the development of dedicated structures is required, as well as particular instruments, systems and processes with which ordinary citizens can enter into disputes (with the government as well as each other), being in possession of the necessary skills and resources. A general culture of language rights must thus be developed, which is an extremely slow, long-term process.

In this regard PANSALB (see Chapter 9) is important, as is the setting up of the *Commission for the Promotion and Protection of the Rights of Cultural, Religious and Linguistic Communities* (Art. 185). A number of seminars and workshops have been held to debate the specific tasks, functions, and composition of this commission, but nothing of substance has as yet emerged.

The constitution is not sufficiently clear about the bases upon which language rights are to be handled. For example, whereas Section 29, on Education, refers to the individual ("Everyone ..."), Constitutional Principle XII refers to "Collective rights (of self-determination)". Given the politicisation of ethnicity in South Africa it is essential that the government provide clarity on the issue.

There are at least three bases upon which language rights can be handled in principle, namely a regional basis in a federal state structure, the basis of the social group, and the basis of the individual.

a.   The territorial principle

Simply put, the territoriality principle means that human rights are handled on the basis of region, as in Belgium and Switzerland, and that a federal system of government is in operation. This approach cannot be followed in South Africa for two simple reasons: (i) The South African state is not significantly federal by nature, and (ii) there is too little congruence between the linguistic distribution and the internal political structures (provincial boundaries), as shown on Map 2.

As regards the first reason: although the present constitution gives the provincial legislatures competence over a number of domains, including cultural affairs, pre-tertiary education and the language policy for the region within its jurisdiction, provincial governments do not have sufficient powers to play a meaningful role regarding language rights outside these specified domains. Furthermore, the central government can easily control the actions of the provincial governments through policy development and its system of financing.

As regards the second: although language distribution is to some degree geographical by nature (see Chapter 3), this only applies to rural areas. Most of the urban areas, particular in Gauteng (where half the country's population resides), are so intricately multilingual that language rights cannot be handled meaningfully on the basis of the territorial principle.

b.   The principle of collectivity

The use of the group as basis for language rights assumes that there is a meaningful relationship between group and language (as, more simply, in the case of religion and gender). However, there are two main factors which complicate a group approach to "promoting and protecting" language rights: the problem of definition, and the politicisation of languages in South Africa.

The issue of definition relates to establishing boundaries between language groups and providing the criteria for determining group membership. In the case of Afrikaans, for example, what counts as "Afrikaans" or the "Afrikaans-speaking group"? Is it a linguistic issue? Is only formal standard Afrikaans considered to be "Afrikaans" or are all the varieties (styles and dialects) of the language included? What do you do with varieties which contain a striking amount of English elements? Is it a cultural issue? If so, what are the relevant culturally distinctive features of "the Afrikaner"? Will an Afrikaans-speaking Indian Muslim qualify to be regarded as "an Afrikaner"? And a black Afrikaans-speaking farm worker from the Northern Cape? A problem in group demarcation is, of course, that membership criteria are easily determined selectively. (A "classic" example of the selective use of membership criteria, is the case of the classification of the Griqua people in the Apartheid era: Though there are historically clear distinctions between the Griqua, who were the original inhabitants of South Africa along with the San, and people of racially mixed origin, the so-called "Coloureds", the Griqua were classified as "Coloured", because they were "not white, not black and not Indian".) It is likely, furthermore, that there is no clear distinction between so-called Afrikaner culture and other cultural identities, and it may not be possible, except for a few superficial differences, to distinguish culturally (attitudes to life, wants and needs, recreational preferences, modes of dress, music taste, and so forth) between five 20 year old urban youths, educated to the same levels, who belong to different racial and language groups. In addition, as we know, cultural groups are not internally homogeneous, and neither has any person a single identity, acting out different roles in different social contexts (the fact of multiple identities).

Similar scenarios can be described for each of the other "language communities". For example, the inhabitants of Soweto are culturally a mixture of many different cultural identities, and a Sowetan probably has cultural features of the Zulu's, the Tswana's, the Pedi's, the Shangaans, the English, and so forth.)

A final consideration in this regard is the fact of socio-cultural engineering. We know, for instance, that what is today regarded as Pedi/Northern Sotho (or

Tswana, or Venda, or Tsonga, and so on) is the product of political (and sometimes also religious) manipulation in the past. Until quite recently, these languages and their groups did not exist. What is today called the "Northern Sotho" people, formerly existed as different tribes or groups of reasonably disparate people. Does it make sense, therefore, to work with the concept of "Northern Sotho language rights on the basis of group rights"?

Though linguistic and cultural communities are realities, and need recognition and protection for their rights, all dynamic communities are linguistically and socio-culturally very diverse in a messy sort of way, which make a group approach to language rights problematical.

A second major factor which complicates the use of the group notion for the recognition of language rights, is the politicization of South African life, in particular regarding its ethno-cultural life. The policy of Apartheid gave ethnicity an extremely negative connotation, so that it is still very difficult to discuss it on public forums. The previous (and still very current) view of South Africa's socio-cultural reality was that it consisted of the sum of disparate cultures, each constituted as a group with distinct boundaries (defined by race and language), within which there was a common loyalty, and with each differing qualitatively from the other groups (the emphasis always being placed on cultural *differences* rather than on similarities — cf. Webb 1994b). This view is clearly directed by 19th century romantic ideas of nationalism and nation, and was used to cultivate patriotism.

It is necessary to create a new discourse on the country's socio-cultural reality, with new meanings to terms such as *language, ethnicity* and *culture*, and to describe a new conception of the country's socio-cultural reality. Until that is done, there will always be a degree of suspicion about the demands for linguistic rights as group rights.

Using the concept *group* as a basis for handling language rights, is problematical.

c.   The individuality principle

The South African constitution is largely directed at protecting and promoting human rights on the basis of personality, the individual. According to this principle the individual is given a free choice about practising his language rights, and about whether he wants to insist on his rights being recognised. This approach is, of course, in the democratic tradition. If this basis is used, it is argued, the deficiencies of the other two approaches are avoided. However, it has problems of its own, in particular the fact that very few individuals have the material and non-material capacity (knowledge and understanding of the rights issue) to insist on their rights. In such a situation, recognising and promoting rights may not be meaningfully possible, thus not providing sufficient protection against the conflict potential of linguistic and cultural diversity.

Although South Africa has a very brief history of human rights protection, there are a few cases where greater clarity can be found about the interpretation of rights by both the government and the Constitutional Court.

A specific language rights issue which has been extensively debated is the question of the obligation of the government to recognise and fund schools which decide to use Afrikaans as the sole language for instruction in single-medium state schools. (Some) Afrikaans-speaking school communities insist that the constitution recognises this right. The government, however, argues that such schools intend to use language to exclude non-Afrikaans-speaking black pupils from admission, and that these schools will thus become exclusive cultural enclaves. They also argue that the constitution does not oblige the state to fund single-medium schools. At most, according to Constitutional Principle XII, such organisations shall be "recognised and protected", whatever this formulation may imply.

In another language rights case, a political party took a local government body to the Constitutional Court, demanding that this body not be allowed to use *only* English for official purposes. The Constitutional Court refused the request.

Clearly, therefore, considerably more debate is necessary about the meaningful basis for the promotion and protection of language and cultural rights.

The management of the country's conflict potential

The remark by Monsour (1993: 132), which has been referred to a number of times, namely that group loyalty is profoundly symbolic and emotional (whereas civic loyalty is rational and conscious), is relevant in a discussion of conflict potential. If a government is corrupt and unjust and individuals are excluded from rewards, they will fall back on group loyalty and migrate or rebel. Given the emotional meaning of languages, it is clearly essential that a state be able to manage the problem potential of multilingualism in order to prevent threats to nation building.

As the events in the former USSR and Eastern Europe show, there are increasing indications that communities are becoming more aware of their separate identities and their rights, especially in the case of minority communities. This development is probably due to a number of factors, including the increasing incidence of globalisation. It is likely that globalisation will psychologically lead to greater *localization* as well as a greater degree of involvement in local affairs and a greater insistence on personal identity and group identity. Governments need to be aware of these developments, since any attempts by the authorities at external re-culturalisation or deculturalisation are bound to result in conflict and national disintegration (as evidenced a number of times in South Africa's history, for instance by the Soweto protests of 1976).

In South Africa there are a number of cases of ethnic nationalism, which is to be expected, given the country's social history and the Apartheid policies of more than forty years. The development of ethno-linguistic awareness, ethnic nationalism and the myth of linguistically and culturally homogeneous communities in South Africa can be illustrated, once again, with the example quoted by Herbert (1992: 2). Herbert (referring to Northern Sotho and Tswana) points out that these two languages were distinguished as separate languages "for political and administrative purposes", that it is difficult to "draw any real boundary between the two" and that "the Northern Sotho 'cluster' contains sufficient diversity to raise some doubts about its essential unity" (see Chapter 1). Two recent and on-going cases of ethnic nationalism are the Zulu's and the Afrikaners. The notion of self-determination, both political and cultural, is still quite strongly present in the case of conservative white Afrikaans-speaking people (who are trying to garner support for their idea of a "Volkstaat", a nation-state), as well as in the case of the Zulu-based cultural and political organisation, Inkatha. It is also possible that other smaller linguistic communities, such as the Shangaan and the Venda, may become more significant role-players in this regard in the future (see Webb & Kriel 2000, on Afrikaans and Afrikaner nationalism).

Somehow the tendencies towards ethnolinguistic ideologisation and mythologisation must be addressed. This is a serious matter, but one which can only be handled through an educational programme directed *inter alia* at nation-building (via the development, for example, of cross-cultural knowledge and tolerance).

It is essential that the South African government takes steps to prevent such developments. This can be done by two measures, namely the legal prohibition of discrimination and the promotion of mutual respect.

If the conflict potential of the country is to be controlled, the statutory prohibition of manipulation and discrimination is necessary, as well as the control of dominance. At the same time the negative potential for ethnic nationalism must somehow be curtailed. If this is to be done, the proposed national language policy needs to be accepted and a very specific plan of implementation developed.

An attitude of tolerance and mutual respect also needs to be promoted in South Africa, and the principle of multiculturalism has to be given concrete substance. This can be done by relating multiculturalism to the notion of nation-building in a very specific way, for example by (a) the meaningful recognition of minority (language) rights, and (b) by promoting an attitude of tolerance.

It is clearly a difficult task, and it can probably only be achieved if the development of a positive attitude towards multiculturalism is seen as part of the socialization process undertaken by the school, the church and parents. It is therefore necessary that the principle of multiculturalism be concretely reflected in school curricula (also for language study).

The protection of linguistic diversity

There are a number of clear indications in South Africa of the likelihood of linguistic and cultural assimilation. Apart from the increasing tendency towards monolingualism in the public and private sectors (Chapter 4), there are clear sociolinguistic signs, for example, the incidence of language shift, code-mixing, code-switching and diglossia, in every case in the direction of English, the starkly dominant language in the country. In so far as linguistic and cultural diversity is a source of wealth, it is in the interests of the country to reverse these tendencies and to ensure space for each linguistic and cultural community.

Two perspectives need mentioning: Firstly, an emphasis on national unity obviously doesn't diminish the need to preserve cultural diversity. The recognition and promotion of cultural identity and diversity can, in fact, facilitate nation-building since it can contribute to spiritual and intellectual decolonization and to the recognition of the value of human kind. Secondly, an emphasis on the recognition and promotion of language and cultural groups must not be confused with Apartheid, or the promotion of separatism.

To summarise the gist of the position taken in this chapter: Language (and language planning) can contribute to nation-building, not through being designated as national languages, but through the contribution it can make to the construction of national integration and national loyalty, and the establishment of the principle of pluralism. It is essential that the principle of pluralism be given substance, and that the tendency towards assimilation be controlled.

The positive promotion of the principles of multiculturalism and multilingualism, the promotion of minority languages, and the development of strategies for handling inter-ethnic conflict are all essential to nation-building. Equally, the notion of multilingualism and multiculturalism as being non-functional, or a hindrance, as something which correlates negatively with economic development and aggravates political sectionalism, and which is costly and inefficient, must be combated.

The role of the school

It is self-evident that the school can be an important instrument in nation-building. As far as language is concerned, this can occur through the language study programmes. In discussions of cultural development in school programmes, the inclusion of a subject called "Ethnic Studies" in the school programme is suggested. But, as Squelch (1992: 187) points out, this is not a good idea. The principle of multiculturalism can only really be established in a meaningful way if it is concretely reflected in the whole school curricula, that is, if all curricula include components focusing on the cultural dimension. Examples of such an approach include: the cultural characteristics of people, how cultural differences arise, how they relate to power relations, the existence, role and dangers of cultural stereotyping and cultural prejudices, the conflict potential of cultural differences (through the ideologizing and mythologizing of cultural identities), and how to deal with conflict. Such a curriculum should also give an understanding of how key social, political and economic institutions work, and how they can be changed. The school programme should obviously not be oriented towards western or Euro-centric views. It should promote the recognition of cultural diversity in a positive way, should reflect the histories, experiences and contributions of cultural and linguistic minorities, should develop positive cross-cultural attitudes, should reduce racial and cultural prejudice, domination and discrimination, should provide skills for meaningful participation in a multi-cultural society, and should empower students to become socio-culturally critical and instruments of social change. Ultimately, such school training programmes should contribute to developing a just and democratic society.

There are of course dangers involved in the inclusion of cultural training in school curricula particularly since it may lead to attempts to promote a particular socio-cultural identity. In South Africa the negative effects of "Christian

National Education" are widely recognized, as is the intellectual colonization of the African people through the excessively dominant role of English, French and Portuguese in Africa. Equally, there is the danger of emphasizing cultural differences at the expense of commonality or by suggesting that cultural differences are innate.

Language planning tasks

There are a number of linguistic and language-related factors which may prove to be obstacles to language and language planning playing a positive role in nation-building. Several of them have already been mentioned, namely the power relations between languages, language-internal conflict, linguistic imperialism and discrimination, the British standard English issue, the marginalization of the minor languages, the low self-esteem of the speakers of the Bantu languages, and linguistic nationalism. A comprehensive national language policy must obviously include strategies which address all these obstacles.

One of the most important immediate tasks of language planners is the need to promote the Bantu languages (see also Chapter 8). Such a programme must aim at facilitating their acquisition of status, economic value and social value, and using them in schools and universities. This implies, as Sow and Abdulaziz (1992: 551) say, "that governments will have to have a clear vision of their goals and needs; they will have to draw up coherent operational programmes and allocate substantial human, technical and financial resources to implementing them." The Government will, as was argued at the end of Chapter 4, need to take a pro-active stance.

Specific language planning tasks which have to be performed if language in South Africa is to be an effective instrument of nation-building include:
- The "normalisation" of the status of Afrikaans and English and their national roles, that is, the legitimisation of Afrikaans, English and the indigenous languages
- The depoliticisation of the medium of school instruction issue (see Chapter 6) as well as the concept of ethnicity
- The training of language practitioners to meet the needs of a new situation, in particular appropriately trained language teachers, language planners, translators, copy-editors, terminographers and lexicographers.

The role of political leaders in civil society

The role of political will in the leadership of the country (as well as among the citizens of the country) is vital to the success of this whole venture.

The tendencies towards increasing monolingualism in South Africa, listed in Chapter 4, suggest that there may be a lack of political will among the political leadership of South Africa to seriously implement the national ideals expressed in the constitution, and that the publicised policy of pluralism may be little more than a symbolic gesture or a strategy to obtain public support, without being intended to lead to any real change in South African society. It may even be that the "élite closure" mentality which existed in Kenya according to Myers-Scotton (1990) also exists here (seeMyers-Scotton: 'Elite closure as boundary maintenance: the evidence from Africa', in Weinstein (ed.), 25–41). One must not forget that politicians and policy-makers are apt to serve their own interests, and that policies are often designed mainly to control society and to maintain power (see Weinstein 1990 and Bokamba 1993).

In studying the implementation/non-implementation of policy, it is necessary to pay direct attention to the political agendas of politicians, and to keep Kashoki's views (1993: 12) in mind: "political will (is) the primary ingredient in utilising the factor of language in any meaningful way in the process of national development".

In this regard it is useful to take note of the example of Afrikaans. It is true that the political history of Afrikaans provides ample examples of how language should *not* be used in a political context (for example its appropriation by its white speakers, and its use for political manipulation and gain). But it does, also, give a useful illustration of the central role of political will in the promotion and development of a language.

The promotion of Afrikaans did not begin with "sociolinguistic fact-finding", research on the social status of the language, the development of language planning skills, or any of the other tasks which language planning scholars usually propose as necessary pre-planning steps (see Chumbow, 1995: 10). The "rise" of Afrikaans began in the eastern Cape in the mid-19th century as part of a political movement (of separatism from the colonial government), and in the western Cape as part of a religious movement (of translating the bible into a language which members of the working class could understand). These movements were not led by government leaders. On the contrary, the English-speaking government as well as the Dutch-speaking cultural leaders were opposed to the use of Afrikaans in public life. The process was driven by community leaders, such as newspaper journalists, teachers and a few church leaders. One of the first (necessary) outcomes of the "movement" was the development of a sense of socio-political identity, which developed into a driving force and a will to promote the language. The development of this political will led to the development of a written form of the language, the establishment of norms and standards and language promotion agencies, that literature was published, and, eventually, that Afrikaans-dominant economic institutions came into being. The government of the time was not involved in these actions.[12] The Afrikaans-speaking community took the task upon themselves to develop the language as an educational, economic and political tool.

The same type of process is necessary in the case of the Bantu languages, especially now that black South Africans have the necessary political power, and are increasingly becoming economically empowered.

Conclusion

The ideas presented in this chapter may be too optimistic and too idealistic, and it may be difficult to give concrete substance to them. Nor is it certain that a language policy directed at nation-building will really contribute to meaningful socio-political change in South Africa. Somehow, however, a balance between the aim of national unity and diversity has to be found, if South Africa is to rid itself of its deep spiritual and intellectual colonialization, and if it is to free its *creative* powers and to make a meaningful contribution to Africa and the rest of the world. One of the conditions for this to happen is that South Africa should relinquish its Euro-centric and colonialist preferences, and accept its African destiny.

This is, presumably, what political leaders mean when they talk about the *African Renaissance.*

Notes

1. At a conference in Brussels, October 1995, which dealt with emerging European identity in the European Union, a director of the Goethe Institute declared that "multilingualism was bad", meaning it was generally an obstacle to effective governance.

2. Partitioning was not the only factor in the divisions between people, of course. Migration and military conflict also played a role.

3. It is probably true that modern-day Europe also no longer thinks of nations in these terms.

4. Janson and Tsonope (1991: 11) regard the concept *national language* as also belonging to "Western culture", contending that the question of a national language has been directed by the language situations in Europe and North America.

5. The information supplied in Heine (1992) differs somewhat. For instance, according to him Senegal's six national languages exist only "as a claim" by Senghor.

6. Monsour (1993: 118–119) points out that the language issue was also largely ignored by the (pre-independence) liberation movements, except for the 'radical' members of the All-African Peoples' Conference of 1958.

7. Afrikaans, as a language of all the socio-economic classes and used by more than three million coloured South Africans, is less of a barrier to vertical integration than English, or any of the other official languages. However, its political meaning is rather a strong deterrent.

8. The position of Afrikaans is complex, given its "colonial" history. Many see it as "African".

9. Remembering of course that "adequate knowledge" refers to more than just the knowledge necessary for basic interpersonal interaction, as argued in Chapter 1.

10. From the African perspective, the Bantu languages have the right to be used in all the usual public functions. To think otherwise is to assume that the use of English in these functions is "normal", "unmarked", which is arrogant.

11. In this chapter the notion "democracy" follows the definition of the NEPI report (1993: 14–15).

12. It is true that the government of South Africa (after 1948, when the Afrikaans-speaking white community attained political power) played a major role in the promotion of Afrikaans, but by that time Afrikaans had already achieved official status and a significant degree of social and economic value.

CHAPTER 6

Growing potential

Language in education

In a newspaper article early in 2000 (*Rapport*, 27 February) the poor state of formal education in South Africa was discussed, in particular the fact that less than 5% of the country's final-year secondary school learners passed with university exemption in 1999. Whereas 25% of the black learners generally obtained exemption in the 1960's (compared to 50% white pupils), the figure at the end of 1999 was lower than 10%. Furthermore, of the 20 000 successful Science candidates in 1999, only 3000 were black. This state of affairs the article partly ascribed to the failure of the government's policies relating to the redeployment of teachers, severance packages (usually accepted by the better teachers who can easily find alternative employment), the reduction in bursaries for study, changes in disciplinary measures and problems with teachers' unions. (Though these factors certainly play(-ed) a role, the article could have focused far more sharply on the effect of the Apartheid policies on the state of educational development. Though difficult to quantify, the role of this factor must have been immense, if one considers the skewed expenditure on "Bantu education", the sub-standard levels of teaching, the disruption caused to education during the struggle against Apartheid — as expressed in the slogan: *liberation before education*, and so forth.)

The question with which this chapter is concerned is whether language is a factor in (poor) educational performance. (The newspaper article refers to a remark on this question by a specialist appointed by the Department of Education to investigate poor performance in Mathematics and Science. According to him language is a factor through the use of "new Latin" as terminology in these subjects! The matter is obviously far more complex than this rather trivial observation suggests, and needs far more incisive attention.)

To start with, specific information is required, relevant to the current situation.

A profile of education in South Africa

Information on language and education was provided in Chapter 1. That information, complemented by some additional facts, is presented in Tables 6.1 to 6.4 (which are basically extracted from SAIRR 2000: 107–133).

Table 6.1. Levels of education as a percentage of the general population in 1996

Older than age 20, yet no formal education	Some primary education	Secondary education	Passed grade 12	Tertiary education
19.5%	24.5%	34%	16%	6%

Source: SAIRR 2000: 107–133

Table 6.2. Comparison of selected educational performance indicators for the country as a whole and for two provinces, as a percentage of the relevant population for 1998

Educational indicators	Country-wide	Gauteng	Northern Province
Literacy[1]	64	79	51
Pass-rate for grade 12	49	56	35
Matriculation exemption	13	16	7
Un- or under-qualified teachers	26	?	?

Source: SAIRR 2000: 107–133

The differences between Gauteng and the Northern Province in Table 6.2 obviously correlate with the urban-rural contrast, and the industrial and economic prosperity dimension.

The information provided in Tables 6.1 and 6.2 is not broken down according to race. If it were possible, it would certainly show that the educational position of black South Africans lags behind their counterparts from the other races. This is apparent from information supplied by the former Department of Education and Training (abbreviation: DET), which was responsible for the schools for black learners (commonly called "Bantu education"):

– of the 5 million persons older than 4 years of age who had had no formal education in 1994, 3.5 million (70%) were black
– 98% of the white learners obtained endorsement (that is, matriculation exemption, and could obtain admission to university study) in 1992, against 44% of the black learners
– 0.01% of the teachers who were professionally unqualified in 1992 were white, against 99.9% who were black

(Source cannot be specified more precisely)

Further information on the unsatisfactory state of educational development in South Africa is provided by statistics on literacy and numeracy in South Africa obtained in an all-African survey, contained in Tables 6.3 and 6.4:

Table 6.3. Cumulative results for literacy task, selected provinces, 1999, in percentages

	Gauteng	KwaZulu/Natal	Northern Province	Western Cape	Total (for 9 provinces)
75–100	30.01	19.84	4.93	28.87	12.82
50–75	32.72	26.16	23.72	35.56	26.78
25–50	32.47	42.17	53.79	28.13	47.14
0–25	4.8	11.83	17.56	6.44	13.27
MEAN RESULT	60.94	51.4	42.75	60.68	48.10

Source: Strauss & Burger: 2000: 7

Table 6.4. Cumulative results for numeracy task, selected provinces, 1999, in percentages

	Gauteng	KwaZulu/Natal	Northern Province	Western Cape	Total (for 9 provinces)
75–100	3.19	1.62	0.69	3.94	1.45
50–75	15.95	9.11	4.65	20.08	8.83
25–50	47.71	48.24	39.86	47.65	45.79
0–25	33.15	41.03	54.80	28.34	43.83
MEAN RESULT	26.70	31.00	25.87	37.93	30.02

Source: Strauss & Burger: 2000: 8

In these two tables, columns two to six contain the distribution of learners evaluated for literacy and numeracy in percentages per province. In the Northern Province, for example only 4.3% of the total number of learners evaluated for literacy scored more than 75% for the task, whilst only 0.69% of them obtained marks above 75% for numeracy. 71.35% and 94.66% of these learners scored lower than 50% for literacy and numeracy respectively, and can thus not be regarded as either adequately literate or numerate. South Africa thus has a long way to go educationally if it is to develop the potential of each learner fully, which is an essential requirement if the country wishes to grow economically and to become competitive on the global market.

There are obviously many domains in which the problems need to be addressed. For example, basic educational facilities need to be provided, such as school buildings, desks and books; teacher training must be radically upgraded, and a culture of learning must be established. A particularly relevant issue is the educational framework within which planning is to occur, called "outcomes-based education" (abbreviated OBE), which will be discussed below.

Before a discussion of the basic features of this "new" education philosophy, it is necessary to briefly keep in mind some aspects of the over-all state of transformation and reconstruction in formal education in South Africa.

First of all, South African education is in a state of radical transition. The administrative and organisational character of the entire educational system had (has) to be restructured — from a fully racialised system into a non-racial system; a new culture of formal education had (and has) to be established (with new values, new standards and norms, new attitudes, new expectations, new ways of thinking and doing things); new managers have to be trained and have to acquire experience; classrooms are, for the first time, significantly non-racial,[2] teaching is also, for the first time, multicultural, and the inequalities of the past, including linguistic inequalities, have to be redressed. Furthermore, new policies have to formulated and implemented, new syllabuses have to be compiled, and teachers have to be trained to handle new situations. Then, also, the culture of non-learning ("no education without liberation"), protest and a general rejection of authority, which was (understandably) so prevalent during the struggle against Apartheid, has to be replaced by its opposite. Concurrently, the suspicion, mistrust and tension between (racial) groups, built-up over centuries, have to be resolved, and teachers', learners' and parents' attitudes, beliefs, expectations and stereotypes have to be changed. Developing new language-in-education policies and plans of implementation, and translating these policies and plans into concrete reality, is an enormous task, which may possibly only become meaningful after a number of generations have passed through the educational system. Introducing a new educational philosophy and an appropriate language-in-education policy and plan, has to occur within the context of this concurrent radical educational reconstruction.

A new education philosophy

In line with the language planning approach followed in this book (see Chapter 2), language-in-education policy and planning development needs to be located in the macro-contexts mentioned earlier, and in the over-all educational philosophy, called *Outcomes-based Education* (OBE, see Department of Education. 1997, and Gultig *et al,* 1998). OBE, as in other countries where it is found (such as the USA and England), has as its starting point "the intended results of learning in terms of knowledge, skills and values rather than the prescription of content to be learnt" (Gultig et al 1998: 9).

OBE is structured around a number of critical outcomes and sets of specific outcomes (for each of a number of learning areas). The South African Qualifications Authority (SAQA) has proposed the following critical outcomes:

Learners will:

1. Identify and solve problems and make decisions using critical and creative thinking
2. Work effectively with others as members of a team, group, organisation and community
3. Organise and manage themselves and their activities responsibly and effectively
4. Collect, analyse, organise and critically evaluate information
5. Communicate effectively using visual, symbolic and/or language skills in various modes
6. Use science and technology effectively and critically showing responsibility towards the environment and the health of others
7. Demonstrate an understanding of the world as a set of related systems by recognising that problem-solving contexts do not exist in isolation
Source: Department of Education, 1997: 12–13

As an example of the *specific outcomes* (SO), the first four of the seven outcomes proposed for the *language, literacy and communication* learning area are listed:

SO1: Learners make and negotiate meaning and understanding. (For example, identify and clarify the key message in a text; create the meaning of a written text and make inferences; construct meaning through interaction with other language users; identify variation in meaning due to personal, social and cultural differences; understand how context affects meaning; identify and evaluate speaker's point of view critically; reason about the interpretation of a text)

SO2: Learners show critical awareness of language usage. (For example, identify purpose, audience and source of a text; explain how socio-cultural ideas and values are transmitted through language; recognise the relations between linguistic varieties; demonstrate how languages change over time and place; identify, analyse and respond to the manipulative use of language; identify ideologically driven and biased language, and respond to it effectively)

SO3: Learners respond to the aesthetic, affective, cultural and social values in texts. (For example, respond to the artistic effects of texts; recognise and describe the literary effects of texts; express an opinion on texts and justify such opinions; relate opinions on texts to those of others)

SO4: Learners access, process and use information. (For example, be able to select information and organise it into new coherent wholes from a variety of sources and situations, identify the information needed; define the aim of the information search; locate, access and select information; evaluate the accuracy and relevance of information; apply organisational skills; develop reasoned arguments; process information and present results)

Summarised from: Department of Education, 1997: LLC-3

Even a superficial look at these outcomes demonstrates that they refer to quite advanced skills. For example, "negotiating meaning" refers to the ability to discover the logic/coherence of a text (identify key elements and the main purpose of a text), and the ability to integrate the information contained in a text with existing knowledge (that is, integrate text with context). This outcome also presupposes a high level of interpersonal collaboration and thus an ability to interact meaningfully with discourse participants (e.g. pupils with teachers), that is, a specific social skill. Furthermore, many of the expected outcomes are "reflexive" or meta-linguistic and meta-textual by nature, since they require the ability to identify, analyse and respond to the manipulative use of language; to identify ideologically driven and biased language and to respond to the aesthetic, affective, cultural and social values in texts.

Consider also the first specific outcome for the *technology* learning area:

SO1: Understand and apply the technological process to solve problems and satisfy needs and wants. (For example: identify and explain problems, needs and wants; consider the range of possible solutions; make an informed choice; develop a plan for the solution of a problem; effect a solution; evaluate solutions and communicate the process)

Source: Department of Education, 1997: TECH-3

From the quoted specific outcomes it is clear that OBE sees educational development as more than just concerned with learning particular content, perception in general or with "mere" associative thinking. OBE is directed at skills development, understanding, and a high level of cognitive ability. It aims at developing **conscious** thought, the type of thought typical of active learning, that is, abstract, objective thought. It wants to develop advanced cognitive and meta-cognitive skills, such as the processes of *analysis* and *control* (planning, monitoring, and evaluating). Educational development thus involves the following high-level skills:

- Finding information (storing, categorising and retrieving relevant information)
- Solving problems (identifying problems, analysing them, determining possible solutions, and managing the implementation of proposed solutions)
- Reasoning (finding plausible and coherent explanations for phenomena)
- Discovering patterns and rules (theory-building)
- Designing and creating, and
- Evaluating points of view or proposals critically

In addition to cognitive and meta-cognitive skills, OBE is also explicitly directed at affective skills (such as developing critical attitudes and a sense of responsibility), and social skills (such as the ability to co-operate and interact with others regarding their needs and wants).

These high-level cognitive, affective and social skills do not, generally, develop in an unguided, "spontaneous" way. They need to be developed in the context of well-structured educational programmes, and their development is directly dependent on language. Language is important in cognitive, affective and social development in at least two ways, namely (a) as a facilitating developmental instrument, and (b) in the development of specifically linguistic proficiency.

Language as a fundamental instrument in educational development

From a language planning perspective, it is necessary to determine the linguistic knowledge and skills necessary for acquiring and developing the knowledge, understanding and skills which learners are expected to acquire and to develop across the curriculum during the school programme. This requires information about the interrelationship between language and cognition, which can then be used in the debate about the language of learning and teaching (abbreviated LoL/T) best suited to the needs of the learning situation as well as the linguistic proficiency (in the first and the second language) which learners require in order to develop educationally and to be regarded as educationally developed.

The *interrelationship* between language and cognition is at least as follows:

a. *Concept acquisition*, at the heart of learning, involves more than just learning the names of concepts; it also involves understanding the concepts, internalising them cognitively and using them in different contexts.

b. Formal learning also requires the development of *reasoning* processes, for example, learning to argue mathematically, historiographically or linguistically, thus acquiring specific patterns of scientific discourse.

c. Related to the preceding, learners need to be able to present arguments in a coherent form and to express relations such as additive, adversarial, temporal or causal. To do this, competence is required in the use of connectors such as *furthermore, namely, similarly, yet, however, although, on the other hand, then, after which, previously, finally, thus, therefore, consequently, because of, since, if ... then*, and so on. Using elements such as these appropriately, requires considerable linguistic skill, especially in text construction. In addition, learners need a command of academic terms such as *name, give, state, describe, discuss, explain, determine, compare, distinguish, define, clarify, criticise, draw a flowchart*, and so on.

d. The linguistic basis of learning activities is also apparent from the fact that, in order to access information from sources, learners have to be able to read texts closely, distinguishing main points from supporting material (that is, construct a mental map of a text), organise information extracted from texts into new coherent wholes, and so on. Understanding and interpreting texts are complex skills, where language proficiency is central. "(I)nformation", Lanham (1986) writes, "got from (a) text is at very least incomplete ... (F)rom the linear progression of propositions in (a) text the reader must create a non-linear structure of inter-relationships..... A statement of theme is seldom overtly present in the text and has to be constructed from it". Furthermore, understanding a text requires "the ability to apply cognitive processes to the world of our experiences ... to link new information to existing relevant concepts, ...(thus to interact constructively) with the information in a text". (Page references unavailable.)

e. Fifthly, educational development requires effective communication in the learning situation. As Hernandez (1993: 356) points out, meta-cognitive skills are acquired "through social interaction where comprehensible communication occurs and active awareness of these comprehension problems and problem-solving strategies is demonstrated (by the teachers)". Children learn, he says, "when they are engaged in social learning activities where communication and meaning serve central functions" (see also Clark 1996, conference paper, page reference unavailable).

f. Finally, it is important to remember that communication or social interaction is not the only function which language performs in the learning context. Language is also an instrument with which:
  – Value systems are acquired and expressed, and views and perceptions are formulated
  – Personality and a sense of community and culture is developed (since language underlies learners' sense of who they are, their self-esteem and self-confidence)
  – Solidarity and institutional loyalty is constructed, and
  – Personality and cultural differences are understood and handled.[3]

The importance of linguistic skills in educational development becomes greater at higher levels of mental activity, that is, in more abstract, objective and symbolic thinking, as Hernandez (1993) points out. Furthermore, as Gelman and Medin (1993158) demonstrate: perception, language and conceptual knowledge mutually interact to determine task performance, with conceptual development involving the interactive influences of all three. Equally, in social development, growing language skill allows social interaction to become more complex, enabling people to respond more appropriately to cohorts in the learning and the vocational context.

Given that language performs a fundamental role in academic performance, it is important to discuss issues such as the LoL/T, language study (as first, second or foreign language), and the language requirements for certification. Also requiring discussion is the impact of certain sociolinguistic phenomena on educational development.

The LoL/T issue

The LoL/T issue in South Africa will be discussed under seven headings: the current language-in-education policy, current practice, language proficiency realities, an alternative option for South Africa, the international debate on LoL/T, available research findings on the issue, and the need for further research.

The current language-in-education policy

The national language-in-education policy of South Africa is described in the South African constitution (1996), the South African Schools Act of 1996, a language-in-education policy document and a proposed language-in-education implementation plan. The latter two documents were announced in July 1997 and were subsequently discussed at a national forum in May 1998.

The South African constitution stipulates (Section 29) that

> (2) Everyone has the right to receive education in the official language or languages of their choice in public educational institutions where that education is reasonably practicable. In order to ensure the effective access to, and implementation of this right, the state must consider all reasonable educational alternatives including single medium institutions, taking into account (a) equity (b) practicability and (c) the need to redress the results of past racially discriminatory laws and practices

The Schools Act determines (in summarised form) that:

a.   The provinces must formulate their own language-in-education policies (subject, of course, to national policy)
b.   The governing body of a (public) school determines the school's language policy (subject to any relevant provincial acts)
c.   The use of language policy for racial discrimination is prohibited, and
d.   The use of a language proficiency test for the purpose of admission to the school is also prohibited

The provisions of the 1997/98 language-in-education policy documents of the central Department of Education can be summarised as follows:

Aims

The Education Department declares itself committed to three aims, namely (a) the promotion of multilingualism (which means developing the 11 official languages, establishing respect for all the languages of the country, and developing the skills needed for communication across the boundaries of colour, language and region), (b) countering the disadvantages resulting from the mismatches between home languages and languages of learning and teaching, and (c) building a non-racial nation and contributing to citizens' full participation in society and in the economy.

The LoL/T policy

The policy describes four basic guidelines:

a.   It accepts the principle of *additive* multilingualism, that is, first languages (such as the Bantu languages) may not loose ground in the process of gaining non-first languages (such as English in South Africa)
b.   It accepts any official language as possible LoL/T

c. It stipulates that learners (in practice: parents and school authorities) may select their LoL/T on entering a school, accepting that their choice may differ from the language policy of the school concerned, and

d. It describes the bases upon which disputes about the LoL/T must be handled (the principles of rights, equity, redress and practicability), as well as the way in which such disputes must be resolved (consultation with the Member of the Executive Council for Education for the province, the Pan South African Language Board, and an appeal for arbitration)

In the case of a LoL/T being requested which is not available in a particular school, the policy states that such a request will be regarded as *reasonably practicable* if it is supported by cost-effectiveness and the required learner/teacher ratio, that is 40 learners per class in grades 1 to 6, and 35 in grades 7 to 12.

The policy documents do not recommend any specific LoL/T model, but do suggest that two such models are considered practical: the use of a first language as LoL/T (with the requirement that an additional language also be studied), and a structured bilingual approach, by which they presumably mean dual medium schools (since they say that this model implies a "two-way immersion" — paragraph 4.1.5).

Multilingualism

The policy document expresses quite a strong position on multilingualism. It obligates schools to promote multilingualism by requiring of them that they stipulate how they will implement it, and it suggests that they (i) use more than one LoL/T and/or (ii) offer additional languages as fully-fledged subjects, and/or (iii) apply special immersion or language maintenance programmes (particularly in cases where learners' home languages are not used as LoL/T). Schools are urged to share human resources in this regard.

Policy implementation assessment

The policy documents also contain directives for assessing policy implementation. The Department proposes that language managers be appointed in school districts and that these officials monitor the language policy implementation of schools actively, for instance with questionnaires to stakeholders, and with interviews. They also propose that the Pan South African Language Board be approached to assist in the implementation assessment process.

It is clear that the language-in-education policy and plan of implementation contain a number of positive features, also from the point of view of the government's philosophy of pluralism. However, the two documents also possess several rather serious shortcomings. This is particularly clear if one evaluates them from the perspective of what needs to be understood by the notion *policy.*

The requirements for an effective policy were discussed towards the end of Chapter 2, following Human (1998: 150–2), a stance reflected in the report of the Working Group on Educational Research and Policy Analysis (1997: xiv–xv).

Given this conception of policy, given the aims the Education Department has set for itself regarding language-in-education, and given the sociolinguistic character of the country, the proposed policy is not entirely adequate, despite its positive features. This can be illustrated with reference to a number of issues.

Language policy development by governing bodies

Though the policy document lists the principles to be followed in formulating school language policy, it gives no explicit direction on how the governing bodies are to go about developing their language policies, nor does it provide information to guide decision-making. Whilst the philosophy of individual choice and the devolution of decision-making accord nicely with a democratic approach to policy-making, it is essential that decision-makers be enabled to make informed choices. The two documents, however, give no indication that the Department intends providing this type of (necessary) information. Given the nature of the language political situation and the central role of language in educational development, this is an essential requirement, and a guiding document or localised information sessions are necessary.

Language of learning and teaching directives

Given the strong stand on multilingualism in the policy documents one would expect a clear and comprehensive directive on the LoL/T. This is not the case. On the contrary, the actual policy statement on the LoL/T is unexpectedly general and inexplicit. It reads, simply, that "the language(s) of learning and teaching in a public school must be (an) official language(s)" (paragraph 4.5). This is not a sufficiently helpful approach.

There is also an unexplained ambivalence concerning the notion of multilingualism, expressed in the shifting use of the terms *multilingualism* and *bilingualism.* Compare, for instance: "to promote *multi*lingualism" (4.1.1) vs. "additive approach to *bi*lingualism" (4.1.5) vs. to "establish additive *multi*lingualism as an approach to language in education" (4.3.2) and the "promotion of *bi-* or *multi*lingualism" (5.1.1.1.2) (emphases added). This ambivalence creates the impression that the Department is not sure whether a multilingual approach is feasible, thus reflecting negatively on the philosophy of multilingualism.

Given the sociolinguistic realities of the country and the strong support for multilingualism one would have expected a stronger stand on the LoL/T. In its present form the "policy" will most probably contribute very little to changing the realities expressed by the statistics in Tables 6.5 to 6.7. In fact, its weakness could even lead to increased subtractive bilingualism.

Besides these specific shortcomings the policy documents are also problematical in the following ways:

a. Though the documents raise specific issues (inadequacies of the Bantu languages: par. 5, p. 11 of the second document) they make no reference to vital issues such as changing the negative attitudes to the Bantu languages, the provision of educational material in these languages, improving language teaching methods (in first language teaching, second language teaching and foreign language teaching), providing specialist teachers of English in every school, countering the hegemony of English, and so on.

b. They display a disturbing lack of linguistic insight into the nature of human languages. They state, for example, that the Bantu languages are somehow "semantically and syntactically" inadequate. They are also not careful enough in their reference to the need to develop and expand "'academic', scientific and technological vocabulary". The view they express is an oversimplified one which lends support to the common objection against the Bantu languages, namely that they cannot be used as languages of learning and teaching in the higher grades because they do not have the necessary technical terminology, and hinting (unjustifiably) that this may not happen soon because it takes such a long time to create one's own technical terms.

c. They demonstrate confusion about the language planning philosophy which is appropriate to language-in-education policy development in a multilingual society. The preamble of the policy document suggests that the Education Department wishes to approach the language issue from the perspective of language as a *resource:* it speaks of *additive multilingualism, the equality of languages* and *the promotion of the Bantu languages.* However, the vagueness and indecisiveness of the policy statement itself suggests that in reality the Education Department has thought about the language issue from the perspective of *language-as-a-problem,* or, at best, as a (restricted) *right*. The Bantu languages, they seem to believe, are only considered important for personal, cultural and religious use.

d. They fail to commit the Department to supplying human and material resources for the implementation of the policy, thus paving the way for a possible failure in policy implementation — as was demonstrated by the inability of the Pan South African Language Board to achieve anything of any significance over the first two years of its existence (see Chapter 8).

The South African language-in-education "policies" in larger or lesser degree display the same weaknesses as those listed by Bamgbose (1991: 111) as typical of the language policies in African countries: "avoidance, vagueness, arbitrariness, fluctuation, and declaration without implementation". *Avoidance* in the policy is found in the number of escape clauses, such as *reasonably practicable, reasonable alternatives, equity,* and *practicability. Vagueness* is found in the fact that some of its basic elements (like *multilingualism*) can be interpreted in different ways. The stipulations are too flexible, with too few details of exactly what should be done. Equally, there is no clarity on *implementation procedures,* in particular: Who has to do what? Which body? When? How? A negative reading of the documents can easily lead one to deduce that the policy is "a declaration without serious intent". Lack of specificity, says Bamgbose (p. 117), effectively gives governments "an alibi for non-implementation".

It is necessary, I think, to keep in mind that the politics of language in South Africa is not situated on an equal playing field. In order to achieve the goals set out in the South African constitution strong steps need to be taken. And these steps need to be prescribed in the language policies of the country. In this regard it is helpful to take note of the views of Wielemans and Berkhout (in press) about the role of policies in transforming public life. They emphasise that policies are not merely simple sets of linear events (for example problem identification, possible solutions, implementation strategies and evaluation procedures) nor a collection of authoritative statements indicating future directions. Policies are, in reality, instruments in the exercise of power and are directed at establishing certain values in a community (p. 2). "Policies should not only be seen as 'things' but also as processes and outcomes, not only as 'text' but also as discourse and effect". This is obviously also applicable regarding language-in-education policies, which must also be implemented in a dynamic process.

The criticisms of the Education Department's language-in-education policy expressed in this chapter should not be interpreted as a plea for government prescriptiveness or strong-arm strategies. Nor does it wish to suggest that policies should have the power of laws. School communities must be allowed free choices and the policy implementation process has to be consultative by nature. The criticism *is*, however, that, given the central role of language in educational development, and given the need for transformation, reconstruction and development, the existing imbalances and the enormity of the task, stronger government action is needed, policy documents must be far more explicit, with clear descriptions of the available options and their consequences, and with a full exposition of the information needed by school communities to make decisions which will be in their own interests in the long run.

Present LoL/T practice

In Africa the major LoL/T is usually the ex-colonial language (English, French or Portuguese), except, in some states, for the first three or four years of the school programme. This is the practice, in spite of the fact that the ex-colonial languages are usually no one's primary language, and in spite of the fact that these languages are generally not known very well (see also Chapter 1).

Before 1976 the policy and practice regarding the LoL/T in South Africa was as follows: In the former DET schools the policy was that the "mother-tongue"[4] should be used during the first 4 years of school, and that a switch to Afrikaans or English could be made from the fifth year of school (previously Standard 3, now Grade 5). In the white schools mother-tongue instruction, thus Afrikaans or English, was compulsory, with coloured and Indian schools being allowed to choose between Afrikaans and English. After 1976, following the Soweto protests, the former DET schools were allowed a free choice of LoL/T from the first day of the school programme. The policy position since 1994 was described earlier.

In practice, schools in the black communities have increasingly favoured English as LoL/T, as a comparison of Tables 6.5 to 6.8 shows:

Table 6.5. Choice of LoL/T in DET schools in the late 1980s

Choice of language of learning	Pupil numbers	Percent
A Bantu language, i.e. a first language	2,632,603	48.00
English (a "second" language) in primary schools	1,338,833	24.40
English (a "second" language) in secondary schools	1,496,529	27.30
Afrikaans and English (both "second" languages)	14,591	00.26
TOTAL	5,482,556	100.00

(Source: DET Report for 1988)

Two points regarding Table 6.5 need to be noted: First, the information it contains dates from the period immediately after the 1976 Soweto protests, when DET schools were able select their own LoL/T, and secondly, almost half of these learners elected to use a Bantu language as LoL/T.

In 1991 a DET survey conducted in 5,017 schools[5] provided the information contained in Table 6.6:

Table 6.6. Choice of LoL/T in DET schools in 1991 in percentages and number of schools

Choice of language of learning	Percentage	Number of schools which responded
A Bantu language	07.35	368
English from grade 1	21.50	1,080
Afrikaans from grade 1	01.48	74
Initially a Bantu language but with a gradual transfer to English	52.87	2,652
Initially a Bantu language but with a gradual transfer to Afrikaans	03.68	185
Initially a Bantu language but with a sudden transfer to English	13.12	658
TOTALS	100	5,017

Source: Heugh 1993 (adapted)

Once again, two points need to be noted. First, that the survey reported on in Table 6.6 was conducted after 1990, when the previous government announced its decision to free Nelson Mandela, unban the African National Congress, the Pan-Africanist Congress, the South African Communist Party, and the other anti-apartheid movements, and to start negotiations about democratic elections. Secondly, that the choice of the English-only option is much the same as in the 1980s, although the Bantu language-only option had lost considerable ground.

The most noticeable fact presented in Table 6.7, which contains information from a time after the advent of a democratic government, is the generally disproportionate relationship between home languages and choice of LoL/T. For example, English is the home language of 13% of the learners in Gauteng province, but the first LoL/T of 66% of these learners. In the same province Sotho, though the home language of 15% of the learners, is not selected at all as LoL/T. The only language which shows a positive correlation between being home language and LoL/T (in each of the provinces included in the table) is Afrikaans.

Table 6.7. Comparison of home language (HL) of pupils with choice of first LoL/T (LoL) in all schools in five provinces as percentages in 1997[6]

Province (Learner totals)	Gauteng (1.45M)		KwaZulu/Natal (2.7M)		Mpumalanga (0.9M)		Northern Province (1.9M)		Western Cape (0.91M)	
	HL	LoL	HL	LoL	HL	LoL	HL	LoL	HL	LoL
Afrikaans	17.5	19.0	1.2	1.6	6.0	6.5	2.6	1.6	60.1	66.0
English	13.0	66.0	10.6	64.3	1.4	61.0	0.4	50.8	19.6	28.0
Pedi	8.3	2.0	–	–	10.8	3.0	56.7	32.8	–	–
Sotho	15.0	–	1.0	–	3.7	0.7	0.3	0.4	0.3	–
Tswana	8.9	2.5	–	–	3.5	1.6	1.5	0.5	0.06	–
Ndebele	2.2	–	–	–	15.6	4.0	1.6	–	–	–
Swazi	2.4	–	–	–	35.2	5.8	0.8	–	0.6	–
Xhosa	6.7	1.6	1.5	0.5	1.5	–	0.2	–	18.6	6.0
Zulu	20.0	8.5	85.0	34.0	16.3	16.8	0.8	0.6	–	–
Tsonga	3.6	–	–	–	–	–	22.7	6.9	–	–
Venda	1.2	–	–	–	–	–	11.8	6.3	–	–

[a] Home language according to the 1991 census.
Source: Education Ministry Information Service (EMIS), Education Department

Although the three sets of figures (in Tables 6.5–1980s, 6.6–1990, and 6.7–1997) are not wholly comparable, for obvious reasons, it is clear that there has been an increase in the choice of English: whereas an average of about 25% of the pupils in DET schools were taught in English in the late nineteen-eighties, more than 60% of the schools in the four provinces outside the Western Cape selected English as first LoL/T in 1997. This last table, especially, shows the dominance of English. In addition, the tendency to choose English as LoL/T is found mainly in the black communities, for which it is a second language.

   If one wants to come to any kind of critical evaluation of the LoL/T situation, one has to determine the reasons for the choices of LoL/T and their justification.

The debate regarding the LoL/T issue in South Africa

The major argument presented in favour of using English as LoL/T is that it ensures access to the job-market. The main language of the workplace is English, and without a thorough knowledge of it, occupational access is severely restricted. In addition, it is argued, English it is an international language, with a very high level of prestige, ensuring people's respect, it is a language of wider communication in South Africa, and the lingua franca in all the major domains of public life (for example the political debate, education, the economy and social advancement), that it provides access to all the important rights and privileges in the country, and that it is educationally fully developed (with teaching and reading materials in all subjects). Using English as LoL/T, it is argued, is essential for improving English language proficiency. In addition, the Bantu languages are said to have no economic value (that is, do not provide access to the job market and other rights and privileges), are not adequately equipped for use as languages of learning and teaching (since they lack technical registers and do not possess the necessary textbooks nor adequate general reading material), are appropriate only for the lower functions, such as social interaction, cultural practice and religion, that their use in the schools as instruments of learning and teaching will be very expensive, since teachers will need to be trained to teach in them, text-books and other teaching material will have to be developed, and, finally, that their extended use as languages of learning and teaching will continue the segregationism of the former government and thus lead to continued division and subordination.

It is relatively easy to counter these objections. Firstly, the main argument, though true, is not a necessary and sufficient reason for opting for English as LoL/T: proponents of the use of the Bantu languages as LoL/T in no way suggest that the acquisition of English is not of primary importance to South African learners. On the contrary, it is generally accepted that knowledge of English is vitally important, and that the government should be obliged to ensure that every learner in the country has the opportunity to acquire it. Secondly, a number of the points of view, though valid in themselves, are not relevant to the issue. For example, it is true that English is an international language, but this is irrelevant to the choice of learners' LoL/T (as shown by the fact that very few non-English-speaking European countries have opted for English as LoL/T in their primary and secondary schools). Thirdly, it is not true that using English as LoL/T automatically leads to improved English language proficiency, as is shown later. Fourthly, some of the arguments are valid and relevant to the issue at hand, but only temporarily so. For instance, it is true that the Bantu languages are at present not adequately developed as LoL/T, but this can be quite easily rectified, given the resolve to do so. Fifthly, arguments such as the one suggesting that the use of the Bantu languages will promote segregationism are not applicable in a meaningful democracy.

The main point in the whole issue, however, is not addressed in the pro-English stance. This is simply that, in order to use a language effectively for learning purposes, a rather high-level proficiency in that language is required (see the argument at the beginning of this chapter). Allowing for exceptions in the higher socio-economic classes of the major urban areas, black South African learners generally do not have the English competency required by OBE. Though a reasonable percentage of these learners have basic interpersonal communicative skills, very few are able to use English effectively for higher order cognitive development in a learning environment.

How proficient are black learners in English?

A discussion of this question must be framed within the distinction which the educational linguist Jim Cummins (1979) makes between *basic interpersonal communicative skills* (BICS), and *cognitive academic language proficiency* (CALP), for the simple reason that BICS is obviously not enough, as indicated in the discussion of the skills required for educational development in relation to OBE. So the question which now needs to be addressed is whether black learners have the required proficiency in English for "OBE purposes".

The general impression one gets from moving around South Africa engaging in informal conversation in English, is that many black South Africans know English well enough for basic interpersonal communication in urban areas. One gets by in English on city streets asking for directions, negotiating parking, directing inquiries at reception desks in post offices, municipal offices, government departments, and so forth. However, as will be shown further down, English proficiency in South Africa is generally not adequate for the purposes of formal learning. Educators with experience in black classrooms, for instance in colleges for vocational education and training, report that learners' faces are mostly "blank" (uncomprehending) when technical, business or academic concepts are explained to them, that these learners very seldom participate in any classroom discussions, and that they perform poorly in assessment situations.

In Chapter 1 the general inadequacy of the English proficiency of learners was demonstrated, in particular their lack of functional literacy[7]. Similar information is available from many sources.

For example, Macdonald (1990) shows that former DET primary school learners had an average English vocabulary of 300–700 words after the fourth grade whereas the syllabus for the 5th grade required a vocabulary of 3000, and a survey undertaken for an organisation called READ showed that rural learners (of whom there are more than 5.6 million) had the reading and writing skills contained in Table 6.8:

Table 6.8. Percentage of 1,898 learners in grades 5, 6 and 7 in 20 rural schools in the Western Cape, the Eastern Cape, KwaZulu/Natal, the Free State, the Northern Cape and Gauteng (former DET schools) who had adequate reading and writing skills, as in 1996

	Grade 5	Grade 6	Grade 7
Average reading skills	33.6	38.5	45.5
Average writing skills	7.5	12.6	19.3

Source: Le Roux and Schollar, 1996: 12–13

Furthermore, tests performed by Messrs. Hough & Horne, a firm of consultants on literacy and communication skills, to assess the English language skills of urban tertiary students with a measure called *ELSA* ("English literacy skills assessment"), provided the results in Table 6.9.

Table 6.9. % of urban tertiary learners with English as L2 and as LoL/T, with adequate English literacy skills in 1998 by year of passing grade 12 (total N: 5 924)

1990	1991	1992	1993	1994	1995	1996	1997
51	35	33	31	28	25	24	22

Source: *Unit for language skills development*, Report, University of Pretoria

In 2000, the *Unit for the Development of Language Skills* at the University of Pretoria assessed the Afrikaans and English literacy skills of students in different faculties. Their findings are given in Table 6.10. The difference between the percentage students who need remediation in Afrikaans and English is due to the fact that for many of the latter English is a second language.

Table 6.10. Language skills assessment as % of first-year students in four faculties at UP, 2000

	Total N tested		% Who need remediation	
	Afrikaans	English	Afrikaans	English
Humanities	459	369	27	42
Law	155	145	21	56
Natural Sciences	564	302	14	28
Economics & Business Management	821	665	26	42
TOTAL	1,999	1,481	12.8 (n=256)	40.4 (n= 599)

Source: *Unit for Language Skills Development* Report, University of Pretoria

Table 6.11 provides the results of similar tests conducted in 1999 in the case of students who are speakers of Bantu languages:

Table 6.11. ELSA evaluations of the English literacy skills of randomly-selected first-year students who are speakers of Bantu languages at the University of Pretoria (expected literacy level: Grade 12) in 1999

(Number of students assessed)	Average level as a grade	Lowest/ Highest grade
Faculty "A" (33)	Grade 9	5/12
Department A (24)	Grade 8	5/11
Department B (24)	Grade 8	6/12

Source: *Unit for Language Skills Development* Report, University of Pretoria

The point Table 6.11 makes is that the pre-tertiary education system in South Africa produces learners who qualify for admission to university study (that is, have passed grade 12 at a particular level) and are thus expected to possess the linguistic knowledge and skills required for effective study (grade 12 level), but in actual fact are well below that level (and thus cannot handle the tasks they are expected to deal with on linguistic grounds). (Webb, 2002, deals with the role of language in the development and assessment of academic competencies at the University of Pretoria.)

Finally, as illustrated in Chapter 1 from an exam question answer of a masters student who is a teacher of English, the lack of English language proficiency is also found at the post-graduate level.

The inadequate proficiency in English is not restricted to South Africa, of course. In Kenya the mean pass-mark of students for English at the end of primary school in 1992 was 48% in the "objective" paper (the language paper), and 30% for the composition paper. The mean pass-marks for English at the end of secondary school in 1991 were: 36.6% for English Composition, 31.9% for English Grammar, and 17.6% for English Literature (Kembo-Sure, 1997: 50–51). In Nigeria 55.4% failed English in the 1994 senior certificate examination (Bamgbose, 2000: 81.). Similar experiences are reported for the Ivory Coast. (See also footnote 3, Chapter 1, regarding French in the Ivory Coast.)

The use of an ex-colonial language as LoL/T has rather serious consequences. In Democratic Republic of the Congo (the former Zaire), where French is also the sole medium of instruction, writes Bokamba and Tlou (1977), only 30% of the primary school entrants complete the first four grades, attaining basic literacy, and only 5% of all elementary school children gain admission to secondary schools. "Today", they write, "as it has been in (the) past 20 years or so, the national wastage rate of elementary school graduates in Zaire varies between 62–74%, and that of secondary schools between 90–94%." They conclude that "the present language policies of Sub-Saharan states constitute a major obstacle to the development of generalized education in Africa", and their argument that these policies "will restrict access to post-primary education to a small minority of Africans, and will lead to a considerable waste of potential human resources" (1977: 35), is fair comment.

In South Africa, the consequences of an inadequate proficiency in English are equally easy to demonstrate. It is reflected in various ways, such as drop-out rates, low pass rates and low mean pass-marks, examples of which were provided earlier. As an example: in the former DET schools in South Africa, the drop-out rate in 1988 for Std. 3 pupils (the grade in which the switch to English as LoL/T occurred) was almost double that for Std. 2 pupils (57 000 against 29 600), and the total drop-out rate for the first four school years in the same year was 307 500 (SAIRR 1990: 828 survey for 89/90).

Generally speaking, minority language children suffer various serious consequences as a result of their inadequate proficiency in the dominant LoL/T. Lemmer 1991: 169 lists the following:
- Poor academic achievement
- A poor foundation for cognitive development and academic progress
- Poor self-image and lack of self-confidence
- Emotional insecurity/anxiety
- Cultural conflict, and
- Little effective parent involvement

One can, of course, argue that the abolition of Apartheid education will lead to a (dramatic) improvement in the English language proficiency of black pupils. This may be true in the case of (higher) middle-class families in the major urban areas where pupils have extensive exposure to English (the school, society in general, the electronic media), and whose parents can afford to enrol their children in the (better) formerly white schools, but it is certainly not likely in the case of less-affluent families in (less) urban areas. In rural areas, where there is almost no exposure to English, where a knowledge of English is not an existential necessity, where literacy is low and very few people have radios and television, where society is generally non-English and where parents are extremely poor, English language proficiency is unlikely to improve.

In this regard it is interesting to take note of the situation in India, as described by the Indian sociolinguist, Debi Pattanayak. Pattanayak pointed out (in 1994) that attempts to teach English to the Indian population have been made for more than 200 years, yet only 2–4% of the Indian population know English today. In fact, there are still 400 million illiterate persons in India. A similar situation is likely to persist in South Africa, where conditions for acquiring an adequate knowledge of English are not favourable in many areas, where the education situation is presently rather poor (with overcrowded classrooms, the absence of the basic facilities (desks, books), an absence of a culture of literacy, and so on), where the knowledge which black teachers have of English is often also inadequate (note the example quoted in Chapter 1: Odendaal 1984 found that 69.4% of the teachers in KwaZulu had obtained between 40% and 49% for English in their final school examinations), and where, from all reports, the actual teaching practice in English classrooms is unlikely to change matters, since teachers generally seem to use a grammar method, rather than a communicative method.

Is the use of a Bantu language as LoL/T not a better choice?

Given now that black learners, particularly in the rural areas, but also in urban areas, generally do not know English well enough to be able to develop cognitively (as well as affectively and socially) to their maximum potential if English is used as LoL/T, it seems common sense to consider the use of the Bantu languages as LoL/Ts in a serious light. Besides the fact that black learners will then be learning in a language they know very well (which means the objectives of OBE can be more easily achieved), the use of these languages will also make parent involvement in learners' formal education possible, and the cultural and emotional transfer from home to school and back will be less traumatic.

Opponents of the proposal that the Bantu languages be used as LoL/T argue that such an arrangement would mean that black learners would not become adequately proficient in English, that the Bantu languages play no role in economic life (and therefore need not be studied as subjects at school), and that, if children were to learn through these languages, they would have to relearn everything once they start to work, and would therefore be badly disadvantaged, that the Bantu languages do not have the necessary status, that educational materials have not been adequately prepared in these languages, and that these languages lack technical terms and registers.

These views cannot generally be sustained. First of all, using a Bantu language as LoL/T does not imply that the acquisition of English must be neglected, as stated earlier. On the contrary — proponents of this policy stance strongly support the radical upgrading of English study. Secondly, it is common sense that knowledge, understanding and skills can only really occur effectively through a language one knows reasonably well. Thirdly, knowledge, understanding and skills are in principle not language-bound — once acquired they can be used in whatever language one knows well enough; they are transferable.[8] Fourthly, well-developed knowledge, understanding and skills lead to more efficient learning in general. Part of the skills a learner acquires is the skill to learn ("learning to learn"). This means that better developed understanding and skills will lead to quicker and more effective learning, also in regard of the acquisition of English. Finally, Bialystok & Majumder (1998) demonstrate that subtractive bilingualism leads to the underdevelopment of the necessary cognitive and academic proficiency, which suggests that learners' bilingualism should be balanced, that they should have an "effective" proficiency in both languages. In the South African language political context this means that the Bantu languages need to be maintained, and that the stigma attached to them should be combated (additionally because parent involvement in the process of educational development is vital). Using a Bantu language as LoL/T is therefore not a bad idea, or one which is detrimental to learners' educational development or future professional life.

There are three rather serious obstacles to the acceptance of a policy of using the Bantu languages as LoL/T: the social status of these languages (see again later); the association of such a policy with the Apartheid ideology of mother-tongue education, which means that the use of the Bantu languages as LoL/T is still seen as a strategy to subordinate black South Africans (and, of course, as a divide-and-rule measure); and the fact that parents are generally quite ill-informed about the LoL/T debate. It may be useful, therefore, to take note of the international debate about the use of first languages/home languages as LoL/T, and the available research findings.

The LoL/T debate at the international level

In 1951, a UNESCO report recommended on psychological, social and educational grounds that children be taught in a language they know effectively, which will normally be the mother-tongue of the child. This recommendation applies to the whole school programme. Fasold (1984: 293ff.) gives a critical assessment of the UNESCO recommendations. One of the remarks he makes is that there is no clear empirical evidence to support either mother-tongue instruction or instruction through a second language. This is not surprising, since the issue cannot really be empirically tested. There are simply too many variables, non-controllable factors. Besides the language of instruction there may also be: the degree in which there is a culture of learning in the community; social class; the home environment; the literacy levels of parents; urban vs. rural environment; the motivation of learners; the quality of teacher training; the social meaning of the languages used; and so on, which all play a role in determining educational success. The role of language in this regard is probably impossible to "prove" in any scientifically meaningful way. Logically and experientially, however, it is simple common sense: one cannot develop educationally unless one can understand the material through which development needs to take place. The point is therefore not that instruction through a first language is the superior LoL/T, but that a language (any language) which the child knows effectively (for the purposes of cognition) should be used for education and training.

Fasold proposes a more considered approach to the selection of an appropriate LoL/T. He suggests that three basic questions be answered when a LoL/T policy has to be formulated. These are:

Can the language under consideration perform the task? Is it codified and standardised? Does it have the necessary technical terms and registers? Are there textbooks available in the language and does it possess sufficient general reading material?

Can the LoL/T policy be implemented in practice? Will such a policy work? Are there teachers who can teach in it?

Does the policy meet the needs of the various sectors of the community involved? Will pupils really be able to learn in the chosen LoL/T? Will the use of a particular language as LoL/T facilitate or obstruct the learning of other languages? Will school-leavers be better off by having used it as LoL/T? Is the language generally acceptable in the community and does it have the required status? Are the needs of society in general met, for instance their need for status? Will the selection of a language enhance national conciliation or be detrimental to it?

The answers to all these questions in the South African context are positive regarding the Bantu languages. Where this is not the case, it is only so in the short-term, and all the official Bantu languages can be developed to meet these requirements. Three further remarks need to be made. Firstly, dealing with these issues in a scientifically justifiable way is probably as difficult as answering the question about which language to use as LoL/T. Secondly, it is strange that Fasold does not place more emphasis on the most fundamental question of all: *Does the child know the LoL/T well enough in order to operate in it on an abstract level, and will he or she be able to develop his/her creativity in it?* And thirdly, one has to remember that the issue of LoL/T in South Africa, like practically all questions, must be answered within the context of the need for (radical) social transformation.

Research findings on the issue

Elsewhere in Africa

The issue of using an ex-colonial language as LoL/T is as problematic elsewhere in Africa as it is in South Africa (see the earlier remarks concerning school results in Nigeria and Kenya). Both Bamgbose and Sure link these results with the language-of-learning-and-teaching factor.

African sociolinguists have undertaken at least three projects on the issue.

The best-known project is probably the so-called Six-Year Primary Project of the University of Ife in Nigeria, discussed by Bamgbose (1984 and 1998). The project was "designed to compare the use of Yoruba as a medium of instruction for the full six-year duration of primary education for all subjects (except English) with the use of Yoruba as a medium for the first three years and a change-over to English as a medium thereafter" (1984: 88). Provision was made for an experimental group and four control groups for comparative purposes. The results of the project were quite definitive: The experimental group performed significantly better than the other groups in Yoruba (naturally), in the subjects science, social and cultural studies and mathematics, and, also, in English.

Of note, too, are the findings of Eddie Williams regarding reading in English in primary schools in Malawi and Zambia (1996). In the article Williams writes that he investigated

> how the language in which formal education is conducted affects learners' reading ability. Malawi and Zambia offer a suitable context for such an investigation in that in Malawi, Chichewa is the medium of instruction for years 1 to 4, with English a taught subject, whereas in Zambia, English is the medium of instruction from year 1, with one of seven local languages as a taught subject. An English language reading test, and a local language reading test (Chichewa in Malawi, and the almost identical Nyanja in Zambia) were administered to the same year 5 learners from 6 schools in each country. The results indicate there is no significant difference in English language reading ability between learners in each country, but large differences in favour of Malawi in local language reading ability. These results are consistent with research on minority groups suggesting that instruction in L1 reading leads to improved results in L1 with no retardation in L2 reading. In both countries, however, reading ability in English is unlikely to be at a level to

allow learning through the medium of English for most pupils. This is related to pedagogic practices which give insufficient attention to meaning. The role of English in these countries is largely driven by political perceptions of effective strategies for unification and modernisation. However, its dominance in the education system may work against the individual primary school child's cognitive development in general, and their reading proficiency in particular. (p. 182)

Finally, the findings of the Working Group on Educational Research and Policy Analysis (1997) on languages of instruction must be mentioned. They were tasked with answering the question: "What is the 'best' language of instruction policy in Africa?" (p. xiii). Their finding was that

> With regard to language and cognitive development, a large body of research has demonstrated the importance of instruction in the mother tongue in the early years of a child's education.[9] Experience in Africa and many other parts of the world show that cognitive development is achieved faster if the mother tongue, rather than an LWC (language of wider communication), is used as the LoI (language of instruction) in primary education.

Furthermore:

> Based on the overwhelming evidence in support of mother-tongue LoI in and outside Africa, the consensus among linguists is that
> – Cognitive gains can be derived from using the child's home language as the LoI in early education; and
> – Where the home language is different from the LoI used in the class-room, the LoI may create pedagogical and cognitive problems. (p. 37)

Outside Africa: the USA and Peru

The LoL/T issue has, of course, been researched in many communities of the world, such as in Europe (for example the Dutch and Belgian minorities), Canada, the USA and in east Asia. The problem in every case is that the contexts of these studies very often differ crucially from the South African situation, so that their findings are not automatically applicable in South African contexts. Nevertheless, something might be learned from a large-scale study conducted in the USA.

W. P. Thomas and V. P. Collier (1997) report on a research project involving 700 000 language minority pupils in five large urban and suburban school districts in various regions of the United States where large numbers of minority language students attend public schools. They made use of school records from 1982–1996, aiming to discover the links between student achievement outcomes and instructional data, and to examine what factors most strongly influenced these students' academic success.

Thomas and Collier found that there were three key predictors of academic success which appeared to be more important than any other variables and were more powerful than student background variables or the regional or community context of the pupils. One of these is instruction in the learners' first language. They concluded that academic instruction through students' first language should be followed for as long as possible (with instruction through the second language (English) for part of the school day). They furthermore found that:

- children in two-way bilingual classes (L1 and L2 pupils in the same bilingual class, working together at all times) outperform their counterparts who are schooled monolingually in the upper grades of elementary school
- these gains were sustained throughout schooling in middle and high school, even when the programme did not continue beyond the elementary school years
- non-English-speaking pupils in these schools outperformed pupils who were native speakers of English in tests in both the first language and the second language as from the 7th grade of the school programme
- non-native speakers of English in schools which used the two-way developmental bilingual education programme scored considerably higher than the average performance of native-speakers of English in traditional schools, and that pupils in late-exit bilingual education programmes in which English as a second language was taught through academic content, also performed (slightly) above the average, and
- pupils in other types of programmes, such as early-exit bilingual education (where academic instruction is given in two languages for the first two to three years with a subsequent transition to majority language), all performed progressively poorer than the average performance of native-English students in traditional schools

They thus found that where quality, long-term, enrichment bilingual programmes using current approaches to teaching, such as two-way bilingual education and late-exit development bilingual education, were fully implemented, language minority students were able to develop their cognitive and academic potential to such an extent that they were academically successful in their high school years.

The work of Nancy Hornberger (1987, 1989, 1994) on the use of indigenous languages in education in Peru is equally applicable to the issue of using first languages as LoL/T in South Africa. Hornberger discusses a bilingual education project in Puno in rural Peru in which Quechua (which had been kept on the margins of the national education system) was introduced as LoL/T alongside Spanish in a dual-medium system. The project was directed at the maintenance approach to bilingual education (rather than a transitional approach), with Quechua used as LoL/T throughout the primary school. An additive approach to bilingualism was therefore followed rather than a subtractive one.

The use of the minority language Quechua as LoL/T produced a number of significant gains, such as the development of the vernacular and the production of written material in it, the promotion of cultural integration, overcoming cultural discrimination, the reduction of illiteracy, and the better use of educational opportunities. Furthermore, there was also greater pupil participation in class-room talk, more meaningful reading behaviour, concepts and logic were stressed in arithmetic classes rather than step-following and memorisation, and generally there was more content-orientation and skills development. Clearly, therefore, a maintenance-directed model of bilingual education in this rural Quechua community had clear educational advantages.

However, reports Hornberger, despite the educational successes, the policy as such was not successful. There was considerable community resistance and eighty schools eventually withdrew from the project. Though some of the reasons for the withdrawal were logistic (for example the transfer of teachers and their replacement by unequipped teachers), and others had to do with wrong decisions (the inclusion in the project of urban schools where Spanish was better known), a major reason for the policy failure was the strong prejudice against the use of a vernacular language in education. The community traditionally saw the school as a non-Quechua institution, in which Quechua was inappropriate.

The question is what South Africa can learn from this experience, and whether it suggests that a policy promoting the use of the Bantu languages as LoL/T will predictably fail. This is a possibility, of course, but need not be the case. What can be learned is what the likely problems are with such a policy, suggesting that policy developers should devise strategies aimed at avoiding similar problems in South Africa. In this respect the case of Afrikaans can once again be used to illustrate an opposite possibility: At the beginning of the twentieth century there were strong governmental pressures against the use of Afrikaans in schools, and the language was linguistically, functionally and socially more restricted (and stigmatised) than any present-day Bantu language. Despite these circumstances, the Afrikaans-speaking communities were able to develop the necessary political will to insist on its use in schools and to manage its social adaptation into a effective educational instrument[10], and today it is as useful as English in the South African educational context.

It seems, in summary, that the South African Department of Education would be wise to provide strong pro-active support for the use of the Bantu languages as LoL/T, especially since such a policy is directly in line with the political philosophy upon which South Africa is being built.

The need for local research

The biggest challenge in South African education regarding the LoL/T issue is to convince learners, parents, teachers and school governing bodies to accept the Bantu languages as LoL/T in a significant way. Hard, empirically and theoretically sound information is essential for such a challenge. For this purpose a research project has been set up by the *Centre for Research on the Politics of Language* (*CentRePoL*) at the University of Pretoria, called *Language, educational effectiveness and economic outcomes* (see Webb and Grin, 2000). The executive summary of the research proposal is as follows:

Motivation
The impetus for the project on Language, educational effectiveness and economic outcomes is the continuing socio-economic inequality between groups in South African society. This inequality, to a large extent, is the result of unequal conditions of access to education and training, resulting in an inadequate level of generic and technical skills among large tracts of the country's workforce.

Core idea
The core idea of the project is that unequal educational conditions (which themselves lie at the root of socio-economic inequality) can in significant part be traced back to language, because languages play a fundamental role in the educational process, both as instruments of learning and teaching, and as subjects in their own right. Language is, to a large extent, the key to educational effectiveness.

Educational effectiveness and the language of learning and training
First, the acquisition of knowledge and the development of cognitive, affective and social skills occur primarily through a linguistic communication process (between learner, educator and learning materials). This linguistic communication is a high-level process presupposing abstract, objective and symbolic thought. Therefore, considerable language proficiency is required if learners are to realise their individual potential fully.

In South Africa, the main LoL/T is English. However, available information on the language proficiency of black learners indicates that for many, English is not an effective instrument of knowledge acquisition and skills development, and that improving English language skills for all learners, up to the point where high-level communication can efficiently take place in English, may not be an achievable goal within a reasonable time horizon. It follows that, for reasons of educational effectiveness (and the influence of the latter on occupational success and socio-economic equality) serious consideration should be given to the use of learners' first languages, in particular African languages, as languages of learning and training. Learners already have oral fluency in those languages when they enter the education system, and there is no reason to presume that these languages cannot be effective instruments of learning and teaching.

Educational effectiveness and languages as subjects

Second, first and second languages ("L1" and "L2") constitute important subjects in the education system, and their importance is growing in a globalising, yet diverse world, with increasing strategic importance placed on communication abilities. First-language competence at a high level is essential to effectively develop superior skills such as negotiating meaning, managing information, identifying and analysing problems, formulating solutions, etc. Second-language proficiency, particularly in English, is an essential instrument for occupational success, inter-community relations and effective political participation, particularly in the case of South Africa.

However, available evidence indicates that even if oral proficiency in L1 is good, literacy in L1 is generally inadequate, thereby hampering the acquisition of high-level language-related abilities. At the same time, as noted above, proficiency in English is often too low for an effective use of this language in essential communication tasks, thereby significantly hampering effective participation in political and economic life. It follows that, along with an increase in the role of African languages as languages of learning and teaching, the teaching of African languages and English as subjects needs to be upgraded, as part of a general effort at increasing the effectiveness of the education system.

Application: the case of vocational education and training

In order to examine these issues more closely, the project will focus on vocational training, particularly in light of the strategic importance of this part of the education system, its closer relationship with the labour market, and the possibilities of immediate positive consequences in terms of matching between learners' actual skills and the skills required on the market.

The project therefore includes the development of experimental syllabuses stressing the role of African languages as languages of learning and teaching for selected subjects, as well as the upgraded teaching of L1 and of English as subjects. A pilot group of vocational school students will be invited to follow these experimental syllabuses, on a voluntary basis. Three technical colleges in the Pretoria region have agreed to co-operate in the project.

In addition to information about the overall effectiveness of alternative approaches to the roles of languages in the education process, the project is expected to generate highly valuable information on the didactics of African languages as languages of learning and teaching, the didactics of African languages as subjects, and the teaching of English as a second language in the educational and cultural context of South Africa.

Cost, cost-effectiveness, and policy implications
Available evidence from other countries indicates that: (1) the use of the first language as a LoL/T improves educational outcomes; (2) the cost of using one more language as a LoL/T is moderate, and is in the region of 5% of total per-capita spending on education; (3) offering education and training through the learners' first language usually generates a net gain; (4) the teaching of languages, including English as a second language, generates high rates of return, both at the private and the social level.

One important part of the proposed project is therefore devoted to the evaluation of the costs and benefits that can be associated with an increased role for African languages as languages of learning and teaching, and with an improved instruction of African languages and English.

The project will provide an information base and evaluation instruments to help assess different policy options regarding the role of languages in the South African education system. These results are intended as complements to the political perspectives on education and language issues, and as useful tools to improve the contribution to both effectiveness and fairness in South African society.

Scientific background
The project is a novel and interdisciplinary one, and rests on strong scientific bases, principally from the following areas of research: (1) the linguistics of language education; (2) the economics of education; (3) the economics of language.

The project is a three-year project, starting in 2002.

Concluding remarks on the LoL/T issue

The critical remarks made earlier about the Department of Education's language-in-education proposal (see above: **The LoL/T issue: The current language-in-education policy**) contain a number of suggestions for a more effective handling of the LoL/T issue, for instance that means need to be devised so that parents and teachers can take more informed decisions about the language policy of a particular school. One aspect which has not been given enough emphasis is the need to take far more note of the sociolinguistic realities of the country.

A single generalised policy statement is not wise. In the South African context different categories of sociolinguistic situations exist, which make different demands on language-in-education policies and practice. At least the following sociolinguistic category types can be identified:

A. The larger urban areas (Johannesburg, Pretoria, Durban, Pietermaritzburg, Port Elizabeth, Bloemfontein and Cape Town)
– where English and/or Afrikaans have strong dominating presences
– where a second language (Afrikaans, English or both) is the language of economic and social power
– where there is a high level of exposure to the second language and a strong incentive to learn it
– where the Bantu languages generally do not have a strong sociolinguistic presence functionally or prestige-wise, but are nevertheless still significantly present, albeit in different degrees (e.g. from five in Pretoria and Johannesburg, to one in the other larger urban centres)
– where there are urban varieties of particularly the Bantu languages (but also of Afrikaans and English), and
– where strong urban identities have developed and there is a resistance against "traditional ways of life".

B. Smaller urban areas (Pietersburg, Potchefstroom, Rustenburg, Kroonstad, Ladysmith, Newcastle, Grahamstown, Kimberley, Mmabatho, Stellenbosch) and larger towns in rural areas (Potgietersrust, Middelburg, Bethlehem, Vryheid, Kokstad, Queenstown, Worcester)
– where Afrikaans generally has a stronger presence than English
– where people are not exposed to English as a second language to a significant extent
– where the Bantu languages may be far stronger statistically speaking
– where children are generally not significantly literate, and
– where teachers are often not very well-trained or exceptionally proficient.

C. The deep rural areas (Nongoma, Thohoyandou, Botshabelo, Engcobo, Bisho)
– where both Afrikaans and English are largely absent (even in the electronic media), except in the Northern Cape, where Afrikaans is dominant
– where one Bantu language (and possibly Afrikaans) is usually dominant
– where there is little substantial (non-symbolic) incentive to learn either English or Afrikaans
– where children grow up in a largely illiterate environment
– where there is still a strong attachment to non-western cultural patterns, and
– where teachers are generally poorly trained and not adequately proficient

Given these categories (with further sub-categorisation probably possible), it is likely that consideration should be given to advocating different models for the choice of a LoL/T policy, for example single-medium schools (with strong support for high-grade programmes for the acquisition of other languages), parallel and dual medium schools, schools with a policy of transfer (gradual or sudden) from one LoL/T to another (preferably as late as possible), and, possibly, even multilingual schools (with unstructured or structured code-switching). The only LoL/T model which is totally ill-advised in rural areas in South African sociolinguistic conditions is the submersion model, where learners are confronted with an LoL/T which they do not know at all from day one of the school programme. (See Garcia in Coulmas 1995.)

Each of these models has relatively clear advantages and disadvantages, of which serious note needs to be taken. These advantages and disadvantages are educational, political and linguistic, and they need to be considered in that order of priority.

The issue of LoL/T policy in tertiary education has not been discussed at all. This is currently an important topic of debate in South Africa, especially in the traditionally Afrikaans-dominant universities (such as the University of Pretoria). Political changes and subsequent policy changes have led to large numbers of black students being admitted to these formerly mainly white institutions. Since these students do not know Afrikaans well at all, and prefer English as LoL/T, these universities have had to adapt their language policies quite radically. The process is still underway. An overview of the debate and the issues involved can be found in Webb 2000c, with a more specific discussion of the situation at the University of Pretoria in Webb (2002).

Language certification requirements

A second major issue which a language-in-education policy has to deal with, is the matter of what language study learners are expected to complete if they are to qualify for certification.

Before April 1994 all students were expected to pass Afrikaans and/or English in order to obtain a Std. 10 (grade 12) certificate or to obtain university admission. This has now changed.

The Education Department's proposed policy on the study of languages is formulated as follows:

4.4.2 From Grade 3 onwards, all learners shall offer their LoL/T and at least one additional approved language as subjects
4.4.4.2 From Grade 5 onwards, one language must be passed, and
4.4.4.3 From Grade 10 to Grade 12 two languages must be passed.

From the point of view of *multilingualism* this policy decision is disappointing, for various reasons:

First of all, it is unlikely to change anything, with many pupils (even black pupils) opting for English and Afrikaans, the two languages with the most economic value in the country. (Preliminary research in KwaZulu/Natal urban areas, where Afrikaans is relatively unimportant, has shown a surprising preference for Afrikaans as a school subject, see Khalawan, 2000.)

Secondly, it can in no way contribute to establishing multilingualism in the country, since learners are only obliged to study two languages (as before 1994), and, more seriously, these two need only be passed during the last three years of the school programme. During the first four years of school study, languages need not be seriously studied at all. One could see this policy decision as an explicit contradiction by the Department of its own stated aim of promoting multilingualism: The policy requires the successful formal study of only *one language* up till the ninth year of school. It therefore, in fact, **strengthens** the monolingual practice which the government is gradually allowing to become a reality.

Thirdly, there is no indication that the Education Department has realised that the only proven way of improving pupils' proficiency in English in South African is by employing specialist teachers of English in all schools.

Language study

The third issue which language-in-education policies need to deal with, is the matter of language study, in particular language curricula. However, the policy and policy implementation documents of the South African Education Department pay no attention to this question. This is strange for a number of reasons. Firstly, language teaching is one of the most serious issues in the language-in-education situation. This is true of first-language teaching (particularly in the case of the Bantu languages, see later on in this chapter) and second-language teaching (particularly the teaching of English).[11] Secondly, language teaching (as L1, L2 or as L3) is probably the most effective way of achieving the objectives which the Department set for itself regarding language-in-education. This is the case in first-language study, since it is in this subject that a wide range of skills can effectively be mastered and practised, given learners' existing proficiency in these languages. At the same time, self-esteem and self-confidence, which are so necessary for educational success, can be built up. Second and third language study can also make a significant contribution to the promotion of multilingualism in the full sense of the word, since such a decision can lead to better inter-group communication. Language teaching can also contribute directly to the promotion of the Bantu languages, it relates directly to individual and societal development, it can play a central role in the social reconstruction of the country and it can provide useful support in any nation-building project. As a society in transition, South Africa has a unique opportunity to make its language learning curricula (at all levels) part of its reconstruction programme, and to promote new values and norms, new attitudes and convictions, and new visions for a new country (as pointed out briefly at the end of Chapter 5).

The matter of curriculum development is being given comprehensive attention outside strict policy formulation (as part of the introduction of the outcomes-based approach). In the absence of full details about this work, it is not possible to describe the present situation meaningfully, or to give a critical overview of the topic. All that can be done at this stage is to comment generally on aspects of possible language curricula from a language planning perspective.

The major task of first-language teaching and study

One of the frequently heard objections by black learners (their parents and teachers, and even the headmasters of schools) against studying their first languages, is that "they already know these languages, so why waste time in studying them. They could rather use this time for the study of English". This is a totally misinformed position, which becomes clear if one tests its relevance for the study of Afrikaans or English as first languages.

The major task in first-language study is the development of the linguistic skills needed to handle and execute the cognitive, affective and social skills required as life-skills and for effective and efficient professional and vocational performance. First-language learners need to develop their linguistic abilities to negotiate meaning and to manage information at the high levels demanded by a globalising, competitive yet diverse world, to identify, analyse and select solutions to problems, to be able to co-operate effectively with cohorts in team-work situations, to acquire the values necessary for successful professional life, to act critically in a responsible way, to communicate effectively with a wide range of people in a wide-range of contexts and for a wide-range of functions, including, especially the ability to read and write in these positions, and so forth.

The criticism that first-language study is irrelevant can only be true if the curricula, the teachers and the didactic methods make it so. First-language study is potentially a meaningful, personally and socially extremely relevant experience.

The role of first language study in social transformation

The role of first-language study in the transformation of public life occurs on the basis of the intimate relationship between language and the socio-cultural order in a country, being both reflective and constitutive of the socio-cultural reality of which it is part. This is neatly expressed by scholars such as Halliday and Kramsch.

Halliday (1978: 1) for instance, points out that "the construal of reality is inseparable from the construal of the semantic system in which the reality is encoded..... Language is the main channel through which the patterns of living are transmitted to him, through which he learns to act as a member of a 'society' — ... and to adopt its 'culture', its modes of thought and action, its beliefs and its values. ... A child creates ... his mother tongue in interaction with ... people who constitute his meaning group." When people talk to one another they do not only exchange information, they"... act out the social structure, affirming their own status's and roles, and establishing and transmitting the shared systems of value and knowledge (via the social meaning of language forms)." And further (p. 3): language does not only express the social system; it symbolises the social system actively ... "representing metaphorically in its patterns of variation the variation that characterises human culture."

Kramsch (1993: 4) is as direct about the relationship between language learning and the socio-cultural reality in which it is imbedded: language acquisition, she says, is the acquisition of "the unspoken ideological substratum of the educational system, the community, the peer group, the family."

Clearly, therefore, language study can play a significant role in contributing to the transformation of South African society.

The social responsibility of language teaching

The language teacher should also be directed at promoting the principle of multilingualism and multiculturalism, and an awareness of the use of language in social (and political) manipulation, discrimination and exploitation — that is, the fact that languages are embedded in the power structures of the society: language teaching should be "critical language teaching".

Similarly, an important aim of language teaching should be to contribute to national conciliation and national integration (Chapter 5) — through the dissemination of knowledge about languages and the development of tolerance and respect for other language communities.

Given these aims language syllabuses directed at social reconstruction and development should cover the following themes:

– The sociolinguistic reality of the country
 The language syllabus should aim at providing students with a knowledge of the multilingual situation in the country, i.e. the number of languages in the country, their place and role in national life, and their general demographic, functional and symbolic distribution. The nature of the languages as languages of Africa should also be discussed. Language teaching should show how the country's languages reflect its socio-cultural reality — the values and norms, attitudes, perceptions and opinions of the different communities in the broader society.

– The promotion of cross-cultural communication
 In a complexly structured society it is essential to specifically develop cross-cultural communicative ability (see Ndoleriire, 2000). This involves at least the following:

 i. Knowledge of the country's socio-cultural history, i.e. the cultural traditions from which people may have emerged (such as *ubuntu*, initiation practices, ancestral spirits, Christian (Calvinistic) theology, the liberal tradition), and what the effect of these traditions may be on language, language choice and language use in South Africa

 ii. The ability to construct and interpret discourse/texts in culturally appropriate ways, including an understanding of culturally determined discourse conventions (like greetings, address forms, reference systems, discourse initiation and discourse termination) and a knowledge of conversational practice in the society (such as the functions and use of code-switching and di- and multiglossia)

iii. The skills needed to handle barriers to cross-cultural communication and to repair cases of communication breakdown, in particular:
- Conflicting interpretative schemata, which occur when differing cultural contexts have different contextualisation cues so that listeners misinterpret the communicative intent of speakers. In such cases, says Chick (1990), participants find it difficult to establish and maintain conversational co-operation
- Negative attitudes and stereotypes
- Mutual distrust between members of opposing groups. As Gumperz (1982: 30) says: situations in which minority and majority groups interact may be such that power relationships prevent misunderstandings from being recognised. The situation in South Africa is a good example of this. Chick (1995: 238) points out that the relations of domination and dominated and superiority and inferiority between white and black relatively, which the policy of Apartheid made practical reality, led to social distance and a-symmetrical power relations, which in turn led to ignorance of one another and of each other's communicative conventions, which again led to misinterpretation of each other's intentions and abilities, to stereotyping and discrimination, and further separation …

- Knowledge and insight into the role of language in national integration
An obvious aim of multicultural language teaching is nation-building and the promotion of a common national loyalty (see Chapter 5). This can be achieved through:

- the development of individual and societal multilingualism
- exposing pupils to the cultural diversity of the country and promoting respect and tolerance for different ways of speaking
- discussing the role of language in the maintenance of a socio-psychological and cultural identity
- demonstrating the creative potential of cultural contact, for instance through the challenges it brings to cultural practices and beliefs
- emphasising the equality of all languages and cultural patterns of behaviour, the legitimacy and authenticity of all the other linguistic varieties, the absence of hierarchies (in principle) between languages or cultural customs, and challenging the hegemony of any one language and any one culture; and

- providing pupils with a knowledge of and an insight into the divisionary and conflict potential of language nationalism — see Webb and Kriel, 2000

An important tool in achieving these aims is the use of language textbooks in which the socio-cultural worlds of the different communities of the larger language community are reflected, in which the so-called non-standard languages are presented in a non-stigmatised way, in which the names of characters are representative of the whole speech-community and in which stereotypes are avoided (Esterhuyse, 1986).

- Manipulation, discrimination and exploitation

As illustrated in Chapter 1, South Africa provides good examples of the use of language for manipulation, discrimination and exploitation, since its languages, like languages the world over, have been used as political instruments, as means of dividing the broad community and controlling it, and as means of controlling access to the country's rights and privileges.

In so far as South African society is hierarchically stratified in terms of particularly race and class, but also gender and age, languages and language varieties, language forms, ways of speaking, and so forth, have become indices and symbols of social groups, and the power or powerlessness of their members. Learners need to be made aware of the potential of language for the exercise of power. (See below for some illustration of the educational consequences of the marginalisation of non-standard varieties.)

The impact of specific sociolinguistic phenomena on educational development in South Africa

In conclusion, it is useful to take note of a number of specific sociolinguistic phenomena which have an impact on language-in-education, that is on the LoL/T issue, the question of language and certification, and language curricula. Some of these phenomena are the following:

Ethno-cultural manipulation: the potential for cultural imperialism and assimilation

Given the close relationship between language and culture, it is, of course, possible to use language for manipulative purposes (see particularly Philipson, 1992). Note for instance, the following remark by Tollefson (quoted in Webb

1991: 8): "the assumption that English is a tool for getting ahead — and that teaching English is empty of ideological content — is an example of ideology. In general, the belief that learning English is unrelated to power, or that it will help people gain power, is at the centre of the ideology of language education." Note also the following remark by the South African author, Njabula Ndebele (1987)[12]: "… we cannot afford to be uncritically complacent about the role and future of English in South Africa, for there are many reasons why it cannot be considered an innocent language. The problems of society will also be the problems of the dominant language of that society, since it is the carrier of a range of social perceptions, attitudes and goals. Through it, the speakers absorb entrenched attitudes."

A good example of this matter is provided by the earlier teaching of Afrikaans, which was used to promote a particular view of life and of the world, as Esterhuyse (1986) demonstrated for the subject as a whole, and Strydom (1987) demonstrated for the teaching of Afrikaans literature.

Esterhuyse discusses a number of examples of the strong cultural bias in Afrikaans language teaching, mentioning:

– The exclusive focus on Afrikaans as a European language, thus denying its African character
– The focus on Afrikaans as the language of only white people
– The exclusive focus on standard Afrikaans
– The negative attitudes towards non-standard Afrikaans
– The ideologising and mythologising of Afrikaans, leading to a defensive over-protectiveness of the language, prescriptiveness, and a self-defeating obsession with "purity", "correctness", and "deviations from the norms"

Language teaching must explicitly avoid being used as a tool for cultural indoctrination or the centralisation of some linguistic communities at the expense and marginalisation of others.

The politics of standard languages

Standard languages play an important role in modern public life, particularly in multilingual and multi-dialectal societies, where governments are responsible for communicating effectively with their linguistically diverse citizens. It is thus necessary to consider standard languages a bit more closely.

First of all, the concept *standard language* needs to be distinguished from the concept *language standardisation*, the first being the product and the latter the process. Definitions of the two concepts often differ in detail (see Cluver 1996: 352–360, 482–90 and 618–624 for bibliographical references), but variously mention particular features. In the case of *standard language* the features include: being codified, existing primarily in written form, legitimated by authorities, used in formal domains, used across community boundaries and accepted as a norm by members of the constituting language communities. *Standardisation* refers to the process whereby the standard language is established. The process is usually deliberate (see Matthews, 1997: 352), with prescribed norms for appropriate usage in formal contexts, but to different degrees, as in the case of Afrikaans, which was strictly controlled, compared to (British and American) English, which was established less deliberately. Standardisation is furthermore also usually associated with power, and the linguistic variety of the economically and politically most powerful community often constitutes the basis of the ensuing standard language. Finally, standard languages can exist at different levels of standardisation, particularly as regards the acceptance of the norms, their knowledge in the relevant community, and their use by community members. This is the case in South Africa, for example, where standard Afrikaans is more strongly established (accepted and used) than standard Tswana, which is still widely contested, is not known throughout the community, and is not used in formal contexts (see Nfila, in preparation). Obviously, this aspect of language standardisation is political in nature, a fact which is also evident from the refusal (especially in the apartheid era) by states such as Lesotho and Botswana to accept the standardised varieties recognised in South Africa.

Given the importance of standard languages, one of the main aims of the language teacher is to develop learners' linguistic skills in the standard language, to develop their confidence in its use, to develop their command of its stylistic and registral resources, to develop their ability to construct coherent and cohesive texts in it, to interpret standard language texts critically, and to use the standard language for a wide variety of public functions, such as academic debates, business negotiations and public speaking. Learners need to acquire functional and sociolinguistic competence in the standard language. However, this task of the language teacher is not as simple as it may seem. Given the preceding discussion it is fairly obvious that language standardisation and standard languages can have negative consequences in the educational context. Some of these are discussed next.

Firstly, language standardisation can (through the determination of the standard variety's norms) lead to linguistic alienation, even, maybe, to language-internal conflict. This is what happened in some degree in the case of Afrikaans: Standard Afrikaans became so differentiated from the vernacular Afrikaans of the Western Cape that the two varieties are, in some contexts, in conflict with each other (see below). The differentiation is the consequence of a strong drive towards "purism", and, in the case of Afrikaans, a commitment to "free" the language from all possible (and impossible) traces of English. It is likely, also, that considerations of race played a role, since the non-standard varieties of the language (Cape Afrikaans and Orange River Afrikaans) are used mainly by non-white speakers. Since the standard language is an instrument of power, intra-linguistic differentiation inevitably leads to the centralisation of the standard and the marginalisation (and stigmatisation) of the non-standard varieties.

Afrikaans is, of course, not the only language in South Africa which exhibits language-internal conflict. The same situation also pertains in the case of the Bantu languages, for instance Zulu, which is dominated by the rural variety, resulting in urban Zulu-speaking pupils finding it difficult to pass Zulu as a school subject. Another example is the "conflict" which has developed between standard Pedi (school Pedi) and the Pedi spoken in the urban communities of Pretoria (which has even been given a name: "Pretoria Sotho"; see Schuring 1983). There is also a serious debate about English, with the English Academy supporting an "international" standard, and with other voices pointing to the possibility of such a standard becoming a barrier to social and economic advancement (see Titlestad 1996, Webb 1996 and Webb 1997, for a discussion of some of the issues involved).

A second, related negative aspect of standard languages is that they can become appropriated by the dominant group, and then used to serve sectional interests. Afrikaans is once more an example of this action, as explained by Pokpas, a linguist from the Western Cape. Pokpas' view (personal communication) is that the white speakers of Afrikaans developed the type of language they spoke in the former Zuid-Afrikaansche Republiek (the old South African Republic) and the Orange Free State Republic into a standard form, and because they had the economic and political power their variety of Afrikaans became the language of the school, political power, social mobility and the higher occupational opportunities.[13] On the other hand, the Afrikaans of the Cape working class communities (the coloured communities) became stigmatised, with the result that it did not function as a tool of access to job opportunities. Its speakers became powerless. In addition standard Afrikaans was used to include certain people into the dominant group, and to exclude others, mainly on the basis of race. Standard Afrikaans became the symbol of

Afrikaner nationalism and was appropriated by its white speakers as their exclusive property.

A third problematic aspect of language standardisation is its possible negative educational implications: If the linguistic and social distance between the standard and the non-standard varieties become too large, pupils who grew up in non-standard environments easily develop linguistic insecurity, negative self-esteem and, finally, begin to fail scholastically. This is what happened with speakers of African-American English (Black English/Ebonics) in the USA and also with speakers of Cape Afrikaans (see van den Heever 1987 and de Villiers 1992).

Several proposals have been made about managing language-internal conflict. Firstly, there was the suggestion that "language enrichment programmes"[14] be instituted. This was later abandoned despite huge financial investment. Another proposal was that non-standard forms be recognised as part of the standard (van Rensburg 1992). However, unless this proposal has the support of the dominant forces in the speech community it is unlikely to succeed (see Webb 1998). Thirdly, there was the proposal that both standard and non-standard dialects be recognised for teaching purposes, and that pupils should (initially?) be allowed to use their (non-standard) variety in school situations, with a gradual transfer to the standard language. But this approach simply amounts to a postponement of the problem. A more promising approach in my view, is the following:

- Accept the priority of the standard variety, also for language teaching purposes, retaining it as the target language of study
- Recognise the integrity and legitimacy of the non-standard variety in a meaningful way, accepting that it has a fundamental socio-psychological role
- Insist on non-discriminatory and supportive attitudes from all teachers, making sure that they are informed about the nature and extent of language-internal "conflict"
- Equip language teachers with the linguistic knowledge and expertise to handle the relationship between the standard and the non-standard varieties, and train language teachers to guide pupils in a linguistically informed way towards the standard variety
- Promote a sociolinguistically informed view of the concept "language error"
- Include, as an important subpart of the programme, a section on the relativity of the standard languages, i.e. challenge their sociopolitical dominance

The low standing of the Bantu languages

The low standing of the Bantu languages in the communities in which they are used as primary languages is apparent from the refusal by their speakers to use these languages as languages of learning and teaching, and also from the striking lack of enthusiasm for their study as first languages. As mentioned earlier, parents and pupils report not seeing any sense in studying them on the grounds of the fact that they "already know" them, and therefore do not need to study them. It is also apparent from reports from teachers that the less able teachers and the junior staff members are often tasked with their teaching (see Masinge 1997). Given this state of affairs it is obvious that serious attention needs to be given to the teaching of the Bantu languages as first languages, and that their curricula need radical revision (especially regarding their social and cultural relevance), appropriate teaching material needs to be developed urgently, and their teachers need to be trained (or retrained). Simultaneously, a rigorous promotional campaign is needed (see Chapter 8).

A serious, related matter is the question of the costs of producing teaching material in nine different standard Bantu languages. Besides the fact that discussions about such costs are often exaggerated, since material in Venda, for example, need not be produced to the same degree as for Zulu, and for the latter to the same degree as for English, the question of the harmonisation of the Nguni and Sotho languages merits mention. The fact is that if these two language families were each to be harmonised (see Alexander 1989), it would be possible to produce textbooks in only two languages, one for all the Nguni-speaking learners and another for all the Sotho-speaking learners, and the costs would be decreased considerably. Unfortunately, however, the issue is generally misunderstood, and has become quite emotionalised, making it difficult to debate it. The matter will be discussed more fully in Chapter 8.

There are a number of signs of a movement towards promoting the Bantu languages. The LANGTAG report devoted a chapter to the issue, and the Pan South African Language Board has a special committee to deal with it (see Chapter 9, as well as Ambrose, Read and Webb, 1998).

Training language teachers

The training of language teachers at teacher training colleges and universities obviously needs more comprehensive coverage than can be provided in this chapter. The syllabus for these training programmes needs to include topics such as the nature of language and language knowledge, the role of factors such as language acquisition, human learning, cognition, personality and the socio-cultural context in L2 study. A discussion of teacher training programmes would also have to cover language teaching methods, in particular communicative language teaching. I would like to conclude this chapter with a short discussion of one aspect of the linguistic training of prospective language teachers, namely the need to give them a training which is relevant to Africa.

A superficial analysis of linguistics training in African universities shows a seemingly uncritical acceptance of European and USA linguistics in practically every sense of the word. The theoretical frameworks used in linguistics programmes in African universities come from there, the syllabus content and organisation are determined by them, the topics discussed and the examples used are European/British and American, and the text-books used are from Europe and America. They determine what constitutes "a linguistic problem", and how it should be approached. But what is the relevance of these approaches for Africa? Are the intricacies of X-bar theory really of primary interest to undergraduate linguistic study in Africa? Is it really crucial to focus on the details of the early history of English? Is it morally justifiable to give long courses on British, American, Australian and New Zealand English whilst English in Africa is beset with problems which need discussion and research and is the source (along with French and Portuguese) of serious problems in language communities in Africa?

African linguists, it seems to me, also suffer from intellectual and spiritual colonisation. It is necessary to reverse this situation: to design syllabuses and course contents appropriate to Africa, to decide in African terms what a linguistic problem constitutes, what the best linguistic methods are to handle the problems which have to be solved, and how research should be done in specifically African contexts. There may be very substantive questions which are typically African and which require sophisticated linguistic training. For example:

- The knowledge and skills necessary to enable African graduates to handle the linguistic and linguistically related problems of African societies (see Chapter 1, for example)
- The problems of defining language and dialect with reference to Bantu languages (including African English)
- The theoretical aspects of "the word", debated with linguistically interesting material from the Bantu languages
- The difficulties of language norms and standardisation, illustrated from the heart of present-day Africa

- Courses on East African/South African/West African English/French/Portuguese: their origin, spread, features and status vis-à-vis British English/European French/Portuguese
- The problems the ex-colonial languages are causing, and their relation to larger and smaller Bantu languages
- How it was possible (through what policies and implementation strategies) for English (and French and Portuguese) to obtain such an overwhelming hegemony
- Language and power in Africa, and the promotion of critical language awareness
- Language planning in multilingual societies (a field in which Africa can make a unique contribution)
- Cross-cultural communication, and politeness phenomena in African communities, and so on.

Rather than "canonising British English and British/American linguistics", linguistics in Africa can be given *an African voice* and students can be equipped with the knowledge and the intellectual skills needed to handle the multitude of (real) problems in African linguistic communities (see Webb and Kembo-Sure, 2000). It is obviously not necessary for African linguistics to be cut loose from Europe or the USA. That would be foolish, and would eliminate African linguistics from participating in and contributing to international discourse. It is obviously essential to retain extensive contact with Western (and other) linguists, and to remain part of the international scene. What is needed, though, is specifically African training programmes.

Notes

1. Literacy statistics often vary because of differences in the definitions used and, probably, in the assessment instrument.

2. The learner distribution in a primary school in central Pretoria by home language in 1999 (as percentages of the learners in the school) illustrate this point: English 30, Sotho 17, Tswana 16, Zulu 10, Xhosa 9, Pedi 7, Afrikaans 4, Venda 3, Tsonga/Shangaan 2.6, remainder 1.4. (Total 610.) (Potloane 2000: 86.) Before 1994 the school was all-white.

3. Given that by far the majority of South Africa's learners come from social worlds which do not match the world of the school and which could even be fundamentally in conflict with it, these functions of language are fundamental (see Webb, 2000c).

4. The term *mother-tongue* is generally avoided in the South African language debate,

because it (as well as the concept) has become stigmatised due to its direct association with the Apartheid policy. In South Africa the terms used are *home language, primary language* and *first language*. In this monograph the concept "language-known-well" is preferred, on the grounds that in multilingual societies learners often know more than one language well-enough to be able to learn through it.

5. Details of the survey method (relating to the reasons for the sample size and the way in which the schools were approached) are no longer available.

6. One's interpretation of the statistics in Table 6.7 should reflect an awareness of the following problems: that it is not certain what, exactly, is meant by "first choice of LoL/T", that the second and third choice of LoL/T are not available, that there is no distinction between primary schools and secondary schools, or the different grades, and that there is no distinction between rural and urban schools.

7. The term *functional literacy* technically refers to literacy at grade 8 level. Less technically speaking, it refers to the ability of a person to "control his or her own life" satisfactorily.

8. This position obviously does not mean that one can apply one's (professional) knowledge in a language one does not know (or is in the process of acquiring), nor does it mean that technical skills acquired in a particular language can easily be practised in any other language. If one has learnt the technical terms and discursive elements and conventions of, say Mathematics, in English, it will obviously be difficult to "do" Mathematics in another language, say French. However, knowledge of and skills in the principles and processes of Mathematics can obviously be transferred to French, once the applicable French terms have been acquired.

9. They do not motivate why their finding should apply only to the "early years".

10. This process of adaptation was well underway by 1948, when the Afrikaans-speaking white voters gained political power in South Africa. The successful promotion of Afrikaans as a LoL/T is therefore not a consequence of Apartheid policies, although it is true that Afrikaans was later strongly advantaged by these policies.

11. The distinction between studying a language as L1, L2 or L3 has been one of the recent topics of debate in South Africa, with educational linguists (Young, 1988: 8; Barkhuizen & Gough, 1996: 459) arguing that the distinction supports apartheid, implies that black learners are not able to assimilate western language and culture, and implies a deficit view of language competence. A core syllabus committee for English, set up in 1993, recommended that the distinction be dropped in the case of English, but that "the differences between mother-tongue and non-mother-tongue learners of English" be acknowledged by calling the latter "bilingual learners of English" (Murray & van der Mescht, 1996: 256).

12. The purpose of this quote is not to imply that Ndebele is opposed to English in any way.

13. Achmat Davids on "The coloured image of Afrikaans" also used terms such as "linguistically subjecting", "impose their language", "forced to speak" and "appropriated by its white speakers". (Unpublished.)

14. These programmes obviously arose out of the conviction that non-standard varieties are linguistically inferior, that their speakers are cognitively deprived, needing to be "enriched". This is unfounded, as we know.

CHAPTER 7

Spreading the wealth

Language and economic development

The state of the South African economy is not very satisfactory, as is shown by information provided by the *South African Institute for Race Relations* (SAIRR, 1998: 400) and their two-monthly publication *Fast Facts*, July, 1998:

a. The *high rate of poverty.* In 1997, 61% of South Africa's black people was poor compared to 1% of the white people. (Being poor meant having less than ZAR353 available per month per adult, or ZAR 948.55 per household of four.)

b. *Inequality in the distribution of wealth.* In 1997, the bottom 40% of households accounted for 11% of the country's consumption, whilst the top 5.8% of the population accounted for 40%. (Average per capita income: white South Africans: ZAR 21 218; Asian: ZAR 7 087; coloured: ZAR 3 931; black: ZAR 2 369.)

The black communities in the country are (still) economically marginalised, and it is necessary that everything possible be done to close the gap in material wealth and to change its skewed distribution. Attempts in this regard should form the bottom line in policy development and planning on all public issues, including language.

There are obviously a number of reasons for the poor state of the South African economy, such as inadequately educated and trained workers,[1] the turmoil brought about by transformation, and the violence and corruption in the country. As sociologists of language we naturally have to ask whether *language* plays any part in the poor economic performance of the South African society, and, if so, whether we can contribute in any way to a resolution of the problem through language planning.

To respond to this question we need to take note of the interrelationship between language and economics, consider the facts relevant to the matter in South Africa, and then reflect on ways in which language planning may contribute to a possible resolution.

The interrelationship between language and economics

The study of the interrelationship between language and economy is only about 30 years old, and is covered in little over 100 scientific articles (Grin 1996: 18), which means that data-based knowledge about the interaction is restricted. Although there is a lot of on-going work in Canada and the European Union, as well as Australia and New Zealand,[2] considerable research still needs to be done, especially since language and economy are both extremely complex phenomena, each constituted by numerous variables, many of which cannot be separated in such a way that their relationship with others can be easily determined. Furthermore, linguistic variables can often not be translated into the quantitative format required for establishing positive correlations with non-linguistic factors.

Some understanding, though, has been obtained about certain areas of interaction. Grin (1994) lists the following topics which have been researched with some success:
- The impact of language knowledge (for example, English in Switzerland) on earnings, particularly regarding the level and nature of language skills (whether they are oral or written, and whether they are active or passive skills) (p. 26)
- The positive effect of public spending on minority language promotion regarding output and income as well as employment (p. 24), and
- The fact that economic inequalities can be language-based (p. 27).

Economists have as yet done very little work on the effect of ethnic and linguistic factors in economic performance. This is especially so in the case of Africa. In fact, "the problem of economic development in less-developed countries has never been studied in connection with language variables" (Grin 1994: 24).

It is likely, though, that language is basic to effective economic performance. This is particularly so in the sense of language being a *facilitator* or a *barrier* to economic activity. Language can facilitate or hinder economic activity in various ways, for instance in regard to the effective distribution of information in the workplace, the organisation of workplace co-operation, the productive utilisation of workers' knowledge and skills, the effective delivery of services to the public, gainful buying and selling, and so forth. The sections below will deal more specifically with the role of language in economic life. First, the role of language as a production factor (training, management and workplace security) will be discussed, and then as a consumer factor — buying and selling, and service delivery (see particularly Grin & Vaillancourt 1996: 46).

Language as a production factor

Language as a production factor refers to its role in vocational training, the management of the workplace and the security of the working environment.

Vocational training

If South Africa is to become a serious player in the tertiary economic sector,[3] the *education and training* of workers drastically need attention. Knowledge must be made available, vocational skills need to be developed, the ability to utilise economically relevant resources as well as information technology has to be developed, and the values and norms of economic competitiveness have to be inculcated. The central role of language and economic literacy in achieving any one of these aims is obvious.

Language is central to all levels of educational development (see Chapter 6), since it is an instrument for the transfer of knowledge and the development of specialised skills and attitudes. This is also the case in vocational training. The modern workplace is situated in the Information Age, the Knowledge Era, which is characterised by economic activity that is knowledge based and knowledge driven.[4] Workers at almost every level need to be able to handle information. Equally, they have to be trained to adapt to new workplace developments, they must have the skill to continue learning and training. The cognitive, affective and social skills needed for effective functioning in the work place obviously also require high-level linguistic skills, such as the ability to understand, interpret and evaluate work-directed texts[5], identify problems (Why does the engine overheat?), analyse them, obtain relevant information, devise solutions and manage their implementation, co-operate with colleagues (both subordinates and superiors), assume leadership, work in a team, and so forth. Furthermore, in order to perform tasks effectively, workers have to possess meta-cognitive (or reflexive) skills, which also require a high level of linguistic proficiency.

Two aspects of language as a production factor which need to be considered are firstly, that the language proficiency required for effective vocational and professional training is not of the nature relevant to basic interactional communication; it is a type of proficiency at a reasonably high level of linguistic skill (see Chapter 6). Secondly, there is the fact that performing work-related tasks requires a specialised language knowledge, namely the ability to conduct oneself linguistically appropriately in one's occupational domain, that is, one has to know the occupational register, and possess the required vocational linguistic skills. In the case of the world of finance, for example, one must have adequately internalised concepts such as *profit* and *loss, budget, investment, balance sheet, income statements, profit margin, debtors, creditors, efficiency, productivity,* and so on, in an adequate way, and be able to argue in ways appropriate to this domain. Furthermore it has to be kept in mind that discourse in workplace communication in South Africa, is usually culturally sensitive. Different cultures have different socio-cultural rules for speaking, for instance for who may speak about what, to whom, when and how (see Hymes, 1972, Wolfson 1992 and Chick 1992). Evidence of this fact is seen quite clearly in situations in South Africa where black people have to "compete" with white people in verbal interaction in "westernised" contexts, for instance in post-graduate training courses. Whereas white students freely participate in classroom discussions it is often very difficult to get black students involved. They sometimes seem hesitant to disagree with lecturers, with "people of authority", and to be critical.

Linked directly to the preceding aspect is the matter of vocational literacy. Literacy must not be understood as simply the technical ability to read and write a (simple) text. In a modern workplace, characterised by technologized information and a new style of co-operation between managers and workers, literacy covers a knowledge of how production works, co-ordinating and controlling the production process, handling "organization charts, job descriptions, work plans, machine operating instructions, procedures manuals, and performance evaluations, as well as devices for budgeting and productivity calculation." (Darville, 1998: 4.)

Language and management

In a 1987 survey of the use of Xhosa in Eastern Cape industry, Kruger (1987) (see also Chapter 1) found that:
a. Only 4% of the white managers knew Xhosa
b. Nearly 50% of the training officers couldn't speak Xhosa, and 22% used only English for training purposes

c. 60% of the organisations did absolutely nothing to encourage white employees to learn Xhosa or about the Xhosa
d. 50% of the organisations did not make information on pension schemes, insurance and savings available in Xhosa, and
e. Only 20% of the labourers interviewed preferred English as a workplace language.

(LANGTAG Report, p 105)

Effective management requires effective vertical communication (e.g. between managers and workers), and horizontal communication (e.g. between workers, or between management and labour organisations negotiating issues such as wages and conditions of service). This is obviously even more so in cases where workplaces are pluri-cultural. Findings like those of Kruger above suggest that maximally effective communication, effective management and thus effective economic performance are unlikely in the industries concerned. If one further considers the movement away from the older Fordist management styles towards a network approach, which places great emphasis on participation and joint ownership, it is clear that the language of the factory and the industry is an important element in workplace efficiency and productivity (see also Darville, 1998).

The effective functioning of the workplace is also conditioned to some extent by the degree to which workers' sense of their work roles and role relations is appropriately developed, and the appropriate values, attitudes, standards and norms (such as a work ethic and a sense of proper time management), the ability to organise people and to get tasks performed successfully, have been developed. These skills are all co-determined by the constitutive role of language-in-training and language-in-use.

Secure work environment

A presidential commission of the South African government found in 1996 that the major factors restricting productivity enhancement were not related to labour market regulations or legislation, but were "more attitudinal", related to the relations between supervisors and supervised, management and unions, and inadequate worker participation.

Language, as we know, is a central instrument of enculturation, of socialisation (see Halliday in Chapter 6). Values, norms, standards, beliefs, attitudes, ways of thinking, and so forth, are all also established through language. The bonding role of language, its separating and symbolic functions and its role in the construction of identity can all be contributing elements in the development of occupational security. An appropriate language policy for the workplace can contribute to a positive institutional culture and the development of a sense of ownership among the workers.

Another way in which language can promote security in the working environment is by contributing to avoiding accidents and conflict in the workplace, for example in the communication of safety information. Lo Bianco (1996) quotes an example from a Melbourne construction company that employs workers from a variety of linguistic backgrounds, but that thought that it would be more effective and simpler to communicate with the workers in English:

> Elaborate safety information was (however), imperfectly communicated, safety jeopardised, and accidents, miscommunication and conflict resulted. A change in strategy, using the naturally occurring affinity groups among the workers and utilising management with knowledge of the relevant languages, or worker-leaders in language groups … was judged by management to be more effective and less costly than denying the diversity that existed. Similar stories abound. The Australian Tax Office … was able to reduce workplace conflict by more productively understanding culture and language issues relevant to its workers and making appropriate, negotiated workplace changes that made general operations more efficient and effective as well as harmonious. (p. 38)

Finally, the role of language in workplace transformation should also be kept in mind. One of the key components in transformation is effective multilateral communication along both the vertical and the horizontal axes (Agunga 1996, Robinson in Madiba 1996, Melkote and Kandath 1996 and Mukasa 1996). As emphasised in Chapter 4, true social reconstruction can only take place if a government (or management) can communicate its views, beliefs, convictions, wishes, values and norms to the citizens of a country/workers, and if these people can, equally, communicate their views, beliefs, wishes, expectations, convictions, values and norms to the government of the country/management. As in the case of good governance open channels of communication lead to greater institutional legitimacy.

Language as a consumption factor

Language knowledge (including knowledge of more than one language) and linguistic skills are commodities, and can be "sold", or used for obtaining work. In this paragraph the role of language in the job market, including the convention industry, tourism and insurance, as well as service delivery will be discussed.

The job market

Language can play a role in creating work, obtaining appointments and removing obstacles to employment opportunities in general.

The possibility of language-related job creation is apparent from the large (international) language industry, that is, the existence of large numbers of people who earn their living through language and language-related or language-based skills: language teachers, translators, interpreters, copywriters in advertising, publishers, workers in printing shops, employees of recording studios for audio-visual materials, language-education software producers, etc. In 1989, for instance, the English language learning industry is reported to have had a turnover of 6 billion pounds sterling. (LANGTAG Report, p. 109.) Of course, only a few select languages can support an industry of this size, namely those for which there is a large-scale demand, the economically super-valuable languages (see discussion of this concept below), but profit can even be made out of economically less significant languages, as Sproull (1996) reports. Gaelic-generated activity in Scotland, he mentions, generated an output of 16 million pounds sterling in 1991/92, and more than 700 full-time jobs.

Language can also be a factor in providing or removing obstacles to employment opportunities. South Africa provides many examples of language as a basis for (economic) discrimination, and even of exploitation. An example of the first comes from Afrikaans and English, notably in cases where competence is demanded in a specific variety of these languages (the standard form), whereas comprehensibility in no way necessitates such a requirement (as has now become obvious from news journalists speaking on national television in South Africa who use "Black South African English", the "typical" way in which many black South Africans speak English). This issue is important, since it is quite widespread, with many employers regarding what is called black South African English as an indication of a lower level of development and even as a sign of cultural and cognitive backwardness. Language-based stereotypes and prejudice are quite marked features of employment situations, despite being generally unfounded. Another example of language as a barrier to trade comes, surprisingly, from the present South African government's handling of contracting opportunities for small business initiatives. It is said that one of the problems in the promotion of Small, Micro and Medium Enterprises (SMME's) is the difficulty of gaining access to information on mainstream funding by the public sector. However, despite a statement by the minister of public works in July 1996 that "Black-owned SMME's had been particularly disadvantaged through poor access to information on governmental contracting opportunities, tender and contract conditions" (SAIRR 1997: 256), a member of his department (ironically) announced in February of the same year that all tender documents would be in English, in an attempt "to involve more small black businesses in the process" (ibid, p. 261). Clearly, this is a contradictory, counter-productive and self-defeating move; a barrier.

The convention industry, tourism and insurance

Language is an important marketable commodity in areas such as the convention industry and tourism. As Lo Bianco points out (1996: 36): "Tourism is arguably the biggest single industry in the world. It's the biggest employer in the world, it's the fastest growing industry (in Australia)." This is also potentially true for South Africa, with its wide variety of languages and cultural practices. Tour guides, it seems, should be trained in giving tourists access (in English) to the wealth of the folklore, traditions and histories of the Zulu, the Venda, the Tswana, and so on, explaining, even, something about the languages of these communities.

Language also has an important role in the insurance industry and related services. In this regard Lo Bianco (1996) remarks:

> To properly compete in these new industries in which consumers are sovereign it is necessary to know (the consumers). This is true for insurance as it is for tourism, as indeed it is for any human servicing industry in which the mores, values and sociology of the consumer society is critically important to the marketing of products, to their design. Imagine the knowledge ... that is needed to devise insurance packages for people, the cultural knowledge and the linguistic skills to gain that knowledge in the first instance. (p. 36)

Niche markets

The question of niche markets can also be considered. In discussing them, Lo Bianco (1996: 22) observes:

> In the seamless or linked economy competitive advantage accrues to those able to locate, or create, niches, i.e. those segments of the economy which give a distinc-

tive advantage and in which it is possible to command clear competitive advantage, either because of privileged information, skill, capacity, cost regimes or some other factor. Cultural production, or, more simply, the co-operative utilisation of cultural knowledge, assists in niche marketing and niche production.

Service delivery

Languages are also indispensable instruments in the effective and meaningful provision of services, for example in adult education, agriculture, health, legal assistance, recreation and social welfare. This is particularly true in South Africa in the case of communities who use indigenous languages. Lo Bianco points out that "the commercialisation of medical, insurance, and valuation, educational and virtually any other service available domestically is greatly enhanced by the addition of (a) language facilitation service" (1996). And as stated earlier, economic services, such as the issue of tenders for government projects, as well as the forms to be submitted, must be available in the Bantu languages.

Something similar is true in the case of development projects. Given that such projects typically involve communication between unequal parties (socially, economically and educationally powerful ones and socially, economically and educationally powerless ones), a situation intensified by the inherited context of 'highly stratified and unequal social and economic structures' (Melkote and Kandath 1996: 6), the role of development communication in the Bantu languages becomes more and more crucial, both in regard to the determination of the needs and wishes of these particular communities, and the delivery of services.

Language as a barrier to economic development in South Africa

Given the discussion above, the next question this chapter wants to pose is what the role of language and multilingualism in economic development in South Africa is, in particular whether the language factor is a facilitator or a barrier. To debate this question, one first has to consider the linguistic character of the workplace.

This issue has not yet been investigated systematically across a broad spectrum, but there is little doubt that English will be found to be by far the dominant language of formal economic activity, with it being used in almost all domains and at all levels of economic activity. This is apparent from the language policy decisions referred to in Chapter 4, namely that several large industries (the Post Office, Telkom, the South African Broadcasting Corporation, South African Airways, the Land Bank, ABSA — one of the larger banking institutions in the country, and so on), have all opted for an English only policy, or were in the process of doing so. It is even probable that a knowledge of English is a general requirement for appointment in most occupations above the level of unskilled labourer. Afrikaans is also a language of the workplace, but it is likely to be mainly the case in less formal communication and in the provision of services to the public. The Bantu languages are even more restricted in their role than Afrikaans, and are probably used only in the (low-level) informal sectors and for personal communication between workers in the workplace.

Table 7.1 (adapted from information in SAIRR: 2000: 257) gives a subjective (and certainly over-simplified) description of the language distribution across occupations.

Table 7.1. Likely language distribution across occupations

	%	Language most likely to be used formally	Likely language use in informal contexts
Legislators, senior officials, managers	4.0	English	Mainly English
Professionals	9.4	English	Mainly English and Afrikaans
Technicians and associated professionals	5.9	English	Mainly English and Afrikaans
Clerks	7.8	English	Any of the 11
Service workers, shop and market sales workers	8.9	English	First language (L1)
Skilled agricultural & fishery workers	3.9	English	L1
Craft and related trade workers	14.0	English	L1
Plant & machine operators & assemblers	7.0	English	L1
Elementary occupations (domestic service, labourers)	26.1	Afrikaans	Bantu language
Unspecified	13.1	?	?

(Breakdown according to the 1996 census.)

Insofar as this analysis has any value, the central role of English in economic activity in South Africa is obvious, and it is clear that a knowledge of English is of exceptional importance, particularly for getting a job, for occupational mobility and for economic activity in general. Any future language plan directed at economic development must obviously include measures to ensure the adequate acquisition of English (also in formal education and vocational training).

However, only about 25% of the South African population has an adequate proficiency in English for the purposes of effective economic activity (see Chapter 3). These people are, furthermore, mainly members of the higher socio-economic classes. Nationally, 75% black South Africans are not proficient enough in English to be able to use it as a meaningful instrument of economic activity (see also Chapters 1 and 6).

Given this information, English is clearly a barrier regarding access to information, the effective development of knowledge, understanding and skills in individual people, and the free and open participation in economic activity. One can argue, of course, that the English language proficiency of black South Africans can be improved, especially since Apartheid has now been scrapped. However, given South Africa's specific sociolinguistic conditions, it is unlikely that the majority of the South African people will, in the foreseeable future, acquire the necessary high-level proficiency in English to overcome the barriers, and thus be able to operate gainfully in South Africa's economic life. This will then mean that the present poverty levels and the disparity in the distribution of wealth will persist in South Africa, with the same communities as before having to continue to bear the brunt.

The Bantu languages can also be seen as barriers to meaningful economic participation. However, they act as barriers in another way: despite the fact that they are the languages the majority of South Africans know adequately, they are not used significantly in the economy, and therefore also do not provide access to meaningful economic activity. Their *non*-use is thus a barrier (albeit in a reverse sense).

The Bantu languages and economic development

Two issues will be discussed in this paragraph: objections against the use of the Bantu languages, and the advantages of their use for economic development.

Objections against the use of the Bantu languages in economic activity

The objections against the use of the Bantu languages in economic activity include the following: that they have no economic value, that a policy of multilingualism will be too expensive to implement and maintain profitably, and that the extended use of the Bantu languages will lead to a decline in English language proficiency.

a.   Economic value of the Bantu languages

Sociolinguists often argue in favour of multilingual language policies on the basis of the *resource value* of languages. However, Grin and Vaillancourt (1997: 48–49) point out that the notion *linguistic resource value* is often used metaphorically, referring in the main to the cultural or religious value of a language. In a discussion of the utilisation of languages for economic development the notion should rather be defined in economic terms, and the term *economic value* used. This term will then refer to the costs and benefits of languages. These benefits and costs will, however, not be restricted to material benefits and costs, but will be described in both market and non-market terms. If we distinguish (as Grin, 1997, does) between private and social market and non-market costs and benefits, the economic value of (the Bantu) languages can be described with reference to the aspects discussed above, as in the following:

Private market benefits
> The value of the language for:
>> access to vocational training programmes
>> getting a job (as an interpreter, teacher, and so on)
>> getting promotion
>> negotiating higher wages
>> having access to goods
>> information exchange
>> communication with diverse workers, clients and markets in management and trade
>> access to industries such as tourism and insurance
>> being able to handle situations of cultural difference as well as cultural conflict
>> accident prevention
>> providing better service delivery

Social market benefits
> The value of the language for:
>> more effective workplace communication and better management
>> effective, efficient and productive work
>> occupational security
>> workplace loyalty, perceptions of ownership

selling products

use in advertisements[6]

increasing company profits

Private non-market benefits

The value of the language for:

minimising discrimination and exploitation (in training institutions, the workplace)

the pleasure of being a speaker of the language

the respect obtained for knowing more than two languages

acquiring access to entertainment (on television and films)

Social non-market benefits

The value of the language for:

harmonious inter-community relations

sense of social cohesion

identity construction

Private market costs

The costs of acquiring proficiency in a language

Social market costs

The costs of an over-supply of speakers of second and third languages (thus lower wage potential)

Private non-market costs

The cost for the language of:

having a stigmatised, non-legitimised language as L1

having to use a second language in all public domains

being discriminated against for not being adequately proficient in the L2

having to acquire knowledge and skills through an L2

Social non-market costs

The cost for the language of:

negative attitudes to multilingualism, causing conflict

being a member of a stereotyped language

It is obvious that the use of the Bantu languages for economic development is (at least partially) dependent on their economic value: the higher their economic value, the more likely it is that they will be used for economic activity. However, in the South African context this equation contains an apparent internal contradiction since the economic value of a language depends upon the economic prosperity of its speakers: the more economically successful the community is, the higher the economic value of its language, and vice-versa.

A systematic analysis of the economic value of the Bantu languages of South Africa still has to be made.

The economic value of languages is reflected in their linguistic character, for instance: their stylistic and registral breadth and depth, their patterns of use in the economic domain, the extent to which they are known (or studied) as second or foreign languages, the total amount of investment that has been made in them (as indicated by their orthographic and lexical standardisation), the number and quality of their bilingual dictionaries, the number of translated texts into them,[7] the degree to which they are used in electronic processing, for example in word processing, spell checkers, machine translation and man/machine communication (for example in commercial banks and airports), the size of the industry they support (teacher training programmes, and the production of teaching materials, translators, interpreters, journalists, copy-editors, and so forth; see also Coulmas, 1992: 89).

An important question in the context of this chapter is how the Bantu languages can acquire economic value. This issue will be discussed further down.

b.   Multilingualism will be too costly to implement

The objection that a multilingual approach will be too costly to implement is often expressed, and it is true that formal multilingualism will cost money (see the end of Chapter 4). However, two issues need to be kept in mind in calculating costs. Firstly, costs should not be determined only in (simple) material terms, for instance by counting the number of words in texts to be translated, calculating the salaries of translators, and determining the cost of paper, ink and word-processing facilities. There are many more serious costs which need to be considered in the equation such as, as Lo Bianco (1996) points out, "tragic workplace accidents in which immigrant workers (can be) injured or killed, ...or suffer higher rates of mental illness and disadvantage at school" (p. 19). Coulmas (1992: 124–125) makes essentially the same point: "Language training for industry and commerce can be a considerable burden for a company, but those who hesitate to make the necessary financial outlays have to ask themselves which is more costly, language training or losses and forgone gains brought about by lack of language proficiency".

The second issue is the reverse of the first: the costs of a *monolingual* policy can in itself be high. It would mean that workers' proficiency in English would need to be extensively upgraded. Given the present proficiency levels in South Africa this may not be feasible, it would be very expensive, and, in the meantime, the same people would continue to be excluded from meaningful participation in economic activity as before. The question of cost-benefit analysis is discussed more fully below.

c. Decreased English language proficiency and the need for retraining
The use of the Bantu languages as languages of vocational education and training will mean, it is said, that black South Africans will be deprived of the opportunity of acquiring English, which is, as we saw, essential in the South African economic context (see the earlier reference to English in Tanzania). Furthermore, it is said, using the Bantu languages as languages of training will mean that future workers will not be able to function properly, because the language of the workplace is English.

Both these arguments are questionable. As argued in Chapter 6 (in the section on the use of a Bantu language as LoL/T), the use of the Bantu languages as languages of training does not mean that there should be less emphasis on the learning of English. On the contrary, the proponents of the use of the Bantu languages support the radical upgrading of the teaching of English as an L2 in the vocational training programme. Furthermore, research has shown that the improved learning skills developed through the use of an L1 as language of training is directly beneficial to all learning, also learning an L2 or foreign language (see Chapter 6). Secondly, using a Bantu language as language of training will not restrict workers in a serious way, even if the dominant language of the workplace is English, simply because knowledge, understanding and skills (as well as the required work attitudes, values and norms) are in principle not language bound: if you have learnt bookkeeping skills, or learnt how to manage a clothing factory, to landscape a garden, to repair faulty electrical circuits, or to read an engineer's design for buildings or roads, you can perform these skills in any workplace, even one in which a language is used in which you did not acquire the required skills, provided you know the language used "well enough", and you would probably even be able to explain to someone else in a satisfactory way how these tasks should be performed. Knowledge, understanding and skills are transferable, and can be applied in whatever language one knows, with, possibly, some degree of "re-" training in performing in the other language.

It seems sensible, therefore, that vocational training be provided in the Bantu languages (with high-quality English language teaching), on the supposition that such an arrangement will lead to higher knowledge, understanding and skills; that this, in turn, will mean better vocational performance, which should eventually lead to better employment opportunities; and, finally, be economically advantageous (the higher earnings gradually distributed throughout the benefiting community).

Advantages of using the Bantu languages in economic activity

It is true that all industries and businesses with global objectives presuppose highly developed skills in (mainly) English, and that leading role-players need a high level of proficiency in English. However, global competitiveness (and attracting investment) is only really possible if the *skills* required for effective manufacturing, trading and service provision are fully developed right down to the lowest level of economic activity. The development of these vocational skills will only take place effectively if they are developed through the medium of the Bantu languages.

Furthermore, a policy which utilises the Bantu languages as languages of the workplace can contribute significantly to secure and positive work environments. This can happen in a variety of ways. Besides the emotional security which the recognition and use of workers' L1s provide, the use of a language which is known well by workers can contribute to avoiding accidents and conflict in the workplace, as pointed out above.

There is also a large need for linguistically informed insurance and tourism workers as well as language professionals (text-writers, document designers, copy-editors, translators, interpreters, language managers, journalists, public relations workers, and so on), especially if the policy of state multilingualism is seriously implemented.

Finally, the use of the Bantu languages in the workplace could probably also contribute to lessening discrimination, and even exploitation, and cases such as the use of Fanagalo[8] in the mining industry as communication medium at the lower levels of work, would not occur.

Language planning for economic development in South Africa

It was argued above that the Bantu languages will only become effective factors in economic activity if they possess economic value. However, to achieve such a state their first-language speakers have to acquire economic prosperity. The situation is thus a classic example of a planning paradox: for A to become B, C must become D, but C can only become D if A has become B. A Catch 22 situation, thus.

Given the strong hold of non-African forces on the economy (global and local), it is rather unlikely that the speakers of the Bantu languages will gain enough economic power to ensure that their languages acquire economic value in a natural way. So, the only way in which something can be done about changing the situation is through government intervention, that is through language planning. This is possible if the government is prepared to take some bold steps ("bold" in the South African language political context).

There are many language policy decisions which the government (at all three levels) can take to promote the economic value of the Bantu languages, for example:

a. The government can ensure that all government-developed multilingual language policies include measures directed at economic development.

b. All government policies which have a bearing on economic development and in which language obviously has a central role, such as the *Reconstruction and Development Programme* (RDP) and the *Growth, Employment and Redistribution* policy (GEAR), the labour policies of the Department of Labour, information on taxes and interest rates, the HIV/AIDS policies of the Department of Health, the language-in-education policies of the Department of Education, should explicitly specify the role which language should have in them.[9]

c. Insofar as the government is responsible for (or has some say in) vocational education and training programmes (such as the training provided in vocational colleges, the training programmes of the Department of Labour, and those of South Africa's National Business Initiative) they (the government) need to make it possible that the Bantu languages are available as languages of learning and teaching (see Webb and Grin, 2000).

d. As major employer institutions the government can contribute to greater efficiency, effectiveness and productivity through the greater use of the Bantu languages for maximal intra-institutional communication

e. The government can ensure the more effective distribution of information through the use of the Bantu languages for providing information about health, pensions, contracts, and so on. Equally, it can prescribe their use on all official forms (such as income tax forms).

f. Government services (health, transport, communication, water and electricity, general utilities) must be available in the languages of the communities being served

g. All government development projects (agriculture, SMME's/small business) must be handled in the languages of the communities targeted

h) As major employer institutions, the governments at all three levels can create a large number of language and language-related jobs. The government can demand the removal of all language-related obstacles to appointment and promotion in public administration. In fact, it can demand a knowledge of the Bantu languages for appointment and promotion, it can use them in the description of employment conditions (working time, maternity rights, child labour, sick and annual leave, protection of part-time and contract workers), and it can provide significant tax incentives for employers who make significant use of these languages. (See Grin 1996: 32, who proposes that a set of incentives be provided to workers in both the public and private sectors to utilise the minority languages in their workplaces; see also Bamgbose 1998).

As regards the *private sector*, it may be useful for them also to consider the use of the Bantu languages for more effective management, training, social binding and identity construction (i.e. the symbolic function of languages), particularly if the firm is not managed in the old-fashioned pyramid-style.

Although government can't intervene in the private sector, it can encourage private sector institutions to make greater use of the Bantu languages in at least four ways:
a. by prohibiting discriminatory language policies and practices
b. by providing tax incentives for activities which are directed at the economic promotion of the Bantu languages (and it could even consider imposing taxes on the excessive use of English in the economic domain)
c. by demanding the use of the Bantu languages in contracts for government projects, and
d. by insisting that the private sector contribute to the development of the work force through skills training through the Bantu languages

The labour sector is predominantly non-English and therefore many of the measures proposed above will be to its direct benefit, and workers' unions should, logically, insist on the use of the Bantu languages for all training programmes, all work contracts and all communications with workers by management (e.g. regarding safety regulations in the mining industry). They should also take note of the enormous advantage they will have were they to insist that all negotiations involving them should be undertaken in a Bantu language. The unions have a particularly important role to play, since the greater use of the Bantu languages will clearly be in the direct interests of the majority of their members.

An issue which is obviously of central importance is the likely costs involved in a language policy which is directed at the formal utilisation of the Bantu languages in economic activity.

A cost-estimate analysis is an essential component of any planning process, and is directed at identifying the items of cost and of benefit contained in the policy proposal, and measuring (i.e. quantifying) these costs and benefits, thus providing policy decision-makers with a rational basis to decide about the policy options (see Chapter 4, and Thorburn, 1971, Jernudd, 1971, Grin, 1996, and Webb and Grin, 2000).

It is not possible to provide an explicit, detailed cost-estimate of any language policy proposal, for a number of reasons. Besides the fact that specific policy details and specific sociolinguistic details are necessary and that a large degree of expertise is required, any proposal involving language policy necessarily refers to factors which cannot be expressed in precisely quantifiable terms, such as the participating, separating, bonding and symbolic functions of languages. Examples of such items are the value for black South Africans of a knowledge of English, the cost of combating the resistance against the use of the Bantu languages in high-function public contexts, the benefits attached to a recognition of people's human dignity through the recognition of their languages, the costs of misunderstandings (and possibly accidents and even death) due to inadequate language proficiency, the personal satisfaction of being able to use a second language very well, the costs of language-related labour strikes (and protests against the enforced use of a language in the public domain, as in 1976 in Soweto), the costs of poor skills development in vocational training incurred through the (inadequate) use by an Afrikaans-speaking instructor of English as the LoL/T with black learners for whom English is also an L2, and so forth.

Accepting, for the argument, that the Department of Education decides that learners in vocational colleges in South Africa should be trained through the medium of a Bantu language (see the large research project described in Webb and Grin, 2000, discussed in Chapter 6), one would have to calculate the costs and benefits of such a decision. The cost-items would have to include items such as the costs of:

- enabling white instructors to acquire the relevant Bantu language (alternately, the cost of training speakers of Bantu languages as instructors in vocational training programmes)
- the translation of learning materials into the Bantu languages
- developing and establishing technical terminology and vocational registers

in the Bantu languages
- changing attitudes to the use of the Bantu languages for high-function purposes
- allaying fears about the "loss of English"
- radically upgrading English L2 teaching and learning
- introducing the study of L1s and reconstructing their curricula into programmes which can be significantly relevant to their learners.

Benefit items to consider include better trained workers (with better vocational understanding and higher levels of vocational skills), a more effective and more productive workforce, higher wages for the better trained workers, wider economic advantages and the eventual fairer redistribution of wealth, higher job satisfaction and more secure work environments, the promotion of the self-esteem of workers and their linguistic communities, followed by an increase in the economic value of the Bantu languages, the restoration of (more) symmetric power relations and, hopefully, the possibility of contributing to the resolution of the language-related problems discussed in Chapter 1.

In conclusion to this paragraph, a few comments on the policy implementation process. First of all, one must accept that the realisation of the goals of such policies will take a long time, and will have to be gradually implemented from the lower levels of economic activity to the higher levels.

Secondly, a policy of multilingualism will not be successfully implemented in South Africa if the communities are not directly involved in all relevant respects, for example by taking direct note of their needs, their views, their attitudes and their linguistic competencies; by involving them in the development of policy; by conducting awareness and information campaigns; and by engaging them in projects as part of policy implementation (such as vocational literacy programmes and projects directed at the development of business skills). A language policy designed to promote the Bantu languages has to have a bottom/up component to complement the necessary top/down component.

Thirdly, given the complexity of the language issue and the enormity of the task, a comprehensive and meaningful policy of multilingualism can only be successfully implemented if there is a strong and clear directive from government and if it is overseen by strong government structures with the maximum authority. As Human (1998: 36) points out: large specialised organisations and institutions are necessary if the state is to penetrate society in a significant way.

It will be very difficult to persuade business and government leaders to consider a multilingual approach since they are generally hesitant to embark on ventures with no guaranteed end-product. However, the fact that the continued use of English as dominant language of economic life is demonstrably a barrier to general economic development, the fact that its sole use will not allow the realisation of the country's economic aims, the fact that this country has a constitutionally entrenched commitment to recognising and realising multilingualism and the fact that the country is comprehensively multilingual in character, make it incumbent upon authorities to find creative ways and means of utilising multilingualism and multiculturalism as developmental resources.

The successful promotion of the African languages as languages of the economy will not be easy. The impact of language policies on language behaviour should never be over-estimated (as they unfortunately often are), both on practical and theoretical grounds. In practice, language policies are only as effective as the commitment of the people managing their implementation. Furthermore, language policies are subject to social, economic and political forces. A language cannot, for example, simply be given economic value or social status by decree (or policy, or some other external language planning measure), as it were. In the interrelationship between language and economic, political or social power, the latter three factors take precedence. As mentioned earlier, the economic value and the social status of a language depends on the economic power and the social status of the communities who use these languages. Unless the speakers of the African languages therefore acquire economic power themselves, their languages will remain economically valueless.[10]

The need for research

In order to address issues in the field of language and economy in South Africa in an informed way, research on a number of matters is necessary. These include:

a. Micro-level studies of the many ways in which "language affects the behavior of actors in a market economy" (Grin 1996: 33)

b. The effect on the economy of the opposing forces of globalisation and modernisation as opposed to ethnicism and nationalism (Grin 1996: 34)

c. The role of cross-cultural communication in economic performance

d. The upper limit to the number of languages which can be used in an economic context so that the benefits (productivity, conflict resolution, social well-being) exceed the material costs (Grin & Vaillancourt 1996: 52–53)

e. The impact on educational effectiveness and the economic consequences of using the Bantu languages as LoL/T in vocational training, using vocationally relevant L1 teaching programmes, and developing upgraded L2 learning and teaching programmes (Webb & Grin, 2000)

f. The sociolinguistic reality at grass-roots level regarding:
    –   Language use in the private and public sectors — in labour negotiations, in official documents and forms (what are the domains of use of each language for different actors — individuals, corporations, the state, civil society organisations, and so on), and language attitudes (Grin & Vaillancourt 1996: 49)
    –   Language knowledge and skills of workers, language behaviour patterns, language preferences and language prestige/status in the workplace
    –   The degree of vocational literacy in the workplace
    –   The incidence of language-based discrimination in the workplace (including the preference of employers for employees from certain language communities)
    –   The linguistic characteristics of workers in different occupational domains
    –   Attitudes to using indigenous languages in production processes, and in the consumer process

g. Language maintenance and shift in the workplace

h. Communication patterns between buyers and sellers from different linguistic and cultural backgrounds

Much of the argumentation in this chapter is theoretical by nature, and does not really have the power which will be required to persuade government officials and decision-makers in the private sector to promote the use of the Bantu languages in economic activity. What is required is empirical evidence. This is the rationale behind the research project discussed in Chapter 6, set up by *CentRePoL*[11] in collaboration with Dr. François Grin, a Swiss economist, entitled *Language, educational effectiveness and economic outcomes*. The project has been given the full endorsement of the Department of Education and has the financial backing of the Swiss Development Corporation as well several local funding institutions. This project also has the full co-operation of the colleges for vocational education and training in Pretoria.

Conclusion

As quoted in Chapter 1, the South African government's aims regarding economic development were expressed in an article in *The RDP Quarterly Report* in June 1996. According to this article the government's *Growth and Development Strategy* wants to "eradicate poverty, remove wealth disparities between people, de-emphasise racial ownership, foster rapid economic expansion and, in the process, cement social and political peace" (p. 3). This the government wants to do through education and training, job creation and the development of a system within which the poorest members of the community can be drawn "into the economic mainstream". The point this chapter wants to make is that these aims can only really be achieved in South Africa if the Bantu languages are formally used in the economy of the country.

The South African government has, fortunately, made a number of policy decisions (formulated as green or white papers or as draft policies) with which a language policy directed at economic development can be linked. Examples of these are the *Growth, Employment and Redistribution* (GEAR) policy, the green paper on a *Skills Development Strategy for Economic and Employment Growth,* and the green paper on *Employment and Occupational Equity* in 1996 (SAIRR 1997: 328). Note must also be taken of the government's agreement with the governments of Lesotho, Zambia and Zimbabwe in February 1996, to empower small construction enterprises and to collaborate in promoting skills, business education and training in industry. It would make sense if these commitments were to be linked to the meaningful use of the Bantu languages.

Given the uncertain attitudes to a multilingual approach to economic development in public and private institutions, and the strong negative attitudes towards the Bantu languages, a decision by the government to support a language policy directed at utilising the multilingual character of the country for economic development could, at this stage, possibly be seen as a leap in the dark. However, the government is committed to social and economic transformation, and has accepted the task of developing and promoting the Bantu languages, and such a leap is therefore probably worthwhile taking.

Notes

1. According to a recent report on poverty and inequality (prepared for the former deputy president) there is a "strong correlation between poverty and lack of education, lack of wage

income, and unemployment". (SAIRR's issue of *Fast Facts* for July 1998, p. 4)

2. The work of de Swaan (1993, 1998a and 1998b) is also of significance in the study of the relationship between language and economy. de Swaan discusses the competition between the dominant languages in the European Union and proposes a measure of the communication potential of a language. This potential is co-determined by political and economic considerations.

3. A tertiary type of economy is knowledge and information directed, focusing on service provision, tourism and education, all activities which require high information content. In 1990, only 51.2% of the economic activity in South Africa was of a tertiary nature. (Mohr and Fourie, 1995: 125.)

4. The difference between the information age and the knowledge era is taken to be that information has become an intellectual instrument, a tool for participating in economic activity. Work activities are therefore more knowledge based and knowledge driven than earlier.

5. The term *text* is used in its generic meaning, and refers to written or oral formats and any genre, such as instructions, diagrams, figures, maps, and so forth.

6. The chief news editor of the SABC (TV) recently reported that the main English news broadcasts contained between six and eight minutes of advertisements as against only one minute on the Zulu and Xhosa news, despite the latter event having a larger viewer audience.

7. Coulmas (1992: 77–78) remarks: "Translation is to be understood as a long-term investment in the interest of maintaining or increasing the value of the languages involved. Since every translation into a language adds value to it, the totality of all translations into a language can be viewed as an indicator of its value. Furthermore, the translation activity into a language demonstrates how much qualified labour a society can afford to devote to this kind of occupation. The Japanese are both willing and able to apply considerable expenditures in order to make scientific insights and literary works first published in other languages accessible in their own language, and in this way continuously adapt their language to the most recent functional requirements." The translation of publications into a language is also, of course, a reflection of the degree to which the speakers of the target language possess a reading culture, and their relative economic potential.

8. The use of Fanagalo in the mining industry in South Africa was discussed in Chapter 1. The fact that mine workers were recruited from all areas of southern Africa meant that there could be no common language of communication, and mining authorities consequently developed Fanagalo, a pidgin which originated on the sugar cane farms of Natal, as mine language, rather than, say, Afrikaans or English. This fact then meant that no mine worker could hope for promotion in a workplace which was dominated by Afrikaans and English.

9. The RDP, for instance, makes no significant reference to language and its role in social, economic and political reconstruction and development, which is a serious limitation, since language is an indispensable factor in social reconstruction and development, as argued earlier (see also Chapter 1).

10. Language promotion projects, narrowly conceived, that are thus directed specifically at

the languages themselves (for instance by organising literary competitions), have very little significant promotional value.

11. The *Centre for Research on the Politics of Language (CentRePoL)* is located at the University of Pretoria.

CHAPTER 8

Giving voice

Language promotion

Introduction

In this chapter the expression "giving voice" is used to refer to a process whereby citizens are enabled to participate effectively in the public affairs of their country through language. In South Africa this was not possible in colonial times and during the apartheid era because the languages of the majority of South Africans had too little standing as languages of high-level public function. The same majority still have no "real voice", despite the democratisation of the country. The dominant language of public affairs in the country is not known well enough, and the public role of the Bantu languages is almost insignificant.

It is difficult to objectify the degree in which a language "gives voice" to its speakers. One way of determining it is by taking note of the number of books published in the language. The assumption is that publishers generally only publish books for which there is some sort of demand, that is, books which they expect to sell. Information about the publication of books in South Africa is available in a project report of the Department of Information Science (Publishing) at the University of Pretoria, compiled by Rall and Warricker (2000), who obtained their data from the South African National Bibliography. The total number of titles published in Afrikaans, English, the Bantu languages, and multilingually for the period 1990 to 1998, according to the report, is given in Table 8.1 below.

The "voicelessness" of the nine African languages, whose speaker numbers total about 90% of the population, "speaks" for itself from Table 8.1.

"Giving voice" to the people of South Africa will require the promotion of the Bantu languages into instruments which will enable their users to develop educationally to their maximal potential, to obtain meaningful access to the economic life of the country, to participate meaningfully in political processes,

Table 8.1. Total number of titles published in South Africa in Afrikaans, English, the Bantu languages, and multilingually, also as % of the annual totals, 1990 to 1998

	1990	1991	1992	1993	1994	1995	1996	1997	1998	TOTAL
Afrikaans	1295	1189	1236	1159	1092	1137	914	782	733	9537
%	28.1	27.0	26.6	23.7	22.8	22.6	21.4	29.1	20.7	23.8
English	2197	2174	2350	2518	2519	2664	2306	2263	2069	21060
%	47.7	49.3	50.6	51.6	52.6	52.3	54.0	58.2	58.3	52.6
Bantu	372	394	361	470	531	710	662	458	401	4359
lang.' s %	8.1	8.9	7.7	9.6	11.1	14.1	15.5	11.8	11.3	11.3
Multilingual	704	630	683	717	643	500	369	370	333	4949
%	15.3	14.3	14.7	14.7	13.4	9.9	8.6	9.5	9.4	12.35
Other	33	21	17	16	4	21	17	13	10	152
%	0.7	0.5	0.4	0.3	0.1	0.4	0.4	0.3	0.3	0.4
TOTAL	4601	4408	4647	4880	4789	5032	4268	3886	3546	40057

Source: Rall and Warricker, 2000: 21

to raise the quality of their lives, and to enjoy their civil, religious and cultural rights to the full; that is, the Bantu languages need to acquire economic value. In order for this to happen, the Bantu languages need to expand lexically, in particular technologically (corpus planning), their social meaning and general stature need to be raised, especially in communities which use them as primary languages (status planning), and speakers of other languages (in the main speakers of Afrikaans and English) need to acquire a meaningful level of proficiency in them (acquisition planning).

Giving voice to the speakers of the Bantu languages is not a process which can be handled in isolation of the other languages. Language promotion relates directly to the power relations between the languages of the country, and in order to promote the Bantu languages, the power relations between the 11 official languages of South Africa as a group need to be addressed (see the diagram of circles representing the languages and their power relations at the end of Chapter 3). So, promoting the Bantu languages requires that the public role of the two non-Bantu official languages also be considered.

Planning for Afrikaans

In language political terms, Afrikaans has a paradoxical history, sometimes being the "hero", at other times the "villain". But, whatever role one prefers to recognise, one of its achievements was that it "held English in check", thus contributing towards a balanced relation between English and the other South African languages in public life. Since 1994, this has changed quite drastically, and there is no longer a natural language political counter-balance to the overwhelming power of English in the country. Giving voice to the people of the country thus requires that the role of Afrikaans continue to be planned.

The decline of Afrikaans in the public domain since 1994 is indicated by its vastly diminished use in government and semi-government institutions and in companies which operate at a national level, its decreasing use as language of teaching in tertiary institutions,[1] the closure and/or downsizing of university departments of Afrikaans,[2] and the strongly declining student numbers in the remaining departments.[3] The reasons for this decline are obvious — it has lost its economic value, it has to "compete" with 10 other official languages for government support (whereas it was the "most favoured language" in the previous regime), and, still being strongly perceived as the language of apartheid, is probably regarded by many public leaders as a target for reprisals. However, Afrikaans is at present probably the only language in the country which can "challenge" the increasing expansion of English in any serious degree. It was the home language of 14.3% of the total population in 1996, is known as second or third language by many more, it is an established LoL/T at all levels, and is functionally fully developed: thousands of people are employed in the Afrikaans language industry (as teachers, media workers, copy-editors, copy-writers, translators, interpreters, lexicographers and terminographers, and so on). Afrikaans is also the main or only instrument of participation in the rights and privileges of many South Africans, it is an instrument of access to general public resources, it is supported by a large number of promotional agencies (some of which are being transformed into progressive organisations, for example, the *Stigting vir Afrikaans* — "Foundation for Afrikaans", which is being transformed into the *Stigting vir bemagtiging deur Afrikaans* — "Foundation for empowerment through Afrikaans"), and there is still a strongly developed ethno-linguistic consciousness among its speakers (see also Chapter 3 and Webb and Kriel 2000). The Afrikaans publishing industry is also quite healthy, relatively speaking. Despite a smaller over-all production than English (see Table 8.1), more fictional titles per year are published in Afrikaans than in English (or the other language categories), as shown in Table 8.2.

These statistics must obviously be interpreted in the light of the fact that many South African authors of English works of fiction publish overseas, but they do allow two interesting observations: that the market for Afrikaans books is reasonably strong, which means that the language has a reasonable market value; and that the Bantu languages also have more titles than English.

Table 8.2. Number of published titles in South Africa in fictional literature per language, with percentages per genre, 1990–1998

	Poetry	Drama	Prose	**TOTAL**
Afrikaans	293	53	2464	2800
%	30.2	10.9	65.6	53.9
English	302	127	545	974
%	31.1	26.3	14.5	18.7
Bantu languages	342	283	635	1260
%	35.2	58.6	16.9	24.2
Multilingual	34	20	109	163
%	3.5	4.1	2.9	3.1
TOTALS	971	483	3753	5197

Source: Rall and Warricker, 2000: 45–50; Galloway 2000

In addition to these considerations, the considerable emigration of Afrikaans-speaking professionals from the country as well as the renewed (post-apartheid) interest in the language abroad has stimulated the South African Afrikaans industry.[4] It is, I think, in the interests both of "giving all citizens voice", as well as the meaningful establishment of pluralism (and multilingualism) in the country to ensure the continued sociolinguistic vitality of Afrikaans. This means, *inter alia*, that it is in the national interest to continue planning for Afrikaans. The important question is: how (see also Webb 2001e)?

The level of "debate" about the language political position of Afrikaans is generally rather low. Discussions about Afrikaans are often emotional, not sufficiently informed, speculative and directed at recommendations about what "ought to be done" about the language. Often there are no arguments, but only opinions, and when "arguments" are offered, they tend to be based upon a one-sided selection of facts. Furthermore, the promoters of Afrikaans usually compare the position of Afrikaans only with English (forgetting or choosing to ignore the fact that there are 11 official languages at the national level), and use the situation before 1994 as their point of reference instead of the post-1994 position. They often also forget that the white Afrikaans-speaking community has no political authority and that its economic power may also be diminishing. Furthermore, there is a definite suspicion among sceptics about the motives of the Afrikaans movement — that the struggle for Afrikaans is fundamentally an attempt by whites to regain lost power. In modern-day South Africa, a "debate" with these characteristics will contribute very little of any significance to the promotion of Afrikaans.

If Afrikaans is to be effectively promoted, a planning programme has to be constructed within an appropriate framework for language planning, as described in Chapter 2. This requires, *inter alia*, that the programme is conducted within the relevant macro-contexts, is supported by the South African government, is rational and is based upon the sociolinguistic realities of the language. Many of these issues have been discussed, and thus need no further elaboration. It is sufficient to list some of the main questions which a promotional programme in support of Afrikaans should answer. These include:

- How can (the speakers of) *Afrikaans* contribute meaningfully towards combating discrimination, promoting equity and national integration, democratisation, the transformation and the reconstruction of society, and the development of all its people?
- How can (the speakers of) *Afrikaans* contribute towards resolving the language-related problems discussed in Chapter 1? Language planning, it must be remembered, is not only about language, but about people, and should be directed at the socio-economic welfare of all the citizens of the country
- What rights and privileges can *Afrikaans-speaking people* expect in the context of 10 communities who speak the other official languages, and how can these "rights" be recognised without infringing upon the rights of speakers of the other languages?
- What is necessary to ensure access to the rich resources available in and through *Afrikaans* to its speakers as well as to speakers of the other languages?

One of the most important considerations in the planning of Afrikaans is that it should be undertaken within the context of the broader situation. This, it seems, is a difficult issue for role-players in the Afrikaans movement to grasp.

Planning for English

The importance of English in South Africa and its great value for the people of the country have been emphasised a number of times in earlier chapters of this book, and needs no further comment. There is, however, a dark side to the picture, repeatedly pointed out in earlier chapters, which also needs to be considered: the excessively high estimation of English in the country is an obstacle to educational, economic, political and social development and is, additionally, a serious threat to the cultural authenticity of the people of the country, in particular the wealth which resides in their cultural heterogeneity. Arguments in support of this view have been given throughout this book. The existence of this threat does not mean that English should be combated in any serious way. It does mean, though, that the negative effects of English in public life should somehow be controlled. This cannot happen in a natural, spontaneous way for several reasons. Firstly, there is the power of English in the global economy, its central role in the information era and technology, and the strength of global political forces. Secondly, there is the enormous status of English in the national community (and in particular the black communities). Thirdly, there are several mistaken conceptions about language and its role in public life, including the belief that using a Bantu language as LoL/T automatically implies the deterioration of proficiency in English. The fact that it is unlikely that the position of English can be normalised in a natural way means that English must become the object of authoritative intervention. The role of English in formal, public life must be planned.

Once again, the question is: What aspects need attention in English language planning? At least the following can be considered:

a. First of all, its enormous power and dominance need to be constrained. English is not a "neutral" language;[5] it is a dominating language, and it can be a threat to the realisation of South Africa's national ideals and the resolution of its language-related problems. One way of controlling the power of English is by the vigorous promotion of the other official South African languages by, for example, providing incentives for their public use.[6] Another is by restricting the use of English in state departments, for instance through some sort of penalty, and by some sort of language tax in the private sector. Furthermore, information campaigns can be conducted to convince parents, learners and school authorities (such as School Governing Bodies) that English language proficiency will not necessarily deteriorate if L1s are used as LoL/T in black communities. Meaningful support can also be given to L1 teaching in the Bantu languages.

b. A second serious issue is the inadequate proficiency in English as a second language at all levels of public life, including the post-graduate levels. The government needs to work towards the development of upgraded English acquisition programmes. To develop such programmes, the realities of TESOL in South Africa need to be researched. (Such research may possibly find that ESL approaches to English language teaching are ineffective, and that English should rather be taught as a third or a "foreign language", with the syllabuses, didactic strategies and the educational materials of such an approach, for instance with more attention to grammatical competence and vocabulary expansion.[7])

c. Attitudes among leading role-models (such as English teachers) to the English of second-language speakers have to be changed, since sociolinguistically unfounded views about "correct" and "proper" English can have serious educational and economic consequences (see Webb 1997). It will be very difficult to change attitudes to English because of the strong beliefs of leading South African figures in English linguistics in the superiority of British English. In the worst scenario, this attitude can be seen as "the imperialism of arrogance", and is probably a consequence of the fact that L1 speakers of English generally grow up in what is effectively a monolingual world, which makes it difficult for them to empathise with people who have problems with English.

In seems, therefore, that in order for English to contribute to the linguistic transformation of South Africa, some form of affirmative action is required.

Promoting the Bantu languages

A major theme of this book has been that South Africa's transformation, reconstruction and development is at least partly dependent on the public role of the Bantu languages. This requires that the promotion of the Bantu languages be given more attention than Afrikaans and English. If this does not happen, the individual and social development of the majority of the people of the country will be constrained, there could be a continuation of discrimination, manipulation and exploitation, there could be an increase in ethnolinguistic tension in the country and there could be a loss of the country's cultural diversity, as argued earlier.

Following Cooper, 1989, the problem is that the Bantu languages have not been adequately equipped to fulfil any developmental role. They are not linguistically sufficiently adapted (corpus planning), they do not have the necessary meaning or stature (status planning), and they are not known well enough by people who are presently central in each of the major domains (acquisition planning).

The unsatisfactory position of the Bantu languages is manifested, as in the case of Afrikaans, by the enormous decline in the study of the Bantu languages at tertiary level. According to a newspaper report (*Sunday Times*, 4/3/2001,

p. 2), the number of undergraduate students in the Department of African Languages at the University of South Africa dropped from 25 000 in 1997 to 3000 in 2001, whilst their post-graduate student numbers declined from 511 to 53. "Other institutions", the article reports, "confirmed an annual decline of 50%". The situation is particularly bad at the so-called historically black universities (HBU's), generally located within rural, wholly black communities in the country. Student numbers in Departments of African Languages at these universities are extraordinarily low. Given the 1996 Constitution, with its philosophy of pluralism and its language stipulations, this decline verges on the incredible. Drastic language planning action is obviously essential.

Several policy proposals relating to the promotion of the Bantu languages have already been made, and this chapter will therefore mainly be a recapitulation of issues discussed in preceding chapters, with the purpose of making the relevant issues explicit within the framework of the language promotion process.

The following aspects will be discussed: the basic requirement for effective language promotion and the potential contribution of language planning to language promotion, a strategic analysis of the current situation, and a promotional programme.

The basic requirement for effective language promotion

As was pointed out in Chapter 2, language planning, as such, cannot contribute much to the process of language promotion, in and of itself. The prerequisite for the valorization of a language is that the stature of its first-language speakers must increase. Communities need to become successful and acquire self-esteem as well as esteem in the eyes of out-groups. In a Western context, this occurs through achieving political and economic success. When *communities* achieve economic and political power, entities associated with these communities, such as their languages, obviously acquire associated stature.

Accepting this view of language valorisation does not mean that language planning is without value. On the contrary, it can create a necessary supportive and enabling environment, for instance the development of an ethnolinguistic awareness, and can bring about a situation which will add value to languages, so that their speakers develop a sense of self-worth and a feeling of ownership, and become socio-psychologically secure in and through their languages. When this happens, these languages will be used more readily in educational, economic, political and social domains and their speakers will begin to participate in the public affairs of their communities in their own languages. Then they can be said to have *acquired voice.*

A strategic analysis of the politics of the Bantu languages

In order to plan the promotion of the Bantu languages effectively, it is necessary to have a full strategic analysis of each language within the contexts relevant to their use and to analyse and interpret the collected information from a language planning perspective, as described in Chapter 2. This process is presented in a revised format in Figure 8.1.

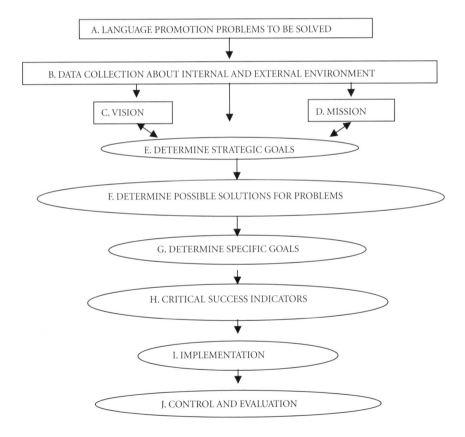

Figure 8.1. Diagram of the strategic planning process

A comprehensive discussion of the strategic planning process for the linguistic transformation of the Bantu languages will not be presented. The following discussion contains preliminary remarks, following the pattern described in Figure 8.1.

A. Problems to be resolved

Some of the basic problems which have to be addressed in the promotion of the Bantu languages are:

- their lack of the status required for use in modern-day urban society, their lack of economic value, and the resistance against their use in high-function public domains
- the possibility that the forces of modernisation and Westernisation will lead to an alienation between rural and urban speakers of a language, with the longer-term consequence of a "loss of a sense of origin, of roots"
- their lack of adaptation to meet the demands of modern technology, e.g. in vocational training and on the internet
- the dominance of English
- the potential for language-internal conflict
- the general lack of Bantu language knowledge by personnel in management positions
- a general inadequate understanding of the fundamental role of (first) languages in public life
- a lack of interest among L1 learners in the study of these languages at all levels
- a lack of political will among almost all leaders to promote these languages
- a lack of commitment among leading officials in state departments to promote them
- a fear of the costs which the promotion of these languages is expected to involve, and
- a fear that the promotion of the Bantu languages will reintroduce Apartheid

Comments upon the first and the last four of these problems follow below.

B. Collection of information about the external and the internal environment

To resolve the problems listed above, information on the following issues is necessary:

External to the promotion of the languages
- the macro-contexts relevant to the promotion of the Bantu languages

- the demands of the information age and the knowledge era, globalisation, increasing technological advances, and the need for "multiskilling"
- a description of educational development in South Africa, in particular the need for technological and vocational education and training
- the language political relations between the Bantu languages, Afrikaans and English
- the needs and requirements of the workplace of the future

Internal to the language promotion programme
- the needs and wants of speakers from the various communities in terms of linguistic knowledge and skills
- the sociolinguistic character of each of the Bantu languages (speaker numbers, the knowledge of the Bantu languages among speakers of languages other than the Bantu languages, attitudes to these languages in all the relevant communities, their standardisation and their codification, etc.; see also Chapter 3)
- language learning aspects: syllabuses, learning materials, didactic approaches
- language management support structures
- the extent of the support of language services, such as lexicographical units, terminographical development, editing, translation and interpretation services

Information on these topics must still be collected. *CentRePoL* is in the process of constructing a sociolinguistic profile of the Bantu languages and a UNESCO languages survey is being compiled for the Department of Arts, Culture, Science and Technology. As an example of the type of the information necessary, see Tables 8.1 and 8.2, as well as 8.3.

Table 8.3. Total number of titles published in South Africa in the Bantu languages by language and year, 1990–1998

	1990	1991	1992	1993	1994	1995	1996	1997	1998	TOTAL
Zulu	61	93	85	91	145	177	200	111	89	1052
Xhosa	54	56	57	107	142	219	141	98	97	971
Tswana	45	40	35	55	56	77	76	57	53	494
Pedi	62	48	31	56	48	81	64	59	56	505
Sotho	51	41	49	40	25	68	91	86	51	502
Swazi	21	33	28	38	24	12	20	6	4	186
Tsonga	27	36	27	45	30	27	26	15	16	249
Venda	48	37	38	31	54	33	31	21	29	322
Ndebele	3	10	11	7	7	16	13	5	6	78
TOTAL	372	394	361	470	531	710	662	458	401	4359

Source: Rall and Warricker, 2000: 22

Further information is needed (for example about the nature of the publications) to enable one to make meaningful observations about the data in Table 8.3. Besides the obvious facts that there *were* publications in every one of the major Bantu languages and that the numbers in each case roughly reflect the order size of the first-language communities, two observations are interesting: that the numbers of publications all "peaked" immediately before, during and immediately after the establishment of democratic government in South Africa; and that there were relatively sharp decreases from 1997. More information is needed to explain these tendencies.

C. Vision
The logic of strategic planning requires that programmes directed at the resolution of the problems listed in "A.", based on the information collected on the topics mentioned in "B." be developed within the applicable vision. This vision is defined by the need to:
- contribute to national transformation and reconciliation
- promote language equity
- develop self-esteem among their speakers
- remove the negative connotations of the Bantu languages by, *inter alia*, promoting their economic value and their use in public domains
- develop the ability among the speakers of the Bantu languages to handle the strong presence of internationalising powers: globalisation, urbanisation and the advent of the Information and Knowledge Era
- develop intellectually through establishing knowledge, understanding and skills, a critical attitude, and adaptability to changing (work) environments ("life-long learning")
- work effectively, efficiently and productively

D. Mission
The mission of agencies directed at the promotion of the Bantu languages includes:
- developing their market value by, *inter alia*, creating language-related jobs
- producing marketable products, such as publications and educational materials
- technologising them
- changing attitudes to these languages
- developing language loyalty among their speakers

- changing language behaviour in their speaker communities regarding patterns of language use and language choice/preference, and
- expanding knowledge of the Bantu languages, their oral literature (also called orature) and literature

E. Decide on strategic goals
Strategic goals could include developing:
- awareness programmes among (government) leaders and role-players in the educational domain
- programmes for educational development, in particular in vocational training and education
- relevant syllabuses for L1 study, and appropriate educational materials
- training programmes directed at the management of information and technology
- programmes to increase proficiency in the Bantu languages among speakers of languages other than the Bantu languages
- ways of reducing the cost of using the Bantu languages for high-level functions
- ways of co-operating with neighbouring countries (Botswana, Lesotho, Swaziland, Zimbabwe), and
- co-projects within the Southern African Development region

F. Determine possible solutions to problems
Possible solutions to the problems listed in "A." are discussed lower down in the paragraph, with reference to the different categories of language planning.

G. Determine specific aims
The specific aims of a language promotion programme is also discussed below in some detail. These aims could include the following:
- the development of explicit language policies and plans of implementation for every government department
- training state administrators to handle language management
- requiring proficiency in the Bantu languages for appointment to positions in the state administration
- training state administrators to use the Bantu languages in performing their work (conducting meetings, writing minutes and memoranda)
- using the Bantu languages on official forms (such as income tax return

forms), government notices and public signs
- making the study of the Bantu languages compulsory in primary and secondary formal education
- gradually introducing the Bantu languages as LoL/T in incrementally higher grades in formal education
- developing educational materials in the Bantu languages
- preparing teachers to use only the Bantu languages as LoL/T, and
- persuading members of parliament to use the Bantu languages in parliamentary debates

H. Critical success indicators

The critical success indicators refer to what must happen to demonstrate that the strategic goals have been achieved. Possible indicators include:
- the increased use of the Bantu languages in high-level functions
- the extensive formal use of the Bantu languages in formal education, including writing examinations
- lower drop-out figures, higher pass-rates and higher average marks in education
- higher levels of work performance and of international competitiveness
- higher earnings among black South Africans
- an increase in the number of publications in the Bantu languages
- more effective public service delivery

I. Implementation

The implementation of a promotional programme (a business plan) is a precise description of what must be done, by whom, when, and with what resources. The content of such a plan depends on the acceptance of specific aims ("G." above), and so cannot really be discussed meaningfully.

J. Control and evaluation

The final part of a language promotional programme needs to describe how the programme's success at specific stages can be determined, on the basis of the critical performance indicators.

Comments on five of the problems to be resolved (see "A.")
Before discussing the content of a promotional programme for the Bantu languages, a few comments on some of the problems that need to be looked at are necessary.

a. *Low self-esteem*
A very important challenge to the promotion of the Bantu languages is their low estimation, coupled with the over-estimation of the ex-colonial languages. African leaders seem to believe that the latter languages are better equipped to serve as administrative, educational, economic and social media, and that they are therefore essential for developmental purposes. The educational and economic meaning of the ex-colonial languages give them so much prestige that it may be very difficult to "replace them" with indigenous languages in the hearts and minds of people. Furthermore, these languages have played such an important role in the genesis of a political consciousness in Africa, and have become the *linguae francae* of national political debates to such an extent that they have come to be regarded as natural candidates for the higher functions in the political arena. This is a central problem for any programme directed at the valorisation of the Bantu languages, that has to be addressed seriously. Given that an African government makes a firm decision to promote its Bantu languages, a vigorous re-education programme and an equally vigorous linguistic and cultural valorisation programme could succeed in placing the relative value of the Bantu languages versus the ex-colonial languages into perspective. (The South African parliament has tentatively set an example by debating a set of laws formulated in Xhosa, and by debating in languages other than Afrikaans and English — personal communication by an MP from the Northern Cape.) As pointed out in Chapter 6, the case of Afrikaans in South Africa provides a good lesson: in 1925, when Afrikaans was declared a national official language (along with Dutch and English), it was a vernacular, that served mainly low functions, with a lower prestige and less adequate linguistic equipment than the Bantu languages of South Africa possess at present. Within three or four decades, however, it was developed into a language of administration, education, economy and social advancement. Obviously, this was only possible because the speakers of the language gained political power in the country, but the essential reason was that its speakers, in particular its intellectual leaders, were driven by the will to promote the language (see Essman, 1987 for a discussion of the ways in which Afrikaans was given economic value).

b. *The lack of political will among the leadership*
Important also is the apparent lack of the required political will among leaders and the lack of commitment by central officials in state departments to the meaningful promotion of the Bantu languages. Judging from language practice in the state administration (see Chapter 4), this is a serious matter. Its serious-

ness is also expressed in a UNESCO report (UNESCO, n.d., p. 121) which suggests that, even though African leaders may have the political will to promote their languages, state and media employees may be unprepared to implement language promotional policies, may have the wrong attitudes, and may be insufficiently trained for such a task. The present South African government leaders must prove that they are serious about the constitution and that they are equally committed to what the current President calls the African Renaissance. If they are, the drive which will emanate from them will surely force civil servants to implement government policy effectively.

c. *The matter of costs*
The question of costs, for example the costs incurred in the development of training material in the Bantu languages and in the time needed for non-Bantu-speaking people (workplace managers, for instance) to acquire proficiency in these languages is obviously an important issue. Yet it must be dealt with insightfully. The view that cost is an insurmountable obstacle in the promotion of the Bantu languages is usually discussed rather one-sidedly. As pointed out in earlier chapters, sceptics seem to forget a number of very relevant aspects of cost-estimation, such as that it is a complex task to undertake; that it can only be undertaken once a clear policy proposal has been formulated; that there are invariably also benefits which need to be taken into account (often difficult to quantify, but of real significance at any rate), and that the costs of promoting the Bantu languages have to be weighed up against the costs of a continuation of the low levels of educational development and the consequent low levels of economic performance (leading, *inter alia*, to a continuation of the present high levels of poverty). Furthermore, some of the costs may be reduced through the use of modern reproduction facilities, and by interstate co-operation, for example with Lesotho, Swaziland, Botswana, Mozambique and Zimbabwe (see also Chapter 7).

d. *The promotion of the Bantu languages and the concomitant promotion of Apartheid*
There is a quite common fear that the promotion of the Bantu languages may lead to the renewed isolation of black communities, their exclusion from international developments in science and technology, and increased conflict (by giving rise to ethnic conflict, or by creating the impression of wanting to divide people in order to control them). Therefore, it is argued, the ex-colonial languages are necessary for the maintenance of order. However, the use of the Bantu languages does not imply the improper or self-disadvantaging diminu-

tion of the role of English in South African public life or the neglect of any of the languages that allow international communication or give access to popular forms of recreation and international science and technology. The case of Afrikaans, once again, is an appropriate counter-example to this fear, as are the many lesser used European languages like Danish, Dutch, Greek and Norwegian. Furthermore, in spite of the aberrations of the apartheid ideology, ethnic awareness is a reality which exists all over the world, also in Africa. Even in South Africa ethnicity existed before the statutory emergence of apartheid. Besides, ethnicity may be a positive force in the life of a national community. The role of ethnicity has to be handled in such a way that its negative effects are neutralized and its positive effects stimulated. This could be done by the acceptance of statutory measures creating a climate of "diversity in unity", and by establishing a culture in which the differences between people are not seen as threats but as sources of enrichment (as discussed in Chapter 5).

The contents of a language promotion programme

As is generally known, language promotion can be facilitated through status, corpus and acquisition planning (Cooper, 1989).

Status planning

Although languages cannot be "given" status, there are a number of measures authoritative persons and institutions can take to facilitate status acquisition. These involve decisions regarding the use of the Bantu languages in higher (or secondary) functions. Examples are as follows:

Statutory and governmental measures
A necessary (though insufficient) strategy for the promotion of a language is its statutory designation as an official language, a national language, a language of the court, the media and education in state-controlled schools. Much of this has been done with the Bantu languages in South Africa, but it is clearly not enough. An essential requirement is the determination to *implement* such a language ideology, as expressed, for example, in language laws, policy formulations, policy directives, and decrees about the official use of languages. This has not been done adequately in South Africa.

The effectiveness of government intervention can be illustrated with two examples from Africa. The first comes from Tanzania. After independence in 1961 and until 1967 English was the major language of official business, the legislature, the court, education, the mass media, and trade and commerce. The Arusha Declaration of 1967, however, oriented the country towards "the people" and Kiswahili was immediately employed for mass mobilization and for the creation of political awareness, and was consciously developed as a symbol of nationalism and patriotism. At the same time a political campaign was begun to discredit English, terming it a "colonial hangover". Kiswahili was made an official language at national level, civil servants were instructed to use Kiswahili,[8] Kiswahili was used as medium of instruction in primary schools and for the teaching of Political Education and Kiswahili in the secondary schools. A task force was also established to plan for the use of Kiswahili as medium of instruction in the secondary schools by 1974. Kiswahili thus came to be used for most of official business, lower education, most of the mass media, trade and commerce, and the primary courts. Today Kiswahili is the "language of national prestige, modernity, the national lingua franca, the language of social promotion and wider acceptance" (Batibo, 1992), and, says Fasold (1984: 274), the language of national unity, i.e. "being Tanzanian". The forceful promotion of Kiswahili led to a decline in the general knowledge of English, which had negative consequences for the country. However, this changed after 1985, as Batibo (1992) reports, when socialism was relaxed, a free market economy was introduced, and the administration was decentralized. There is now a new appreciation of both English and the ethnic languages. The lesson to be learnt from the Tanzanian experience is, therefore, that a balanced language policy must be constructed, and that the value of a world language needs to be officially recognised and supported, in addition to the promotion of the indigenous languages.

The second example comes from Somalia. Although Somalia recently experienced very serious internal political strife, the attempts to promote Somali in the early seventies remains an impressive example of language promotion (Griefenow-Mewis 1992: 127–134). Before the Second World War the Somali's were mainly nomads and farmers, and the country was thinly populated, with few towns. English, Italian and Arabic were used for all public functions. Somali had not been "modernised", and was even without an official orthography. In January 1973 the government announced that Somali would become the official language and the language of education. By May 1974 illiteracy had been largely overcome, and by 1978 Somali was the sole official language and the medium of instruction up to Grade 12.

The obvious question, of course, is how this remarkable feat was achieved. According to Griefenow-Mewis, the following strategies were employed: the nationalization of printing shops and private schools, a three-month course for teaching all teachers, ministry officials, journalists and military personnel to read and write in Somali, a vast expansion of schools and pupils (an increase of 146% in pupil numbers in three years), intensive programmes for teacher training, the use of volunteers from the National Services as teachers throughout the country, programmes for adult education in factory plants and residential areas, a central co-ordinating committee for literacy as well as anti-illiteracy committees in every district, village, army camp and prison, and the use of 20 000 students, teachers, medical, veterinary personnel and agricultural officers in the literacy campaign among the nomads. The reasons for the Somalian success (albeit temporary) lay in three factors: the determination of the government to succeed, the linguistic homogeneity of the country, and the presence of a strong feeling of nationalism in the country.

The point with the Somalian example is not to suggest that the South African government should adopt the same strategies. It can, however, learn from them about the power of political determination. Since 1994, political and military power in South Africa has been completely in the hands of black South Africans, with the ANC obtaining a two-thirds majority in the 1999 election. Black South Africans head the South African National Defence Force and the South African Police Department, every state department including the Department of Education, and also the public broadcasting system. In addition, the constitution provides explicit support for the promotion of the Bantu languages, and there is a reasonable supply of language planning expertise in the country.

The South African government can at least decide to use the Bantu languages for daily activities in the state administration, in government services at local, regional and national level, for communication with the general public (such as for the dissemination of information on national health), as requirements for appointment and promotion in the civil service, and on road signs and tax forms. It can also provide support for the use of these languages in high-function publications (for example through subsidies), and through the creation of occupational opportunities for translators and interpreters in these languages.

The hesitancy of the South African government to provide determined and vigorous support for the promotion of the indigenous languages is not really surprising in the context of Africa. African governments often express their support of the African languages. In 1975 the Intergovernmental Conference on Cultural Policies in Africa, organized by UNESCO with the co-operation of the Organization of African Unity in Accra "recognized and affirmed the irreplaceable role of African languages in any development policy", recommending, *inter alia*, that African states should "choose one or more national languages, gradually increase the use of African languages as vehicles of instruction, establishing departments of African linguistics, setting up specialized language institutions ... supporting literacy training in African languages and collecting oral literature". (UNESCO, n.d.: 16) A similar point of view was taken by the African Ministers of Education in 1976, who also underlined the role of African languages in education. Extensive support has been provided by UNESCO. In 1972 it adopted a ten-year plan to promote these languages, followed in 1978 by a similar decision in Niamey and, more recently, with *Project Horizon 2000*. As a consequence of these views several African countries (like Benin, Ghana, Guinea, Nigeria and Togo) began promoting their indigenous languages strongly. Under Sekou Touré, for example, Guinea recognized eight languages as national languages, and urged their linguistic description and the development of teaching materials and literacy programmes in them. In Ghana nine national languages were recognized, and in Tanzania — one of three African states with a non-colonial language as the medium of official administration, and so on — Swahili was proclaimed a national and an official language. However, these very positive views about the issue and the resultant moves to promote African languages have not been kept up in practice. Romaine (1991: 246), when referring to the failure of African states to promote their indigenous languages meaningfully, quotes A. Mazrui, who pointed out that "post-colonial African governments in fact introduced English at an *earlier* level in the educational system than the British themselves had done" (emphasis added). The following comment by Griefenow-Mewis (1992: 121), though it deals with educational issues, is worth considering in a debate on the promotion of the Bantu languages: she refers to power hungry politicians, writing that "African politicians, who are merely interested in securing the economic and political positions of their own social group, their family or ethnic community ... consider education for their compatriots worthwhile only within the framework which is absolutely necessary in economic terms. They are aware that the basis of their own power is the maintenance of the educational privilege ...". Romaine (1992: 245) makes a similar point. She writes: "In many ... newly independent (African) colonies it has been difficult to oust the colonial language … because it had become the language of indigenous élites, who see it as a way of consolidating their access to the state machinery …". There is no reason to suppose that these observations are applicable to political leaders in South Africa, especially since the ruling ANC have committed themselves to a government of national unity. However, it is a point worth keeping in mind in general terms.

An increase in the economic value of a language

One of the most important determinants of the fate of a language is its economic value, as pointed out in Chapter 7. The most effective way of promoting a language is, arguably, by increasing the economic success of the speakers of that language.

The importance of the economic value of a language is nicely illustrated in Belgium, as is pointed out by Willemyns (1992) as well as Deprez and Wynants (1990). Whereas French has always had a higher status than Dutch in Belgium (as is witnessed by bilingualism patterns: more Flemish were bilingual than Walloons), the industrial development in Flanders caused a shift in the economic centre of gravity towards Flanders (followed by a shift in the political, social and cultural balance of power). As a result Dutch gained in social status in the Walloon community — evidenced by the "ever-growing numbers of non-Dutch-speaking children … in the Flemish kindergartens and primary schools of Brussels" (Deprez and Wynants, 1990: 43).

The connection between language promotion and the economic situation in a country is also illustrated by Kiswahili. Originally, Kiswahili was used only along the coast, but was later used along the trade routes into the interior of the country, and so became the economically dominant language. In this way it eventually became — as a second language, the language of national communication in Tanzania.

The Bantu languages of South Africa also need to achieve economic value. Though this can only really happen when they acquire increased economic power, language planning *can* contribute to the process, for example if the Bantu languages become (or are "made") essential in the work-place at all levels, if a knowledge of them is demanded for access to job opportunities, especially for particular occupations (e.g. teachers and government officials, security services, hospitals, the registration of lawyers, and so on), for promotional purposes and for salary increases. (In Guinea no one can enter the civil service or be elected to any rank in the ruling party without passing an examination in one of their six national languages, UNESCO, p. 138). Eventually, the

Bantu languages should also, of course, become languages of private enterprise (see Chapter 7).

Educational value

The Bantu languages must gradually be developed into indispensable instruments of educational development, as was discussed quite fully in Chapter 6.

An important consideration in the context of education is the role (responsibility?) of universities who serve mainly black communities. As institutions with a clearly defined community service commitment (in addition to their teaching and research tasks), the "historically black universities" need to provide specific support for the languages of these communities. For example: historically Afrikaans universities" generally regarded their departments of Afrikaans as their "flagships", providing them with strong support, well-trained staff and funding for research work. This should clearly be a priority for the HBU's too.

Social value

As regards the development of positive attitudes towards the Bantu languages in South Africa, one needs to keep in mind that positive language attitudes cannot be directly engineered. One cannot force people to feel positive about their languages, or to have a strong feeling of language loyalty. However, it is possible to create an environment which will be supportive of promoting language loyalty, and to find ways of emphasising the positive cultural meanings of these languages. This can be done by several means, for example:

a. By using the school, one of the basic institutions for socialisation in a state, and particularly the language syllabuses to enhance the positive cultural meaning of the languages (see Chapter 6). Valorization presupposes the re-education of a community's citizens, persuading them of the value of their languages and instilling some linguistic pride. The school (and other institutions which transmit the norms, values, beliefs and attitudes of a community) is therefore important[9]

b. By the use, the frequent recognition and expression of appreciation for the value of the Bantu languages by high profile public figures, stressing their importance in promoting national integration, stressing their value for maximal educational development and stressing their role in cultural expression

c. By strongly encouraging the collection of oral literature and the production of literature (also through translations of the best works into and out of the Bantu languages), for example by the establishment of substantial prizes for excellent achievements in this domain. In South Africa, with its strong awareness of the importance of arts and culture, it is feasible that an awareness of cultural wealth could be established in cultural centres, or "community colleges", which can be tasked to collect oral literature (folk tales), record them, and produce plays which are based upon the cultural heritage of the communities

The value of external measures must obviously not be over-estimated. Although they can contribute to the increased status of a language, no amount of formal or external effort to promote a language will have any practical effect unless the speakers of a language *want* to promote their language.

The cultural value of language
There is little doubt that the Bantu languages of South Africa have clear cultural value, since they are central instruments for practising particular cultural acts, and since they are symbols of cultural identity. In the case of Zulu there is even a strong link with "a glorious past". It is reasonably certain that speakers of Bantu languages experience some feelings of loyalty towards them, and that these languages somehow function as symbols of solidarity and distinctiveness (*us* against *them*), thus subconsciously playing a role in *identity construction*. There are signs of emerging ethnolinguistic consciousness (for instance accusations of urban languages being impure, tainted and without integrity), and an awareness in some communities of being "different" (even though their members may not be clear about what these "imagined" differences are).

There are a number of problems regarding the cultural meaning of the Bantu languages which need consideration from a language promotion perspective. One is the possible association of ethno-linguistic consciousness with the segregationist thinking of apartheid, and the other is the rural-urban split, with many young people in urban areas regarding the Bantu languages as symbols of traditionalism and conservatism (even "backwardness"). In black communities it is generally the mixed varieties of the cities (such as Tsotsitaal, isiSoweto and so on) which symbolise progressiveness and modernity, being "with-it" (Schuring 1983). (In Afrikaans a similar situation evolved, as Ponelis, 1992 has described.)

It is important in language promotion programmes to ensure a balance between the promotion of cultural identities and linguistic (or cultural) nationalism, even imperialism. The threat of language-related ethnicism, so real in Africa, has somehow got to be controlled, most likely by legislative means.

Corpus planning

There are a number of corpus planning issues in the Bantu languages which need serious attention if these languages are to be effective for use in high-level functions.

Firstly, there is the demarcation and denomination of the Bantu languages. As pointed out in Chapter 1, the languages in both the Sotho and the Nguni subgroups (Pedi, Tswana and Sotho, and Zulu, Xhosa, Swazi and Ndebele, respectively) came into existence on the basis of the translation of the Bible by rival missionaries, and, later, within the context of political policies. Before the arrival of white groups in the interior of the country (first quarter of the 19th century), these language communities (along with the Tsonga and Venda) did not exist as identifiable languages in the way they do today. The history of their "unification" has not as yet been researched and described adequately, and so it is not really possible to decide whether problems may arise in this connection in the future. However, most of these languages are dialectically quite diverse and it is said that there are dialects in Pedi which differ more from each other than standard Pedi differs from standard Tswana. It is possible that the lack of "linguistic integrity" and "authenticity" in "Tswana" and Pedi" may later have language political consequences.

A second issue, which may be a consequence of the first, is that the Bantu languages are not yet standardised in the full sense of the concept. There have been attempts at establishing standard varieties, and norms for appropriate lexical usage, grammatical structure, pronunciation and orthographical practice have been described. However, the so-called standard varieties have not been accepted across their communities and unlike Afrikaans and English are not widely used. The Swazi community, for instance, used Zulu in their schools until quite recently. According to the post-graduate work being undertaken by Ms. Bonang Mfila at the University of Pretoria, the same situation exists in Botswana with Tswana, where serious objections against the standard variety officially accepted in the country is heard in certain dialect communities. A large amount of work is therefore necessary on this dimension of the standardising process — establishing a clear set of norms and getting these norms accepted and used across the language community (see also the end of Chapter 3).

Thirdly, and also related to the preceding issues, there is the widespread emergence of urban varieties, such as Pretoria Sotho, Isicamto and Tsotsitaal. Pretoria Sotho (see Schuring, 1983; Malimabe, 1990), it is said, differs so much from standard Pedi that Pedi children who grow up in the Pretoria area do not understand the former. That this may in fact not be a linguistic matter but a social phenomenon (in the sense that urban people may have a psychological resistance against the standard variety because of its association with conservatism and traditionalism) indicates the tension (and potential conflict) which exists in the different communities, and also how complex the standardisation issue is. Furthermore, the high prevalence of code-switching also needs research (see Kamwangamalu, 2000, and Abbey Tshinki's masters work at the University of Pretoria, in progress).

A final question regarding standardisation and codification is the question of harmonisation. As described in Chapter 1, the harmonisation of the Sotho and Nguni languages (an idea first proposed in the 1950s and subsequently pursued by Alexander 1989 and 2000) is based upon the linguistic similarities between the languages in each sub-group and upon considerations of cost-effectiveness. The argument is simply that the creation of one *written* variety in each sub-group will mean that publications such as school books can be produced in one linguistic format for all the users in a particular group (one for the Zulus, the Xhosas, the Swazis *and* the Ndebeles), thus minimising the costs of producing the same work in four "different languages". The (reasonably wide-spread) objections against this idea is generally based on a wrong understanding of the proposal. It is thought, namely, that the proposal wishes to replace an existing language or variety, and that the authorities want to take something away from people that they have already made their own. This is not the case, since the proposal relates only to a written variety, to be used in the production of books. It is additive, not subtractive.[10]

It is essential for the Bantu languages that language development centres[11] be established which deal with aspects of corpus development such as standardizing and codifying the languages (producing prescriptive grammars, dictionaries and normative word lists), providing technical terminology and technical registers, and promoting the use of these styles of speaking; disseminating such information via newspapers, radio and television, the schools and language agencies, thus promoting the general use of these terms in the community; and developing the Bantu languages for media usage. The existing National Language Service of the Department of Arts, Culture, Science and Technology in South Africa, in particular their terminography section, and the lexicography centres which are being established for the Bantu languages are important institutions in this context (see also the discussion of the National Language Bodies in Chapter 9).

Corpus development (or planning) is an important activity for a language community, and is basically not undertaken for its own sake, but for the facilitation of development. This is also true of general intellectual development. This point is clearly made by Dirven and Webb (1992: 5): "The development of the autochthonous languages will support the development of the conceptual system(s) of the cultural community. The conceptual system of a community reflects the community's categorization systems, and the paths of its metaphorization processes (which work from spatial experiences into more abstract or more general conceptualizations). If these languages are then used in the secondary domains such as government, administration and education, the need arises to develop their expressive power beyond the colloquial level of the primary domains. This affects the vocabulary of the language, the terminology for all specialized fields, the morphology (compounding, derivation, composite terms), the stylistic varieties, the written code as such and the metaphorization processes, allowing the *exploration* of new mental experiences in art, science and religion."

The technicalisation of the Bantu languages
The majority of the Bantu languages has not been technically sufficiently adapted as regards both technical terms and the necessary technical registers and styles of speaking. It may therefore be useful to devote some attention to their technicalisation.[12]

By way of introduction two issues need to be clarified. Firstly, it must be emphasised that the term *technicalisation* must be used rather than *modernisation*. The reason for this is that the latter concept is reminiscent of the colonial belief that European civilisation and culture is superior to that of Africa and that Europeans are thus morally obliged to "civilise" the "natives" and bring light to "dark Africa". To avoid this implication this monograph operates with the notion that cultures are *different* rather than one being *deficient* or *inferior*.

Secondly, two South African misconceptions regarding the technicalisation of the Bantu languages need to be mentioned. The first is that the Bantu languages cannot be used as languages of learning and teaching (and economic activity) because they do not possess the required technical terms. This argument is, of course, wholly inapplicable, since the Bantu languages, like all other languages, can borrow technical terms from any available source. The second misconception, related to the first, is that technicalisation can only occur through the *creation of new terms* by the communities themselves, or specialised term-creating institutions (apparently for considerations of "linguistic purity"). Proponents of this view, acting on the assumption that this restricted view of technicalisation is valid, then quote examples of clumsy Zulu creations, suggesting that their clumsiness illustrates why the Bantu languages cannot expect to become effective technical languages:

accountancy	ukubhalwa kwamabhuku ezimali ("to be counted in the book of money")
agronymy	isifundo sezolimo ("to learn to plough")
air-conditioning	ukulinganisa ubunjalo bomoya endlini ("to correct throughout the air in the room")
battery charger	umshini wokugcwalisa amabhethri ("machine which fills batteries")

The restricted conception of linguistic technicalisation is obviously wrong, since technicalisation can be brought about in various ways, for example the semantic specialisation or restriction of words from the language itself or its dialects, the redefinition of existing terms, borrowing from related languages, and metaphoric and metonymic extensions and loan translations (see Johnson and Sager 1980: 98–99).

Besides the fact that the restricted conception of technicalisation is linguistically inapplicable, it can also be countered by examples of effective term borrowing in Zulu (demonstrating that technical terminology can be incorporated quite effectively in Zulu):

acid	iasidi[13]
atomic bomb	ibhomu leathomu
bacteria	ibhakthiriya
bank account	iakhawanti yasebhange ("account of the bank")

In these cases, the English terms have been borrowed and indigenised by rephonologisation and the insertion of the required prefixes and suffixes.

Given that speakers of the Bantu languages decide to use these languages in technical contexts, the necessary terms can clearly be acquired almost at will. (What then subsequently needs to happen, is that these newly-acquired terms be standardised, and the usage of the standardised terms be generalised over the communities who need to use them professionally.)[14]

The technicalistion of the Bantu languages can occur in a planned way, and the purpose of the present section is to describe how this could happen, and whether it could happen in the manner of Western languages.

Traditional terminological development

In general, (Western) terminographers work with quite specific views about the nature of technical language, the criteria for the creation of technical terms and the principles, strategies and mechanisms of language technicalisation. Briefly, following Johnson and Sager (1980), some of these views are:

- that a technical/scientific language is a set of terms and discourse conventions which have a very narrow sphere of applicability in terms of topics and situation, and in which the terms have restricted, preferably unambiguous, precise reference
- that a technical/scientific language is characterized by deliberate attempts to impose uniformity of usage
- that it is preferably an international code, with standardized terminological strategies and mechanisms, using fixed procedures, like borrowing from specific languages such as English, Greek and Latin. (In this way, it is argued, technical and scientific communication across language communities can be facilitated.)
- that its terms must obey the principles of *economy* (brevity of form, contextual independence, non-redundancy, orthographic invariance), *precision* (transparency, clear association of term with definition/concept), and *appropriateness* (systematicity, no synonyms, allowing effective communication)

This conception of technical language, which Cluver (1989: 200) calls a "structural" view, thus sees technical language as an independent sub-cultural system.

The question which needs to be asked is whether this view of technical languages is relevant to the technicalisation of the Bantu languages of South Africa. Are there no other considerations which apply in the case of languages in technologically developing countries?

A number of African scholars have discussed this question in the southern African context, for example Matsela & Mochaba (1986), Cluver (1987 and 1989), and Swanepoel (1989). Matsela & Mochaba, for instance, point out that speakers' beliefs and socio-cultural values should be considered in the creation of technical terms, and Cluver argues against the technicist/positivistic nature of the "structuralist" approach to terminological work, emphasising that terms are rooted in human societies and that terminological work should therefore be approached in a sociolinguistic framework. He describes a "sociolinguistic approach" to technical language as recognising that it is part of the socio-cultural identity of a community, that it has a role in everyday life, and that it has an effect in the community (1989: 200). Fishman (1992) also points out that the acceptance of lexical innovations depends, *inter alia*, on their social and cultural fit: they must not clash with the community's need for political and cultural independence and authenticity. The creation or selection of lexical items, he says, therefore requires a thorough knowledge of and an insight into the complex social networks in a community.

The considerations above are clearly important: Given the specific socio-political and sociolinguistic set-up in South Africa, the technicalisation of the Bantu languages cannot wholly take place in the same way as in Western societies. Besides, technical terms are not restricted to hi-tech levels (scientific inquiry, medical research, financial deliberation), but also belong in the lower-level world of tradesmen, motor car mechanics and carpenters. One should beware of constructing an artificial opposition between these diverging points on the technology spectrum. Below, three particular non-linguistic constraints which seem to be directly relevant to the technicalisation of the Bantu languages in South Africa will be mentioned. They are that technicalisation should form part of a community development programme, that it should be culturally contextualized, and that it should be aware of ideological manipulation.

Technicalisation must be directed towards community development
As an aspect of language planning, language technicalisation must be viewed within the broader context of South Africa's socio-political planning. This means that it should contribute to nation-building, the democratisation of knowledge and intellectual skills, and the development of personal and social self-esteem.

As pointed out above, a contribution of this nature requires that one views technical language from a sociolinguistic perspective, and realises that technical languages do not function in an exclusionary way, and do not produce distinguishable sub-cultures. Looked at from a broader perspective, they do not exist separately from the community. This is true in at least two ways:

Lay people play a role in the dissemination and acceptance of technical terms, as can be illustrated by the use of two technical terms in Afrikaans. In Afrikaans the terminological equivalent for AIDS is VIGS, and for VAT ("value added tax") it is BTW. Both Afrikaans terms are, however, associated with the establishment, and are thus resisted in informal contexts by many people. This resistance is expressed by a preference for the English terms. A similar situation is found in black urban communities in the country, who prefer English terms to indigenous terms, thereby signalling their modernity and their freedom from establishment control.

Secondly, technical language plays a central role in the development of the whole community, and should be viewed as an integrated part of the intellectual life of the community, as pointed out in the quote above from Dirven & Webb (1992: 5). In this regard, Kishindo (1987: 107) points out that people are not "passive beneficiaries" of technical and scientific terms. They are, as it were, actors in the drama of their own development. Technicalisation is both a response to social change and an agent of social change. Technical languages must lead to the intellectual liberation of people. They cannot be allowed to be used to obscure meaning or to be used as instruments of exclusion and elitism, as they often are by their nature. (Refer, for interest's sake to the remark by a presidential commission on LoL/T quoted on the first page of Chapter 6.)

If this view of the role of technical language is accepted, it means that language technicalisation must be needs-directed and that it is therefore important to first determine the needs of the community and then to fulfil these needs.[15]

The technicalisation of the Bantu languages should also focus on technical communication between specialist and lay persons[16] and not, exclusively, on the other two communicative contexts (specialists with one another, and lay persons with one another). In present circumstances in South Africa the priority level is not technical communication between scientists and technologists among themselves, but between technically/scientifically trained people and lay people, as happens in school and in the work of agricultural extension officers, health workers and nature conservationists.

Since there is at present little sense in focussing language technicalisation in regard to the South African black communities on high level scientific and technical research and teaching, some of the strict criteria and principles of traditional terminological theory can be relaxed, e.g. unambiguity, brevity of form, uniformity of usage, the abolition of synonyms, links with internationalism and large scale borrowing from foreign sources. (From this viewpoint one therefore has to disagree with the proposal by Swanepoel and Morris (1988) that terminographers in South Africa should rigidly follow internationally accepted terminological methods.)

Technicalisation should be culturally contextualized

In Africa, technicalisation could conceivably lead to Westernisation, with the eventual loss of the indigenous cultural heritage and character, and their sense of origin, of a "past", of "roots". The impact of modern-day technological and scientific development on African communities could be as great as the colonisation of Africa in the 19th and 20th centuries by the European powers, which had an impact that went much further than political and economic colonisation, and included intellectual and spiritual colonisation (Ngugi wa Thiong'o, 1986). Matsela (1987: 84), for example, writes:

> (The use of a foreign medium of school instruction) generally continues some degree of debilitating colonial mentality with a resultant longing for the continuance of the dominant language, and a seeming blindness to, or fear of what would result from its removal or from the linguistic liberation of the colonial culture it imposes, as well as from its replacement by the younger, more dynamic, even if economically less effective, community or local language.

Deculturalisation (or Westernisation) through the technicalisation of the Bantu languages of Africa is a possibility because (as argued above) the world of science and technology is not a separate, independent cultural system, with links only with the international world. The close link (see also Cluver 1989: 203, 228) between the two worlds can easily be demonstrated with reference to the relationship between technical language and the general vocabulary:

a. Structurally the vocabulary of a language forms a continuum, ranging from the vernacular items, through the technical terms used by lay people in everyday communication, to the technical language used in school, and ending with the more generally localized technical language and the more specific, international technical language of experts.

b. The mechanisms and products of lexical expansion often end up in the general vocabulary, as in the case of the words *lekchera, meneja* and *msaikoloji* in Kiswahili (Ohly 1987: 61).

Although it is true that culture is dynamic and that it inevitably changes according to the social, political and economic forces operative in a community, language planners should be aware of the possible impact of language technicalisation on the cultural integrity of local communities, and of the fact that it may lead to the dominance of rationalism (and the subjugation of intuitiveness) and then to cultural alienation, or even, cultural death. If language planners were not aware of this possibility, and allowed the "law of the jungle" (or the "survival of the fittest principle") to control the fate of language, the rich cultural diversity of Africa could be destroyed.

A question of central importance is therefore: how can cultural alienation through language technicalisation be controlled?

One of the answers is obvious: via language technicalisation from indigenous sources (see Ouane 1991, Mochaba 1987, and Swanepoel 1989: 90). The usefulness of indigenous sources is not surprising, since many of the phenomena for which technical terms are necessary, such as illnesses, plants, animals, insects, and so forth, are widely known in local communities, form part of folk taxonomies and therefore already have names. Furthermore, most local communities have highly specialized registers, for example for traditional religion (ancestral spirits), healing by traditional healers, and the terms for secret emotive and sensitive cultural practices like the initiation ceremonies in African communities.[17] What is needed is that more use should be made of these sources, as Ohly (1987: 6) suggested. (There are many examples of the use of indigenous terms in the southern African Bantu languages, see Mochaba (1987: 140) for Sesotho, and Jafta (1987: 132–7) for Xhosa).

Objections, have, of course, been made against the use of indigenous sources. Swanepoel (1989: 93), for instance, points out that specific terms sometimes cause problems. He refers to the term *isiphuphutheki* for "telecommunication satelite", saying that, before terminologising, the Zulu word means "roaming about in space", "permanently flying object bound for nowhere", and that its use as a technical term requires reconceptualisation. I would doubt that this is necessarily a problem, since it seems to me that technical terms can be created by a conscious decision to use a particular word (or phrase) as a technical term, as the referent for an object or concept newly come across.

A second objection raises the issue of the costs involved. Some argue that public funds should rather be used for research and technical development than for creating and disseminating new terms. Besides the fact that the funds involved in the two areas are probably highly incomparable, it is also a short-sighted objection since it could lead to the continued dependence of the speakers of the Bantu languages on the West.

A third more serious objection against the view that technicalisation should make use of indigenous sources is that in the present political context of South Africa arguments in favour of the indigenisation of technical languages may be seen as a badly disguised attempt to promote ethnic nationalism and therefore apartheid, or to ensure that the control of power remains in white hands by dividing the national community (see the earlier discussion at the end of the section headed **A strategic analysis of the politics of the Bantu lan-**

guages, in the subsection which contains *comments on five problems*). Given our immediate past history this is a difficult matter to handle.[18] Possibly it can be countered by continually emphasising the real motivation, viz. the protection of the cultural integrity of the communities and the rich cultural heritage of the country, and the effective technicalisation of African communities.

Technicalisation should be aware of ideological manipulation

Technical language, with its built-in potential for elitism and exclusivism, is potentially subject to ideological manipulation.[19] This may have been the case in South Africa. In South Africa the terminological development of the Bantu languages was controlled by 10 language boards (see further Chapter 9). They compiled and published lists of terms and translation equivalents and then expected the schools under the control of the Department of Education and Training (which was responsible for "Bantu" education) to use only these terms. According to Nkondo (1987), the terms used in the so-called white schools and created for Afrikaans and English were used as points of departure for the technical terms compiled and disseminated in this way. Although the terminological policy of these language boards and the terminology lists they produced were good on face value, these bodies were seen in progressive quarters as instruments of apartheid and therefore viewed with suspicion, and not regarded as serving the interests of the people concerned (see Chapter 9 for a brief critical overview).

To summarise: the technicalisation of the Bantu languages is essential for many reasons. One of these is that it is necessary for the purpose of national development. To perform this function technicalisation needs to be linked to specific community needs, to be integrated into the cultural character and the conceptual life of communities, and to become part of their metaphorization processes, that is, be integrated linguistically.

How should language technicalisation take place?

Given the above constraints the final matter to be discussed is how language technicalisation should be handled in the new, emerging situation.

It is important, first of all, to remember that language technicalisation cannot be undertaken in isolation. It must be explicitly seen as part of a larger context. For instance:

– Language technicalisation presupposes the existence of a technicalised culture, in which a need exists for technical language

- Language technicalisation in South Africa must be an integrated part of a larger policy of language promotion (Cluver, 1989). Such a policy should be directed at the resistance in black communities against the use of their languages in high function situations, for example as media of instruction, as objects of study and research, and as high profile languages of the printed and electronic media
- Language technicalisation must take direct note of the sociolinguistic features of the South African community, for instance the excessively low self-esteem of some linguistic communities, and the excessively high esteem for others, language attitudes and preferences, and so forth
- Language technicalisation is directly dependent on the existence of a dedicated infrastructure, including training programmes, buros for terminography, schools as disseminating agencies, professional associations and research centres (see also Chapter 9)

Secondly, language technicalisation can only be effectively handled by institutions with authority which also have the necessary legitimacy. Given the present socio-political situation this means that a democratic, "bottom-up" approach should be used in language technicalisation, that is, an approach which directly involves the "consumers":[20] individuals (for example technologists and the people who have to use the terminology at ground level), communities and concerned organisations. The creation of technical terms must occur on the factory floor, as it were, in the context of work. There are, however, also other ways in which non-terminologists can be involved in term creation, as Kunene and Sukumane (1987) show in referring to term-creation competitions for Swazi.

Finally, it is essential that the co-operation of the schools as well as the media, in particular the radio in South Africa, be obtained for the dissemination and establishment of technical terms.

If the speakers of the Bantu languages develop the determination to become a technological society, language technicalisation can be easily accomplished. There are many examples of success in similar situations. Ohly (1987) refers to Tanzania, Kenya, the Arab countries, Malaysia, India and Israel. One can also look at the Afrikaans community, which, having had the necessary political will, created 140 000 technical terms and produced 130 technical dictionaries (Cluver mentions 265 technical dictionaries and lists) in 290 technical domains in little over 50 years.

Acquisition planning

The third and last area of language promotion is acquisition planning.

This area of language promotion refers both to the study of the L1 and the acquisition of an L2 or a foreign language. Both areas are of particular importance in the South African context, since (a) there is a resistance among first-language speakers of the Bantu languages against the study of their own languages as L1s, (b) Asian, coloured and white South Africans generally have a totally inadequate knowledge of the Bantu languages, and (c) there is too large an incidence of linguistic intolerance.

Language acquisition was discussed in Chapter 6, and is not considered any further here.

Conclusion

In devising a language promotion programme, the fact must be kept in mind that such a programme has very little power of its own. External changes to languages,[21] or statutory measures to change the functional allocation of languages in a country do not have the power to effect social and cultural changes. As Fasold (1984: 286) points out: "There is … a vast difference between the power of 'natural' social change, … and the relative puniness of official planning." The interaction between language and society is generally the other way round: language valorization is a function of political and socio-economic transformation. Socio-psychological, socio-cultural, economic and political forces are more basic to linguistic transformation than language policies, language laws or language statutes.

However, it is also not wise to rely solely on the power of social, cultural, economic or political forces in a community. As pointed out earlier, if these forces were allowed to determine the fate of communities and their languages in an uncontrolled way, one could easily have a situation in which the "laws of the jungle" reign supreme. The sensible thing to do is to adopt programmes aimed at educational, political, economic, social and cultural change and then to adopt statutory measures, that will support and facilitate these programmes.

Finally, a reminder that a decision to promote the Bantu languages of South Africa does not (indeed, *should* not) imply that English will have no role in the public life of the state. South Africans must be able to study English for the purpose of international trade and diplomacy, and in order to gain access to the higher levels of scientific and technological activity, as well as world literature and recreation in general.

It is presumably easy to find fault with many of the ideas in this section by pointing out that the costs involved in training and employing terminologists (for research and development work) and terminographers will be large, that there are simply too many languages in the country to cover, that the social status of the Bantu languages is excessively low, that it will be difficult to get the Bantu languages used for high functions (or even as media of instruction in secondary schools), and that term creation and implementation is an extremely slow process, and so forth. However, before these "objections" can be considered seriously, they need to be supported by theoretical considerations, facts and justified cost-estimates.

Notes

1. Before 1994 five of the 21 universities in South Africa taught only or mainly in Afrikaans. Now only one university still uses mainly Afrikaans, and there is increasing pressure from the Minister of Education that only English be used. In fact, a special committee was appointed in March 2001 to report on the issue.

2. The Department of Afrikaans at the University of the Witwatersrand, one of the country's foremost universities, whose Afrikaans Department was one of the best in the country in the 1950s and 60s, has been closed, whilst the departments at Natal University and the University of Cape Town have been radically downsized and/or reorganised.

3. The Department of Afrikaans at the University of Pretoria, the largest residential university in the country, which housed about 1500 students in 1981, housed 387 in 2001 (Willemse, public lecture).

4. There seems to be a growing international demand for Afrikaans books (particularly children's books) and music.

5. See also Tollefson (1991), who points out that viewing a language as "neutral" is itself an ideology (and also Romaine, 1992: 245).

6. Language management in Somalia and Tanzania, discussed later in this chapter, illustrates the possibility of success, provided the political will is present.

7. The rationale behind such a stance could be that the use of English as LoL/T requires a better developed grammatical competence, which is difficult to acquire in contexts where there is very little exposure to English outside the school.

8. According to Fasold (1984: 272) government policies such as the following contributed to the spread of Kiswahili: the transfer of civil servants, for limited periods of time, to regions whose language(s) they did not know, thus compelling the officials to speak

Kiswahili, and the establishment of *ujamaa* villages in which people from diverse language backgrounds lived.

9. There are, of course, dangers in such an approach, viz. the possibility that the (state) schools may be manipulated to promote the ideology of the dominant group, the ruling elite. Obviously, this possibility must somehow be combated, for instance by statutory means (see also Chapter 6).

10. At the end of April 2001, the *Centre for Advanced Studies of African Society* (CASAS) (e-mail: bankie@casas.co.za, and website: www.casas.co.za) presented a two-day conference on "Harmonization and Standardization of Southern African Languages".

11. Such as those of Ghana (the Bureau of Ghana Languages and the Institute of African Studies), Nigeria (the Centre for Language Development), Somalia (the Somali Language Committee) and Tanzania (the Institute for Kiswahili Research, and Bakita).

12. Technicalisation requires two types of activity: (a) the acquisition of terms, and (b) the development of technical varieties, discourse genres. The latter process is naturally very important. In the same way as scientific disciplines like Mathematics, History and Chemistry have their own typical ways of presenting material, and mathematicians, historians and chemists know what a "fact" in their disciplines is, how technical terms should be used, what counts as an argument or a proof, how deductions should be made, and how scholarly discourse should be structured, so there are appropriate ways of handling technical discourse in all areas of professional activity.

13. There is a glottal stop between the first two vowels, and vowel insertion after the final consonant of the English loan, since Zulu, like the Bantu languages in general, prefers a CV syllable structure.

14. This process may have been taken too far in the Western world, since technicalisation has led to Western societies becoming scientifically orientated and technicalised in their everyday ways of thinking and their patterns of living. The Western world seems to have become dominated by rationalism.

15. A remark by Fishman, 1992 accords nicely with this view. He points out that the socio-psychological needs of young people also have to be met, and that there is little sense in stressing the traditional culture to people leaving home to build a life in the big city. A technicalised language should also enable young people to play meaningful roles in the modern urban world. Traditionalism must also not outweigh modernity in term-creation.

16. The effective distribution of technical information is obviously not only a function of technical terms. For example: information on HIV/AIDS in South Africa is far more a question of effective "cross-cultural" communication, than a matter of technical terms. If the world's greatest expert on the pandemic were, for argument's sake, a North European, and (s)he were contracted by the South African government to help convey information on this illness to teenagers in rural KwaZulu/Natal, the chances that (s)he would be effective would be zero, even with a very good interpreter. Besides the style of communication, the authenticity of the speaker, her/his relations with her/his audience, her/his standing in the community, and many other factors, would probably obstruct the transfer of the required information.

17. This practice has been called the "indigenous" university of the local communities, since manhood, legal rights (like being permitted to marry) and human rights (like being an accepted member of the community) are dependent on participation in them.

18. Corpus planning/lexical expansion can, of course, form part of a political struggle. This happened in the case of Afrikaans, with a strong emphasis on purism and a strong stand against Anglicisms, since anglicization was seen as undermining the cultural autonomy and integrity of the Afrikaans-speaking (white) group. However an excessively negative and selective stand against linguistic borrowing can be detrimental in the long run, as Ponelis (1992) points out.

19. School text books and prescribed books are particularly effective instruments of cultural manipulation.

20. A good example is the establishment of the Pedi legal language project. Pedi-speakers who were concerned about the non-use of Pedi in courts of law initiated the development of legal terminology.

21. Even in the case of norm determination, for example decisions by language boards about spelling forms.

CHAPTER 9

Steering the course

Language management

Introduction: a framework for management

In general terms, management can be described as the set of activities under-taken to ensure that the goals of an organisation are achieved in an effective and efficient way. In language planning terms language management refers to the actions and strategies devised to achieve language policy objectives.

In a settled situation, where a comprehensive language policy and language plan is in place, language planning and language management obviously differ, with the latter referring only to the management of the implementation plan. However, in South Africa, where language policy and language planning devel-opment is still in progress, language management has to refer to the entire process involved, that is, from the strategic analysis stage (the identification and definition of the major language problems which need to be resolved, the decision about the language planning framework to be used, the analysis of the relevant external and internal environments, the description of the language planning vision and mission, and the formulation of general and specific language policy goals — see Chapters 2 and 8), through the strategic planning stage, that is the description of the specific plan of implementation, to the actual management of the implementation of the language policy and plan.

In this chapter, a description of the institutions and structures responsible for language management in South Africa will first be given, and then a provisional evaluation will be given of the South African management process guided by the framework described in Fourie and Zsadanyi (1995: 135–165). As a preface to the two topics, a brief explanatory illustration of general and language management tasks will be given. Ideally, the work of a language management body should be used as an illustration. However, the process of language standardisation will be used as if it were a project which needed proper management.

According to Fourie and Zsadanyi (1995: 142) management tasks include planning, organising, leading and controlling, each with specific sub-activities. In the area of language management these tasks and sub-tasks can be illustrated as in Table 9.1:

Table 9.1. Framework for language management (LM)

Management tasks	General illustration	LM example: language standardisation (= LS)
PLANNING		
Strategic planning	Specify objectives needed to achieve mission	Sociolinguistic analysis of the language; define bases for LS, and norm determination. Determine aspects to be standardized (orthography, spelling; pronunciation; grammar; lexicon.) Select members of LS body. Determine norms. Codify standard.
Functional planning	Indicate marketing and resource strategies for achieving objectives	How are LS decisions to be disseminated? (Teachers; publishers; media.) How is progress to be evaluated?
Tactical planning	Short-term programmes	Press releases, circulation of provisional decisions for comment. Arrange information meetings with teachers, publishers, media; include decisions in language curricula, text-books
ORGANISING		
Responsibility; authority	Who are the responsible bodies, and what is their authority?	Ensure (legal) authority for LS-body; determine speaker needs, wants; ensure legitimacy, transparency, accountability; involve speakers in decision-making; avoid accusation of serving own interests. Consult experts.
Delegation	How can tasks be distributed?	Outsource tasks (e.g. educational material). Get expert comments on proposals.
Co-ordination	How can the activities of collaborating units be synchronised?	Liaise with related bodies, central language planning body, education department; joint meetings of LS-units; regular reports & evaluation of reports
Assignment of tasks	What is to be done	Develop business plan
Allocation of resources	Who, when, how	Provide required funds, staff, time
LEADING		
Leadership	Ensuring effective performance	Secure experts as advisors and evaluators; require frequent reports; build team spirit, create sense of ownership.

Motivation	What strategies are required to motivate units to achieve goals?	Emphasise importance of task, e.g. for educational development & cost saving, e.g. on text-book production.
Disciplining	Influencing sub-ordinate's behav-iour for effective performance	Set performance indicators. Frequent meetings; regular report backs on achievement of goals.
Communication	Ensure co-operation among working units	Organise training workshops; discussion groups. Meetings with agencies, speakers.

CONTROLLING

Setting standards	Define expected performance of each unit	Train members of LS-bodies. Ensure understanding of bases for norm de-termination, norm selection, role of standard language in society.
Measuring performance	Reporting on performance	Evaluate on basis of performance indi-cators. Review processes & products on regular basis.
Evaluating deviations	Determining differ-ences between stan-dards & performance	Audit speakers' language behaviour in formal public contexts following policy implementation
Rectifying deviations	Revising strategies	Adapt earlier norm decisions; train teachers, editors.

Adapted from: Fourie and Zsadanyi (1995: 142–160)

Description of the institutions and structures for language management in South Africa

A brief historical note

Before 1994, language management was conducted in a reasonably systematic manner, but selectively. The government had a specific political ideology, a clear vision about the role of language in public life, and knew exactly what had to be done to realise their aims: how the use of particular languages should be promoted, how that of others should be restricted, what developmental projects were required for which languages, what organisational structures were needed, who should be responsible for doing what, and so on. The major concern of the pre-1994 governments was the promotion of Afrikaans (and English).[1]

The responsibility for the corpus development of **Afrikaans**, for example, was given, by legislation, to the *Suid-Afrikaanse Akademie vir Wetenskap en*

Kuns (the South African Academy for Science and Art), which, despite its name, was exclusively directed at promoting the interests of Afrikaans. A language committee of this body determined the spelling and lexical norms of the language (since 1927), whilst a literary committee handled literary awards. The *Akademie* and both its committees are still operative. As regards the lexicographical development of Afrikaans, the government funded a dictionary unit for the *Woordeboek van die Afrikaanse Taal* (the dictionary of the Afrikaans language) which, since 1925, when it first started its work, has managed to cover entries for the first twelve letters of the alphabet (up to the letter L), published in nine volumes, totalling 6 878 pages. A large number of private organisations were (and still are) actively involved in the promotion of Afrikaans, such as the *Federasie van Afrikaanse Kultuurliggame* (Federation of Afrikaans cultural organisations) in Johannesburg and the *Stigting vir Afrikaans* (Foundation for Afrikaans) in Pretoria (which is now being completely transformed, and relocated in the Western Cape).

No South African body was ever formally appointed to manage **English** in any way, although there were, of course, a number of institutions who awarded literary prizes (but not as part of an organised language promotion action). The norms and standards of English were "determined" in Britain. Challenged by the black writer, Njabulo Ndebele (Ndebele, 1987), the *English Academy of Southern Africa* entered the national debate on the norms of English in South Africa rather actively (in 1987), as described also in Chapter 1. English language teaching has received huge support, especially by the British Council and United States government agencies, but also by (private) centres such as the *English Language Teaching Information Centre* (ELTIC) in Johannesburg, and the *Molteno Project* in Grahamstown, Eastern Cape. (There are said to be more than 70 bodies in South Africa which support the development of English second language teaching.) The *Dictionary Unit for South African English*, established in 1970 at Rhodes University in Grahamstown, which was not funded by the government, is also noteworthy.

In addition to these language-specific bodies, a number of state institutions provided services to both Afrikaans and English, such as the (former) State Language Services and the National Terminological Service, both situated in the predecessor of the Department of Arts, Culture, Science and Technology, and the language-specific committees of the former South African Broadcasting Corporation. Language management was also undertaken by municipalities, semi-state institutions such as the Electricity Supply Commission, the South African Transport Services, the Iron and Steel Corporation and telecommunications bodies, as well as by private organisations such as banks and the publishing industry.

The promotion of the **Bantu languages** was regarded as the responsibility of the so-called homeland governments (whether as "national states" or as "self-governing regions"), and the Department of Education and Training (DET, the former national department responsible for "Bantu education"). The argument was that Afrikaans and English were the (only) official languages of the Republic of South Africa, and that the interests of the Bantu languages were the responsibility of the "future governments" of their speaker communities. (Morally, the position of the South African government was questionable, to say the least, since many millions of speakers of the Bantu languages lived and worked in the Republic of South Africa (that is, "outside" the homelands), which justified, one would think, a far bigger commitment, both materially and symbolically, by the South African government to the Bantu languages.)

The pre-1994 governments appointed ten language boards under the joint supervision of the DET and the homeland governments, one for each of the nine main Bantu languages, but two for Xhosa, since Xhosa was the major language of two separate "national states", the Transkei and the Ciskei. These language boards were responsible for the development of teaching material at primary school level, the provision of prescribed school books, the standardisation of orthography and spelling, lexical expansion (terminology) and standardisation, and the promotion of literature in these languages through literary awards. The (complicated) history of these boards is directly relevant to the present language management situation, but cannot be dealt with in this chapter (but see Masunga, 2000). Of importance to note is that they were perceived as instruments of Apartheid, especially in progressive circles, and became totally discredited, losing all their legitimacy. A former Deputy Minister of the Department of Arts, Culture, Science and Technology, the well-known Winnie Mandela, made the following remark in her opening address at the *Languages For All Conference: Towards a Pan South African Language Board* (27–28 May 1994):

> The term "language board", though, conjures bad memories (sic). We are reminded of the language boards of the apartheid era. Language boards which were not structured and created democratically. Language boards which were not accountable to anybody. Language boards which prescribed terms for use on radio and television without consulting the users of the language themselves. Language boards which catered for writers who ensured that their own books were prescribed as setworks in the DET schools.
>
> (Beukes and Barnard 1994: 4)

The final group of bodies involved in language management were (and still are) the associations for language professionals. These include the *African Languages Association of Southern Africa* (ALASA), the *Linguistics Association of Southern Africa* (LSSA), the *Southern African Applied Linguistics Association* (SAALA), the *South African Association for Language Teaching* (SAALT), and the *South African Institute for Translators and Interpreters*.

After 1994, a major change occurred in language management in the country, and it became more comprehensive, with formal attention being given to all the official languages, in particular the Bantu languages, and with a clear intention of handling language management equally systematically, less selectively than before (except for the necessary correction of past imbalances), and on a national basis.

Language management institutions in modern-day South Africa

There are three types of language management institutions in South Africa, namely the legislative bodies (parliament, the provincial legislatures and local government councils), national, provincial and local governing departments, and dedicated language management bodies, such as the *Pan South African Language Board* (PANSALB).

Legislative bodies

Using parliament as an example, legislation, as is known, follows a particular path, described in Table 9.2 in a simplified way:

Table 9.2. The path of legislation through parliament

Needs identification	Decision by Cabinet to attend to the needs	Proposals by the public service
Discussion documents	Green paper	Approval by Cabinet
Draft bill	Tabled in parliament/first reading	Referred to portfolio committee
Second reading	Approval by parliament	Signed by President
	Law	

Based on: Taljaard and Venter, 1998: 54

Language policy follows a similar route. Along this route, the portfolio committee of parliament (and its equivalents at the other levels) is an important body since it does most of the work on bills and policies: it debates bills and policies, consults the public via public hearings and the media, makes recommendations to parliament (even to the extent of changing the contents and principles of a bill), and acts as parliamentary watchdog on all aspects of a minister's and state department's domain: "In terms of the rules of parliament committees must 'monitor, investigate, inquire into and make recommendations relating to any aspect of the legislative programme, budget, rationalisation, restructuring, functioning, organisation, structure, personnel, policy formulation or any other matter it may consider relevant" of the government department assigned to it. (The portfolio committees) are the engine-room of the new parliamentary democracy" (Taljaard and Venter, 1989: 34).

In the case of language policy, the portfolio committee of the Department of Arts, Culture, Science and Technology, is thus of core importance, also as far as the management of language policy is concerned.

State departments

As the administrative executive institutions of the national, provincial and local governments, governing departments house the country's major managers, viz. the directors-general, deputy directors-general, chief directors, directors, deputy directors and assistant directors. In South Africa, the state department which is tasked with handling language matters is the Department of Arts, Culture, Science and Technology — DACST (see also Chapter 4). This is the Department which has to develop the national language policy and oversee its implementation. It is responsible for all the management tasks listed in Table 9.1: planning, organising, leading and co-ordinating language management activities, ensuring effective performance, setting standards and evaluating implementation performance.

A full language management analysis must analyse and evaluate DACST's work in this regard. One has to determine its exact task description, the plans already in place, its organisational structure, its human and material resources, its achievements, and so forth. In the absence of the relevant information, this cannot be done, and only provisional observations can therefore be made.

DACST houses a directorate for language services which "consists of four translation and editing sections for the official languages, one for foreign languages, and a language planning section" (Annual Report, 1997: 26). All six of these sub-directorates are important in language management, but the language planning sub-directorate is obviously central.

In the recent past, the language planning sub-directorate has focussed on the development of a language policy, has established a telephone interpreting service for medical service in the country (TISSA), has presented a number of language planning workshops, supported a rather large language awareness campaign, began compiling a data-base on language planning, and has published a number of reports on language issues. The central issue, the development of a national language policy, was discussed in Chapter 2. As described earlier, a draft bill has been submitted to the Cabinet. However, the Cabinet referred the proposed policy back for further consideration, and this, along with the usual constraints on national budgetary cycles, may mean that a comprehensive national policy may only become applicable in about 2005. Yet the LANGTAG report was already accepted by Cabinet in 1996.

Important, though, is the strategic planning undertaken by the language planning sub-directorate since the formulation of the South African Languages Draft Bill, reported on by its deputy director at a conference in Pretoria (11 September 2000) which dealt with language policy development at local government level (see Beukes, 2000). According to Beukes' handout the sub-directorate has formulated a set of strategic goals, identified special focus areas and developed an action plan detailing proposed activities, actors and timeframes. The strategic goals are: individual empowerment through the promotion of language rights, the development of the indigenous languages, the development of a regulatory framework for language in the public service, supporting economic development, supporting the learning of languages, and promoting the indigenous languages for use in technology. The special focus areas identified are the Public Service, the administration of justice, education, the public media, legislatures and the Bantu languages. The activities they envisage to undertake are the promulgation of the languages bill, a Language Practitioners Council bill, awareness campaigns, audits of official multilingual documentation, a language code of conduct, the establishment of language units in national and provincial government departments, the development of the indigenous languages, terminology development and the establishment of language museums. The actors they intend to co-operate with are PANSALB (see below) and the Department of Public Service Administration. The timeframes they have in mind cover the period 2000 to 2005.

The language planning sub-directorate of DACST has produced the following reports:

1996.   *Towards a National Language Plan for South Africa. Final Report of the Language Task Group.* (229 pages)

1996.   *Lexicography as a Financial Asset.* (159 pages)

1996.   *The Economics of Language.* (46 pages)
1997.   *Trading with francophone Africa.* (55 pages)
1997.   *The Feasibility of Technical Language Development in the African Languages.* (123 pages)
1997.   *Standardising the Designation of Government Departments.* (89 pages)
1999.   *Marketing Linguistic Human Rights.* (94 pages)

The *Translation and Editing Services* and the *National Terminology Services* (which was restructured into the **National Language Service** in 1997), are both, of course, making important contributions to language management. This is particularly so in the case of the National Terminology Services, which produces technical terms and also undertakes training in terminology development. Examples of its work are the Basic Health List in all 11 languages; the AIDS Awareness Campaign Terminology in all 11 languages; the Zoo Project, the Building Dictionary, Primary Schools Projects, the Political and Related Terminology Project in Afrikaans and English, Police Terms in Afrikaans, English and Pedi, and Legal Terminology in Afrikaans, English and Sotho.[2]

The language planning sub-directorate of DACST is too small to handle language management effectively and it needs to be assisted by similar sub-directorates in all national, provincial and local government departments. The work of these sub-directorates should then be co-ordinated by the sub-directorate in DACST.

The Pan South African Language Board (PANSALB)

In the history of South African language management, PANSALB is quite unique: it is a single, legally-constituted body, dedicated to language planning, with a national obligation, and responsible for 11 official languages.

The concept of PANSALB was developed in the course of a series of meetings of linguists and language workers, the first of which was a conference organised by the National Language Project in Cape Town in 1992, and followed by conferences of the Linguistics Society of Southern Africa (Pretoria, 1993), the Southern African Applied Linguistics Association (Stellenbosch, 1994) and, eventually, by the Languages For All Conference (Pretoria, 27–28 May 1994), co-hosted by the former Department of National Education and the African National Congress' Department of Arts and Culture. These deliberations, in particular the last one (which was attended by about 400 delegates representing all stakeholders in the country, and which is arguably *the* major event in the history of language planning in South Africa), eventually led to a white paper on PANSALB, which was made public, and about which any interested party could submit comments during a meeting of the parliamentary portfolio committee responsible for language in Cape Town. Following these public hearings, PANSALB was established on the basis of the Interim Constitution[3] by an act of Parliament in 1995 (Act number 59 of 1995).

PANSALB is thus a constitutionally prescribed language management body,[4] envisaged to be independent of the government (subject only to the constitution and accountable to Parliament), and tasked to act as a watchdog on all language policy and planning issues in the country. To emphasise its political independence, its founding was handled by the former Senate (and not the National Assembly).

Given the importance of this body, various aspects relating to it such as its objectives and its composition are discussed in detail below.

Task and aims of PANSALB

Two reasons are given for the establishment of PANSALB, provided in the preamble to the act promulgated for its establishment, namely that the constitution (Act No. 200 of 1993, that is, the Interim Constitution), provides for the recognition of the principle of multilingualism, and the fact that

> "provision is to be made for measures designed to achieve respect, adequate protection and furtherance of the official South African languages and for the advancement of those official languages which in the past did not enjoy full recognition, in order to promote the full and equal enjoyment of the official South African languages and respect for the other South African languages used for communication and religious purposes." (Government Gazette, Vol. 364, No. 16726 of 4 October 1995, page 2.)

PANSALB came into existence towards the end of 1996.

The enabling act describes the aims of PANSALB as follows (adapted from Act No. 59 of 1995), published in Afrikaans and English:

a. To promote respect for and ensure the implementation of the following principles referred to in the Constitution:
   i. The creation of conditions for the development and for the promotion of the equal use and enjoyment of all the official South African languages,
   ii. the extension of those rights relating to language and the status of languages which at the commencement of the Constitution were restricted to certain regions;
   iii. the prevention of the use of any language for the purposes of exploitation, domination or division;
   iv. the promotion of multilingualism and the provision of translation facilities;

> v.   the fostering of respect for languages spoken in the Republic other than the official languages, and the encouragement of their use in appropriate circumstances; and
>
> vi. the non-diminution of rights relating to language and the status of languages existing at the commencement of the Constitution;
>
> b. to further the development of the official South African languages;
>
> c. to promote respect for and the development of other languages used by communities in South Africa, and languages used for religious purposes;
>
> d. to promote knowledge of and respect for the other provisions of and the constitutional principles contained in the Constitution dealing directly or indirectly with language matters;
>
> e. to promote respect for multilingualism in general; and
>
> f. to promote the utilisation of South Africa's language resources. (1995: 4)

A number of these points are materially (but not in principle) at variance with the 1996 constitution, in particular the non-diminution stipulation (a(vi) above), and will probably be corrected in a revision of the legislation on PANSALB.

The independence of the board

The act is quite explicit about the necessity of the board to be independent and impartial. It stipulates (pp. 4–6), *inter alia:*

> (1) The Board, individual members of the Board and officials of the Board shall serve impartially and independently and exercise, carry out and perform their powers, duties and functions in good faith and without fear, favour, bias or prejudice, subject only to the Constitution and this Act and accountable to Parliament.
>
> (2) No organ of state and no member or employee of an organ of state or any other person shall interfere with the Board, any member thereof or a person appointed under Section 10 in the exercise, carrying out or performance of its, his or her powers, duties and functions.
>
> (3) All organs of state shall afford the Board such assistance as may reasonably be required for the protection of the Board's independence, impartiality, dignity and effectiveness in the exercise, carrying out and performance of the Board's powers, duties and functions.

Composition of the board

The act determines (p. 6) that the board shall have 13 members, plus a Chief Executive Officer who will have the same rights and duties as the other board members.

    An interesting feature of PANSALB is that 12 of its members have to be language workers, whilst one has to be a legal expert who has a special knowledge of language legislation. The language workers represent the following professions: interpreting, translation, terminography/lexicography, language teaching and language planning. In addition, the board has to include five persons who have a special knowledge of language matters in South Africa.

Further requirements include that the members should be "broadly representative of the diversity of the South African community; and be supportive of the principle of multilingualism."

Powers and functions of the board

The act stipulates (pp. 10–14) that the board's functions include the following. It:

1. a. shall make recommendations with regard to any proposed or existing legislation, practice and policy dealing directly or indirectly with language matters at any level of government, and with regard to any proposed amendments to or the repeal or replacement of such legislation, practice and policy;

   b. may advise any organ of state on the implementation of any proposed or existing legislation, policy and practice dealing directly or indirectly with language matters;

   c. may monitor the observance of any advice given in terms of paragraph (b.);

   d. shall make recommendations to organs of state at all levels of government where it considers such action advisable for the adoption of measures aimed at the promotion of multilingualism within the framework of the Constitution;

   e. shall actively promote an awareness of the principle of multilingualism as a national resource;

   f. shall actively promote the development of the previously marginalised languages by —

      i. developing, administering and monitoring access, information and implementation programmes; and

      ii. undertaking such studies for report on or relating to language development as it considers advisable

   g. may in respect of equitable, wide-spread language facilitation services, issue directives on and monitor (i) applicable standards determined by the Board for such services; and (ii) the rendering of such services;

   h. may investigate on its own initiative or on receipt of a written complaint, any alleged violation of a language right, language policy or language practice;

   j. may, having regard to the constitutional provisions and principles dealing directly or indirectly with language matters in general, and to the Constitution in particular —

      i. monitor the observance of the constitutional provisions regarding the use of language;

      ii. monitor the contents and observance of any existing and new legislation, practice and policy dealing directly or indirectly with language matters at any level of government;

      iii. assist with and monitor the formulation of programmes and policies aimed at fostering the equal use of and respect for the official languages, while taking steps to ensure that communities using the (other) languages referred to in the Constitution have the opportunity to use their languages in appropriate circumstances;

  k. may establish, compile and maintain databases including, but not limited to, databases of (i) all legislative measures dealing with language matters; and (ii) every policy and practice of any institution or organ of state dealing directly or indirectly with language matters.

2. The Board may —

  a. initiate studies and research aimed at —

      i. promoting respect for the official languages of the Republic, and their equal use and enjoyment;

      ii. promoting respect for the (other) languages referred to in the Constitution;

      iii. the development of the previously marginalised languages of South Africa;

      iv. the non-diminution of rights relating to language and the status of languages existing at the commencement of the Constitution;

      v. promoting multilingualism in South Africa;

      vi. promoting the utilisation of South Africa's language resources; and

      vii. the prevention of the use of any language for the purposes of exploitation, domination or division;

  b. advise on the co-ordination of language planning in South Africa;

  c. facilitate co-operation with language planning agencies outside South Africa; and

3. The Board may commission any person or body of persons or institution to conduct research and prepare publications on its behalf and may for this purpose make resources available to any such person or body of persons or institution.

4. For the purposes of this section, the Board may provide any person or body of persons with financial or other assistance.

5. The Board shall initiate or investigate legislation, policy and practice dealing directly or indirectly with language in general and the provisions of the Constitution dealing directly or indirectly with language at any level of government, or cause it to be investigated, and may submit recommendations thereon to any legislature or organ of state.

7. If the Board deems it necessary, it may advise the Government to provide individuals or groups who are adversely affected by gross violations of language rights with financial and other support.

8. The Board shall in the manner prescribed by the Board by notice in the Gazette and the Provincial Gazette establish —
   a. a provincial language committee in each province to advise it on any language matter in or affecting any province
   b. a language body to advise it on any particular language, sign language or augmentative and alternative communication if no such language body exists or if an existing language body does not serve its purpose.

The Board's relationship with organs of state

The Act stipulates (p. 14) that the Board should "strive to promote close co-operation between itself and organs of state or any person or body of persons or any institution involved in the development of language and the promotion of language rights", and it may "consult and work closely with any person or body of persons who has special knowledge of and experience in the language problems of South Africa".

The mediatory role of the board

The Act determines (p. 18) that the board has to mediate on matters concerning (alleged) violations of language rights, language policy or language practice, adding that this service must be rendered free of charge. In cases where allegations of these violations are found to be substantiated the board has to attempt:

(i) to resolve and settle (the) dispute; or

(ii) to rectify any act or omission arising from or constituting a contravention or infringement of legislation or alleged contravention or infringement of legislation, language policy or language practice, or a violation of or threat, or alleged violation of or threat to any language right.

Accountability of the board

The act determines that the Board has to publish reports of its activities on a quarterly basis, and that it is responsible to parliament. The legislative bodies of the country (parliament, provincial legislatures and executive bodies at all levels of government), it says, has to take the reports of the board "into account".

Funding
Finally, the activities of the Board is to be financed by Parliamentary awards. At this stage a remark about the financial resources of PANSALB is appropriate. Detailed information on the initial budgetary position of PANSALB is not available, but it was publicly reported as being unsatisfactory. In fact, the government initially failed to provide any notable funding to the Board, and members were not even paid for their services during the first nine months of their work (p.c. by a member of the Board). In May 1998 however, it was announced that ZAR 11m. would be made available to PANSALB. Indeed, the 2000 annual report states that the government grant for the year ending March 2000 was just over ZAR 12 million (but that the 1999 award was only ZAR 4.2m.). Of the 2000 government award, ZAR 1.7m. was spent on salaries and remuneration (1999: ZAR 0.97m.), ZAR 1.4m. on projects (1999: ZAR 0.92m.), ZAR 0.7m. on dictionary units (1999: nothing), and ZAR 1.8m. on conference fees (1999: ZAR 0. 4m.) (PANSALB 2000: 47).

The organisational structure of PANSALB
Given the information contained in the Act, the organisational structure of PANSALB can be represented diagrammatically as follows:

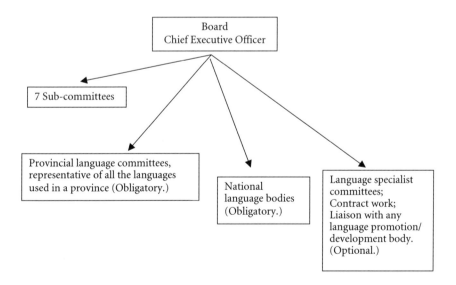

Figure 9.1.   The organisational structure of PANSALB

Remarks:

1. The seven sub-committees referred to deal with: language status promotion; language rights and mediation; provincial and other language committees; language-in-education; translation and interpretation; terminology, lexicography and place names; and the promotion of literature
2. The National Language Bodies are tasked to promote, develop and extend the use of the languages for which they are responsible; promote multilingualism, and survey, record and standardise new terminology

An evaluation of PANSALB

From the description of PANSALB given above it is clear that it has both positive and negative features.

Its positive features include:

Firstly, that the appointment of the members of PANSALB was/is not based on language or ethnicity. There are at least three reasons why it was wise not to base the composition of PANSALB on linguistic or ethnic representation, namely: both features were central bases upon which the apartheid structures were built; language and culture both have a strong conflict potential in the country (which could mean that a language-based board could become a site for adversarial actions); and the constitutional objective of promoting multilingualism may be better achieved by a body that is not based upon separated language interests.

A second positive feature is that the members of PANSALB are all experts. Given that the language issue is a complex question, that it is necessary to understand the political nature of language planning (e.g. the politics of language standardisation), that a great deal of research must still be commissioned if effective language planning is to be accomplished in South Africa, and that the development and evaluation of language policy and planning implementation is a specialised task, it is clearly important that sociolinguists and legal experts be members of the major language management body in the country.

A third positive feature is that PANSALB is conceived as part of the political process in South Africa. As a political activity (though obviously not in the party political sense of the word), language planning must facilitate ideals such as effective state administration, nation-building, the establishment of a non-discriminatory society, and so on. This is achieved by making PANSALB accountable to Parliament, the National Council of Provinces (the former "Senate"), the Provincial legislatures and local government bodies (i.e. the elected representatives of the people).

Fourthly, PANSALB is designed to have legitimacy. It was established through a process of proper consultation with all interested parties, and its members were (and are) appointed in a wholly transparent manner. Its aims and functions are also clearly directed at serving the interests of the people of the country. In addition, it is a constitutionally prescribed institution, a legally established body and a body with national recognition. It is unlikely that the criticisms levelled by Ms. Winnie Mandela about the former language boards (see above) will be made against PANSALB. It has, in principle, the necessary legitimacy.

Fifthly, since it can establish special interest or issue committees and can consult any other expert or body with particular expertise (such as the English Academy or the "Suid-Afrikaanse Akademie") it can acquire professional authority and standing.

During the first few years of its existence, PANSALB was not very productive, and even struggled to set up the necessary administrative structures. The reason for this was the absence of an adequate budget which it could control according to its own needs and beliefs. The situation was so serious that the first vice-chairperson of PANSALB (the best-known language planning scholar in South Africa) resigned from his position, reportedly because of frustration at constantly being hamstrung by the lack of meaningful government support. During this period PANSALB was only really able to make public statements and/or press-releases expressing its concern about matters such as the proposal that English be made the main language of parliament (April 1998) and that it be the main language of the court (October 1998), the government's apparent lack of political will to give concrete support to the principle of multilingualism (in an open letter to the President in June, 1997), and the neglect by the South African Broadcasting Corporation and the South African Airways of languages other than English. However, no official body seems to have paid any serious attention to any of these public actions.

Since the beginning of 1999, PANSALB has been able to complete quite a number of tasks. It has succeeded in defining its position within the larger governmental context, extending its administration, establishing the seven sub-committees mentioned above, and funding research projects. The annual report for 1999/2000 lists the following as achievements:

– The establishment of provincial language committees, national language bodies, and lexicographical units for each of the official languages
– Setting up a regulatory body for the translation and interpreting profession

- Commissioning a sociolinguistic profile of South Africans
- Commissioning research directed at the promotion of the Bantu languages, and
- Handling complaints about language rights

Source: *Annual Report June 2000*: 4–5

Eight provincial language committees were established, their (12) members appointed, and a two-day workshop held to discuss their tasks and their relationship with PANSALB. Fourteen national language bodies were formed (the 11 official languages, the Khoi and San languages, Sign language and the heritage languages),[5] and nine lexicography units were founded (for all the official languages except Sotho and Venda; and with members elected to seven of the nine), located at different tertiary institutions. Discussions were held about language policy with the Departments of Land Affairs and Housing, a memorandum was submitted to the President about obstacles to the promotion of multilingualism, and the issue of the language of record of the court was dealt with. Several meetings were organised, including:

- A workshop on a professional council for language workers (1999)
- A workshop on the promotion of previously marginalised languages (1999)
- Training workshops for national lexicography units and lexicon computerisation (1999)

Several research projects were funded, including projects on subtitling, language use and client behaviour, learners' perceptions of the teaching and learning of Xhosa, literacy, the situation of the deaf in tertiary institutions, a language audit of the Khoe and San languages and the translation of the work of a South African writer. PANSALB received 60 complaints about language rights between 1 April 1999 and 31 March 2000, lodged by private individuals, private sector and state department employees, political parties and voluntary organisations, and co-operated with the Department of Arts, Culture, Science and Technology, the Department of Constitutional Development (on the proposed Commission for the Promotion of the Rights of Cultural, Religious and Linguistic Communities), several independent national institutions (such as the Human Rights Commission and the Commission on Gender Equality), produced a multilingual newsletter and developed an official website (at http://www.pansalb.org.za). In addition, the sociolinguistic survey commissioned by PANSALB on language use and language interaction in South Africa was completed and presented to the media on 7 September 2000: *Summary of the findings of: A sociolinguistic survey on language use and language interaction in South Africa*, 11 pages.

The negative face of PANSALB

From the perspective of what language planning has to achieve in South Africa (see Chapter 1), the main negative aspect of PANSALB is that it has very little real power. Even a superficial reading of the enabling legislation makes this clear: PANSALB activities are restricted to *making recommendations, advising* the government, *monitoring* language policy behaviour, *promoting* language-related matters, *undertaking studies, investigating* complaints about violations of language rights and *compiling* databases. The only "executive" powers it has relate to establishing language management structures, developing language promotion programmes, initiating research on language political issues and deciding on the funding for such research. PANSALB is, essentially, a "soft" policy instrument. If one considers the magnitude of the language issue in the country and the fundamental role language plays in public life, it is unlikely that PANSALB can be expected to make any really meaningful contribution to the linguistic reconstruction and transformation of South Africa. This evaluation is apparent from the fact that, despite all the work PANSALB has completed over the past few years, there is still no sign of significant changes: the Bantu languages still have a very low status among both first- and non-first-language speakers, the parents of (black) school children have a larger overriding desire to have their children taught through the medium of English, the Bantu languages still require serious corpus development attention, there is still an underlying culture of linguistic (and cultural) intolerance, the languages of the country are still heavily politicised, far too little is still known about the sociolinguistics of the Bantu languages, there is still a serious under-availability of language management workers, and so on. Furthermore, the practice of monolingualism (and, in effect, discrimination and marginalisation on linguistic grounds) seems to be increasing,[6] government departments are continuing to develop their own language policies,[7] apparently without feeling obliged to involve PANSALB in a meaningful way (see Chapter 4). Also it is not clear that the Board has been able to assist any outside person or bodies who needed assistance on serious language matters in any significant way, there is no certainty that the language management structures it has been able to establish will make any real difference, its reports are not distributed effectively (for instance to professionally interested bodies) or made accessible to the general public, for whom language matters are of crucial importance.

Given the universal self-interest of politicians, given the economic, political and social forces of assimilation, and given the difficulties of turning a complex situating 180 degrees around, it is essential that a body such as

PANSALB be given as much power as possible, even to the extent of it being able to take the government to the constitutional court. This power it does not possess, and so it is relatively powerless, with no government department, no political leader and no company or firm in the private sector obliged in any way to pay any attention to the advice of PANSALB, that is, to the advice of language experts on language matters.

It is also unclear whether PANSALB has really been able to contribute to making language management a bottom/up process to complement the necessary top/down approach it has to follow. As a body which is part of the structures of state (created and funded by the state) it functions, obviously, in a top/down fashion. However, it is essential that the opposite dimension of management also be recognised, which means essentially that the needs and wants of the citizens of the country be met. How can this be done? There are probably a number of ways, including obtaining the views of institutions that are in touch with the linguistic needs and wants of South Africans, consulting regularly with the language-using public and their language representatives (for example at local, regional and national seminars and workshops), and taking note in a systematic way of opinions expressed in the media (for example by a full-scale analysis of newspaper editorials, readers' letters, news reports, and so on).

A preliminary evaluation of language management in South Africa from the perspective of strategic management

An evaluation of language management in South Africa has to cover the language management work of the legislative bodies, DACST and PANSALB. The main question such an evaluation will attempt to answer is whether these three institutions can guide language policy and planning activities via management.

The nature and importance of strategic management

As described in Chapters 2 and 8 and the beginning of this chapter, effective management needs to be preceded by a strategic analysis and strategic planning. Equally important is an understanding of the nature of language and its interrelationship with public life, and a knowledge of the theoretical aspects of language planning (particularly, an understanding of the restricted role of language planning in society). Language managers need to understand the relationship between planning and change, transformation and reconstruction. Meaningful policy implementation furthermore also requires the availability of authoritative bodies, and staff trained in language management. Self-evidently, the unconditional support of the government for language management is required through the provision of human (e.g. language management specialists), infra-structural (offices, equipment) and financial resources.

Naturally, it is important to remember that language management differs from the management of a state department or a business firm. The former's objectives can often not be defined in the same precise, measurable fashion, and can usually not really be achieved in a specified manner or time-frame, particularly since its main tasks may involve (as in the case of South Africa) changing citizens' attitudes, beliefs, expectations and behaviour patterns, and effecting social, educational, economic and political transformation. A strategic planning approach to language management can, however, make a very positive contribution to an effective enterprise. A strategic planning approach directs one's thinking, compels one to take note of specific aspects in the processes being planned. It also provides a clear framework for making non-ad hoc and non-arbitrary decisions and for motivating these decisions and it forces the planner to build in control and evaluation measures, such as performance indicators, thus enabling one to identify deviations and obstacles in time. In addition, it enables one to determine priorities which are essential in deciding which research and development projects warrant support and funding and which are peripheral to the main task at any one particular moment. As a rational exercise, strategic planning also enables one to rule out irrelevant demands and emotional appeals, and brings a high degree of transparency to the management activity. An analysis and evaluation of language management in South Africa from the perspective of management by strategic planning is clearly a worthwhile exercise.

The importance of a strategic planning approach to managing the language factor can be illustrated by the experience at the University of Pretoria.

The University of Pretoria was formerly an almost wholly white, Afrikaans-speaking university. Since 1990, its student profile has changed drastically however, and today 40% (or more) of its students prefer to be taught in English, which is the second language of most of them. The University has consequently decided to provide instruction in Afrikaans as well as English, and has developed a language policy to regulate the language factor. The *policy* it developed is reasonably adequate, particularly in its recognition of the language rights of the (academic staff and also of the) students to choose their language of learning and teaching (LoL/T). The language policy is also backed-up by a serious commitment to handling the language issue at the university. However, the policy is not accompanied by a proper strategic plan, a clear delineation of problems, a specification of priorities or the collection of relevant information. There is no sufficient plan of policy implementation management. As a result, there are still serious problems such as students selecting an LoL/T which they do not know well enough, therefore consistently performing at least 15% below their potential, or worse: failing,[8] not being able to develop a proper understanding of scientific concepts, principles and processes and to internalise them effectively, probably experiencing a degree of linguistic alienation resulting in a restriction to their participation in academic interaction, and being exposed to discrimination by lecturers because the latter have not been made aware of the relativity of linguistic norms. Many teaching staff members, furthermore, are unwilling to duplicate course work in both LoL/Ts, because of time constraints,[9] thus unfairly "compelling" students for whom English is a second language to demonstrate their knowledge, understanding and skills in English. Finally, lecturer-student relations are sometimes also affected detrimentally in the case of Afrikaans-speaking lecturers who make grammatical mistakes in English and have an Afrikaans pronunciation of English.[10] The long-term impact of the language question on students' future is obvious.

An evaluation

From the discussions earlier in this chapter of the legislative bodies responsible for language matters,[11] DACST and PANSALB, it is clear that an impressive amount of work has been accomplished and that language planning has been seriously handled in South Africa: a general identification of the broad problems has been made, general policy-like decisions have been made, management structures have been developed, a strategic plan of some sorts has been developed, and some of the necessary resources have been made available. However, there is too little clarity about the vision and the related mission, the information necessary for meaningful policy development has not yet been sufficiently collected, and there is (thus) no formally accepted comprehensive national language policy as yet. Consequently, there cannot really be any adequately defined objectives and tasks, a proper plan of implementation, cost-effective analyses or an appropriate budget.

Proper planning in a managerial sense is thus not really possible. This means that a (full) evaluation of language management in the country is also not possible, and one can only make provisional comments. Despite the provisional nature of the situation, such comments could make some contribution to the on-going construction of effective language planning and management.

The language management situation in the country will be discussed under the task categories mentioned at the beginning of this chapter, namely *planning, organisation, leadership* and *control*.

Planning

As indicated earlier, DACST has evolved a strategic plan. However, the information provided by Beukes (2000) is too sketchy to allow a proper evaluation of it. No similar plan has been produced by PANSALB, as far as is publicly known. Any evaluation of the management activities of DACST and PANSALB must therefore be based on the work they have carried out. Is there any evidence from the work they have done, the projects they have initiated and supported, and the research they are funding, that they have a clear over-all strategic plan?

The answer to this question is either "no" or a qualified "no". The issues in strategic analysis and planning (such as the macro-contexts of language planning, the vision and mission within which it needs to be conducted) have been discussed in this book and need not be repeated. Instead, comments will be made on a few *central* issues:

a. *The gathering of sociolinguistic information*

As mentioned earlier, PANSALB commissioned a sociolinguistic profile of South Africans in 2000. The work was undertaken by MarkData (Pty) Ltd., and an 11 page summary of the survey findings was presented publicly in September, 2000. A "stratified probability sample of 2160 South Africans over the age of 16 was drawn from all social categories, rural and urban" (PANSALB 2000b.1) The survey contains a good deal of valuable information, covering matters such as the proportion of respondents who felt accommodated in their own home language in public domains (p. 3), the overall distribution of language use in the workplace and in the educational setting (p. 5), attitudes to language policy (p. 7), and levels of understanding of languages other than their own (p. 9). However, this survey is not nearly sufficient for the purpose of effective language planning. A detailed sociolinguistic characterisation of each (official) language is essential (see Chapter 8: "A STRATEGIC ANALYSIS OF THE POLITICS OF THE BANTU LANGUAGES").

In addition to the preceding information, detailed information on language policy and planning work/projects underway at the various research and development centres is also essential. If language management is to be handled effectively, it is necessary that a register be compiled about all the applicable work in the country, that is, which institutions are involved in the language management domain, what projects are underway and what training programmes are being offered, so that the strengths and weaknesses of the field can be identified. Such an audit has not been done, and inquiries have suggested that no institution is equipped (with the required knowledge and expertise or the authority) or willing to undertake the survey. It is perhaps necessary that PANSALB or DACST elect a particular institution to perform this task, and empower it with the necessary authority and means.

b. *Language planning priorities*
Language planning must obviously be guided by the priorities demanded by its objectives and the facts of the situation. Such priorities can be determined logically and theoretically (that is, from the perspective of the politics of language), or pragmatically (in terms of what can be realistically attained, that is, from the perspective of management). These two lists may differ, and the items they include obviously need debate. Logically, the following can be considered as priorities for language planning in South Africa:

General issues
a.   The need to convince the politicians of the country that the language issue, being directly concerned with development and transformation, is of fundamental importance, so that the political will to implement the policy of linguistic pluralism can be developed
b.   The need to undertake information campaigns (e.g. among the parents of school-going children about the best LoL/T for the pupils, and among school-teachers about the educational consequences of the stigmatisation of languages and linguistic varieties), and awareness campaigns (e.g. to make the South African population aware of the importance of language and of multilingualism)
c.   The need to stimulate debate on issues such as language and power, language policy and economic development, and fallacies about language (e.g. that the Bantu languages can only be used as media of school instruction once they possess technical terms)

Language planning issues

d. The need to co-ordinate language policy development inter-departmentally, for instance by arranging a conference of all organised language management bodies, in order to co-ordinate their programmes

e. The need for the development and implementation of training programmes directed at producing language management specialists

Status development issues

f. The need to address the attitudes towards and the perceptions of the Bantu languages

g. The need to institute actions aimed at depoliticizing the language situation

Corpus development issues

h. The need for the development of literacy programmes in the Bantu languages

i. The need to co-ordinate the standardisation and codification of the Bantu languages, including the acceptance of these standards and their general use

Research and development issues

j. The need to encourage co-operation with researchers and language management experts and stimulate research about the sociolinguistic character of the Bantu languages and patterns of language use, language attitudes, language shift, linguicism, and so on

Examples of a list of priorities from the perspective of language management is listed in Table 9.3 below.

The question now is what the priorities of DACST and PANSALB are. One way in which one may determine their priorities, is the list of workshops they organised and the research projects they funded. The DACST and PANSALB workshops were listed above, and according to these events they seem to regard the following issues as high priorities:

DACST:

language policy development, lexicography, language and economic activity, language technologisation, language rights

PANSALB:

translation and interpretation, language promotion, lexicography and the functioning of the language committees.

As regards research projects:

PANSALB has funded (and is funding):
    projects on subtitling
    language use and client behaviour
    learners' perceptions of the teaching and learning of Xhosa
    literacy
    the situation of the deaf in tertiary institutions
    a language audit of the Khoe and San languages, and
the translation of the work of a South African writer

It is not known whether DACST has funded any outside research.

If this list is compared with the lists in Table 9.3 there is a clear difference. Many of the supported projects hardly qualify as priority issues, in my view. A strategic plan must decide which of the lists and the items in them deserve priority treatment.[12]

Table 9.3. A strategic issues map[13]

Making a Bantu language a government	H	
appointment[14] criterion	I	
Prohibit language-based discrimination	G	
Promote language management training	H	
Co-operate with sociolinguistic researchers		
Co-ordinate language policy development		
Conduct audits of sociolinguistic information	C	
Produce sociolinguistic profiles of all official languages	O	
Promote individual multilingualism	N	
Convince political leaders about language planning	T	Combat conflict — standard/
Standardisation, codification of the Bantu languages	R	non-standard Afrikaans
Develop upgraded English teaching as an L2	O	
Promote the Bantu languages as LoL/T and as subjects	L	
HIGH IMPORTANCE		*LOW IMPORTANCE*
Technologise the Bantu languages	L	Combat conflict: standard
Develop cross-cultural communication skills	O	English — black SA English
Conduct information campaigns about LoL/T	W	
Promote literacy in the Bantu languages		
Conduct language awareness campaigns	C	
	O	
Change language attitudes	N	
Depoliticise the country's languages	T	Contain language nationalism
Change a-symmetric power relations	R	
	O	Protect cultural identities and
Address Africa's intellectual and spiritual colonisation	L	diversity

Source of idea: Human, 1998: 130–132

Organisation

As stated earlier, the existing official language management structures are DACST's sub-directorate for language planning, PANSALB and its seven committees, the National Lexicography Units, the Provincial Language Committees and the National Language Bodies, co-ordinated by PANSALB. Beukes (2000) refers to language units in each national and provincial government department and centres for language development and research which have to be created in terms of the proposed language bill (but do not yet exist). In addition there are the non-governmental organisations mentioned at the beginning of this chapter.

An interesting matter is the apparent difference in the thinking of DACST and PANSALB regarding the structural organisation of the language planning field. The seven sub-committees of PANSALB (for language status promotion; language rights and mediation; provincial and other language committees; language-in-education; translation and interpretation; terminology, lexicography and place names; and the promotion of literature) and the strategic "goals" of DACST (more properly: "focus areas"): language rights, language services, indigenous language development, language policy development, language and economic activity and language learning differ quite markedly, with the views of DACST being slightly more justified from a language planning perspective. However, both "divisions of labour" are rather ad hoc, and neither is properly based on the logic of language planning as a field of professional activity. The DACST organisational structure mixes language planning categories, domains and language service, whilst PANSALB mixes language planning considerations, language policy development, domains of language usage and language services, sometimes grouping differing issues together, and at other times distinguishing between issues which belong together. A more justified division of work would be:

> policy development;
> language promotion
>> status planning (including the promotion of literature)
>> corpus planning (including lexicographical and terminological
>>> development, as well as place names), and
>> acquisition planning (including language-in-education);
> language management (language committees);
> domains of usage (including the economic, educational, political/
>> public service and socio-cultural domains (rights and media-
>> tion); and

> language services (translation, interpretation, document design and editing).

A matter of greater immediate importance is the apparent lack of co-ordination regarding language policy development. As described in Chapter 4, state departments at national and provincial levels (and possibly also at the local government level) each seem to be developing language policies without any serious liaison with other state bodies tasked with language management (such as DACST and PANSALB[15]), with some departments even acting in conflict with the constitutional stipulations in this regard. This is clearly an undesirable state of affairs. The requirement that PANSALB should be consulted in such matters has obviously been ineffective, and it is necessary to oblige government departments legally to co-ordinate their language policy development. DACST, the responsible department, should give priority to resolving the confusion.

Equally important is the fact that there is no definite separation of language-related departmental functions. Firstly, DACST and PANSALB seem to overlap in the work they undertake, and secondly, the Department of Constitutional Development is also somehow involved in language policy development. The latter department, in fact, was responsible for organising the workshop which eventually led to the establishment of LANGTAG, and has also been given the responsibility for getting the *Commission for the Promotion and Protection of the Rights of Cultural, Religious and Linguistic Communities* established. It is, as yet, not clear what the relationship between this commission, DACST and PANSALB will be and how their functions are to differ.

It is common sense that all language management bodies in the country, both state-controlled and private, university research and development centres as well as NGOs must somehow be integrated into a network of institutions which co-operate to achieve the national objectives. This should not be taken to mean that there should be more central control, but duplication, fragmentation, bureaucracy and waste must somehow be avoided, and the available resources (expertise, time, energy, funding) effectively used.

Serious attention is also needed to develop tertiary level formal training facilities for language managers (courses/programmes, training bodies, syllabuses, appropriate training norms and standards, incentives, and so on), that is for language planners, translators, interpreters, lexicographers, language teachers, and so on. The under-availability of language management professionals may become a serious problem, and suitable training programmes need to be facilitated, developed, and supported.

A final remark concerning the organisational aspects of language management is that communities also need to be involved in the process. This does not mean that the entire process should literally be a bottom-up process, but it does mean that state intervention and a programme of action will only succeed if it has the support and participation of the public. Frequent consultation between the managers of language policy and plans and their assumed beneficiaries is essential.

The task of leading language management
As repeatedly stated in this book, it is reasonably certain that a strategic analysis will find that the majority of the country's political leaders and corporate decision-makers do not support the philosophy of multilingualism in a practical sense. This is apparent from the views listed in Chapter 4 (see the section headed "Language policy and practice in government institutions") that only one language be used in parliament, the South African National Defence Force and the court, and the similar decisions considered by parastatal bodies (the Post Office, Telkom, the South African Broadcasting Corporation and South African Airways) as well as institutions in the private sector (the Landbank and the ABSA banking group). The government has, as indicated earlier, been made aware of the increasing movement towards monolingualism, but do not really seem to be concerned (see the statement by a former minister responsible for language policy, also quoted earlier, in Chapter 4, that the official status of languages should not be confused with the *use* of these languages).

A fundamental leadership task to be performed by language management in South Africa is to educate decision-makers in all domains. It is essential that language managers market their ideas, for instance through information and awareness campaigns. In this way some of the misconceptions in public life can be combated, such as the conviction that linguistic pluralism is impractical and will be too costly to implement, that English is superior and Afrikaans bad, and that the Bantu languages are incapable of performing any public function of importance. Similarly, a culture of multilingualism and language respect can be supported as well as a meaningful conception of language rights. Frequent public communication is crucial and necessary for civilian participatory decision-making and the promotion of feelings of ownership, and an awareness, understanding and appreciation of language in South Africa.[16] It is not easy to influence public opinion. A discussion of the language issue on television or the radio will probably have little substantial effect since most people regard language as a "soft" issue, relating "only" to culture and to human rights with very little meaning for individual people. It is thus necessary to stress the impact of language on economic performance and on people's earnings (see Chapter 7). The language issue must repeatedly be marketed as an economic matter.

Control

A first issue in the context of control is the matter of authority, and executive power. In this regard, language management in South Africa is seriously hamstrung. Language management bodies/institutions in South Africa have very little power or influence, as stated earlier. Both DACST and PANSALB should therefore be given more power so that they can be more pro-active, and take greater leadership and control roles.

Control in the context of management implies the development of management standards and norms, and performance indicators. In the absence of an adequate national language policy (and thus also language policies at provincial and local levels of government, as well as in state departments) it is not possible to specify criteria for the measurement of effective policy implementation. Equally, deviations from policy prescriptions and plans of implementation can also not be identified or justified. Nor can they be rectified or can strategies be revised. The existence of the constitutional language stipulations is simply not enough to allow the realisation of the multilingual and pluralist ideal.

Language management needs to be conducted professionally, and thus has to meet the requirements for effective and efficient management (as is the case in corporate and public management, and any other form of management). This implies formal evaluation, and refers to both internal evaluation and external evaluation. The first has to do with the evaluation of the effectiveness and the efficiency with which a language management institution performs its work. This can, of course, be handled in the usual way, through explicit business plans, control measures and the production of reports about the progress of the work undertaken. The evaluation of achievement management is also necessary, both top/down (superiors of subordinates) and bottom/up (subordinates of superiors). External evaluation has to do with the degree in which the ultimate objectives of language management have been attained: changing peoples' language behaviour, their attitudes and their beliefs. This can obviously not be measured in any easy way, for instance by comparing "achievements" against targets. It can only really be determined by a study of the actual patterns in people's language behaviour and through an analysis of their preferences, attitudes and beliefs.

Furthermore, the language planning programmes of DACST and PAN-SALB have to be made known and publicly evaluated. This can be done through research on the results of language management activities (through interviews and questionnaires) and the delivery of regular reports made available to the public, NGOs, as well as government institutions. In addition, specialist consultants can be appointed to evaluate the effectiveness of DACST and PANSALB, and newspaper reports, letters and editorials can be analysed in a routine manner to obtain information about public perceptions of language management.

Conclusion

The logic which underlies any academic exercise requires that a definition of the problems to be investigated be given, that the conceptual framework within which these problems will be dealt with be clearly specified, that appropriate information be gathered, analysed and interpreted, and that proposals be formulated for the resolution of the problems investigated on the basis of the collected data and within the selected conceptual framework. This is also the logic of this book.

The final questions of this chapter must therefore be:

Can the current management of the language issue in South Africa contribute towards solving the language-related and language problems (Chapter 1) of the country?
Can the management of the language issue in South Africa contribute towards the necessary linguistic reconstruction and transformation of the country?
Can the management of the language issue in South Africa contribute towards the educational, economic, political and social reconstruction and transformation of the country?

Despite the notable progress which has been made in the area of language management in the country, the answer to these questions, given the present state of language politics, is no.

What then is necessary for the resolution of these problems from a language planning perspective? Clearly: strategic planning, language policy development and pro-active, vigorous plans of implementation, and, above all: the political will and determination of those in power, those elected to serve the interests of the citizens of the country, those elected to change, reconstruct and transform society — the government. They form the central cog of the machine. They are at the heart of the matter.

But neither strategic language planning nor the required political will really seems to be present. At least, not for the moment.

Notes

1. The more fervent supporters of the Afrikaans cause object quite angrily against the contention that Afrikaans was disproportionately advantaged in the time of Apartheid. Technically, they may have some case, but morally, not much.

2. A central question, of course, is whether these terms have been effectively disseminated, and are actually used in the workplace.

3. Thus before the present 1996 Constitution, which differs in detail from the Interim Constitution regarding the language stipulations (see Chapter 3).

4. Interestingly, in the final Constitution (of 1996) the chapter devoted to "State Institutions Supporting Constitutional Democracy", Chapter 9, makes no reference to PANSALB. It is not clear what one can deduce from this "omission".

5. The following quotation from a speech of the chairperson of the Khoe and San National Language Body provides some insight into the attitudes prevailing in (some of) them: *Although the forces of violence wanted us to be silent in recognising our language and identity, it is with a great sense of pride and dignity that we have finally reclaimed our linguistic heritage and identity in this country* (PANSALB Annual Report, June 2000: 17).

6. Ironically, its own annual report for 1999/2000 does not set an example of multilingualism: the main report (pp. 14 to 64) is only in English. The "word from the chair" is also provided in only four languages, not eleven.

7. This may change once a national language policy has been accepted by Parliament.

8. The university does provide a programme directed at helping beginner students to develop their academic literacy skills, but no programmes are available to enable other students to develop their LoL/T proficiency.

9. Staff members sometimes justify their decision to teach only in English with the argument that English is the language of the professional world, unaware of the effect of an inadequate proficiency in the LoL/T on effective educational development, as well as the fact that knowledge and skills are cross-linguistically transferable (see Chapter 6).

10. From an interactional sociolinguistics perspective one would ordinarily not focus on linguistic mistakes. However, the situation referred to is a formal instructional one, where the symbolic function of language is important.

11. Since these committees are not planning bodies in the usual sense, they will not be discussed any further.

12. A personal comment: The author was involved in the evaluation of applications to PANSALB for research funding at the end of 2000. No directives were provided for the evaluation task on the basis of priorities.

13. A strategic issues map distinguishes between what is of immediate importance, and what can be effectively accomplished, and thus between issues which are high on importance, but low on control (regarded as *vital issues*); those which are high on both dimensions (regarded as *operational issues*); those low on both dimensions (*emerging issues*); and those low on importance and high in terms of control (*maintenance issues,* because solutions are in place).

14. Alignment (left, central, right) is also intended to signify degrees of control and importance.

15. PANSALB does report liaisons with government bodies/state departments (see earlier). What the nature and, more importantly, the impact, of the liaisons was has not been made known.

16. The establishment of provincial and national language bodies and the subsequent involvement of many concerned community leaders will, hopefully, remedy the situation.

Bibliography

Abbot, G. 1996. Development, education, and English language teaching. In Hedge and Whitney (Eds.). *Power, Pedagogy and Practice.* Oxford: Oxford University Press. 43–52.

Adegbija, E. 1994. *Language attitudes in sub-Saharan Africa.* Clevedon: Multilingual Matters Ltd.

Adendorff, R. 1995. Fanakalo in South Africa. In Mesthrie (Ed.), 176–192.

Adendorff, R. & T. Nel. 1998. Literacy and middle-class privilege in post-apartheid South Africa: Evidence from planning time sessions at a church pre-school. In Kamwangamalu (Ed.). 197–226.

Africa Institute. 1996. *Africa at a glance. Facts and figures.* Africa Institute of South Africa. Pretoria.

African National Congress Language Commission. 1993. Towards a democratic language policy for South Africa. Paper presented at the International Culture and Development Conference. Johannesburg.

Agunga, R. 1996. Communication: The missing element in Africa's development struggle. Unpublished conference paper. 6–9 September. Pretoria: Human Sciences Research Council.

Alberts, M. & P. Mtintsilana. 1988. *Leksikografiese ontleding van Afrikaans en Afrikatale-leksikons.* [The lexicographic analysis of Afrikaans and African language lexicons.] Pretoria: Human Sciences Research Council.

Alexander, N. 1989. *Language policy and national unity in South Africa/Azania.* Cape Town: Buchu Books.

Alexander, N. 1990. Afrikaans and language teaching in a free South Africa. *Language Projects Review* 5(3). 13–14.

Alexander, N. 1995. Language policy and planning in South Africa: The need for a coherent national plan for languages. In an unpublished workshop report of the Department of Constitutional Development. 1995.

Alexander, N. 2000. The African Renaissance, African languages and African education. Paper presented at a conference on language policy in Africa: The African Renaissance as a challenge for language planning. 30 March to 1 April. Institut für Afrikanistik. Universität Leipzig.

Ambrose, M., J. Read & V. Webb. (Eds.). 1998. *The role of the African languages in democratic South Africa.* Unpublished workshop report. University of Pretoria.

Ammon, U. & M. Hellinger. (Eds.). 1992. *Status change of languages.* Berlin/New York: Walter de Gruyter.

Ammon, U., N. Dittmar & K. J. Mattheier. (Eds.). *Sociolinguistics: An international handbook of the science of language and society.* Berlin. New York: Walter de Gruyter.

Andersen, Benedict. 1991. *Imagined communities.* London: Verso.

Andrzejewski, B. W. 1983. Language reforms in Somalia and modernisation of the Somali vocabulary. Fodor and Hagège (Eds.). Vol. 1. 69–84.

Angélil-Carter, S. (Ed.). 1998. *Access to success. Literacy in academic contexts.* Cape Town: University of Cape Town Press.

Appel, R. & P. Muysken. 1987. *Language contact and bilingualism.* London: Edward Arnold.

Apronti, E. O. (Date unknown.) Sociolinguistics and the question of a national language: The case of Ghana. In *Studies in African Linguistics Supplement.* 1–19.

Arcand, J-L. 1996. Development economics and language: the earnest search for a mirage? In Grin (Ed.). 1996c: 119–158.

Bailey, R. 1995. The Bantu languages of South Africa: towards a socio-historical perspective. In Mesthrie (Ed.). 1995: 19–38.

Bak. N. (Ed.) 2000. *Making OBE work?* Conference proceedings of the conference on OBE organised by the Western Cape Education Department. December 1999.

Bamgbose, A. 1984. Mother-tongue medium and scholastic attainment in Nigeria. *Prospects,* Vol. XIV. No. 1. 87–93.

Bamgbose, A. 1991. *Language and the nation. The language question in sub-Saharan Africa.* Edinburgh: Edinburgh University Press.

Bamgbose, A. 1994. Pride and prejudice in multilingualism and development. In Fardon & Furniss. (Ed.). London and New York: Routledge. 33–43.

Bamgbose, A. 1998. Language as a resource: An African perspective. In Ambrose, Read and Webb (Eds.), 5–21.

Bamgbose, A. 2000a. *Language and exclusion. The consequences of language policies in Africa.* Hamburg: LIT.

Bamgbose, A. 2000b. Multilingualism in Africa: challenges and responses. Paper presented at the Linguistics Society of Southern Africa conference, January 12–14. Cape Town.

Bamgbose, A. 2000c. Language and the African Renaissance: Lessons from the South African experience. Paper presented at a conference on language policy in Africa: The African Renaissance as a challenge for language planning. 30 March — 1 April, Institut für Afrikanistik. Universität Leipzig.

Barkhuizen, G. & V. de Klerk. 2000. Language contact and ethnolinguistic identity in an Eastern Cape army camp. In Kamwangamalu (Ed.). 95–118.

Barkhuizen, G. & D. Gough. 1996. Language curriculum development in South Africa: What place for English? *TESOL Quarterly* 30. 453–471.

Barkhuizen, J. H., H. F. Stander & G. J. Swart. (Eds.). 1992. *Hupomnema. 'n Feesbundel opgedra aan prof. J. P. Louw.* [A festschrift in honour of Prof. J. P. Louw.]. Department of Greek. University of Pretoria.

Barkon, E. & E. Avinr. 1995. Academic difficulties and early literacy deprivation: The case of Ethiopians in Israel. In *Language, Culture and Curriculum,* 8 (2). 201–209.

Batibo, H. M. 1987. The challenge of linguists in language development: The case of Kiswahili in Tanzania. *Proceedings of the 3rd LASU (Linguistic Associations of Southern African Universities) conference.* University of Zimbabwe. (Exact date unknown.)

Batibo, H. M. 1992a. The conflict between elitist, national and ethnic loyalties in language attitude and use: The case of Tanzania. Paper presented at the University of Duisburg. Germany, March.

Batibo, H. M. 1992b. The fate of ethnic languages in Tanzania. In Brenzinger (Ed.).

Batibo, H. M. 1995. The growth of Kiswahili as language of education and administration in Tanzania. In Pütz (Ed.). 57–80.

Baucom, K. 1978. *Report to the vice-chancellor on adult literacy and language instruction in South Africa.* Johannesburg: University of the Witwatersrand.

Baucom, K. 1978. The needs for literacy in commerce and industry. In Hauptfleisch (Ed.). *Literacy in South Africa.* Pretoria: Human Sciences Research Council. 27–33.

Bennett, J. A. (Ed.). 1995. *Managing Tourism Services.* Pretoria: J. L. van Schaik.

Berg, J. S. (Ed.). 1999. *Geskiedenisatlas van Suid-Afrika. Die vier noordelike provinsies.* [Historical atlas of South Africa. The four northern provinces.] Pretoria: van Schaik Publishers.

Beukes, A. 1991. Training translators in post-apartheid, democratic South Africa. *Language Projects Review* 6 (3/4). 26–29.

Beukes, A. 1995. Language policy in Australia. In an unpublished workshop report of the Department of Constitutional Development. Ms.

Beukes, A. 2000. The language policy and plan for South Africa. Paper presented at the *Language Summit* conference organised by the City Council of Pretoria. 11 September 2000.

Beukes, A. & M. Barnard. (Eds.). 1994. *Proceedings of the languages for all conference: Towards a Pan South African language board.* Dept. of Arts, Culture, Science and Technology. Pretoria.

Beukes, E. P. 1996. The economics of language. A response to Gideon Strauss's: The economics of language. In Strauss, Leibrandt, Beukes and Heugh. 1996: 33–37.

Bialystok, E. & S. Majumder. 1998. The relationship between bilingualism and the development of cognitive processes in problem solving. *Applied Psycholinguistics* 19. 69–85.

Bird, A. 1984. The adult night school for blacks on the Witwatersrand, 1920–1980. In Kallaway, P. (Ed.). *Apartheid and Education.* Johannesburg: Ravan. 192–221.

Blatchford, M. F. 1991. Bush English, or why Sindiswe can't read Wordsworth. *Language Projects Review* 6(3/4). 24–25.

Bloor, M. & T. Bloor. 1990. The role of English in resurgent Africa. In *British Studies in Applied Linguistics 5. Language and Power.*

Bokamba, E. G. & J. S. Tlou. 1977. The consequences of language planning of African states *vis-a-vis* education. In Kotey & Der-Houssikian (Eds.). 35–53.

Bokamba, E. G. 1993. The politics of language planning in Africa: Critical choices for the 21st century. Unpublished paper presented at the Linguistics Society of Southern Africa conference. July. University of Pretoria.

Botha, K., J. Esterhuyse, R. Gouws, T. Links & J. Pienaar. 1989. *Ruimland. ("Spacious land"–* School text-book series for Afrikaans.) Cape Town: Maskew Miller Longman.

Botha, K. 1990. Afrikaans en empowerment. [Afrikaans and empowerment.] In *Karring* 1:5–9. University of the Western Cape. Bellville.

Botha, K. 1990. The ideological and methodological challenges facing language textbook writers: towards creating a new research model. In Chick (Ed.). 1990a. 493–508.

Botha, L. 1989. *Cross-cultural communication in industry: study of the problem of meaning.* Unpublished M. A. thesis. UNISA. Pretoria.

Brenzinger, M. (Ed.). *Language Death: Factual and Theoretical Explorations.* Berlin: Mouton de Gruyter.

Breytenbach, B. 1984. *The true confessions of an albino terrorist.* Johannesburg: Taurus.

Brown, D. (Ed.). 1997. *Education policy and language learning for a multilingual society.* Conference proceedings. Education Policy Unit. University of Natal, and the Centre for Education Policy Development. Evaluation and Management. Durban.

Brown, D. 1988. The basements of Babylon: language and literacy in South Africa. *Social Dynamics.* 14(1). 46–56.

Brown, D. 1988/9. Speaking in Tongues: Apartheid and language in South Africa. In *Perspectives in Education.* 10(2).33–46.

Brown, D. 1989. Language and literacy on the South African mines. In *Language Projects Review.* 4(2). 17–18.

Brown, D. 1995. The rise and fall of Fanakalo: Language and literacy policies of the SA gold mines. In Webb (Ed.). 1995. 309–328.

Brunfaut, T. & K. De Bruyn. 2000. Het bicultureel onderwijsmodel van Foyer. Een mogelijke implementatie van CI en CLIP. University of Antwerp. [A bi-cultural instructional model. A possible implementation of Complex Instruction and Co-operative Learning in the Intercultural educational Project.] Unpublished student report.

Bureau of Literacy and Literature. (Date unknown.) *Papers.* CPAS Archives. University of the Witwatersrand.

Buthelezi, Qedusizi. 1989. South African Black English: a myth or reality? In van der Walt. (Ed.). 38–61.

Cahill, S. & G. D. Kamper. 1989. *Die stand, plek en rol van Afrikaans as tweede taal in die breë kurrikulum van sekondêre skole van die Departement Onderwys en Opleiding.* [The status, place and role of Afrikaans as a second language in the broad curriculum of the secondary schools of the Department of Education and Training.] Pretoria: Human Sciences Research Council.

Calteaux, K. 1996. *Standard and non-standard African language varieties in the urban areas of South Africa: Main report for the stanon research program.* Pretoria: Human Sciences Research Council Publishers.

Calteaux, K. 2000. The Pan South African Language Board's guidelines on municipal language policy. Paper presented at the Pretoria City Council's language summit. 11 September. Pretoria.

Capotorti, F. 1979. *Study on the rights of persons belonging to ethnic, religious and linguistic minorities.* New York: United Nations.

Carbaugh, D. (Ed.). *Cultural communication and intercultural contact.* Hilsdale: Erlbaum.

Carstens, A. & Grebe, H. (Eds.). *Taallandskap.* [The language landscape.] Pretoria: van Schaik Publishers.

Chaffee, J. 1997 (Fifth print.). *Thinking critically.* New York: Houghton Mifflin Company.

Chamber of Mines. 1938 and 1985. *Fanakalo dictionary.* Johannesburg: Chamber of Mines Health and Safety Committee.

Chick, K. 1985. The interactional accomplishment of discrimination in South Africa. In Carbaugh (Ed.). 225–252.

Chick, J. K. 1995. Interactional sociolinguistics and intercultural communication in South

Africa. In Mesthrie (Ed.). 230–241.

Chick, K. (Ed.). 1990a. *Searching for relevance. Contextual issues in applied linguistics in Southern Africa.* Durban: Southern African Applied Linguistics Association.

Chick, K. 1990b. Introduction to Chick, Keith. (Ed.). 1990a. ii-xii.

Chisholm, L. 1984. Redefining skills: black education in the 1980s. In Kallaway (Ed.). 387–410.

Chisholm, L., S. Motala and S. Vally. (Eds.). 1999. *Review of South African education.* 1996–1998. Wits Education Policy Unit. University of the Witwatersrand. Johannesburg. 1–35.

Chumbow, B. S. 1997. Language planning and national development: The case of Cameroon. Ms.

Clark, J. 1996. Task-based learning: purposes, processes and ever-improving knowledge and language. Paper presented at the 24th Annual Conference of SAALT. Johannesburg. July.

Cloete, F. & H. Wissink. (Eds.). 2000. *Improving public policy.* Pretoria: van Schaik Publisher.

Cluver, A. de V. 1987. A sociolinguistic approach to the study of technical languages. *Logos* 7.2 13–20.

Cluver, A. de V. 1988. Towards a post-positivistic model of technical languages. *TermNet News.* 20. 1–10.

Cluver, A. de V. 1989. *A manual of terminography.* Pretoria: Human Sciences Research Council.

Cluver, A. de V. 1990. The role of the language teacher in the information society. In Chick (Ed.). 1990a. 469–492.

Cluver, A. de V. 1992a. Language planning models for a post-apartheid South Africa. *Language problems and language planning.* 15, 2. 105–136.

Cluver, A. de V. 1992b. Language planning in South Africa. In *South Africa in the nineties. Prospects for solutions.* Pretoria: Human Sciences Research Council. 10–11.

Cluver, A. de V. 1992c. Language policy and the language professions. In Kruger (Ed.). 1992. *Changes in translating domains.* Pretoria: University of South Africa. 5–10.

Cluver, A. de V. 1994. *A dictionary of language planning terms.* Pretoria: University of South Africa.

Cluver, A. de V. 1996. *A selected bibliography of language planning in South Africa and general sources.* Pretoria: University of South Africa.

Coetzee-van Rooy, S. 2000. Cultural identity and English second language proficiency. Unpublished paper presented at the Linguistics Society of Southern Africa conference, July. Pretoria: University of South Africa.

Cole, D. T. 1953. Fanakalo and the Bantu languages in South Africa. *African Studies.* 12(1).1–14.

Combrink, J. G. H. 1991. Die toekomstige status en funksies van Afrikaans. [The future status and functions of Afrikaans.] *Tydskrif vir Geesteswetenskappe* 31 (2) [Journal for the Humanities.] 101–112.

Cooper, B. 1991. The national literacy co-operation — an update. *Language Projects Review.* 6 (3/4). 44–47.

Cooper, R. 1989. *Language planning and social change.* Cambridge: Cambridge University Press.

Coulmas, F. 1992. *Language and economy.* Oxford: Blackwell.

Craib, C. 1984. *Work communications on a gold and a coal mine.* Auckland Park: HRL. Chamber of Mines.

Crawhall, N. 1990. Why is language standardisation an issue for workers and peasants? *Language Projects Review* 5(4). 4–5.

Crawhall, N. 1991. Language and materialism. *Language Projects Review* 6 (1/2). 40–44.

Crawhall, N. 1992. Women, men and language difference. *Language Projects Review* 7(4). 25–27.

Crawhall, N. 1998. Going to a better life: Perspectives on the future of language in education for San and Khoe South Africans. Paper presented at the World Congress of Comparative Education Societies, July. University of Cape Town.

Crawhall, N. (Ed.). 1992. *Democratically speaking. International perspectives on language planning.* Cape Town: National Language Project.

Crossley, S. 1989. South African Indian English: grammatical features. In van der Walt (Ed.). 79–92.

Cummins, J. 1979. Linguistic interdependence and the educational development of bilingual children. *Review of Educational Research* 49. 221–251.

Dale, P. S. 1976 (Second edition.). *Language development. Structure and function.* New York: Holt Rinehart and Winston.

Darville, R. 1998. Competitiveness — and equity? — in adult literacy. Paper presented at the *World Congress of Comparative Education Societies.* Cape Town. July.

Davey, L. & C. van Rensburg. 1993. Afrikaans — sy ondergang in Tlhabane. [Afrikaans — its demise in Tlhabane.] *Tydskrif vir Letterkunde* 31 (3) [Journal for Literature.] 25–40.

Davids, A. 1987. The role of Afrikaans in the history of the Cape Muslim community. In du Plessis & du Plessis (Eds.). 37–59.

de Klerk, V. (Ed.). 1996. *Varieties of English around the world. Focus on South Africa.* Amsterdam/Philadelphia: Benjamins.

de Klerk, V. 1999. To be Xhosa or not to be Xhosa ... That is the question. Paper presented at the annual conference of the Linguistics Society of Southern Africa, July. Pretoria: Unisa.

de Klerk, V. & G. Barkhuizen. 1998. Language attitudes in the South African National Defense Force: Views from 6SAI. In Kamwangamalu (Ed.). 155–179.

de Roo, R. 1995. Europe of the cultures. Paper presented during a visit by masters students of the Catholic University of Leuven, November. Brussels.

de Swaan, A. 1993. Introduction, and The evolving European language system: A theory of communication potential and language competition. In de Swaan (Ed.). Special issue of the *International Political Science Review.* 14 (3). 241–255.

de Swaan, A. 1998a. A political sociology of the world language system (1): The dynamics of language spread. *Language problems and language planning.* 22.1. 63–75.

de Swaan, A. 1998b. A political sociology of the world language system (2): The unequal exchange of texts. *Language problems and language planning.* 22.2. 109–128.

de Villiers, A. 1992. Die implikasies van taalinterne konflik in Afrikaans vir opvoedkundige prestasie. [The implications of language internal conflict in Afrikaans for educational achievement.] In Webb (Ed.). 1992. 285–316.

Deacon, J. 1996. (Exact title of paper unknown.) Paper dealing with the paleo-anthropological excavation of Klasies River. Presented at the Khoe-San conference, March. Pretoria.

Degenaar, J. 1994. Beware of nation-building discourse. In Rhoodie and Liebenberg (Eds.). 23–29.

Department of Arts, Culture, Science and Technology. 1996a. *Lexicography as a financial asset*. Pretoria.

Department of Arts, Culture, Science and Technology. 1996b. *The economics of language*. Pretoria.

Department of Arts, Culture, Science and Technology. 1996c. *Towards a national language plan for South Africa. Final report of the Language Plan Task Group*. Pretoria.

Department of Arts, Culture, Science and Technology. 1997a. *Annual Report*. Pretoria.

Department of Arts, Culture, Science and Technology. 1997b. *Standardising the designation of government departments*. Pretoria.

Department of Arts, Culture, Science and Technology. 1997c. *The feasibility of technical language development in the African languages*. Pretoria.

Department of Arts, Culture, Science and Technology. 1997d. *Trading with francophone Africa*. Pretoria.

Department of Arts, Culture, Science and Technology. 1999. *Marketing linguistic human rights*. Pretoria.

Department of Arts, Culture, Science and Technology. 2000. *Language policy and plan for South Africa. Final draft*. Pretoria.

Department of Bantu Education/Departement van Bantoe-onderwys. 1972. *Zulu. Terminologie en spelreëls No.3./Terminology and orthography No.3*. Pretoria: Government Printer.

Department of Constitutional Development. 1995. *Workshop: Constitutional rights — language*. Compilation of papers presented at a workshop on language planning held in Cape Town on 16 February 1995.

Department of Education. 1997a. *A programme for the transformation of higher education*. Education White Paper 3. Government Gazette. Vol. 386, no. 18207. Pretoria.

Department of Education. 1997b. *Education statistics*. Pretoria.

Department of Education. 1997c. *Outcomes-based education in South Africa — Background information for educators*. Pretoria.

Department of Education. 2000a. *Curriculum research and development. Review 2000*. National Centre for Curriculum Research and Development. Pretoria.

Department of Education. 2000b. *Language in the classroom. Towards a framework for intervention*. National Centre for Curriculum Research and Development. Pretoria.

Department of Education. 2000c. *The role of learning support materials in C2005*. National Centre for Curriculum Research and Development.

Deprez, K. & A. Wynants. 1990. Flemish primary schools in Brussels: which prospects? In Gorter, Hoekstra, Jansma & Ytsma (Ed.). 43–52.

Deprez, K. & T. du Plessis. (Eds.). 2000. *Multilingualism and government. Studies in language policy in South Africa*. Pretoria: van Schaik Publishers.

Desai, Z. 1990. Impressions of the Harare language workshop. *Language Projects Review* 5(2). 26–28.

Dirven, R. 1990a. Attitudes towards English and Afrikaans in South Africa. In Nelde (Ed.). 1990. 216–226.

Dirven, R. 1990b. Contact and conflict linguistics in Southern Africa. In Chick (Ed.). 1990. 16–51.

Dirven, R. & V. Webb. 1993. (2nd edition.) *Introduction to the LiCCA research and development programme.* Duisburg and Pretoria: University of Duisburg.

Djité, P. 1993. Language and development in Africa. *International Journal of the Sociology of Language.* 100/101. 149–166.

du Plessis, H. G. W. 1989. Die anatomie van taalbeplanning. [The anatomy of language planning.] *Koers* 54(3). 272–289.

du Plessis, H. 1992. *En nou Afrikaans?* [What now, Afrikaans?] Pretoria: J. L. van Schaik.

du Plessis, H. and T. du Plessis. (Eds.). 1987. *Afrikaans en taalpolitiek: 15 Opstelle.* [Afrikaans and the politics of language. 15 essays.] Pretoria: Human & Roussouw.

du Plessis, L. T. 1991a. *Die evaluering van taalbeplanningsprosesse en aanbevelings vir die oplossing van taalbeplanningsprobleme in Afrikaans.* [The evaluation of language planning processes and recommendations for the resolution of language planning problems in Afrikaans.] Unpublished dissertation. University of the Free State.

du Plessis, T. 1991b. Myths about language loyalty. *Language Projects Review* 5.4. 17–18.

du Plessis, T. 1992. Veranderende opvattings rondom Afrikaans sedert die sewentigerjare. [Changing views about Afrikaans since the seventies.] In Webb (Ed.). 1992: 91–118.

du Plessis, T. 1999. Multilingualism and government in South Africa. Unpublished paper presented at an annual conference of the Linguistics Society of Southern Africa. Pretoria: Unisa. July.

du Plessis, T. and A. van Gensen. (Eds.). 2000. *Taal en stryd 1989–1999. Gedenkbundel.* [Language and struggle 1989–1999. Commemorative volume.] Pretoria: van Schaik Publishers.

du Preez, E. 1989. Geolinguistics: multilingual and language distribution. In van der Walt (Ed.). 1989: 93–103.

Dua, H. R. (Ed.). 1996. Politics of language conflict: Implications for language planning and political theory. *International Journal of the Sociology of Language.* 118. 223 pp.

Dwyer, C. 2000. *Language, identity and nationhood: Language use and attitudes among Xhosa students at the University of the Western Cape, South Africa.* Unpublished dissertation. University of the Western Cape: Bellville.

Eastman, C. 1983. *Language planning: An introduction.* Novato: Chandler and Sharp.

Eastman, C. 1992. Sociolinguistics in Africa. Language planning. In Herbert (Ed.). 1992: 95–114.

Eastman, C. (Ed.). 1993. *Language in power.* Special issue of *International Journal of the Sociology of Language* 103.

Elaigwu, J. I. 1992. Nation-building and changing political structures. In Mazrui and Wondji. 435–498.

Ellis, C. S. 1987a. *Literacy statistics in the RSA: 1980.* Pretoria: Human Sciences Research Council.

Ellis, C. S. 1987b. *Statistiek oor taal en geletterdheid in die werksituasie.* [Statistics on language and literacy in the job situation.] Unpublished ms. Pretoria.

Emenanjo, E. N. 1989. Planned and spontaneous modernization of standard Igbo vocabulary. In Fodor & Hagége (Eds.). Vol. 4: 221–232.

Essman, M. J. 1987. Ethnic politics and economic power. *Comparative Politics.* 395–418.

Esterhuyse, J. 1986. *Taalapartheid en skoolafrikaans.* [Language apartheid and school Afrikaans.] Johannesburg: Taurus.

Esterhuyse, J. 1995. Attitudes to the cultural content of Afrikaans school text-books and syllabuses. In Webb. (Ed.). 253–260.

Fardon, R. & G. Furniss. (Eds.). 1994. *African languages, development and the state.* London and New York: Routledge.

Fardon, R. & G. Furniss. 1994. Introduction. Frontiers and boundaries — African languages as political environment. In Fardon and Furniss. (Eds.). 1–29.

Farrell, J. D. 1978. Black labour: Problems in labour relations. *South African Journal of Labour Relations.* June. 9–26.

Fasold, R. 1984. *The Sociolinguistics of Society.* Oxford: Basil Blackwell.

Ferguson, C. A. & S. B. Heath. (Eds.). *Language in the USA.* Cambridge: Cambridge University Press.

Fermino, G. 1994. Language and education in Mozambique. Paper presented at a conference on the use of indigenous languages in education. September. Maputo.

Finlayson, R. & E. Clayton. 1995. Local markets, domestic services, family and friendship networks. In Webb (Ed.). 371–377.

Fishman, J. A. 1971. *Advances in the sociology of language.* The Hague: Mouton.

Fishman, J. A. 1983. Prefatory remarks. In Fodor and Hagège. Vol. 1. 1–9.

Fishman Joshua. 1989. *Language and ethnicity in minority sociolinguistic perspective.* Clevedon: Multilingual Matters.

Fishman, J. 1990. *Reversing language shift.* Clevedon: Multilingual Matters.

Fishman, J. A. 1992. Three dilemmas of organised efforts to reverse language shift. In Ammon & Hellinger (Eds.). 285–293.

Fodor, I. & C. Hagége. 1983. *Language reform. History and future.* (Vols. 1–3). Hamburg: Buske Verlag.

Fodor, I. & C. Hagége. 1989. *Language reform. History and future.* (Vol. 4). Hamburg: Buske Verlag.

Fourie, J. H. & T. Zsadanyi. 1995. Managing the tourist industry. In Bennett (Ed.). 135–165.

Fourie, P. C. 1977. Gesonde verhoudings tussen wit en swart werkers as basis vir verhoogde produktiwiteit. [Good relations between white and black workers as basis for increased productivity.] *Bedryfsleiding.* 8(1). 31–34.

French, E. 1982. *The promotion of literacy in South Africa: A multifaceted survey at the start of the eighties.* Pretoria: Human Sciences Research Council.

French, E. 1986. *The potential of television in the promotion of adult literacy.* Pretoria: Human Sciences Research Council.

French, E. 1990a. English: Medium of instruction or enemy of instruction? *Language Projects Review* 5(3). 23–25.

French, E. 1990b. The baleful influence of "linguistics" on adult literacy work. In Chick (Ed.). 547–569.

French, E. 1991. The literacy challenge: How to work creatively through the transition. *Language Projects Review* 6(3/4). 39–44.

Freund, B. 1991. South African gold mining in transformation. In *South Africa's Economic Crisis*. David Phillips. 110–128.

Galloway, F. 2000. Comments on a round table presentation on "Multilingualism, publishers, readers and the question of literary language in Africa: For whom are stories told and books written?" Paper presented at the 16th Congress of the International Comparative Literature Association. *Transitions and transgressions in an age of multiculturalism*. Pretoria. 13–19.

Garbers, J. G. 1990. Die wetenskapstaal in Suid-Afrika. [The language of science in South Africa.] In *Tydskrif vir Geesteswetenskappe* [Journal of the Humanities.]. 30(3). 220–246.

Gardiner, M. 1990. Language and the state in a future South Africa. Unpublished paper. Centre for Development Studies. University of the Witwatersrand.

Gelman, S. A. & D. L. Medin. 1993. What's so essential about essentialism? A different perspective on the interaction of perception, language and conceptual knowledge. In *Cognitive Development*. 8. 157–167.

Gilbert, A. J. 1979. *The present need for better manpower management: implications for job evaluation, management and training*. Johannesburg: Council for Scientific and Industrial Research, National Institute for Personnel Research.

Goody, J. (Ed.). 1981a. *Literacy and traditional societies*. Cambridge: Cambridge University Press.

Goody, J. & I. Watt. 1981b. The consequence of literacy. In Goody (Ed.). 1981a: 27–68.

Gorter, D., J. F. Hoekstra, L. G. Jansma & J. Ytsma (Eds.). 1990. *Fourth international conference on minority languages*. Vol. II. Western and Eastern European Papers. Clevedon: Multilingual Matters.

Government Communication and Information Service. 1999. *South African Yearbook*. Pretoria.

Government of the RSA. 1996. *Constitution of the Republic of South Africa*. Pretoria: Government Printer.

Grabe, W. (Ed.). *Annual review of applied linguistics XIV*. 254–273. Cambridge: Cambridge University Press.

Graff, H. (Ed.). 1981a. *Literacy and social development in the West*. Cambridge: Cambridge University Press.

Graff, H. 1981b. Literacy, jobs and industrialization: the nineteenth century. In Graff (Ed.). 1981a: 232–260.

Griefenow-Mewis, C. 1992. Status change of languages in sub-Saharan Africa. In Ammon and Hellinger (Eds.). 100–139.

Grin, F. 1990. The economic approach to minority languages. *Journal of Multilingual and Multicultural Matters*. 11 (1–2).

Grin, F. 1991. Territorial multilingualism. *Language and Society Papers. Series: Linguistic Decisions*. Number LD15.

Grin, F. 1992a. European economic integration and the fate of the Lesser Used Languages. *Language and Society Papers. Series: Linguistic Decisions*. Number LD17.

Grin, F. 1992b. Towards a threshold theory of minority language survival. *Kyklos.* 45 Fasc.1: 69–97.

Grin, F. 1994. The economics of language: match or mismatch? *International Political Science Review* 15(1). 25–42.

Grin, F. 1996a. Economic approaches to language and language planning: an introduction. In Grin (Ed.). 1–16.

Grin, F. 1996b. The economics of language: survey, assessment, and prospects. In Grin (Ed.). 17–44.

Grin, F. (Ed.). 1996. *Economic approaches to language and language planning. International Journal of the Sociology of Language.* 121.

Grin, F. 1999. On the costs of minority language education. Paper presented at the European Centre for Minority Issues. Flensburg. (Date unknown.)

Grin F. 2000. Effectiveness, cost-effectiveness and democracy: a background paper. Paper presented at the conference on *Evaluating policy measures for minority languages in Europe: Towards effective, cost-effective and democratic implementation.* European Centre for Minority Issues. Flensburg, May.

Grin, F. & F. Vaillancourt. 1997. The economics of multilingualism: Overview and analytical framework. In *Multilingualism. ARAL 17.* 43–65.

Grin, F. & F. Vaillancourt. 1998. *Language revitalisation policy: An analytical survey.* The Treasury, New Zealand.

Grobler, E., K. Prinsloo & I. J. van der Merwe. 1990. *Language atlas of South Africa: language and literacy patterns.* Pretoria: Human Sciences Research Council.

Gultig, J. (Ed.). 1998b. *Understanding outcomes-based education. Teaching and assessment in South Africa. Learning Guide.* Cape Town: Oxford University Press Southern Africa.

Gumperz, J. J. 1978. The conversational analysis of interethnic communication. In Ross (Ed.). 13–31.

Gumperz, J. J. & J. Cook-Gumperz. 1981. Ethnic differences in communicative style. In Ferguson & Heath (Eds.). 430–445.

Gxilishe, D. S. and D. H. van der Vyver. 1987. Language training in industry with special reference to the Cape Town metropolitan area. *Per Linguam: A journal of language learning.* University of Stellenbosch.

Haarman, H. 1995. Preface. *Sociolinguistica.* 9.

Haasbroek, P. 1995. Socio-economic policy and democratisation in South Africa. In Rhoodie and Liebenberg (Eds.). 215–224.

Hall, S. K. P. 1984. *Attitudes of black employees towards the use of different language media in the mining work situation.* Johannesburg: Chamber of Mines.

Halliday, M. A. K. 1978. *Language as social semiotic.* London: Edward Arnold.

Hanekom, E. 1988. *Die funksionele waarde van Fanakalo.* [The functional value of Fanakalo.] Pretoria: Human Sciences Research Council.

Harlech-Jones, B. 1990. *You taught me language. The implementation of English as a medium of instruction in Namibia.* Cape Town: Oxford University Press Southern Africa.

Hartshorne, K. 1992. *Crisis and Challenge. Black education 1910–1990.* Cape Town: Oxford University Press Southern Africa.

Hauptfleisch, T. 1977a. *Language loyalty in South Africa. Volume 1: Bilingual policy in South*

Africa — opinions of white adults in urban areas. Pretoria: Human Sciences Research Council.

Hauptfleisch, T. 1977b. *Language loyalty in South Africa.* Vols. 2–4. Pretoria: Human Sciences Research Council.

Hauptfleisch, T. (Ed.). *Literacy in South Africa.* Pretoria: Human Sciences Research Council.

Heine, B. 1979. *Sprache, Gesellschaft und Kommunikation in Afrika.* München: Weltforum Verlag.

Heine, B. 1992. Language policies in Africa. In Herbert (Ed.). 23–36.

Heinecken, L. 1998a. Inequality and diversity: SANDF officers' attitudes towards integration, affirmative action, gender and language. Paper presented at a conference of the Centre for Military Studies. Stellenbosch. (Date unknown.)

Heinecken, L. 1998b. Social equality versus combat effectiveness: An institutional challenge for the military. Paper presented at the annual conference of the South African Political Science Association. University of Pretoria. September.

Herbert, R. K. 1975. (Ed.). *Patterns in language, culture and society: sub-Saharan Africa.* Working Papers in Linguistics No. 19. Ohio State University.

Herbert, R. K. 1992. Language in a divided society. In Herbert (Ed.). 1–22.

Herbert, R. K. (Ed) 1992. *Language and society in Africa. The theory and practice of sociolinguistics.* Johannesburg: University of the Witwatersrand Press.

Herberts, K. & J. G. Turi (Eds.). *Multilingual cities and language policies.* Åbo Akademi University. Social Science Research Unit. Publication No. 36.

Hernandez, J. S. 1993. Bilingual cognitive development. *Educational Forum* 57(4). 350–358.

Heugh, K. 1990. Language policy and education. *Language Projects Review* 5(3). 15–17.

Heugh, K. 1993. Not so straight for English. *Bua!* (Formerly *Language Projects Review*). 8(2). 31.

Heugh, K. 1995a. Trading power. *BUA!* Vol. 10 (1). 22–24.

Heugh, K. 1995b. Comments on language policy clauses in the Constitution of South Africa. In an unpublished workshop report of the Department of Constitutional Development.

Heugh, K. 1995c. Shifting the paradigm: language policy, implementation and results. In an unpublished workshop report of the Department of Constitutional Development.

Heugh, K. 1995d. Why is the water so muddied? A response to Gideon Strauss's: The economics of language. In Strauss, Leibbrandt, Beukes and Heugh. 1996. Department of Arts, Culture, Science and Technology: Pretoria. 38–46.

Heugh, K. 1998. The new language in education policy: South African perspectives on implementation. Paper presented at the Education Department's conference on language policy and implementation. Pretoria. May.

Hill, L. A. & A. A. Archer. 1988. Communication and labour relations in South Africa — a strategic approach. *Industrial Relations Journal.* 2nd quarter. 43–58.

Hornberger, N. H. 1987. Bilingual education success, but policy failure. *Language in Society* 16. 205–226.

Hornberger, N. H. 1988. *Bilingual education and language maintenance: A Southern Peruvian Quechua case.* Dordrecht, the Netherlands: Floris Publications.

Hornberger, N. H. (Ed.). 1989. *Bilingual education and language planning in indigenous*

Latin America. Special Issue of the International Journal of the Sociology of Language. 77.

Human Sciences Research Council. 1981. *Education provision in the RSA: Report of the Main Committee of the Human Sciences Research Council investigation into education.* Pretoria: Human Sciences Research Council.

Human Sciences Research Council. 1985. *Investigation into intergroup relations.* Pretoria: Human Sciences Research Council.

Human Sciences Research Council. 1986. *The role of language in Black Education.* Pretoria: Human Sciences Research Council.

Hubbard, H. 2000. Discourse: Language in context. In Webb & Kembo-Sure (Eds.). 245–267.

Human, P. 1998. *Yenza.* Cape Town: Oxford University Press.

Hymes, D. 1972. On communicative competence. In Pride & Holmes (Eds.). 269–293.

Jafta, N. 1987. The development of terminology in Xhosa: A case study. In *Logos 7.2* 127–138.

Jansens, J. (Ed.). *Knowledge and power in South Africa: Critical perspectives across the disciplines.* Johannesburg: Skotaville.

Janson, T. 1988. A language of Sophiatown, Alexandra and Soweto. In Romaine (Ed.).

Janson, T. & J. Tsonope. 1991. *Birth of a national language. The history of Setswana.* Heinemann: Botswana.

Jernudd, B. H. 1971. Notes on economic analyses for solving language problems. In Rubin & Jernudd (Eds.). 263–276.

Jernudd, B. H. 1993. Planning English language acquisition in ESL and EFL societies: development and maintenance of languages and cultures. *Journal of Multilingual and Multicultural Development.* 14 (1–2). 135–149.

Jernudd, B. H. & J. das Gupta. 1971. Towards a theory of language planning. In Rubin & Jernudd (Eds.). 195–216.

Johnson, R. L. & Sager, J. C. 1980. Standardisation of terminology in a model of communication. *International Journal of the Sociology of Language.* 23. 81–104.

Joseph, J. E. & T. J. Taylor. (Eds.). *Ideologies of language.* London: Routledge.

Joubert, J. 1996. The distribution and emancipation of languages: Using GIS in challenges to development efforts, cultural diversity and communication strategies. Paper presented at the International Culture, Communication, Development Conference. Pretoria: Human Sciences Research Council. August/September.

Kallaway, P. (Ed.). 1984. *Apartheid and Education.* Johannesburg: Ravan.

Kamwangamalu, N. M. (Ed.). 1998. *Aspects of multilingualism in post-apartheid South Africa. A Special Issue of Multilingua.* 17 (2–3).

Kamwangamalu, N. M. (Ed.). 2000a. *Language and ethnicity in the New South Africa. International Journal of the Sociology of Language.* 144.

Kamwangamalu, N. M. 2000b. Apartheid and ethnicity: Introductory remarks. In Kamwangamalu. (Ed.). 1–6.

Kamwangamalu, N. M. 2000c. The New South Africa, language and ethnicity: prognoses. 137–138.

Kapp, R. 1998. Language, culture and politics: The case for multilingualism in tutorials. In Angelil-Carter. (Ed.). 21–34.

Kashoki, M. E. 1990. *The factor of language in Zambia*. Lusaka: Kenneth Kaunda Foundation.

Kashoki, M, E. 1993. Some thoughts on future language policy for South Africa *vis-à-vis* the *Language plan of action for Africa*. Paper presented at the Linguistics Society of Southern Africa conference. University of Pretoria. 3–5 July.

Kembo-Sure. 1991. English in Kenya. Moi University. Unpublished manuscript.

Kembo-Sure. 1997. Language development and integration in Kenya since independence. Unpublished manuscript. University of Pretoria.

Khalawan, P. 2000. *Attitudes among the black matriculants in the Durban community towards Afrikaans as matric subject*. Unpublished masters thesis. University of Zululand.

Khamisi, A. M. 1992. Developing an indigenous language for education in a multilingual setting: A case for Tanzania. Paper presented at the UNESCO Institute for Education Seminar on *Post-Literacy and Basic Level Education*. Hamburg. 19 May.

Khati, T. 1992. Intra-lexical switching or nonce borrowing? Evidence from Sesotho-English performance. In Herbert (Ed.). 181–196.

Khubchandani, Lachman M. 1999. The non-native phenomenon in a plurilingual ethos: English snowflakes in Indian tropics. Paper presented at a conference (particulars not available).

Kishindo, P. J. 1987. The state of scientific terminology in Chichewa. *Logos 7.2* 103–114.

Kotey, P. A. 1975. The official language controversy: Indigenous versus colonial. In Herbert (Ed.). 18–26.

Kotey, P. R. A. and H. Der-Houskian (Eds.). 1977. *Language and linguistic problems in Africa. Proceedings of the VII conference on African linguistics*. Columbia. South Carolina: Hornbeam Press.

Kotze, E. F. 1987. A black perspective on Afrikaans. In Young (Ed.). 169–183.

Koul, Omkar N. 1999. Multilingualism and local government in India. Paper presented at the conference on Multilingual cities and towns in South Africa — challenges and prospects. Council for Scientific and Industrial Research. Pretoria. 10 October.

Kramsch, C. 1993. *Context and culture in language teaching*. Oxford: Oxford University Press.

Kruger, A. (Ed.). 1992. *Changes in translating domains*. Pretoria: University of South Africa.

Kruger, A. 2000. Linguistic empowerment: the role of municipal interpreters. Paper presented at the Pretoria City Council's Language Summit. Pretoria. 27 August.

Kruger, W. J. 1989. *A preliminary investigation of the language problems in the industries of Port Elizabeth and Uitenhage*. Pretoria: Human Sciences Research Council.

Kumalo, M. B. 1987. Revised current and proposed new terminology in language description and Izulu literature. *Logos 7.2* 147–166.

Kunene, E. C. L. & J. Mulder. 1992. Linguistic considerations of some cultural attitudes in SiSwati. In Herbert (Ed.). 335–344.

Kunene, E. C. L. and J. G. B. Sukumane. 1987. Borrowing and neologism as a means of bridging the gap between foreign concepts/experiences and Siswati terminology in applied branches of knowledge. *Logos 7.2* 115–126.

Laitin, D. 1989. Language politics and political strategy in India. *Policy Sciences* 22. 415–436.

Laitin, D. 1993. *Language repertoires and state construction in Africa*. Cambridge: Cambridge

University Press.

Lang, K. 1993. Language and economists' theories of discrimination. In Eastman (Ed.). 165–183.

Langenhoven, H. 1995. Enabling economics: a policy perspective. In Rhoodie & Liebenberg (Eds.). 234–239.

Lanham, L. W. 1986. Another dimension of readiness to learn in the second language. Paper presented at the conference on *The role of language in black education.* Pretoria: Human Sciences Research Council. February.

Lanham, L. W. & K. P. Prinsloo (Eds.). 1978. *Language and communication studies in South Africa.* Cape Town: Oxford University Press.

Lanham, L. W. and Macdonald, C. A. 1979. *The standard in South African English and its social history.* Heidelberg: Julius Groos Verlag.

Lass, R. 1995. South African English. In Mesthrie (Ed.). 89–106.

Leger, J. 1991. Coal mining: past profits current crisis? In *South Africa's economic crisis.* David Philip. 129–155.

Leibbrandt, M. 1995. Comments on Gideon Strauss's: The economics of language. In Strauss, Leibbrandt, Beukes & Heugh. 1996. Department of Arts, Culture, Science and Technology: Pretoria.

Lemmer, E. M. 1991. Addressing the needs of the black child with a limited language proficiency in the medium of instruction. In le Roux. (Ed.). 143–170.

le Roux, J. (Ed.). *The black child in crisis. A socio-educational perspective.* Vol. 1. Pretoria: J. L. van Schaik Publishers.

le Roux, N. & E. Schollar. 1996. *A survey report on the reading and writing skills of pupils participating in READ programmes.* Report prepared for READ Educational Trust. Braamfontein.

Lo Bianco, J. 1996. *Language as an economic resource.* Language Planning Report No. 5.1. Department of Arts, Culture, Science and Technology: Pretoria.

Louw, J. 1963. *Xhosa grammar.* Pretoria: Nasou.

Louw-Potgieter, J. & J. Louw. 1991. Language planning: Preferences of a group of South African students. *South African Journal of Linguistics* 9(4). 96–99.

Lubbe, J. W. 1999. Addressing failure rates through language: Idealism, reality and pragmatism. *The NAETE Journal.* Vol. 14. Pretoria: University of South Africa. 1–10.

Lubisi, C., V. Wedekind, B. Parker & J. Gultig. (Eds.). 1998a. *Understanding outcomes-based education. Teaching and assessment in South Africa. Reader.* Cape Town: Oxford University Press Southern Africa.

Luckett, K. 1990. Some reflections on pre-school language policy for a non-racial and democratic South Africa. *Language Projects Review* 5(2). 29–33.

Mabasa, H. 1996. Submission to LANGTAG on behalf of the Committee of marginalised languages. Pretoria.

Macdonald, C. A. 1989a. *Crossing the threshold into Std. 3.* Pretoria: Human Sciences Research Council.

Macdonald, C. A. 1989b. Developing primary science materials to facilitate language and conceptual development. In van der Walt (Ed.). 119–129.

Mackenzie, C. 1990a. Njabulo Ndebele and the challenge of the new. *Language Projects*

Review 5(3). 29–33.

Mackenzie, C. 1990b. Njabulo Ndebele, *Fools and other stories* and the language of black resistance. *Language Projects Review* 5(1). 22–25.

Madiba, R. 1996. The African languages and development. Paper delivered at the conference on Culture, Communication and Development. Pretoria: Human Sciences Research Council. August/September.

Makgoba, W. M. (Ed.). 1999. *African renaissance.* Cape Town: Mafube & Tafelberg Publishers.

Malimabe, R. M. 1990. *The influence of non-standard varieties on the standard Setswana of high school pupils.* Unpublished masters thesis. Rand Afrikaans University. Johannesburg.

Mankomo, P. 1990. Drawing from our experiences — Xhosa conversation course. *Language Projects Review* 5(1). 14–15.

Manpower, Department of, and the National Training Board. 1989. *The Human Sciences Research Council/NTB investigation into training in communication in the workplace.* Pretoria: Human Sciences Research Council.

Marivate, C. T. D. 1993. The cultural significance of the indigenous languages in a post-apartheid South Africa. In Swanepoel & Pieterse (Eds.). 59–64.

Marschak, J. 1965. Economics of language. *Behavioral Science* 10. 135–140.

Masinge, 1997. *Teaching Xitsonga as a first language.* Unpublished MA thesis. University of Pretoria.

Masunga, S. 2000. *Language management in South Africa: A case study with Xitsonga.* Unpublished MA thesis. University of Pretoria.

Matsela, Z. A. 1987. The problems of modernizing the development of Sesotho scientific/technical terminologies. *Logos* 7.2 79–102.

Matsela, Z. A. & Mochaba, M. B. 1986. Development of new terminology in Sesotho. *South African Journal of African Languages. Supplement.* 6. 136–147.

Matthews, P. H. 1997. *Oxford concise dictionary of linguistics.* Oxford: Oxford University Press.

Mawasha, A. L. 1986. Medium of instruction in Black education in Southern Africa. In Human Sciences Research Council. 13–30.

Mazrui, A. M. 1996. Language policy and the foundations of democracy: an African perspective. In Dua (Ed.). 107–124.

Mazrui, A. A. & C. Wondji (Eds.). 1992. *Africa since 1935. General history of Africa. VIII.* California: Heinemann. UNESCO.

Mboweni, T. 1995. The socio-economic conditions for the democratisation of South Africa. In Rhoodie & Liebenberg (Eds.). 228–233.

McKay, S. L. 1989. Language teaching: a need for socio-political awareness. In van der Walt (Ed.). 1–18.

McCormick, K. 1989. *English and Afrikaans in District Six: A sociolinguistic study.* Unpublished dissertation. University of Cape Town.

Meintjies, E. 1991. Translating for a new and progressive South Africa. In *Language Projects Review.* 6(1/2). 35–39.

Meintjies, F. 2000. Language and labour. In du Plessis and van Gensen (Eds.). 101–117.

Melkote, S. R. & K. P. Kandath. 1996. Reconceptualization of the role of communication in development: A focus on the organizational value of DSC. Paper presented at the conference on Culture, Communication and Development. Pretoria. August/September.

Mesthrie, R. 1989. The origins of Fanagalo. *Journal of Pidgin and Creole Language.* 4(2). 211–240.

Mesthrie, R. 1991. *Language in indenture: a sociolinguistic history of Bhojpuri-Hindi in South Africa.* Johannesburg: Witwatersrand University Press.

Mesthrie, R. 1992a. *A lexicon of South African Indian English.* Leeds: Peepal Tree Press.

Mesthrie, R. 1992b. *English in language shift. The history, structure and sociolinguistics of South African Indian English.* Johannesburg: Witwatersrand University Press.

Mesthrie, R. (Ed.). 1995. *Language and social history. Studies in South African sociolinguistics.* Cape Town: David Philip.

Mesthrie, R., J. Swann, A. Deumert & W. L. Leap. 2000. *Introducing sociolinguistics.* Edinburgh: Edinburgh University Press.

Ministry of Education of Botswana and UNESCO's International Centre for Technical and Vocational Training. 2000. *Enhancing access to effective technical and vocational education and training.* Unpublished project report. Gaborone. Botswana.

Mkatshwa, Father S. 2000. Language and the national democratic struggle. In du Plessis and van Gensen (Eds.). 32–41.

Mmusi, S. O. 1987. *Language planning policy and its associated problems in black education in South Africa.* Unpublished master's thesis. Southern Illinois University.

Moatlhodi, S. M.1998. *The study of cultural conflict in D. P. Moloto's novels.* Unpublished master's thesis. Rand Afrikaans University.

Mochaba M. B. 1987. "Shift in meaning" in Sesotho modern terminology. *Logos 7.2* 139–146.

Mohr, P. & L. Fourie and Associates. 1995. *Economics for students.* Pretoria: J. L. van Schaik.

Mokoena, B. 1990. Language and international relations. Working paper of the ANC Harare conference on the Language Future of South Africa.

Monsour, G. 1993. *Multilingualism and nation-building.* Clevedon: Multilingual Matters.

Moodley, K. 2000. African Renaissance and language policies in comparative perspective. *Politikon.* 27(1). 103–115.

Mosha, M. 1983. Loan-words in Luganda: A search for guides in the adaptation of African languages to modern conditions. In Fodor and Hagège (Eds.). Vol. 2. 505–521.

Msimang, C. 1992. *African languages and language planning in South Africa.* Pretoria: Inaugural lecture: University of South Africa. Pretoria.

Msimang, C. T. 1993. The future status and functions of Zulu in the new South Africa. In Swanepoel & Pieterse (Eds.). 29–41.

Mukasa, S. G. 1996. A cultural and communication approach to development and multiculturalism in context. Paper presented at the conference on Culture, Communication and Development. Human Sciences Research Council. August/September.

Murray, S. & H. van der Mescht. 1996. Preparing student teachers to teach English first and second language — problems and challenges. In de Klerk (Ed.). 251–267.

Mvula E. T. 1992. Language policies in Africa: The case for Chichewa in Malawi. In Herbert (Ed.). 37–48.

Mzamane, M. 1990. *Towards a national language policy in post-apartheid South Africa.* Southern African Research Programme. Unpublished seminar paper.

National Commission on Higher Education. 1996. *A Framework for transformation.* Pretoria.

National Education Co-ordinating Committee (NECC). 1990. *Readings from a workshop held in Harare from 21–24 March 1990.* Cape Town: National Language Project.

National Education Policy Investigation. (NEPI). 1992. *The Framework Report and Final Report Summaries.* A project of the National Education Co-ordinating Committee. Cape Town: Oxford University Press SA/NECC.

National Education Policy Investigation. (NEPI). 1993. *Language.* Cape Town: Oxford University Press SA/NECC.

National Language Project. 1991a. New school language policy. *Language Projects Review* 6(1/2). 34.

National Language Project. 1991b. Towards harmonisation. *Language Projects Review* 6(1/2). 10–11.

Ndebele, N. S. 1987. The English language and social change in South Africa. *The English Academy Review* 4. 1–16.

Ndoleriire, Oswald K. 2000. Cross-cultural communication in Africa. In Webb & Kembo-Sure (Eds.). 268–285.

Nelde, P. H. (Ed.). 1990. *Language attitudes and language conflict.* Plurilingua IX. Bonn: Dümmler.

Nfila, Bokang. (In preparation.) *Standard Setswana in Botswana.* Masters thesis. University of Pretoria.

Ngugi wa Thiong'o. 1986. *Decolonizing the mind. The politics of language in English literature.* London: James Currey.

Nkondo, C. P. N. 1987. Problems of terminology in African languages with special reference to Xitsonga. *Logos 7.2* 69–78.

Noor Mohamed, R. 1998. *Taalverskuiwing in die Afrikaanssprekende Indiërgemeenskap in Pretoria.* [Language shift in the Afrikaans-speaking Indian community in Pretoria.] Unpublished doctoral dissertation. University of Pretoria.

NTB investigation. 1990. *Technological development and training.* Pretoria: Government Printer.

Nyamnjoh, F. B. 1996. The role of culture in African development: Some general reflections. Paper presented at the conference on Culture, Communication and Development. Human Sciences Research Council. August/September.

Odendaal, M. S. 1986. Die milieu binne die skool. [The milieu inside the school.] In Human Sciences Research Council. 57–84.

Official South African trade unions directory and industrial relations handbook. 1989. Johannesburg: Richard Havenga.

Ohly, R. (Ed.). 1987. *Professional terminology in African languages, theory and practice. Workshop papers.* Academy. Windhoek. Namibia. *Logos.* 7.2.

Ohly, R. 1987. Corpus planning, glottoeconomics and terminography. *Logos 7.2* 55–68.

Oladejo, J. A. 1993. How not to embark on a bilingual education policy in a developing nation: The case of Nigeria. *Journal of Multilingual and Multicultural Studies Development.* Vol. 14 (1 and 2). 91–102.

Omotoso, K. 1994. *Season of migration to the south.* Cape Town: Tafelberg.

Ouane, A. 1991a. Language standardization in Mali. In von Gleich & Wolff (Eds.).

Ouane, A. 1991b. L'harmonisation des langues maliennes: entre l'intégration nationale et régionale. In Ouane & Sutton. (Eds.). 99–114.

Ouane, A. & P. J. Sutton. (Eds.). Special issue of the *International Review of Education.* Vol. 37 (1). Unesco Institute for Education. Hamburg.

Pan South African Language Board. 1997. *Annual report.* Pretoria.

Pan South African Language Board. 2000a. *Annual report.* Pretoria.

Pan South African Language Board. 2000b. *Summary of the findings of: A sociolinguistic survey on language use and language interaction in South Africa.* Pretoria.

Pattanayak, D. P. 1991. *Language, education and culture.* Central Institute for Indian Languages. Mysore.

Pattanayak, D. 1994. Interview. In *Bua!* National Language Project. Cape Town.

Peirce, B. N. 1990. People's English in South Africa. *Language Projects Review* 5(1). 7–9.

Peirce, B. N. 1991. On language, difference and democracy. *Language Projects Review* 6(3/4). 21–24.

Pendelbury, S. 1983. English for special purposes: new approaches to language training. *Training and Development Forum.* 1(2). 15–18.

Pennycook, A. 1994. *The cultural politics of English as an international language.* Harlow: Longman.

Phetha, T. R. 1984. *The use of Fanakalo in training on a gold and a coal mine.* Auckland Park: HRL. Chamber of Mines.

Phillipson, R. 1992. *Linguistic imperialism.* Oxford: Oxford University Press.

Pieterse, H. J. 1993. Taalbeplanningsmodelle vir Suid-Afrika: 'n oorsig en voorlopige sintese. [Language planning models for South Africa: A survey and a preliminary synthesis.] In Swanepoel & Pieterse (Eds.). 124–143.

Pokpas, L. & A. van Gensen. 1992. Afrikaans en ideologie in taalbeplanning: 'n stryd van standpunte. [Afrikaans and ideology in language planning: A clash of viewpoints.] In Webb (Ed.). 1992. 165–180.

Polomé, E. C. 1983. Standardization of Swahili and the modernization of the Swahili vocabulary. In Fodor and Hagège (Eds.). 53–77.

Ponelis, F. 1992. Standaardafrikaans in oorgang. [Standard Afrikaans in transition.] In Webb (Ed.). 1992. 65–84.

Pool, J. (Undated). Language planning and identity planning. Mimeo.

Pool, J. 1990. Language regimes and political regimes. In Weinstein (Ed.). 241–261.

Poulos, G. 1990. *Linguistic analysis of Venda.* Pretoria: Via Afrika.

Pool, J. 1991. "A tale of two tongues". Unpublished manuscript. Department of Political Science. University of Washington. Seattle.

Poulos, G. & L. Lourens. 1994. *Linguistic analysis of Northern Sotho.* Pretoria: Via Afrika.

Prah, K. 1995a. *African languages for the mass education of Africans.* German Foundation for International Development. Bonn: Education, Science and Documentation Centre.

Prah, K. 1995b. *Mother tongue for scientific and technological development in Africa.* German Foundation for International Development. Bonn: Education, Science and Documentation Centre.

Pride, J. B. & J. Holmes. (Eds.). *Sociolinguistics.* Harmondsworth: Penguin.

Prince, D. 1984. Workplace English: approach and analysis. *The ESP Journal.* 3(2). 109–116.

Prinsloo, D. & J. C. Steyn. 1999. The influence of language legislation on language shift in traditional South African cities. In Herberts & Turi (Eds.). 147–160.

Prinsloo, K. P. 1972. *Die tweetaligheid van twee groepe universiteitstudente en hul ingesteldhede teenoor die tweedetaal: 'n voorondersoek tot 'n landwye opname.* [The bilingualism of two groups of university students and their attitudes to the second language: a pilot study for a nation-wide survey.] Doctoral dissertation. University of Pretoria.

Prinsloo, K. P. (Ed.). 1985. *Language Planning for South Africa. South African Journal of Linguistics. Occasional Papers* 2. 124 pages.

Prinsloo, K. P. 1990. Veranderings en eise op die breë taalgebied in Suid-Afrika. [Changes and demands in the broad area of language in South Africa.] Paper presented at the annual meeting of the Linguistics Society of Southern Africa. Bloemfontein. July.

Prinsloo, K. P. 1991. Language and government in a changing South Africa. Paper presented at the First International LiCCA (Languages in contact and conflict in Africa) conference. University of Pretoria. April.

Prinsloo, K. 1999. The gap between language policy and its application in a new South Africa.: A tale of two cities. In Herberts & Turi. (Eds.). 161–170.

Prinsloo, K. P. & C. van Rensburg. (Eds.). 1984. *Afrikaans: stand, taak en toekoms.* [Afrikaans: state, task and future.] Pretoria: HAUM.

Prinsloo, K., Y. Peeters, J. Turi & C. van Rensburg. (Eds.). 1993. *Language, law and equality.* Pretoria: University of South Africa.

Prinsloo, M. & M. Breier. (Eds.). 1996. *The social uses of literacy. Theory and practice in contemporary South Africa.* Studies in written language and literacy 4. SACHED Books and John Benjamins. Amsterdam/New York.

Pütz, M. (Ed.). 1992. *Thirty years of linguistic evolution.* Philadelphia/Amsterdam: John Benjamins.

Pütz, M. (Ed.). 1994. *Language contact and language conflict.* Amsterdam/ Philadelphia: John Benjamins.

Pütz, M. (Ed.). 1995. *Discrimination through language in Africa? Perspectives on the Namibian experience.* Berlin: Mouton de Gruyter.

Raath, A. W. G. 1990. Die toekoms van Afrikaans in die lig van konstitusionele vraagstukke. [The future of Afrikaans in light of constitutional issues.] Paper presented at the conference on language planning. University of Pretoria. March.

Radise, J., A. Wainwright & J. K. McNamara. 1979. *The attitudes of black and white employees to the use of Fanakalo on the mines.* Auckland Park: HRL. Chamber of Mines.

Ragavan, C. R. 1998. English language teaching in South Africa. *Bulletin. News for the human sciences.* Vol. 4 no. 6. Human Sciences Research Council: Pretoria. 2–3.

Rall, P. & H. Warricker. 2000. *Trends in book publishing in South Africa for the period 1990 to 1999.* Unpublished project report of the Department of Information Science (Publishing). University of Pretoria.

Ramaliba, T. Z. (In preparation) *Language-internal conflict in Tshivenda.* Doctoral dissertation. University of Pretoria.

Rammala, J. R. (In preparation.) *Language planning and social transformation in the Northern Province: The role of language in education.* Doctoral dissertation. University of Pretoria.

Rand Mines Training Centre. 1980, 1983. *Reports, 1980, 1983.* (Adams report and Watters report).

Ranney, A. 1987. (Fourth edition.). *Governing. An introduction to Political Science.* Englewood Cliffs: Prentice-Hall.

Rapport (Sunday newspaper). 2001. African languages on the decline. 27 February.

Reagan, T. G. 1985. On 'sharp edges and watertight compartments': problems of language planning in the South African context. In Prinsloo (Ed.). 58–70.

Reagan, T. G. 1986. *A sociolinguistic model for the analysis of communication and communications problems in industry.* Pretoria: Human Sciences Research Council.

Rhoodie, N. & I. Liebenberg. (Eds.). 1995. *Democratic nation-building in South Africa.* Pretoria: Human Sciences Research Council.

Ribbens, R. 1990. Language organisations and language planning. In Chick (Ed.). 124–140.

Ribbens, I. R. (Ed.). 1990. *Taal en bedryf.* [Language and industry.] Pretoria: Human Sciences Research Council.

Ribbens, R. & T. Reagan. 1995. Trade, industry and the business community. In Webb (Ed.). 289–308.

Roberge, P. 1990. The ideological profile of Afrikaans historical linguistics. In Joseph & Taylor (Eds.). 131–49.

Roberge, P. 1995. The formation of Afrikaans. In Mesthrie (Ed.). 68–88.

Robinson, C. D. W. 1994. Is sauce for the goose sauce for the gander? Some comparative reflections on minority language planning in north and south. *Journal of Multilingual and Multicultural Development.* 15 (2/3). 129–145.

Robinson, C. D. W. 1996. *Language use in rural development. An African perspective.* Berlin: Mouton de Gruyter.

Robinson, C. D. W. Language policy from the bottom up? Reclaiming language use in Africa. [Further particulars unavailable.]

Romaine, S. 1988. *Pidgin and creole languages.* London: Longman.

Romaine, S. 1992. The status of Tok Pisin in Papua New Guinea: The colonial predicament. In Ammon & Hellinger. (Eds.). 229–252.

Ross, E. L. (Ed.). 1978. *Interethnic communication.* Athens: University of Georgia Press.

Ross, E. L. 1978. Interethnic communication: an overview. In Ross (Ed.). 1–12.

Rousseau, A. H. 1990. Die eise wat die werksituasie aan standerd 10-leerlinge stel ten opsigte van Afrikaanse en Engelse vaardigheid. [The demands of the work place on Std. 10 learners with regard to proficiency in Afrikaans and English.] In Ribbens (Ed.). 12–26.

Rousseau, A. H., S. Lombard & G. D. Kamper. 1989. *Die eise wat die werksituasie aan skoolverlaters stel ten opsigte van Afrikaanse en Engelse taalvaardigheid.* [The demands of the work place on Std. 10 learners with regard to proficiency in Afrikaans and English.] Pretoria: Human Sciences Research Council.

Rubagumya, C. M. (Ed.). 1990. *Language in education in Africa. A Tanzanian perspective.* Clevedon: Multilingual Matters.

Rubin, J. & B. Jernudd. (Eds.). 1971. *Can language be planned? Sociolinguistic theory and practice for developing nations.* Hawaii: University Press of Hawaii.

Ryan, C. 1996. Contribution in *RDP quarterly report.* Pretoria: South African Government Printer.

South African Communication Service. 1996. *South Africa Yearbook.* Pretoria: Government Printer.

South African Institute of Race Relations. 1990. *Race relations survey, 1989/90.* Johannesburg.

South African Institute of Race Relations. 1996. *Race relations survey for 1995/6.* Johannesburg.

South African Institute of Race Relations. 1997. *Race relations survey for 1996/7.* Johannesburg.

South African Institute of Race Relations. 1998. *Fast facts.* July.

South African Institute of Race Relations. 2000. *Race relations survey, 1999/2000.* Johannesburg. (Millennium edition).

South African Law Commission. 1991. *Project 58: Group and human rights.* Interim Report. Pretoria: Government Printer.

Sachs, A. 1993. The ANC's language policy and the position of Afrikaans. Paper presented at the Seminar on promoting Afrikaans. University of the Free State.

Scheffer, C. J. 1987. Promoting and managing terminological activities in South Africa. *Logos 7.2* 31–34.

Scheffer, P. 1983. *Afrikaans en Engels onder die Kleurlinge in die Kaapprovinsie, in besonder die Skiereiland.* [Afrikaans and English among the Coloureds in the Cape Province, particularly in the peninsula.] Pretoria: Human Sciences Research Council.

Schuring, G. K. 1979. *A multilingual society: English and Afrikaans amongst blacks in the RSA.* Pretoria: Human Sciences Research Council.

Schuring, G. K. 1985. *Kosmopolitiese omgangstale. Die aard, oorsprong en funksies van Pretoria-Sotho en ander koinétale.* [Cosmopolitan vernaculars. The nature, genesis and functions of Pretoria Sotho and other koiné languages.] RGN-verslag. [Human Sciences Research Council Report.] Soling-7. Pretoria.

Schuring, G. K. 1990. Taalbeplanning vir 'n nuwe Suid-Afrika. [Language Planning for a new South Africa.] Paper presented as a research presentation. Pretoria: Human Sciences Research Council.

Schuring, G. K. 1992. Die moontlike toekomstige posisie van Afrikaans op skool. [The possible future position of Afrikaans in schools.] In Webb (Ed.). 249–272.

Schuring, G. K. 1993. Sensusdata oor die tale van Suid-Afrika. [Census data on the languages of SA.] Unpublished working document. Human Sciences Research Council.

Schuring, G. K. & C. S. Ellis. 1987. Shared languages and 'language gaps' in South Africa: an analysis of census data. *South African Journal of Labour Relations.* 11(3). 37–45.

Schuring, G. K. & M. K. Yzel. 1983. *'n Veeltalige samelewing: 'n Ondersoek na die taalsituasie in die Suid-Afrikaanse swart gemeenskap. Deel 1.* [A multilingual society: an investigation into the language situation in the South African black community. Part 1.] Pretoria: Human Sciences Research Council.

Seifert, K. L. & R. J. Hoffnung. 1987. *Child and adolescent development.* Boston: Houghton Mifflin Company.

Selman, R. 1993. A second language in the classroom: Are we missing the boat? *Montessori*

LIFE 5 (1). 31–32.

Shabalala, S. 1995. Response to Haasbroek. In Rhoodie & Liebenberg (Eds.). 225–227.

Shane, S. 1989. *Trade union development in sub-Saharan Africa.* Pretoria: Human Sciences Research Council.

Skutnab-Kangas, T. 2000. Global diversity or not: the role of linguistic human rights in education. Paper presented at the 25th Anniversary of the Seminar on language and education. University of Barcelona.

Slabbert, S. 1994. Isisoweto. Ek slaan al die tale. [Isisoweto. I use all the languages.] *Bua!* Vol. 9. No. 1. 4–9.

Slabbert, S. 1995. A re-evaluation of the sociology of Tsotsitaal. In Webb (Ed.). 143–167.

Smit, J. 1995. Language practices in central government departments, security services and provincial administration. In Webb (Ed.). 209–218.

Smith, L. E. (Ed.). 1987. *Discourse across cultures. Strategies in World Englishes.* New York: Prentice Hall.

Smith, L. E. 1987. Introduction: Discourse strategies and cross-cultural communication. In Smith (Ed.). 1–6.

Sonn, F. A. 1990. Die toekoms van Afrikaans. [The future of Afrikaans.] *Acta Varia 1.* Bloemfontein: University of the Free State.

Sotashe, P. 1992. Looking for language boards. *Language Projects Review* 7(4). 7–8.

South Africa (Republic). 1988. *Standard industrial classification of all economic activities* (SIC). Fourth edition. Pretoria: Central Statistical Service.

South Africa (Republic). 1989. *South African labour statistics.* Pretoria: Central Statistical Services.

South Africa Bureau for Information & Department of Foreign Affairs. 1990. *Official Yearbook of the Republic of South Africa.* Pretoria: Bureau for Information.

Southey, P. 1990. Junior primary language policy. *Language Projects Review* 5(3). 19–21.

Sow. A. & M. Abdulaziz. 1992. Language and social change. In Mazrui & Wondji. (Eds.). *General history of Africa VIII. Africa since 1935.* Heinemann. California. UNESCO. 522–552.

Sproull, A. 1996. Regional economic development and minority language use: the case of Gaelic Scotland. In Grin (Ed.). 93–118.

Squelch, J. 1993. Towards a multicultural approach to education in South Africa. In le Roux (Ed.). 171–201.

Stanley, J. (Ed.) 1990. Australian language education for industry. *Language is good business. Proceedings of the conference: The role of language in Australia's economic future.* Canberra. NLLIA.

Stanton, P. J., C. J. Aislabie & J. Lee. 1992. The economics of a multicultural Australia: A literature review. *Journal of Multilingual and Multicultural Development.* 13 (5). 407–421.

Statistics South Africa. 1998. *Census in brief.* Report No. 1: 03–01–11. Pretoria.

Statistics South Africa. 1999. Unpublished information supplied on order in electronic format.

Steyn, J. C. 1980. *Tuiste in eie taal.* [At home in one's own language.] Cape Town: Tafelberg.

Steyn, J. C. 1987. Afrikanernasionalisme en Afrikaans. [Afrikaner nationalism and Afrikaans.]. In du Plessis & du Plessis (Eds.). 73–96.

Steyn, J. C. 1990. Menseregte en taalregte. [Human rights and language rights.] *South African Journal of Linguistics.* 8(1). 39–47.

Steyn, J. C. 1991. Taalkroniek: taalstatus, taalbeleid en taalregte. [Linguistic chronicle: language status, language policy and language rights.] *Tydskrif vir Geesteswetenskappe.* [Journal of the Humanities.] 30(4). 303–10.

Steyn, J. C. 1992. Die behoud van Afrikaans as ampstaal. [The retention of Afrikaans as official language.] In Webb (Ed.). 201–226.

Steyn, J. C. 1993. Taalideologie en taalbeleid in die Suid-Afrikaanse geskiedenis — oorwegings in die ampstaaldebat? [Language ideology and language policy in South African history — considerations in the debate on official language?] *Acta Academica Supplementum* 1993. Bloemfontein: University of the Free State.

Stoltz, E. 1982. *Gepidginiseerde Afrikaans in wit-swart interaksie.* [Pidginized Afrikaans in white-black interaction.] Master's thesis. Rand Afrikaans University. Johannesburg.

Strauss, G., M. Leibbrandt, E. P. Beukes & K. Heugh. 1996. *The economics of language.* Language Planning Report no. 5.3. Department of Arts, Culture, Science and Technology: Pretoria.

Strauss, G. 1996. The economics of language. Diversity and development in the information economy. In Strauss, Leibbrandt, Beukes & Heugh. 2–28.

Street, B. 1984. *The theory and practice of literacy.* Cambridge: Cambridge University Press.

Strydom, F. 1987. Die onderrig van Afrikaans in 'n geïdeologiseerde situasie. [The teaching of Afrikaans in an ideologised situation.] In du Plessis & du Plessis (Eds.). 189–206.

Strydom, H. A. & J. L. Pretorius. 1999. Language policy and planning: How do local governments cope with multilingualism? Paper presented at the conference on Multilingual cities and towns in South Africa — challenges and prospects. October.

Strydom, L. (In preparation.) *A sociolinguistic profile of Atteridgeville and Mamelodi, Pretoria.* Doctoral dissertation. University of Pretoria.

Sunday Times. 2001. Report: Declining interest in the African languages. 4th March.

Swanepoel, J. 1990. Taalaanbieding aan die technikon: Vraag- en aanbodsituasie. [Language teaching in the technikon: needs and response.] In Ribbens (Ed.). 39–52.

Swanepoel, P. H. 1989. *Special language issues in black education. Report on a study of the provision, use and acquisition of special language.* Department of Education and Training. Pretoria.

Swanepoel, P. H. 1991. *Die liefdesverhouding tussen Afrikaans en die Afrikaanssprekende: 'n blik deur die oë van Mater Matuto. [The love relationship between Afrikaans and the speaker of Afrikaans: a view through the eyes of Mother Matuto.]* Inaugural lecture. Unisa. Pretoria.

Swanepoel, P. H. 1992. Taal, emosies en die toekoms van Afrikaans. [Language, emotion and the future of Afrikaans.] In Webb (Ed.). 1992a. 119–164.

Swanepoel, P. H. & H. J. Pieterse. (Ed.). 1993. *Perspektiewe op taalbeplanning vir Suid-Afrika. Perspectives on language planning for South Africa.* Pretoria: Unisa.

Swanepoel, P. H. & R. Morris. 1988a. *Die rekenarisering van terminografiese prosesse.* [Computerising terminographical processes.] Pretoria: Human Sciences Research Council.

Swanepoel, P. H. & R. Morris. 1988b. *Die rekenarisering van leksikografiese prosesse.* [Computerising lexicographical processes.] Pretoria: Human Sciences Research Council.

Tait, N., A. Whiteford, J. Joubert, J. van Zyl, D. Krige & B. Pillay. 1996. *A. Socio-economic atlas of South Africa*. Pretoria: Human Sciences Research Council.

Taljaard, R. & A. Venter. 1998. Parliament. In Venter (Ed.). 23–57.

The Citizen. 1998. 14 August.

The Sowetan. 2000. (Article on HIV/AIDS.) 14 August.

The Human Sciences Research Council/NTB investigation into the training of artisans. 1985. *Report*. Pretoria: Human Sciences Research Council.

The Human Sciences Research Council/NTB investigation into training in communication in the workplace. 1989. *Report*. Pretoria: Government Printer.

Thomas, W. P. & V. P. Collier. 1997. School effectiveness for language minority students. (Handout regarding a research project. Published by the National Clearinghouse for Bilingual Education.)

Thompson, C. 1984. Black trade unions on the mines. *South African Review*. 2. Johannesburg: Ravan. 156–164.

Thorburn, T. 1971. Cost-benefit analysis in language planning. In Rubin & Jernudd (Eds.). 253–262.

Titlestad, P. 1995. English, the Constitution and South Africa's future. In de Klerk, V. (Ed.). 163–174.

Tlou, T. & A. Campbell. 1984. *History of Botswana*. Gaborone: Macmillan Botswana.

Tollefson, J. W. 1991. *Planning language, planning inequality*. London/New York: Longman.

Traill, A. 1995. The Khoesan languages of South Africa. In Mesthrie (Ed.). 1–18.

Traill, A. 1996. The Khoe-san languages. Paper presented at the conference on the Khoe-San. Pretoria. March.

Tsinki, A. (In preparation.) *Code-switching in Setswana in Botswana*. Master's thesis. University of Pretoria.

UNESCO. No date. *La définition d'une stratégie relative à la promotion des langues africaines. Documents de la réunion d'experts qui a eu lieu à Conakry (Guinée)*. 21–23 September 1981.

UNESCO. *Project Horizon 2000*.

Vaillancourt, F. & F. Grin. 2000. The choice of language of instruction: the economic aspects. Paper prepared for the World Bank Institute.

Vaillancourt, F. 1996. Language and economic status in Quebec: measurement, findings, determinants, and policy costs. In Grin (Ed.). 69–92.

van Aswegen, A., U. Holtzhausen & H. Groenewald. 1987. *Die bepaling van die behoefte aan interkulturele opleiding — 'n voorondersoek*. [Determining the need for intercultural training — an exploratory study.] Pretoria: Human Sciences Research Council.

van Baalen, J. 2000. Project management and public policy implementation. In Cloete & Wissink (Eds.). 190–209.

van de Craen, P. & H. Baetens Beardsmore. 1987. Research on city language. In Ammon, Dittmar & Mattheier. (Eds.).

van de Rheede, I. 1992. Die skool, Afrikaans en die kurrikulum. [The school, Afrikaans and the curriculum.] In Webb (Ed.). 273–284.

van den Heever, R. (Ed.). 1988. *Afrikaans en bevryding. Tree na vryheid*. [Afrikaans and liberation. A step towards freedom.] Cape Town: Clayson.

van der Berg, S. 1995. Economic reconciliation as a precondition for sustained democracy. In Rhoodie & Liebenberg (Eds.). 240–250.

van der Merwe, E. G. 1990. Taalbeplanning. [Language planning.] *South African Journal of Linguistics* 8(4). 185–193.

van der Vyver, D. H., J. T. Engelbrecht & D. S. Gxilishe. 1983. The effect of language training on labour relations and productivity in industry. *Intus News/-Nuus.* 7(2). 8–33.

van der Walt, J. L. 1989. (Ed.). *Southern African studies in applied linguistics.* Potchefstroom: South African Applied Linguistics Association.

van Els, T. J. M. 2000. *The European Union, its institutions and its languages. Some language political observations.* Published public lecture. University of Nijmegen.

van Groenou, M. 1993. Interaction between bilingualism and cognitive growth. *Montessori LIFE.* 33–35.

van Jaarsveld, G. J. 1988. *Gesprekstaboes en misverstand: taalhandelinge oor kulturele grense.* [Conversational taboo and misunderstanding: speech acts across cultural boundaries.] Bloemfontein: University of the Free State.

van Rensburg, F. I. J. 1990. Afrikaans se aanspraak op die behoud van sy ampstaalstatus. [The claim of Afrikaans to the retention of its official status.] *Spits* 6(1). 40–99.

van Rensburg, M. C. J. 1991. Wat van 'n nuwe Afrikaans? [What about a new Afrikaans?] *Acta Academica* 23(3). 13–33.

van Rensburg, M. C. J. 1992a. Language planning in Africa and the case of the minority language Afrikaans. Ms. of paper presented at the international conference of the International Academy of Language and Law. Hong Kong.

van Rensburg, M. C. J. 1992b. Die demokratisering van Afrikaans. [The democratisation of Afrikaans.] In Webb (Ed.). 181–200.

van Rensburg, M. C. J. 1996. Die voorwaardes waaronder koloniale tale voortleef: Neder- lands in Indonesië en Afrikaans in Suid-Afrika. [The conditions under which colonial languages continue to exist: Dutch in Indonesia and Afrikaans in South Africa.] *Language matters. Studies in the languages of Southern Africa.* 27.

van Rensburg, M. C. J. 1999. Afrikaans and apartheid. *International Journal for the Sociology of Language.* 136. 77–96.

van Rensburg, M. C. J. & A. Jordaan. 1995. The growth of Afrikaans in Africa. In Webb (Ed.). 107–132.

van Rensburg, M. C. J., T. Links, A. Davids, J. Ferreira & K. P. Prinsloo. 1997. *Afrikaans in Afrika.* Pretoria: J. L. van Schaik.

van Vuuren, D. P. 1995. Unpublished research report. Broadcasting Research Unit. SABC.

van Vuuren, D. P. & A. Maree. 1994. *Report: Language and broadcasting in South Africa. A research perspective.* Broadcasting Research Unit. SABC.

van Wyk, E. B. 1966. *Die Bantoetale.* [The Bantu languages.] Pretoria: J. L. van Schaik.

van Zyl, A. 1990. *Die taalpolitiek van die Federasie van Afrikaanse Kultuurvereniginge (FAK) met spesifieke verwysing na die tydperk 1976–1986.* [The language politics of the Federa- tion of Afrikaans Cultural Organizations with specific reference to the period 1976– 1986.] Unpublished master's thesis. University of Natal.

Venter, A. (Ed.). 1998. *Government and politics in South Africa. An introduction to its institutional processes and policies.* Pretoria: van Schaik.

Verhoef, M. M. 1991. *Taalbeplanning: Die stand en toekoms van taalbeplanning vir Afrikaans in 'n multitalige Suid-Afrika.* [Language planning: The status and future of language planning for Afrikaans in a multilingual South Africa.] Unpublished doctoral dissertation. Potchefstroom University.

Verster, R. 1976. *Kommunikasie met swart werkers — 'n sisteembenadering.* [Communication with black workers — a systems approach.] Bloemfontein: University of the Free State.

Verster, R. 1981. *Interkulturele kommunikasie: die posisie in die munisipaliteite.* [Intercultural communication: the situation in the municipalities.] M A and E. December: 34–35.

von Gleich, U. & E. Wolff. (Eds.). *Standardization of national languages.* Hamburg: UNESCO Institute for Education and Graduate Program for the Study of Language Contact and Multilingualism. University of Hamburg.

Vorster, J. & L. Proctor. 1975. Black attitudes to white languages in South Africa. *Journal of Psychology.* 92 (1). 103–108.

Webb, V. N. 1990a. 'n Menseregtehandves vir Suid-Afrika en die beskerming van taalregte. [A Bill of human rights for South Africa and the protection of language rights.] *Aambeeld.* 18(1). 18–23.

Webb, V. N. 1990b. 'n Taalbeleid vir 'n nuwe Suid-Afrika — Weer eens 'n skandmuur? [A language policy for a new South Africa — A wall of shame once again?] *Communicare* 8(2). 67–70.

Webb, V. N. 1990c. Die begrippe *Volk, Nasie* en *Afrikanerdom*–'n sosiolinguistiese ontleding. [The concepts people, nation and the Afrikaner people — a sociolinguistic analysis.] *Handhaaf.* 29(4). 10–12.

Webb, V. N. 1990d. Die rol van Afrikaans in 'n nasiebouprogram. [The role of Afrikaans in a nation-building programme.] Paper presented at the annual congress of the Afrikaans Literature Society. Durban. September.

Webb, V. N. 1990e. Voorwaardes vir die beplanning van 'n nuwe talebestel in Suid-Afrika. [Conditions for planning a new language dispensation in South Africa.] Paper presented at the language planning conference. University of Pretoria. April.

Webb, V. N. 1991. *Conflict in South African society, and the role of language.* LAUD prepublication. 232. University of Duisburg.

Webb, V. N. (Ed.). 1992. *Afrikaans ná Apartheid.* [Afrikaans after Apartheid.] Pretoria: J. L. van Schaik.

Webb, V. N. 1992a. Afrikaans as probleem. In Webb (Ed.). 3–24.

Webb, V. N. 1992b. Afrikaans: 'n Tuiste vir Afrika. [Afrikaans: A home for Africa.] In Barkhuizen, Stander & Swart (Eds.). 338–350.

Webb, V. N. 1992c. Language attitudes in South Africa: Implications for a post-apartheid democracy. In Pütz (Ed.). 429–461.

Webb, V. N. 1992d. Die statutêre erkenning van minderheidstale in 'n toekomstige Suid-Afrika. [The statutory recognition of Afrikaans in a future South Africa.] In Webb (Ed.). 227–248.

Webb, V. N., R. Dirven & E. Kock. 1992. Afrikaans: Feite en interpretasies. [Afrikaans: Facts and interpretations.] In Webb (Ed.). 25–68.

Webb, V. N. 1993. The national language issue in South Africa. Paper presented at the tenth World Congress of the International Association of Applied Linguistics. Amsterdam. 12 August.

Webb, V. N. 1993/4. Language policy and planning in South Africa. In Grabe (Ed.). 254–271.

Webb, V. N. 1994a. Revalorizing the autochthonous languages of Africa. In Pütz (Ed.). 181–204.

Webb, V. N. 1994b. Language teaching in the context of cultural heterogeneity. Paper presented at the conference on the culture of multilinguality. University of South Africa. Pretoria. August.

Webb, V. N. (Ed.). 1995a. *Language in South Africa. An input into language planning for a post-apartheid South Africa. The LiCCA(SA) Report.* Pretoria: University of Pretoria.

Webb, V. N. 1995b. The technicalisation of the autochthonous languages of South Africa: Constraints from a present day perspective. In Pütz (Ed.). 83–100.

Webb, V. N., K. Heugh, R. Mokate, G. Strauss & G. Puth. 1996a. Language as an economic resource. In Department of Arts, Culture, Science and Technology. 1996b: 89–122.

Webb, V. N. 1996b. Language and politics in South Africa. In Dua (Ed.). 139–162.

Webb, V. N. 1996c. English and language planning for South Africa: The flip-side. In de Klerk (Ed.). 175–190.

Webb, V. N. 1997. Language and development. Paper presented at the Development, Culture and Communication conference. Human Sciences Research Council. September.

Webb, V. N. 1998. Mutilingualism as a developmental resource: Framework for a research program. In Kamwamgamalu (Ed.). 125- 154.

Webb, V. N. 1999a. Language policy and language politics in a pluralist democracy: the South African case. Paper presented at the Second International Symposium on language policy at the Millennium. Bar Ilan University. Israel. November.

Webb, V. N. 1999b. Language study in South Africa: a view from the politics of language. Paper presented at the National Association of Educators of Teachers of English. Pretoria. August.

Webb, V. N. 1999c. Multilingualism in democratic South Africa: The over-estimation of language policy. *Journal of Educational Development* 19: 351–366.

Webb, V. N. 1999d. Policy development and economic empowerment through multilingualism. Paper presented at the conference on Multilingual cities and towns in South Africa — Challenges and Prospects. Pretoria.

Webb, V. N. 1999/2000. The implementation of OBE in the context of the language politics of South Africa. In Bak (Ed.). 190- 207.

Webb, V. N. & M. Kriel. 2000. Afrikaans and Afrikaner Nationalism. *International Journal of the Sociology of Language.* 144. 19–49.

Webb, V. N. & F. Grin. 2000. Language, educational effectiveness and economic outcomes. A research proposal. Centre for research on the politics of language. University of Pretoria.

Webb, V. N. 2000a. The African languages as languages of vocational training. A research project. Paper presented at the annual conference of the Linguistics Society of Southern Africa. Cape Town. 12–14 January.

Webb, V. N. 2000b. Language and economic development. Paper presented at the 17th biennial conference of the German African Studies Association. Institut für Afrikanistik. Universität Leipzig. 30 March — 1 April.

Webb, V. N. 2000c. Constitutional principles and challenges for language policy and language planning in tertiary education. Keynote lecture at the seminar on language policy at the tertiary level, PU (CHE), Vaal Triangle Campus, van der Bijl Park. September.

Webb, V. N. 2000d. Auditing language for language policy development at local government level. Seminar of the Greater Pretoria Metropolitan Council. Pretoria. September.

Webb, V. N. 2000e. The role of cultural factors in academic training. Paper presented at the conference of the project Linguistische afstanden overbruggen. University of Pretoria. October.

Webb, V. N.. 2000f. Ethnolinguistic factors in educational development. Paper presented at a workshop on ethnolinguistic factors in educational development. University of Pretoria. October.

Webb, V. N. 2000g. Die rekonstruksie van die Afrikaanse werklikheid en handboekvernuwing: Repliek op Jan Esterhuyse. [The reconstruction of Afrikaans reality and textbook renewal: A response to Jan Esterhuyse.] In du Plessis and van Gensen (Eds.). 59–68.

Webb, V. N. 2000h. Language as a factor in the struggle against HIV/AIDS. Paper presented at the annual conference of the *South African Association of Public Administration and Management*. Council for Scientific and Industrial Research. 23 November.

Webb, V. N. 2000i. Memorandum to the Department of Labour. Unpublished.

Webb, V. N. & Kembo-Sure (Eds.). 2000. *African Voices. An introduction to the linguistics and languages of Africa*. Cape Town: Oxford University Press South Africa.

Webb, V. N. 2001. Die bevordering van Afrikaans. [The promotion of Afrikaans.] In Carstens & Grebe (Eds.). 164–178.

Webb, V. N. 2002. English as a second language in South Africa's tertiary institutions. A case study at the University of Pretoria. *World Englishes* Vol. 21, No. 1, 49–61.

Webster, E. 1983. "Introduction" to labour section. *South African Review*. 1. Johannesburg: Ravan.

Wedepohl, L. 1984. *A survey of illiteracy in South Africa*. Cape Town: Centre for Extra-Mural Studies. University of Cape Town.

Weinstein, B. (Ed.). 1990. *Language Policy and Political Development*. Norwood, New Jersey. Ablex.

Western Cape Province. 2000. *Discussion document: Draft language policy for the Western Cape*. Unpublished document.

Wiechers, M. 1992. Taalmodelle en die reg. [Language Models and the Law.] In Swanepoel & Pieterse (Eds.). 167–184.

Wielemans, W. & S. J. Berkhout. (In press) Towards understanding education policy: an integrative approach. To appear in *Educational Policy*.

Wilkes, A. 1978. Bantu language studies. In Lanham & Prinsloo (Eds.). 96–116.

Willemse, H., A. Coetzee, L. Pokpas, J. Smith & I. van de Rheede. 2000. Oor bloekombos en (voor-)uitkyk. [On bluegum bushes and looking ahead.] In du Plessis & van Gensen (Eds.). 82–93.

Willemse, H. 1990a. A position paper on language policy in a New South Africa. *New Observations*. 83.

Willemse, H. 1990b. Language policy in a new South Africa: The development of indigenous languages. *Facets* 9(2).

Willemse, H. 1991. Securing the myth: The representations of the origin of Afrikaans in language textbooks. In Jansens (Ed.).

Willemse, H. 2001. Strategiese beplanning vir die Departement Afrikaans. [Strategic planning for the Department of Afrikaans.] Paper presented at the annual prize-giving ceremony of the Department of Afrikaans, University of Pretoria.

Willemyns, R. 1992. Linguistic legislation and prestige shift. In Ammon and Hellinger (Eds.). 3–16.

Williams, E. 1993a. *Report on reading in English in primary schools in Malawi*. Serial No. 4. Department for International Development. London.

Williams, E. 1993b. *Report on reading in English in primary schools in Zambia*. Serial No. 5. Department for International Development. London.

Williams, E. 1996. Mother tongue medium versus second language medium: the effects on the reading proficiency of African pupils. *Triangle* 14. 147–164.

Wilmsen, E. N. & R. Vossen. Labour, language and power in the construction of ethnicity in Botswana. *Critique of Anthropology*. No. 10 (1). 7–37.

Wise, P. & K. Hahndiek. 1995. *Continuous interpretation services from all official languages; background and implications*. Internal memorandum for the South African parliament.

Wissing, D. (Ed.) 2000. *Workshop papers (on) Black South African English*. Collection of papers presented at the workshop on Black South African English during the annual conference of the Linguistics Society of Southern Africa. Cape Town. 12–14 January.

Witthaus, G. 1991. A critical examination of learner-centredness and related concepts in alternative literacy organizations. *Language Projects Review* 6(3/4). 59–64.

Wolff, H. E. 2000. The notion of the "African Renaissance" as developed in speeches by South Africa's President Thabo Mbeki in 1998/1999. Paper presented at the panel discussion on language policy in Africa: The African Renaissance as a challenge for language planning. Institut für Afrikanistik. Universität Leipzig.

Wolfson, N. 1992. Intercultural communication and the analysis of conversation. In Herbert (Ed.). 197–214.

Wood, T. 1995. Attitudes towards future possible official languages. In Webb (Ed.). 187–196.

Working Group on Educational Research and Policy Analysis. 1997. *Languages of instruction. Policy implications for education in Africa*. International Development Research Centre.

Wright, S. 1994. The contribution of sociolinguistics. Eastern Europe. Migration, language rights and education. *Current issues in language and society* 1–6.

Yahya-Othman, S. 1990. When international languages clash: The possible detrimental effects on development of the conflict between English and Kiswahili in Tanzania. In Rubagumya (Ed.). 42–53.

Young, D. (Ed.) 1986. *Language: planning and medium of instruction*. Papers presented at the 5th annual conference of the Southern African Applied Linguistics Association,

Cape Town. 9–11 October.

Young, D. 1988. English for what, for whom and when? *Language Projects Review* 3(2). 8.

Young, D. 1995. English in education in a post-apartheid South Africa. In Webb (Ed.). 235–242.

Young, D. & C. Nuttall. 1989. Demystifying textbook language for ESL learners: towards a text-analysis model. In van der Walt (Ed.). 224–262.

Index